THE GLOBAL AND THE LOCAL

The Global and the Local
Understanding the Dialectics of Business Systems

ARNDT SORGE

OXFORD
UNIVERSITY PRESS

OXFORD
UNIVERSITY PRESS

Great Clarendon Street, Oxford OX2 6DP

Oxford University Press is a department of the University of Oxford.
It furthers the University's objective of excellence in research, scholarship,
and education by publishing worldwide in

Oxford New York

Auckland Cape Town Dar es Salaam Hong Kong Karachi Kuala Lumpur
Madrid Melbourne Mexico City Nairobi New Delhi Shanghai Taipei Toronto

With offices in

Argentina Austria Brazil Chile Czech Republic France Greece
Guatemala Hungary Italy Japan South Korea Poland Portugal
Singapore Switzerland Thailand Turkey Ukraine Vietnam

Oxford is a registered trade mark of Oxford University Press
in the UK and in certain other countries

Published in the United States
by Oxford University Press Inc., New York

© Oxford University Press, 2005

British Library Cataloguing in Publication Data

Data available

Library of Congress Cataloging in Publication Data

Sorge, Arndt.
The global and the local : understanding the dialectics
of business systems / Arndt Sorge.
p. cm.
Includes bibliographical references and index.
ISBN 0-19-927890-3 (alk. paper)
1. Acculturation. 2. Globalization–Social aspects. 3. Social change.
4. National characteristics. 5. Industrial sociology. I. Title.
HM841.S67 2005
306.3–dc22   2004027321

ISBN 0-19-927890-3

1 3 5 7 9 10 8 6 4 2

Typeset by Kolam Information Services Pvt. Ltd, Pondicherry, India
Printed in Great Britain
on acid-free paper by
Biddles Ltd., King's Lynn, Norfolk

Foreword

Arndt Sorge's *The Global and the Local* is a book with a complex agenda. Above all, it undertakes to place 'globalization', probably the most fashionable subject of current public and academic debate, in the context of an unashamedly sociological theory of the development of human societies that covers a somewhat longer period than the time between the 1980s and now. Second, it makes a case for conceiving of societies as open, dynamic, dialectical—i.e. internally contradictory and dilemmatic—historical configurations of social structures and pragmatic actions, rather than as basically closed and consistent systems that are, most of the time, in static equilibrium. In particular, it shows how the specificity of a society is dialectically constituted in its interaction with its wider environment, and becomes vested in long-term national 'metatraditions' that guide but do not determine its continuing reconfiguration over time.

But this is not all. Third, the book argues that the 'societal effect' approach to the analysis of business systems, varieties of capitalism, or economies-in-society, to which Sorge himself has made such important contributions, is entirely compatible with the notion of internationalizing societies with open and moving borders—if only because societies have basically always been internationalizing. Fourth, it demonstrates the value, as well as the high art, of combining abstract theoretical reasoning with empirically grounded analysis of subjects eminently recognizable to practitioners—making theory both listen and speak to everyday experience and opening up the latter to a sort of 'understanding' (see the book's subtitle) that is much more practically useful than the specific prescriptions offered by most 'experts' and asked for by most of their clients. And fifth, quite counter-intuitively for non-German and even many German readers, the book uses the case of Germany, a supposedly highly homogeneous and closed society, as evidence for the universality of moving borders, expanding horizons, incorporation of the foreign into the domestic, and hybridization as the normal mode of social evolution.

So there is, indeed, no lack of ambition in this book. And yet, unlike much of what today comes to us as sociology, it is fun to read, written in a way that combines the very abstract and the very concrete, the principles of general theories and the anecdotes of specific histories, in ways that are enlightening and entertaining at the same time. Those who take the book to heart will find themselves in the possession of a language that can speak about 'globalization' in a non-sensationalist manner without, however, in any way detracting from its significance—in fact, quite the contrary. They will understand much better and more systematically the lasting significance of the local in a world whose horizons of action are expanding. They will be in command of concepts that will not require them to describe social settings as coherent and consistent that are actually contradictory in structure and dialectical in process, or to deny the paradoxical character of many of the choices social actors face in social reality. Instead they will be able to treat dilemmas, contradictions, and unexpected consequences as essential and inevitable elements of social and economic life. Most importantly perhaps, they will recognize when social theorizing becomes too short-term and 'goes off on a tangent', failing to take a longer look and to place what is happening now in the historical and social-structural context that is making it happen.

We are proud that this book was written when its author was a Visiting Scholar at the Max Planck Institute in Cologne. Making this sort of work possible is what research institutes are all about. In a world in which one evaluation committee follows the next, forcing science to produce to ever shorter deadlines and in ever faster programme cycles, this is not always possible. This time, however, it has been. A book like Sorge's, which pulls together the general lessons of long years of research and teaching, will take its time to filter down into everyday social science. In our own work at the Institute, this process began while the book was still being written. Now others can join in.

Wolfgang Streeck
Max Planck Institute for the Study of Societies, Cologne

Preface

Most books have their roots in previously existing, substantive contributions, and in research and data that are considered to be the rawer reflections of a supposedly real world. However, books are also the response to the subjective impulses of an author and his or her personal experience. My experience of growing up in Germany during the immediate post-World War II period was disenchanting. I was surrounded by the rubble of a large town bombed to pieces and by a population shattered by trauma, confusion, guilt, and loss of respect. This was not a context conducive to developing a healthy national identity. What then came naturally to many of us in this generation was the desire for the obliteration of borders and the creation of an international, possibly cosmopolitan identity. This is what has kindled in me and many, many others an interest in foreign languages, culture, institutions, and places.

One of the tangible consequences of this experience is my preference for conducting comparative research between countries and for living and working abroad. Still, the impulse to internationalize myself had to be reconciled with insights about the persistence of national and even local identity. Such reconciliation depended not only on the results of comparative research. On a more personal level, I became aware of the persistence of national identity most intensely at precisely the moment that I started having dreams in English and was not sure if I would ever return to Germany to work and live. The counterpoint to my Anglicization occurred in a small flat in Oxford: as I listened to a Bach cantata on BBC Radio one dreary autumn evening in 1976, I was suddenly emotionally overcome with the awareness of somehow being irradicably German. It had nothing to do with dissatisfaction with any foreign or international arrangement or identity; it was focused on a German ritual associated with late autumn or winter that consisted of listening to a Bach cantata, having a walk regardless of the foul weather, and enjoying coffee and cake afterwards. More than a year later, I was back in Germany enjoying that ritual when I had similar emotional recollections of England.

Grappling with research and theoretical problems, I have benefited most of all from two professional and personal relationships, far more than is evident in the references of this book. I have enjoyed almost thirty years of critique, cooperation, and friendship with Marc Maurice, at Aix-en-Provence. The other major source of inspiration has been Wolfgang Streeck, whom I have known even longer. Much of what I have tried to do here implies an explicit or tacit dialogue with these two men. I also particularly thank Wolfgang for having made it possible to write this book by an invitation to, and hospitality at, the Max Planck Institute for the Study of Societies in Cologne in 2002/3, and for having gone through previous drafts with impressive dedication and precision. I am also indebted to the fellows of the

Institute, notably Fritz Scharpf (as director emeritus), for their help and suggestions, for the work they have done and the discussions we had. In conceiving the argument of the book, it was also of great importance to imagine what René König might have said as an inspiring teacher and integrator of the social sciences whom I feel very lucky to have encountered as an undergraduate.

Over many years, I have greatly profited from working with colleagues in the EMOT programme of the European Science Foundation, which became a standing working group of EGOS, the European Group for Organization Studies. Discussions, notably with Peter Clark, Marie-Laure Djelic, Mike Geppert, Peer Hull Kristensen, Kari Lilja, Ray Loveridge, Glenn Morgan, Sigrid Quack, Ayse Saka, Diana Sharpe, Risto Tainio, and Richard Whitley have had beneficial consequences for this book. I was also stimulated to develop a number of ideas by preparing a paper for, and taking part in, a conference at Montreal in 1995, organized by Jean-François Chanlat, which dealt with the conundrum of societal community in Quebec and Canada. My historical interest was first kindled at St Antony's College and was further encouraged by Peter Lawrence, Eli Moen, and Luchien Karsten; this was nicely balanced by the diversified and thoroughly nomothetic rigour of Arjen van Witteloostuijn. Last but not least, I am greatly indebted to Dona Geyer for having edited the manuscript with great rigour and erudition.

Arndt Sorge
Groningen, June 2004

Contents

I

The Paradox of Internationalization

1.1 Three central themes

This book examines how internationalization affects the economy, work, organization, industrial relations, management, and corporate governance within a larger society. It traces such aspects of internationalization back to processes of societal aggregation, disaggregation, and institution-building, processes which co-evolved with the development of economic activities and their social regulation. Co-evolution means that throughout time characteristics evolve together along different dimensions or in different areas, and interdependencies develop between evolutions in different areas or between different species or types.[2] Hence this study emphasizes broader historical perspectives that are based on general social science theory. These perspectives are geared to explain more recent and topical manifestations in more specific domains.

The book features three major intertwined strands of argument. The first addresses *the way societies become aggregated and disaggregated*. This argument is not only macrosociological. The evolution of societal aggregation and disaggregation requires a consideration of social action and the construction of actors, and an analysis of structures and processes that mediate between actors and societies. In other words, we are poorly served by a macrosociology that focuses on variables and characteristics located at a macro level only. The approach used here leads instead to an analysis of the build-up of societal complexity as related to the fashioning of culture and institutions. It implies the reciprocal constitution and conditioning of societies and actors, as found in the pragmatist and interactionist perspectives developed in the Chicago school of sociology and social psychology.

Such theoretical perspectives then help to establish a basis for theory and research on the *internationalization of social, economic, and political action*. This is the second major strand of argument. It means chiefly that internationalization should be viewed as a central factor in the long-term generation of societal specificity, in the sense of developing distinct societal institutions and culture. Societal distinct-iveness not only results from isolation but also from the internationalization of action. The argument is not that institutions and culture are pervasive (general characteristics applying to the entire societal fabric) or unchanging. Instead, we see that characteristics are differentiated by dimensions and that characteristics which were previously coherent and widely applicable become decoupled; opposing characteristics are allocated to specific situations and thus recombined, and the combination of contrary or divergent characteristics is subject to intense innovation over time.

This argument profits from the interactionist theory of social action and societal aggregation that the Chicago School has developed. It incorporates dialectics and paradox, which in turn help explain why and how things that were linked or separate at one time and in one place become decoupled or linked under different circumstances. Introduced as elements of social action theory, dialectics and para-dox are useful for the analysis of internationalization. This understanding of dialectics is adopted from Rorty; pragmatic dialectics combines contingencies with irony: we can only tentatively indicate, in an ironical way, the fundamentals that we accept.[3] Both internationalization and the build-up of societal specificity are paradoxical. The former also implies and is grounded in the latter, and vice versa. This therefore means that the advance of both is dialectical: internationalization feeds into the build-up of societal specificity; societal aggregation also implies disaggregation; societal integration or coherence implies the recombination of characteristics that are opposite to one another.

These arguments require an analysis over time because they address processes. But they cannot dispense with cross-societal comparison. The latter is a necessary condition, but it is not sufficient for a sound development of both arguments. The analysis must build on a very long-term view because such a view reveals how paradoxical and dialectical societal integration and internationalization are—an aspect that tends to be forgotten in cross-sectional comparisons and studies with a more reduced time horizon. While a short-term analysis reveals temporarily plaus-ible combinations in the form of societal 'models', a long-term perspective exhibits how often and how extensively models have changed through the dialectical construction of culture and institutions.

A long-term perspective can only be developed conveniently by focusing on one society and its internationalization. This leads to the third major strand of argument: *Germany is an excellent example of the interaction of internationalization and societal specificity over time* and of how this specific interaction relates to the differentiation, decoupling, and recombination of characteristics in the cultural and institutional landscape. This is a different Germany from the one that all too often appears in the literature: homogeneous, well integrated, Germanic, orderly, stable. The real and historical Germany is an eminent ethnic and cultural melting-pot, but a melting-pot that has brought forth new regional diversity. It has featured oscillations between overextension of domination and societal disaggregation. It was a late-comer to nation-building because it was an early inter-nation. The oscillation between aggregation and disaggregation, generalization and particularization of norms, and internationalizing and provincializing tendencies has brought forth a unique metatradition. This does not mean long-standing homogeneity or stability. A metatradition implies both a more abstract continuity over time and a rhythm of institutional decoupling and recombination.[4] In this respect, it is dialectical. This metatradition has strongly imprinted itself upon German economic, social, and political institutions and culture. It explains the configuration that Germany's business systems and related institutions have evolved. This configuration has always thrived on internationalization and, in turn, has influenced the particular path of internationalization. A similar analysis could be envisaged for other societies. But now it is time to look at Germany in a different light.

1.2 Globalization?

It is convenient to start the discussion from the broader perspectives that have been developed on 'globalization'.[5] Like many terms that fascinate people for a time, this is a highly general and internally heterogeneous notion. In its present usage, it means that 'something' spans or is being extended all around the globe. In this sense, the term is not new for there have been empires, i.e. large aggregates of people and territories, held together by an integrated set-up of rule and domination, which have stretched all around the world and affected every or nearly every continent inhabited by humans. The Spanish Empire is an example, with large colonies in America, Asia, and Africa. The British Empire encompassed an even greater territorial expanse. Global empires have tended to originate in Europe, and they are linked with the colonization of the rest of the world by Europe. But they have never covered the whole world, since colonization has been a competitive enterprise triggered by major and competing European seafaring nations. The empire of the Russian tsars relied mainly on land-based expansion, and after one tsar had sold Alaska to the United States, one should probably hesitate to call the empire global because it was limited to 'only' two continents and stretched over a coherent land mass. Geographically, Europe is, after all, only a small, warped and contorted appendix to the Asian land mass. Actual boundaries to Asia are hard to define. They are vague and indefinite, and have shifted throughout history, depending on complex and ever-changing composites of cultures and civilizations.[6]

This imperialist state of globalization came to an end with decolonization in the sense of the termination of formal and effective subordination to political rule. Some people would argue that imperialism and colonialism have continued in the form of economic dependency, exerted by some governments, multinational enterprises, and supranational governmental institutions. With or without a connotation of imperialism, the term 'globalization' started to be used much more frequently in the 1990s. It has come to mean a new type of globalization on the basis of an integrated world order, rather than competitive and partial world orders constituted by rival empires. Since the disintegration of the Communist empire, the independence of states in the Soviet Union, and the disappearance of the Warsaw Pact and Comecon, the idea has become widespread that the world is now subject to one set of markets and to global and supranational governmental institutions that enhance markets rather than govern societies, thereby facilitating an unrestricted and more free-floating movement of people, enterprises, goods, money, and information. According to some of the rhetoric, globalization was to be associated with democracy and the rule of law. For the moment, it seems to be dominated by an American influence that puts greater stock in open markets and economic liberalism than in spreading effective democracy. But even the liberalization of markets is occurring only to a point and is being checked by a renaissance of protectionism, despite all the rhetoric and theory to the contrary. The 'level playing fields' so embraced by theoretical and policy-making rhetoric are currently becoming shot through with protective measures, as has often been the case following an onslaught of liberalization.

The globalization of free movement in a liberal and open order, democracy, and the rule of law exists in empirical reality in the form of programmes or questions more than indubitable facts. In addition, if tends to acquire very locally specific meanings and is subject to local restrictions. 'Globally speaking', there is indeed 'something' to the notion of globalization, and it is probably something quite different from earlier types of globalization, but what it precisely comprises and entails is highly questionable. This 'certain something' inherent to globalization needs to be defined and differentiated.

First, globalization is not an end in itself; it is a trend ascertainable over time. It means an extension of the range, borders, or horizon within which certain activities occur that are validated and institutionally supported by market orders. The free flow of goods and people always needs institutional arrangements that legitimate and facilitate it. As a trend, globalization can be investigated empirically. It starts small and does not necessarily achieve any real completion. It is convenient to go through the main dimensions of that certain 'something' which globalization denotes.

International exchange, mobility, and communication themselves comprise a complex set of dimensions. With regard to international trade within Europe and beyond, it is clear but counter-intuitive to globalization enthusiasts that its intensity relative to gross domestic product has not changed very much from the heyday of colonialist globalization around the beginning of the twentieth century until now.[7] There have been sizeable fluctuations, occasioned by dramatic political and regulatory shifts such as war and its aftermath, nationalism, and autarchic movements on the one hand, and the establishment and expansion of free trade areas or supranational communities on the other. But the weight of imports and exports relative to GDP has not changed much in the long run. This is despite the fact that the relevant societal and state entities, such as late nineteenth-century France, the United Kingdom (then Great Britain and Ireland), and Germany, were all territorially larger than they are now. One would expect imports and exports to be less important in larger societies. The population of these countries has increased in the meantime, but the importance of imports and exports has not. This may reveal the limits of globalization, or it may mean that globalization has shifted to another front.

Very often, the extent of globalization in the past has been neglected. With respect to regulation, the period at the end of the nineteenth century had a world order in which currencies were exchangeable, even between competing colonial empires, and their value was mostly fixed to the gold standard. As far as trade and currency standards are concerned, the extent of globalization in this period is hard to rival. Yet, this era of globalization was rudely interrupted by diverse and excessive kinds of nationalism and autarky that reversed developments for a long time. National states thrived as institutions that helped to control and curtail the consequences of the earlier globalization. We know that nationalism and relative autarky superseded liberal globalization once before. How are we to exclude the possibility that a repetition of this cycle, albeit probably not identical in all respects, will happen in the future?

The figures for the period of the late nineteenth century are the first that rely on proper national accounting, so that it is difficult to say whether this measure of globalization represented an unprecedented historical record, or a rather normal state of affairs. *Ceteris paribus*, smaller societies will have larger import and export percentages. Hence, as societies aggregated increasingly into larger nation states and beyond, import and export rates will most likely have fallen, if this drop was not compensated for by a secular increase in the intersocietal division of labour, meaning intersocietal trade. Smaller societies of the past, before the heyday of the late nineteenth-century globalization, traded intensively with neighbours, and it is hard to compare the volume of that earlier trade in the absence of modern national accounting.

For the periods after the emergence of nation states, colonialism, and a standard of national accounting, it is difficult to establish a secular tendency towards a relative increase in the importance of exports and imports. Although trade, in principle, always competes with direct investment abroad in entrepreneurial decision-making, there is not necessarily a negative correlation in the evolution of industries over time. In a regime of convertible and flexible exchange rates for currencies, however, relative prices of factors of production and transport costs will induce enterprises on the whole to substitute direct investment abroad for exporting. This points towards the establishment of multinational enterprises, which will be discussed later.

Mobility was equally high in the past. However, mobility between Europe and the rest of the world at the end of the nineteenth century was marked by emigration rather than tourism. Mobility and communication have increased dramatically and consistently. These are apparently valid indicators showing the fairly monotonous increase of globalization for different and changing reasons. Transport can be promoted by a supranational order to assure safety and efficiency. Examples include the World Postal Union and the ICAO, the International Civil Aviation

Organization. But it is a totally different question whether mobility eventually reduces differences between societies. In colonies there have invariably been tendencies to separate segments of society, with different norms, customs, languages, traditions, and, of course, human physical features. The magnitude of such tendencies may have depended on the ethnic or cultural distance between the colonialists and the colonized. Even long after the demise of formally ordained colonialism, a relative segregation of domestic and immigrant segments, of inhabitants and tourists, nationals and expatriates, is the rule.[8]

Whenever people migrate along certain trajectories and feed into specific places, such as large or growing cities, this will lead to societal segmentation among ethnic, racial, and cultural lines, rather than integration. Where cultural distance is particularly great, such as between Europe and what used to be called the Third World, such segmentation will therefore be strongly evident. Many cities in the 'less developed' world have almost always been larger than European ones, even before colonization. At the time of being 'discovered' and subsequently ravaged by the Spanish at the end of the fifteenth century, Tenochtitlan (now Mexico City) had more than 800,000 inhabitants. The only city in Europe to have reached a similar size (1 million inhabitants) had been first-century Rome. Even for megacities first founded as mere railway depots or military camps, such as Nairobi, their rate of growth has been much more phenomenal in less-developed countries and has led to a population density and concentration which in Europe has been and continues to be rare. It has resulted in urbanization, with societal rifts between urban and rural areas and between ethnicities and cultures.

Communication (media, business, or personal exchange of information) has been subject to drastic increases. But again, this has happened along particular main trajectories rather than randomly or across the board. Despite growth in imports and exports, there have been large and growing spheres of communication that are meaningful only in a domestic context; they can hardly be understood or appreciated by foreigners or different cultures. While North American films, television soap operas, and news channels appear to be fairly widespread, they are only a part of the spectrum. One must not forget that the most important film-producing country in the world is India, and its output is virtually incommunicable abroad except to immigrant segments of society in East Africa and Britain.

Supranational governance, regulations, and standards comprise another complex set of dimensions that have become more diversified and important during and after colonialism and World War I (e.g. the League of Nations and more specific agencies such as the World Postal Union and the International Labour Organization). In a paradoxical way, they achieved increased importance just as the earlier form of global economic liberalism was being countered by nationalism and autarchy. Again the question arises: how are we to exclude the likelihood of this happening again in the future? It has been well said that those who neglect the past are compelled to repeat it. This is another challenge which the book seeks to address.

In the period following World War II, another spate of organizations was founded that included the United Nations and its many subsidiary agencies—the

World Bank, the International Monetary Fund, the Bank for International Payments, and the World Trade Organization at the world level and free trade areas and political communities at the regional level (such as the precursors of the European Union and the eventual Union itself, plus the European Economic Area). The world is thus being governed more and more by an increasingly elaborate, laterally and vertically differentiated network of supranational, governmental, and administrative bodies. While these indubitably absorb either the functions or at least the aspects of the functions previously dealt with in nation states, it is being debated informally or bilaterally whether they have reduced the relative importance or control capacity of lower-level authorities, regulations, and standards.[9] Here again, globalization or regionalization on a smaller scale—the establishment of authorities, regulations, and standards above a level which we classify as national or societal—is ambiguous with respect to upward shifts in the distribution of power and functions. Upward shifts of some competencies tend to go together with or be related to a strengthening of the importance or control capacity of subsidiary authorities.

Multinational enterprises, alliances of enterprises, joint ventures, and other involvement in enterprise capital across borders is another frequently documented set of dimensions that imply globalization. Of course, some of the multinational enterprises that have emerged are truly global in that they have subsidiaries in many countries of the world. Some are also 'globally integrated' to a great extent, meaning they are governed by more uniform and centrally ordained policies. However, most of the truly globally ubiquitous companies are not necessarily globally integrated and centralized, and far less than most of the globally integrated firms are globally ubiquitous. In Europe, most multinationals take globalization to denote a strong and consistent presence on one or two continents, above all in Europe. Often, globalization may amount, more modestly, to regionalization. According to recent rhetoric, the 'trendy' multinational is the 'transnational enterprise', which combines global integration with 'local responsiveness'.[10]

The term 'local responsiveness' attenuates a globalizing trend. We see the term 'globalization' being used to refer to both the degree of global presence and the degree to which policies and practices are integrated and harmonized. In the case of the globally integrated *and* locally responsive firm, it may also happen that global interdependencies between subsidiaries imply very different types of products, firms, practices, and knowledge in different areas or countries. Also, the type of multinational enterprises and the extent of their expansion are radically different in different societies. Some countries, such as Denmark, have very few multinational subsidiaries while others, such as Belgium, have many; some, such as the Netherlands, Switzerland, and Sweden, have produced important and widespread multinationals, and others, such as Austria, hardly any. These examples of small countries show that the meaning of multinationals for them or in them varies considerably despite the strong role of these countries as highly developed and specialized economies in an international division of labour, and despite their similar size (Austria has the same population as Sweden).[11]

In short, globalization means radically different things to different people in different places, and the use of the term runs the risk of confusing a welter of phenomena or tendencies; only a few such notions imply truly global presence or truly global harmonization, and the combination of the two is rare. One of the leading authorities on economic globalization and global enterprise strategy, Alan Rugman, now considers the evidence as pointing towards the 'end of globalization.'[12] Other publications of this author have titles such as 'Myths of Globalization' or 'The End of Global Strategy'. Articles or books featuring the same titles could also have been written in 1914 or 1920. This attests to the fact that history has, at least to some extent, an uncanny habit of repeating itself naturally in new forms. There appear to have been cycles of internationalization and subsequently of national or regional closure.

Little attention is paid to this point in larger debates, whose participants are still fascinated by the latest hype over a new era of globalization. Although North American companies have in many cases been the rhetorical forerunners of globalization and have in fewer cases actually practised it in one sense or another, they are also distinctive in having the overwhelming bulk of their operations concentrated in North America.[13] As much as globalization is undeniable in one sense or another, care has to be taken to use more precise terms and notions. Globalization is far from being a consistent syndrome; it has many different meanings. There is also evidence of reversals among economic indicators of globalization and with regard to the spread of supranational government, regulations, and standards. Globalization consists of such a hotchpotch of different and contrary meanings[14] that I shall replace this term with *internationalization*.

'Internationalization' is not a more precise term and notion than 'globalization'; the main difference is that in internationalization the geographical expansion is more modest and open. However, this is not the only reason for preferring this term to 'globalization'. Arguably, 'internationalization' is less sweeping in its implications. It is possibly a more conservative concept but it does not rule out thrusting globalization along any of its many dimensions. It also alerts us to the fact that the nature of global or international interdependencies differs from one society to another. Paradoxically, internationalization is therefore a national or local phenomenon!

This is how the use of the term should be interpreted here. It alerts us to a number of possibilities without foreclosing on any of them; notably, it is meant to evoke the possibility of geographically, functionally or institutionally more restricted options of internationalization, and it should also alert us to the likelihood of pairing countervailing tendencies: global integration with local responsiveness, supranational competence with national or local power, extensive migration and the mixing of peoples with the formation of subsocietal segments. Unlike manna or air pollution, internationalization does not fall from the heavens, i.e. from an elevated supranational level. It is constructed from the bottom up and is, to some extent, constructed differently to accommodate various societies and economies. In a way, this is postnational internationalization, a type that goes beyond the nation state but does not obliterate it. But then the question is: do we not find a more general pattern over time in which the world oscillates between the strengthening of societal coherence and internationalization?

One of the central questions in the globalization rhetoric and debate is whether it leads to the *assimilation and harmonization of national or more local culture and institutions*. Here again we have a vast field of opposing evidence and interpretations. On the one hand, we have a quasi- or real genocide of traditional cultures and their people; remnants of ethnicities subsist in rural or urban slums, deprived not only of large aspects of their culture but also of their traditional 'mode of production'. The latter is a dialectical unity of 'productive forces' and 'productive relations', as Marx would have said,[15] and that mode of production had been the foundation of a society which had formed and engaged their personalities. This is the dismal aspect at both ends of the convergence and divergence spectrum, where a mode of production that advances internationalization crowds out or annihilates everything that stands in its way and supposedly confronts people with the stark options of passive adaptation, misery, or death. Conceivably, it is a small step from divergence, when a people refuse to converge upon internationally imported practices and therefore suffer the consequences, to partial convergence, which consists of the simultaneous adoption of some Western 'standards' of civilization ranging from alcohol abuse to medical care. Classic cases are those of Native Americans in the United States or Aborigines in Australia, in which these peoples were first massacred and confined to reservations, then became maladapted in one respect, but also well adapted to the downsides of consumerism and public welfare.

On the other hand, we have the glorious end of convergence, where societies adopt and diffuse a technical, business, or socio-organizational template, and successfully compete internationally by attracting new industries and building up new enterprises. Some 'Asian tigers' would qualify for this classification. There is also the glorious side of divergence, where societies specialize in activities that are deliberately engineered to be different from those in other societies in an effort to carve out a niche for themselves—technically, commercially, or legally—that assures and even heightens their distinctiveness with regard to others. This is the Liechtenstein, Delaware, Switzerland, or Luxembourg effect: whether you specialize in money-laundering, favourable taxation and hence company headquarters, or specific types of industrial products, the effect builds on diverging from others in a number of respects. This produces quasi-monopolies or comparative advantage, thrives on specific productive forces, and entails specific productive relations.

In between more distinct situations, we have a vast grey area where societies feature intricate mixtures of convergence and divergence. This is the area that we will focus on in this book. This does mean that the more dramatic side of present-day internationalization will be neglected. Societies in Europe have also experienced the drama and tragedy of internationalization in their history, and these will not be neglected here. But a bitter history notwithstanding, European societies exemplify scenarios that offer more than a choice between passive adaptation and simple reproduction of domestic practices. The theme here is about the

combination of thorough innovation, rather than passive adaptation, with meaningful, rather than mechanically traditional, retention of heritage. Such scenarios
are not only politically suggestive but also more rewarding for students keen on
refinement and precision. It may not be possible to generalize the treatment for
every part of the world in concrete empirical terms. But it is hoped that general
mechanisms can be identified which will, to some extent, elude the specificities of
time and place.

In the search for evidence for and against convergence between societies, we
find that one of the more systematic fields of data collection and interpretation is
concerned with fundamental values, argued to be the foundations of societal
coherence and identity. More geographically extensive and standardized series of
data have been collected and interpreted with regard to such social values in order
to evaluate tendencies of harmonization and assimilation. Social values are taken to
be highly general and all-encompassing fundamental orientations into which
members of a society are socialized. These values influence attitudes and behaviour
in a wide range of domains: familial patterns, work and organization, political
choices, social inequality, lifestyle, and others. The existence of fundamental social
values does not mean that they do not change. Researchers have extensively
documented and interpreted value change. Data on values have been collected
on the basis of standardized instruments across societies. Such studies deal with
'culture' in terms of fundamental values, and thus they are not the same as
ethnographic studies of culture. Ethnographic studies use more qualitative
methods, deal with a larger variety of concrete practices, and emphasize the
intricacies of interpreting symbols and practices in ethnic and cultural communities;
they pay more attention to institutions, a theme which will be developed empirically in the following chapters.

Here, the purpose is merely to indicate that studies of cultural values have
produced findings that reflect on the more general picture of what internationalization means. We have three major sources on the diversity, divergence, or
convergence of values. One is an international consortium centred around Inglehart;[16] another is the European Values Survey started by De Moor at Tilburg and
colleagues in many countries.[17] Hofstede has published prominently on the diversity and change of work-related values,[18] notably in IBM subsidiaries in many
countries of the former First and Third Worlds. IBM subsidiaries, of course, were
absent from the Second World (of state socialism or Communism). These studies
show that values do change over time. Researchers who proposed changes of values
as interesting phenomena and important explanatory factors have never intended
them to be unchanging foundations of human behaviour. The same holds true for
Hofstede. Even though his value scores are often used as if they were immutable,
this is not at all what he intended.

Yet the question is whether value changes exhibit any evidence that societies are
becoming more similar with regard to values. This question is a different one from
asking whether we can see the effect of some tendencies or shifts in different
societies. With respect to the latter question, the answer is clearly that we can.

Tendencies such as individualization occur fairly universally. However, individualization is not the evolutionary opposite of collectivism. Modern individualism is dialectically complemented by the rise of impersonal and bureaucratically governed collectivities, such as the welfare state. The history of individualization is thus one of impersonal collectivities taking the place of personalized collectivities. That may happen in very different forms. There are also some fairly widespread tendencies in 'Western' countries that manifest themselves in very different ways, such as the growing separation of citizenship and several types of inclusion in the community, on the one hand, and religion, on the other. In the United States, a secular societal community exists alongside a strong, organized, and very differentiated religiousness, whereas in Europe it mostly does not. Thus, the acknowledgement of some tendencies which are fairly widespread—although it is largely impossible to ascertain whether some tendencies are truly global or general, even in such a small space as the Western world—makes us aware that different and more particular tendencies exist.

Despite commonalities of tendencies across many societies, there is no overall assimilation of fundamental values whatsoever, be they political, social, or work-related. People are eminently capable of assimilation. This is not refuted by such findings. But they make use of their capability of assimilation in a different way than we tend to imagine. People are naturally born syncretists, meaning that they adapt new beliefs, ideas, practices, techniques, etc. to those they already have. They have an amazing capacity to make things compatible that at one stage or at first sight appear radically different. The pioneer example of this is tribes in the Pacific who found it perfectly natural during World War II to interpret the supply ships of the US Navy not only as useful artefacts but endowed with godly qualities—objects of veneration, which gave rise to the 'cargo cult'.[19] Similar findings are presented by social anthropologists whenever different worlds collide or become enmeshed with each other, such as the 'disenchanted'[20] world of occidental rationalism and animistic world views. Such collisions, hard or soft, produce new amalgamations which have an original quality and represent a synthesis rather than a mixture. Syntheses, to use a chemical metaphor, are different from mixtures in that they imply a reaction of one substance with another. The pioneering example of the cargo cult should not lead us to disparage such syncretism as generically 'under-developed' or unworthy of an enlightened world.

Pidginization or mongrelization is a pervasive foundation of highly sophisticated cultural artefacts. The French language evolved through a process of sophistication and refinement from a crude, vulgar, and mongrelized vernacular which mixed the Latin slang of soldiers and peasants in late antiquity and the early Middle Ages with Celtic and Germanic words and rode roughshod over sophisticated Latin grammar.[21] Likewise, the poetic richness of the English language in terms of nuanced words would have been infeasible had it not emerged from a highly mongrelized concoction of Germanic, French, and Celtic expressions. Even clichés such as 'law and order' reveal subtle nuances: 'law' is a Germanic word meaning traditional norms arising from custom and practice, whereas 'order' derives from Latin and

French words (*ordo, ordre*) meaning an order imposed by rule, in this case that of the Norman and Latinized invaders from France. The Normans themselves were exemplary mongrels: hailing from Norway, this was a northern Germanic tribe that conquered 'Normandy', then accepted feudal allegiance to the king of France, converted to Christianity, mixed with locals, and adopted early French language and culture.

Recently, the amalgamation of different practices and institutions has been discussed under the notion of 'hybridization'. Notably Robert Boyer, in his interpretation of the evolution of socio-economic regimes and modes of production, uses this notion in order to counter the idea that new practices and institutions typically elbow aside older ones.[22] Hybridization does make it clear that something happens which is different from the emulation of a more universal template. But the notion is loaded towards a position in between. This position plays on a geometrical and mechanical analogy: different forces act upon an object in different directions, and the diagonal or resultant of the parallelogram of forces indicates the path the object will take in between the forces. To the extent that natural science metaphors are adequate, my preference is for one from chemistry: the reaction of one substance with another may produce a synthesis which has a quality that distinguishes it from the ingredients that went into the reaction. Salt (NaCl) is a substance quite different from its ingredients (sodium and chlorine) in appearance and with respect to what you can do with it.

Following a collision or explosive experimentation in social, political, and economic affairs, people most certainly interpret many syntheses, particularly once they have settled into a pattern, as leading to a distinctive, original, and integral substance. Larger constellations or ensembles of economic, social, and political institutions that we have come to consider as coherent—in the sense that they fit nicely into a pattern—have resulted, as it were, from chemical experiments that were unpleasant: noisy, smelly, and sometimes lethal.

Again, reacting against the notion of convergence on a more universal template, researchers such as Soskice have suggested that we should consider national socio-economic and political regimes as being path-dependent.[23] This means that national regimes follow a rather consistent path, influenced by something similar to the inherent momentum of existing institutional sets that steer the behaviour of individual and aggregate actors in a distinctive direction. This also means that the direction of any regime—social, political, or economic—is controlled by an earlier direction or momentum and cannot be radically changed.

The question then is whether socio-economic aggregates or complete societies follow a straight and consistent path. They do follow some sort of path, resulting from their own and external momenta, and they do start somewhere and arrive at some other place, but is it a straight path? Might it not be a crooked path, with erratic turns and reversals? That would weaken the applicability of a notion such as path-dependency, because if the path is crooked, the question must then be asked how this comes about. Crooked paths suggest multiple and changing forces, possibly altering in strength and direction over time. In this case, path-dependency is a meaningful concept only if we can deal with the complexities and change in the redefinition of a path, which the literature on path-dependency does not do.

1.3   The nature of dilemmas

Paths are a metaphor from geography, mobility, transport activities, or infrastructure. Whereas roads often twist and bend, modernity seems to have stimulated a preference for straight paths in infrastructure and transport. This is evident not only from a glimpse at the geography of North America or Australia but even from a more traditional and rural area such as Westphalia after the French occupation around the beginning of the nineteenth century: new country roads were constructed that connected one village church to the next in as straight a line as possible. The question is whether we can ascertain this tendency in the evolution of socio-economic or political regimes. Internationalization, like other broad societal tendencies such as individualization or secularization, generates and integrates opposite tendencies or momenta. Individualization has been facilitated by and has resulted in a build-up of organized collective institutions of social solidarity and security. This amounts to a conjunction of opposing but interdependent influences that need to be analysed. The liberation of the individual presumes existential safeguards provided by privilege, thus benefiting only the few, or by right and entitlement instituted in a larger collectivity, thus benefiting the general populace.

Human actors act mainly on the basis of three different motives: they follow affective dispositions, they follow established custom and practice, and they make more deliberate, reflective, or rational choices.[24] When they ponder a decision, they are normally subject to a greater or lesser dilemma. A 'dilemma' is an interesting phenomenon. The term comes from Greek and means that a reflection suggests 'two assumptions'. One should add that it offers at least two assumptions and often many of them, each pointing in different, conflicting directions. Actors generically suffering from dilemmas may thus be led to take crooked paths, yielding to a certain momentum at one time and to another later.

There are dilemmas that arise through countervailing forces and information. In this case, the actor is able to distinguish distinct and different forces and information. These are cognitive dilemmas, and they are typical for actors in social settings, subject to conflicting interests, influences, values, relations, and information about the feasibility of courses of action. This consideration also incorporates the problem of interactivity among humans: information, preferences, and influences are not individually established but are subject to social interaction. This interactivity leads to a multiplication of dilemmas. Faced with overly complex dilemmas, social actors tend to seek their bearings in stylized and general ideas, rough rules of thumb, if and when they rest on articulate ideas; they also rely on intuitive and inarticulate personal knowledge. There is a stark contrast between the overt simplicity of articulated knowledge—every piece of knowledge that we have written down, filed away, or are able to discuss in rigorous terms—and the multiplicity of action dilemmas.

Despite the increasing refinement of social science theories and diagnostics, social actors typically rely on compound notions and terms which are *inherently* dilemmatic. Compound notions such as guiding ideas, principles, rules of thumb, or theoretical terms have the pervasive feature that, upon closer scrutiny, they reveal internal contradictions in addition to contradictions between them. The implication is that the rigorous analysis of courses of action is always confusing and less pronounced and specific than the complexity a problem requires. One immediately enters into a dilemma, even when confronting one and the same piece of knowledge, rule of thumb, guiding principle, or specific interest. There is no need to consider two or more distinct pieces of information or points to generate a dilemma. It is quite enough just to follow one line of thinking in order—upon reflection and in practice—to end up in the middle of a healthy analytical and action dilemma. It is the explicit analysis of courses of action that brings out dilemmas, while tacit and intuitive deployment of activities offers a semblance of comfort and assurance when it is rooted in personal experience and social heritage.

A brief glimpse at some findings reveals that internationalization also turns out to be inherently dilemmatic. This is not only because it is itself one of the crudest terms we can come up with. In internationalization, as in more 'simple' things, actors cope by using tacit and explicit knowledge together.[25] But actors are more aggregated and types of knowledge become attached to the aggregations of actors. Such an aggregate picture needs to be examined from a perspective that puts actors in a prominent position. This is not to become overly preoccupied with the individual as a unit of analysis. 'Structures', i.e. inter-individual forces, are also important. But they are not independent of actors' preferences, concepts, perceptions, and other individual characteristics. Actors 'enact' social, economic, and political forces, or structures; we do not know the structures well enough before they are manifested in practice. What can be said for social actors then applies *a fortiori* to the complexity of aggregated actors and to societal space. Hence, societal orders breed dilemmas to a much greater extent.

The resolution of dilemmas is not principally analytical and contingent upon the arrival of high-tech socio-economic navigation systems that reduce the dilemmatic nature of decisions and action. In one sense, dilemmas never disappear but are reinterpreted so as to make them consistent or of no concern any more. Within processes of change, actors pragmatically enact and legitimate solutions which, at least to some extent, define dilemmas away. This is the pragmatic way of resolving dilemmas. Therefore, when unpacked, any pragmatic resolution contains a great number of internal dilemmas. For example, consider the term and notion of the *Soziale Marktwirtschaft*, the social market economy as a programme and ambiguous reality in Germany. Despite its powerful motivating force, it is full of internal conflicts and contradictions, as are even more technical terms such as 'shareholder value'. These contradictions, which come out when we unpack notions, are the residues of past action dilemmas that are never resolved. In an effort to make them consistent, actors learn to differentiate between situational, personal, and other type of criteria when applying knowledge, norms, and considerations. This must have consequences for the construction of more societal settings, and they need to be explored in the present study on internationalization.

Another way of resolving dilemmas is ideological. Ideologies are great for obscuring internal contradictions, for they impose a coherent framework which suggests that dilemmas can be resolved on their own consistent terms. In state socialism, it was proclaimed that environmental damage would never last long because the regime was the only authority capable of counteracting exploitation. In pure market economies, unemployment would not occur. In thoroughly authoritarian regimes, rulers find it in their own interest to bear in mind the interests of the ruled. By emphasizing the coherence of a framework, ideologies pretend that some sort of generic improvement of knowledge and betterment of the human race is being achieved, but only if the principles of the framework are well understood and correctly applied. Coherent frameworks go hand in hand with single-mindedness. Ideologies may thus instil a sense of purpose and enhance motivation; they may also partially increase the efficiency of a social movement; but they are poor at generating theory to explain the real world. Still, even the most eminent pragmatists have found it useful, in a political role, to engage in ideology or use the services of ideologists. In this way, ideology and pragmatism conflict in logic as well as being complementary in practice.

The concepts of internationalization or globalization have been controlled by both pragmatic and ideological action. It is on the bases of both pragmatism and ideology that they have become salient notions to describe and explain events as well as to motivate people to accept or contest a phenomenon of greater importance. It is a phenomenon that needs to be unpacked in more specific detail. In doing so, doctrines are as important as pragmatic considerations. At this point, it is appropriate to synthesize a plethora of dialectical notions that have been mentioned so far.

Dialectics signifies a phenomenon of simultaneous or successive conflict, interdependence, and complementarity between a statement, notion, motive, or force and its respective opposite. None of these is internally consistent to such an extent that it is not constituted as interdependent and complementary with regard to its opposite. If we express this principle with regard to a specific statement, notion, motive, or force, we call its nature paradoxical. Paradox is a basic and unavoidable fact. In the most specific and restricted but widely applicable sense, it 'consists of two contrary or even contradictory propositions to which we are led by apparently sound argument'; the pursuit of coherence thus unavoidably leads us to paradox.[26] Dialectics is about relations between distinguishable statements, notions, motives, or forces; it therefore presumes a greater amount of analytical decomposition.

Paradox suggests that any individual statement, notion, motive, or force is fundamentally incoherent and needs to be decomposed with the aid of dialectics. There are ways of unhooking us temporarily from dialectics and paradox, by constructing more basic statements or forces that reconcile oppositions, or by conceptually differentiating different statements or forces with regard to domains in which they are applicable and unequivocal. But this is temporary, and further steps of corroboration and logical refinement inevitably reveal new paradox.[27] Although this sounds like a philosophical nicety, it is of everyday relevance in realistic social science and is accepted in organization and management studies.[28]

Dilemmas emerge when we consider paradox from the point of view of the actor(s). As social phenomena, the existence of paradox within motives and forces, and the dialectics between opposing motives or forces, are 'external' to actors to some extent, in the sense that they are intersubjective. The residue of dialectics and paradox in the internal world of actors and their reflection of a world imagined to be external can then be described as dilemma. Dilemma is experienced by actors under social or individual pressure to achieve consistency; its intersubjective and social corollary is dialectics. We experience dilemmas by yielding to a compulsion to achieve coherence.

The first type of contradiction signifies that one statement is not compatible with another in the same text, concept, or theory. The second denotes incompatibility between different texts, concepts, and theories. The third reveals that contradictions are synonymous with conflicts between or internal to social forces or motives within an overall socio-economic or political configuration. Contradictions of the third kind are the spice of evolutionary development, and they lead to syntheses emanating from a reaction of forces conflicting with one another, as explained above. Any set of institutions and any culture imagined to be coherent is actually an original synthesis, specific in time and place, of conflicting elements.

The climax of dialectical complexity is reached when we apply the dialectical principle—that a phenomenon, concept, or theory both conflicts with and complements its opposite—to the dialectical principle itself. This means that dialectics has its limits, that beyond these limits the opposite applies, and that dialectical reasoning and real-world processes both conflict with and complement continuity and consistency.

Actors play an important role in the present approach. Actors are different from agents in that they act out dilemmas, are bound and unbound by paradox, and change rules, norms, and institutions in the process of coming to grips with them. An agent is the dialectical opposite and complement of an actor, and an agent moves within rules and is bound to norms and institutions. Real-world actors are also agents to some extent and vice versa.[29] For actors, institutions are soft whereas for agents they are rigid. In the next chapter, the difference between rigid and soft institutions will be explored. The term 'actors' will be used in the sense of agents and actors combined in dialectical unity, i.e. they are both conflicting and complementary types.

In order to appear legitimate, i.e. to conform with rules and norms or consistent principles, actors gloss over, ideologically and pragmatically, the variety of dialectical phenomena discussed. When they enact ideologies or pragmatism, they segment meanings by different and contrasted situations, persons, institutions, or other contingencies. This means that they tacitly or expressly take one principle, value, statement, or practice to be applicable under specific conditions, whereas the opposite principle, value, statement, or practice is applicable elsewhere. The corollary of such action in the societal fabric is a patchwork of different, contrasting, and complementary behavioural norms and patterns allocated to different places— types of encounters, situations, persons, or institutional domains. This will be referred to as a *partitioning of societal space and combination of opposites* within it. An enduring combination of opposites is, in a way, dialectics that have calmed down after having been more explosive in the past. A central proposition is that internationalization has always informed the construction of society and its specificity; the latter is the residue of internationalization dialectics that have settled down and are then interpreted as coherent. In order to achieve such an interpretation, actors have to perform at least implicitly the indicated act of partitioning and combining. Actors thus exhibit ideology or pragmatism.

1.4 Societal and other perspectives

Internationalization implies a number of factual dimensions or domains of action, and a number of axes of analysis or comparison. First, internationalization occurs over time. This points to questions about how it came about and evolved. The time dimension can be addressed with the aid of recent publications or data sets that supply longitudinal information. But the quality of information has also changed over time. In order not to become dependent on a short-run series of data or a particular period, it is useful to take a long-term view because internationalization has been with us for a long time. Historical analysis may thus add important facets to our picture. It is questionable whether restrictive periodization is a good idea, although it occurs very often when the notion of globalization is used. This happens when globalization is taken to be something very new. As we have seen, this is not so.

To the extent that only a particular dimension of globalization is relatively new, the question is how global something has become. Therefore, we are reluctant to confine our analysis to a brief historical period.

Internationalization also has implications for the internal order of societies. Whatever this may be, we need a concept for investigating this order. In particular, we need one which explicates the 'ingredients' of society: the parts, domains, spheres, and spaces into which society can be differentiated, and the relations between these. This is the societal perspective needed, and it should help relate social, economic, political, and other developments to one another. Given the initial theoretical outline, such a societal perspective must not create a contrariety between society and actors. Societal structures are put in place, maintained, and developed by actors, and the actors, in whatever they do, even in deliberate contestation of social, economic, or political factors or forces, respond to them or take them into account. Structures are what is considered in action. If they are not heeded, they are meaningless. Likewise, actors have to be characterized by the things they take into account, in addition to characteristics that have become part of their personality. Furthermore, the boundary between the two must be rather fluid, if it is to be a meaningful one.

Such a theory is also needed for comparing what happens to societies over time, how their qualities, mechanisms, or identities change. It must fulfil the requirements of comparison across societies. Comparisons are needed to tell us how or the extent to which the institutions and culture of societies converge or diverge, in which spheres this happens and why. But we must also be careful not to develop a societal approach averse to incidental events or shocks. Historiography argues that these are important and that central incidents or accidents may channel, deflect, and target greater forces and movements. In return, greater forces and movements may produce specific incidents or accidents. Greater forces and specific but central incidents should thus always be considered, in principle, as interdependent over time.

In addition to these rather general types of social science theory, we have a number of specific middle-range theories that deal with organization, human resources and their generation, industrial relations, enterprise finance, business systems, and varieties of capitalism. Internationalization potentially affects all of these. Hence a variety of specific theories is needed. However, these theories must be compiled and integrated into the larger theoretical framework. This is indeed an eclectic programme. Eclecticism has its limits where theories or approaches conflict. Although tension is inevitable between sets of theories according to some axiomatic suppositions, or epistemological or methodological characteristics, their insights and findings can often be converted or translated to link up with those in entirely different disciplines, subfields, or approaches. Theoretical contributions are often preoccupied with questions of incompatibility or incommensurability between approaches within a discipline or between disciplines. However, it is possible to link different theories in a discursive manner which specifies the place of theories, i.e. what they do comparatively well in which domain, and which links them with other theories that have comparable strengths in other specifiable domains. An eminent example of a discourse linking theories with such respective strengths and weaknesses has been provided by Peter Clark in organization studies.[30]

In the social sciences, our capacity to explain the world is much greater than is commonly assumed. There are no deterministic or exact explanations, but the explanatory performance of the social sciences as a whole, including business, economics, and history, is very good. The approach used in this book corroborates this argument. We have only to make a serious effort to relate complementary bodies of knowledge to one another. But implicitly, there appears to be an assumption shared by the more informed public and many scholars alike that concrete and specific events or phenomena are best explained by specific theories. As a general supposition, this is questionable. Without rejecting the usefulness of any specific theory, we need to recognize that the objects of social science are invariably specific to time and place. They are highly contextualized, and to explain specific classes of phenomena more fully, their contextual situatedness needs to be taken into account. This leads to the need to bring different theories to bear conjointly on specific objects. That is a central art in social science, although it is dismally neglected in training and in performance standards. Proponents of general sociological theory, for example, tend to be unaware of and inexperienced in specific theories and fields of research, let alone in business, management, and industrial economics. Parallel discussions are thus conducted about the same problem in different disciplines without much contact between them. Narrow specialization by disciplines and their subfields may thus lead to an absence of theoretical discipline.

Bringing different theories to bear conjointly on specific classes of objects is a complex enterprise. Some classic authors have evolved this into a tacit skill combined with extensive academic knowledge. Lesser scholars in more developed fields, such as this author, require specific theories to engineer this combination and intertwining of theories, supported by their own line of research. But even then, disciplines or subfields should not try to reinvent the wheels of others. Even if the wheel offered by another discipline is paradigmically or epistemologically unfamiliar, some adaptation may enable it to fit perfectly well. Like other integrated systems of ideas or the specific notions they use, theories are also inherently dilemmatic. They are more or less congealed and coherent ensembles of other theories that were previously kept separate by jealous guardians of the integrity of older theories and approaches. Marx's theory is, for instance, a synthesis of David Ricardo's labour theory of value, Lorenz von Stein's class theory, and Hegelian dialectics 'put on its feet rather than standing on its head', as Marx claimed. Even a totally different kind of theory, such as rational choice theory, was put together from a multitude of different sources (from thermodynamics via areas in psychology to economics). Any streamlined approach of today has emerged from an eclectic combination of disparate chunks of yesterday.

We can therefore derive a perfectly workable theoretical and empirical synthesis for many social science objects of study. The synthesis may however be a general one to a limited extent only; specific syntheses may be required for different classes of problems. The self-assurance that Marx expressed in his understanding of how history works and what to expect of the future may therefore be inappropriate. Yet it is important not to exaggerate the novelty of phenomena in order to legitimate an entire new class of theory and line of research.[31] There is a temptation to which many social scientists yield—to define a subject area, even that of general theory, as being narrow and specialized, and to plough a narrow furrow of research on a small patch of knowledge. Political scientists, economists, business scholars, and sociologists have thus become accustomed to working independently of each other. However, it is more fruitful to bring diverse, more robust approaches and extant findings together in order to deal with a class of phenomena such as internationalization. Such an operation has to bear in mind situatedness in time and place. Once a more thorough attempt has been made to do this, the specific theories needed to perform the integration will be developed more parsimoniously and are assured of better corroboration. This helps to prevent the balkanization of social science, which has already proceeded by leaps and bounds and is confusing the public, practitioners, and scholars alike.

The conceptual orientation of the book is therefore more general than the theme of internationalization implies. But internationalization is a convenient theme with which to launch judicious theoretical eclecticism and synthesis. The topic is in great need of this, since contributions-come from economics, business and management, sociology, history, and political science, each following different trajectories of research and theory. The emphasis on situatedness in time and place and the complexity of the theoretical programme now have a practical consequence. It is not possible to deal with many countries at the same time in a small book when following such a programme. Instead, a more focused demonstration of the programme, using the example of a particular society within internationalization tendencies, is what we currently need, given the glut of short-term and cross-sectional studies. At the same time, it must not neglect comparative findings.

A good approach to use to integrate such different theories is societal analysis as it was conceived at the Laboratoire de Sociologie et d'Economie du Travail at Aix-en-Provence (LEST).[32] This is an approach deliberately constructed to combine interdisciplinary elements and eclecticism with theoretical cohesion and rigour. Its foundations will be explained in Chapter 2, and it is developed throughout the book. The approach is meant to be distinctive but also non-exclusive. Many readers will undoubtedly suggest that there are further theories that might or should have been used, possibly because they fit even better or add important qualifications. I am very aware of this. But what this suggests is that disciplined eclecticism works. Theories and contributions used here are not meant to be exclusive.

1.5   Germany as a puzzling inter-nation

Which country should be chosen to demonstrate the eclectic approach to internationalization? There are practical and conceptual reasons for the selection I have made. Some practical considerations have had as great an influence as those pertaining to conceptual rigour. I have found it eminently appealing to consider Germany from a distance, as a German who has become a Dutch university teacher and researcher and has more experience working abroad than in his home country, and moreover, who has worked on comparative international projects and at a multinational institute. The resultant personal distance notwithstanding, Germany has remained accessible and increasingly easier to understand because of this distance, not despite it. The alternation between distance and intimacy is, after all, a good approach, within a methodology keen on qualification, yet not against quantification.

With nearly 83 million inhabitants, Germany is the largest country in the European Union. Large countries can presumably escape or evade internationalization longer than smaller ones. Yet, Germany borders more countries than any other in Europe and even more than all others in the world, except Russia and China. It shares borders with Denmark, Poland, the Czech Republic, Austria, Switzerland, France, Luxembourg, Belgium, and the Netherlands. The international diversity which surrounds it is therefore unparalleled. Only the Russian

Federation and China, which are much larger, have the same number of neigh-bours. Germany features strong societal aggregation and international exposure at the same time. Its location and its criss-crossing traffic and transport routes have made it the heart of central Europe. The last thing it has is 'natural borders', something that France has been very keen on through its history.

Germany exemplifies countervailing tendencies of societal extension and aggre-gation on the one hand, and thorough internationalization on the other. It allows us to develop the theme of countervailing tendencies inherent to internationalization. The point is not that Germany is the best case to demonstrate this, but I doubt that many people even think it would be a good choice for such a case-study. There-fore, to prove the contrary is to contradict widespread intuition or widely held opinions and is therefore valuable in making a more general point. As we will see, this theme applies to other countries, too. One might expect smaller countries to exhibit such effects very clearly, possibly even more clearly. People in the Netherlands have suggested this to me. But it is better to make the point in a case which is counter-intuitive. To demonstrate the more specific dialectics of internationalization and nation-building is presumably less surprising for the Neth-erlands because people would expect that to be the case in a smaller society, but not in a much larger one. In addition, Germany also constitutes a case for the occur-rence of internationalization *before* nation-building. It suggests the idea of historical cycles of societal aggregation and internationalization, rather than the simplistic idea that internationalization supersedes the nation state at one or several points in time.

All this may be summed up by classifying Germany as a pioneering and early *inter-nation*. It has a unique and puzzling history of extension and consolidation alternating with partitioning, and it will be argued that this has had a profound effect on the construction of its institutions, including those governing work, organization, the economy, and industrial relations. Many overextended societies have split up or disappeared. Germany is an interesting example of a society that emerged, has nearly split up a number of times, but has never disintegrated. Typifying Germany as an early inter-nation is a response to the analysis of Helmut Plessner, who called Germany the 'belated nation' (*verspätete Nation*).[33] I argue that it was a belated nation because it was an early inter-nation. Germany in its present form is a historical accident, or a sequence of historical accidents, despite its consolidation. Demonstrating Germany's evolution not only serves to repeat and bemoan the predicaments which belated nation-building implies.[34] In a more long-term view, the full weight of German heritage also better prepared this society for internationalization. Its example shows how societies can be aggregated and layered at the same time, inserted into the international division of labour, and subjected to a societal community of an emergent higher order.

Likewise, Germany is a good case with which to demonstrate how continuity and change are interdependent, how severe societal changes occur, not least because of internationalization tendencies, and, despite or even because of these, how actors unwittingly construct a continuous cultural and institutional heritage which in retrospect acquires consistency and coherence. In the terminology of a classic book on varieties of capitalism by Michel Albert,[35] Germany came to exemplify 'Rhenish capitalism', as a socially more embedded form of capitalism subject to participative governance and limitations to the free exercise of shareholder or top management discretionary rights. By terminologically locating all manner of such capitalisms, from Baden-Württemberg to Japan, in the Rhineland, Albert in one way performed a rhetorical trick. Rhenish capitalism was thereby within reach of but separate from France, his native country, and it was more distant from the United States than from France. But it is also true that historically, Rhenish capitalism emerged under French influence and was influential in the modernization of Prussia, to which the Rhineland had belonged since 1815, and of the emerging German nation state, half of which consisted of Prussia.

One might just as well have called this form of capitalism Swabian, Franconian or Saxon. It is—and this will be thoroughly explored in this book—a form of capitalism with different connotations that are not readily reconciled: it features long links of trade and a provincial horizon, and it has become widely applied in Germany although it has no centre or focal point of origin. We would have been equally justified to regard this as Elbe capitalism, thereby highlighting another, more eastern river that linked early places where embedded merchant capitalism, craft, and industrial capitalism thrived between Bohemia and Hanseatic ports on the North Sea and the Baltic Sea. However, I will take my cue from Albert and focus a part of the historical analysis on the Rhineland. The regions of the Rhineland have produced not only this particular form of capitalism but also the Franks and western European feudalism in both France and Germany, as well as, in a broader sense, the major ruling dynasties that became important in German, Austrian, and Czech (or Bohemian and Moravian) history.[36]

To some extent, however, Albert's treatment sends the analysis of varieties of capitalism down the wrong path. It suggests a compact coherence of tradition, institutions, and social values, and it was instrumental in establishing a 'German model' that was to be consistent over time and over institutional manifestations in different societal and economic domains. If this coherence is accepted, then subsequent changes are to be seen as radical changes to this supposed 'model' or its collapse. In this way, both the coherence and the radical change of the supposed model become exaggerated. In empirical fact, there have been many German 'models', and they have changed a great deal over time. One of the more frequently cited students of a German 'model' or 'system' is Streeck. It is helpful to note what he says about the coupling between elements of this 'model':

It is not intended to suggest that the institutional configuration that made up the 'German system' in the 1970s and 1980s was created in one piece, or created for the economic purposes that it came to serve. Some of its elements were pre-Wilhelminian, others were introduced by the Allies after 1945, and still others originated in the politics of the Federal Republic, sometimes drawing on and modifying earlier arrangements, and sometimes not. Moreover, each element, for example, the banking system, was subject to its own historical dynamic. All were and continue to be changing, for their own reasons as well as in reaction to each other, and there can certainly be no presumption of pre-established fit between them, even though one might want to allow for some reinforcement effects of the 'model's' historically contingent, social and economic success. That its parts happened to perform together so well during the period in question must be attributed at least as much to *fortuna* as to *virtu* [37]

This legitimates using quotation marks whenever the term 'model' is mentioned, as Streeck usually does. Quotation marks indicate that models are puzzling because their ingredients are rather accidental concoctions that are readily decoupled and recombined within an evolution. In a societal order, the conceptual puzzle is that, in one way, everything seems to be related to everything else, but in another, arrangements which at one stage appeared closely coupled to one another become dissociated, and new arrangements and new ensembles come forth. This puzzle is not sufficiently resolved by analysis of 'varieties of capitalism' or 'business systems' which amount to path-dependency. These imply that culture and institutions are built up over time and retain a formative influence on the build-up or change of further institutions and culture. At the same time—and a few recent studies to be discussed cogently make this point—it is undeniable that change exhibits note-worthy deviation from institutional and cultural templates or models. If that is so, how can we maintain an explanation that relies on the steady build-up and maintenance of culture and institutions over time? If institutions that are found to be coherent in the literature on the varieties of capitalism do change substantially over time, what point can there be in an institutionalist explanation? Would it then only be a short-run methodological artefact? The challenge is to deal with such puzzles in a conceptually sound way. Is there a way of combining the close interrelatedness of culture and institutions, within a societal ambit and over time, with the pervasive facts of autonomous institutions and social, economic, and political change? Germany has featured some of the most breathtakingly funda-mental changes in history, although Germans have not conducted revolutions in which they cut off the heads of their rulers. Germany has been stylized as having brought forth a 'model', whereas more recently and from a more historical perspective, the stability of such a characterization arguably becomes dubious.

For a time, Germany was known for its particularly authoritarian patterns and for its aggression and conquests. For these reasons, Germans have subsequently ex-pressed considerable self-deprecation, amongst themselves and in the presence of foreigners. This is not the rhetoric I propose to adopt here, not because there is no point in it but because it has become a commonplace. Yet the puzzling question how a country known for idolizing authoritarian father figures and goose-stepping, exalting all things military, and meting out corporal punishment in the family during World War II and the post-war period,[38] could subsequently develop a company and work organization featuring few superiors and a great deal of lateral coordination and co-determination.[39] Has everything changed in society, suddenly or subtly, or have some accounts of Germany's past been exaggerated?

One prevalent impression can be corrected from the start. Throughout history, Germany has not been outstanding at empire-building, not even empire-building within Europe. Consider the following statement from a scholarly article on occupation regimes: 'From time immemorial Germans (Prussians) have occupied Russian territory and Russians German territory, while Poland continually suffered from Russian, German and Austrian rule.'[40] This is wrong on several counts. Germany occupied some tsarist territory for a while during World War I but not much Russian land, and it concluded a peace with the new Soviet Union in 1917, earlier than it did with its western enemies. The only time in history that Germany ever attacked and occupied substantial areas of Russian land was after 1942. Prussia never attacked or occupied Russia, and before 1944, Russia never occupied substantial areas of German territory.

Poland is another story. On the one hand, it has been divided and ruled by Russia, Prussia, and Austria a number of times. On the other, Poland was itself one of the outstanding imperial powers in Europe during the high Middle Ages. In 1519, the territory of the Polish-Lithuanian empire was as large as that of the Holy Roman Empire and included large parts of the Ukraine, Belarus, and smaller parts of western Russia.[41] Historically, in fact, empire-building by Russia is to some extent the reaction to the trauma of occupation inflicted on Russians by the Poles, Mongols, Tartars, and Swedes. In other words, these earlier masters of the game of empire-building taught the Russians what they needed to know. One eminent but now long forgotten empire-builder within Europe was Sweden, which occupied substantial areas of Finland, Russia, and north-eastern Germany until the end of the eighteenth century.

At the end of World War I, Polish forces once again occupied substantial parts of western Russia, Belarus, and Ukraine, which led to a conflict between the new Soviet Union and Poland that was finally settled in 1945 by the Soviet occupation of western Ukraine and eastern Poland. From a long-range historical perspective, Germany has thus been an empire-building country in Europe on a par with Sweden, Russia, France, and Poland. There is nothing peculiar about Germany in this respect, except that it 'only' attempted to build an empire within Europe more recently. Granted, Germany's recent attempt was particularly vicious and out of place, an attempt from which it had to back down, to the advantage of all countries concerned. But when evaluating this over time, it is important to keep in mind the crucial role played by trauma and envy, triggered by foreign incursions that set off particular reactions which at a glance appear erratic or wilful. This will be shown for the cases of Brandenburg-Prussia and Germany, where incursions led to specific reactions. These reactions then interacted with institutional and cultural heritage, and eventually generated a metatradition. In turn, this metatradition became essential for the way this society handled internationalization.

Another widespread cliché is that Germany is a more stable and homogeneous society and less of a country of immigrants. Just the opposite is true. Based on the number of current residents who were born abroad, present-day Germany is a nation of immigrants to the same extent that the United States or Australia are.[42]

Furthermore, it has been subject to international migration throughout its history and its population is a significant mixture of ethnicities. Germany has been known for its 'wonderful capacity of absorption', to quote a concise and masterly work on European history.[43] As in other societies, its aggressive nationalism has been due to the strains produced by consolidation in the face of open and ambiguous boundaries. However, since ethnic or cultural Germans have often migrated and lived abroad throughout the ages, notably in eastern or south-eastern Europe, and were classified as German according to the eastern European practice of distinguishing between citizenship and nationality, German citizenship law made allowances for this by granting German citizenship to foreign ethnic or cultural Germans. In the wake of the two world wars, migration across the borders of any historical Germany has become linked with severe conflict and turbulence, with the onslaught of 'ethnic cleansing' in eastern Europe and with the more painful growth of nation states in this area. Such tendencies have been at the root of both a proclivity to restore and cherish societal order and a high rate of migration. Until recently, the immigration of non-Germans was reluctantly tolerated rather than systematically managed. The fact remains that Germany and Switzerland have the largest proportion of immigrants in Europe.

The discovery that these generalizations about Germany's societal patterns or traits are apparently contestable makes Germany a convenient example for our purposes. It shows that 'opportunity makes strange bedfellows', which means that opposing characteristics are combined, dissociated, and recombined in new ways, and succeed each other over time. Societies do not do things in a uniform way across many domains, institutions, settings, and situations. Instead, they have an uncanny capacity to combine situationally differentiated opposites with one another. Germany affords a magnificent opportunity to demonstrate this. As in the case of other nations, closer inspection shows the necessity of a much more differentiated and situated analysis of opposing general characteristics—characteristics which may nevertheless cohere although they are quite different from one situation to another and although things may look different in another period. As a consequence, Germans have turned out to be eminent pragmatists and ideologists at the same time in resolving the dilemmas they have been faced with and have generated themselves. The argument that opportunity makes strange bedfellows also combats tendencies within various strands of social sciences to overgeneralize across periods, social domains, and situations.

This is societal analysis without a notion of strong, pervasive, general, and lasting identity of specific culture and institutions. It is suitable for adequately dealing with internationalization and its own dialectics. But according to the logic of dialectics, a principle is always interdependent to some extent on its opposite. One therefore has to expect that the partitioning and recombination in societal space which is fundamental for the continuous or radical innovation of concrete institutions and culture does not occur willy-nilly but is related to a more persistent theme. This analysis will focus on the metatradition, the dialectical backdrop of partitioning and recombination. The metatradition immediately invokes these; it cannot be defined without them. While the notion of a metatradition is therefore strongly paradoxical, societies are not very aware of it because they are preoccupied with invoking the constant reworking of heritage. Truly dialectical insights rarely lend themselves to ideologies with popular appeal because they relativize phenomena more than actors in need of a firm grounding will find intellectually practical. The ideas that guide societies thus tend to transform a metatradition into a myth, like a fundamental ideational construction in which opposites are reconciled. In the very plain and clear words of Claude Lévi-Strauss, 'the purpose of a myth is to provide a ... model capable of overcoming a contradiction'.[44] For instance, one myth of modern German nation-building is that Roman legions were defeated by Germanic tribes led by Quintilius Varus from the forests beyond the borders of the old Roman Empire. We will see which contradictions the myth sought to reconcile.

1.6   An overview of the empirical treatment and the argument

In the next chapter, we lay the cornerstone of the theoretical foundation by introducing a framework in which the construction of societies and actors are interrelated. While this framework uses historical examples of societal aggregation and disaggregation, it is more conceptual. It introduces the notion that societies are normally layered entities. It directs us towards the concept that the expansion of horizons of action is different from the extension of society, and that the extension of societal horizons tends to be interdependent on provincialization. Internationalization is part of such dialectics. Germany exemplifies how the overextension of rule and the emergence of transnational society carry over into provincialization.

Chapter 3 is more historical and shows how the interplay of internationalization and provincialization produces a tradition that becomes a more national one, although it implies a strong dose of provincialization. To be consistent, traditions are analytically separated from metatraditions. The latter are more abstract, stable over the longer run, and inclusive of substantial changes. This explains how paths of development become crooked and yet relate to an overarching leitmotiv. The cultural and institutional sets that prevail at certain periods are shown to result as much from internationalization as from the reproduction of domestic heritage or repertoire. Internationalization sharpens domestic characteristics rather than weakening them. The period in this analysis starts at a time when there was no Germany and concludes at about the end of the Thirty Years' War, when Germany was still a dubious entity. What happened during this period is identified as the formation of a South Germanic bedrock, as opposed to the North Germanic (Scandinavian) bedrock.

Chapter 4 then takes us from that period up to the present and also refers extensively to social, economic, and political history. In this chapter, we see how long-existing economic and social metatraditions took shape under the influence of internationalization, which is denoted here as 'foreign incursions'. The main argument is that Germany developed a unique alternation and combination of liberal and non-liberal practices and institutions, which were periodically elaborated, differentiated, combined, dissociated, and recombined into ever new ensembles. This metatradition has remained surprisingly consistent despite drastic changes in the political order. The result is that most of the institutions now considered as being very German are in fact either 'domesticated' foreign imports or reactions to international political and economic challenges, wars, conflicts, and occupations that have occurred over centuries.

This is the more historical and conceptual setting on the basis of which the discussion of the governance of work systems is developed in Chapter 5. Work systems are considered from the end of World War II until the present, a period for which we have methodologically rigorous comparisons between societies in Europe and between Germany and the United States. In view of the unique combination of liberal with non-liberal (corporatist) practices, work systems are linked to free international goods markets but are themselves highly regulated, in the sense of being under corporatist influence and subject to statutory regulation. On this basis, they exemplify unique combinations of hierarchical, professional, and lateral types of coordination and control. While these combinations are mostly considered to be based on domestic institutional heritage, they have been stimulated by the US government of occupation and its policies and by economic internationalization, culminating in GATT and the European Union.

Chapter 6 deals with management and corporate governance and focuses more on relatively recent tendencies concerning financial internationalization and shareholder-value orientations. Here the emphasis is shifted to an even stronger degree from the distant past to the topical present. Americanization is shown not to be new but to have had its heyday in the post-war years. Furthermore, the basic mechanism in which internationalization and domestic societal specificity co-evolve is operating as it did in the past. This means that internationalization implies the translation of imported practices into a domestic order and a recombination of established patterns with new ones. Compared with changes in the past, the recent ones are less substantial, and the reversibility of some of them is likely.

As the book proceeds, different aspects are emphasized. General theory is the main focus of Chapters 2 and 3; the historical (social, economic, and political) emphasis emerges in Chapter 3 and culminates in Chapter 4. In Chapters 5 and 6, the emphasis shifts increasingly to more recent findings that relate to more specific middle-range theories and subject areas. Despite these various emphases, the central intention throughout the study is always to link them: for example, general theory and history in Chapter 3; organization and management studies, industrial relations, and history in Chapter 4. Furthermore, the general theoretical theme is also translated into applications specific to work, management, organization, and industrial relations in the appropriate chapters.

Of course, the book is not an encyclopaedic treatment of everything mentioned; that would be pretentious. It is an exercise in cross-disciplinary analysis which does not pretend to be complete with regard to internationalization, general theory, specific theories and strands of research, or socio-historical Germany across the ages. The point of the exercise is not to reconstruct a general social science, as if its differentiation could be superseded and replaced by one integrated framework. There is no intention of bringing monolithic grand theory back to the centre stage. The assumption and conclusion is that there is no centre stage but bridges are very important in a landscape of concepts and research which resembles an archipelago.

The last chapter sums up the highlights of the analysis and generates some conclusions that are possibly more widely applicable. It shows that we can work very well with a concept of society becoming both more layered and more distinctive, not despite but because of internationalization. It is a concept in which action in society is tightly coupled, but institutions are regularly decoupled and recombined into novel forms and constellations. Societal integration is thus distinct and different from institutional stability. Integration implies institutional change but always revolves around some key metatraditions. Societal integration makes for paths around a metatradition, but the paths are crooked and winding, which exemplifies institutional change.

Societal integration and differentiation and internationalization therefore emerge as a patchwork. This means that different and opposed patterns are patched together to create a tapestry of society and internationalization. However, the patchwork metaphor is decidedly not a post-modernist one, as if anything was possible and institutions and culture could be patched together in a haphazard way. There are firm regularities governing the patching-together of societal order and its internationalization, the endogenization of foreign institutional and cultural imports, and the ongoing cultivation of domestic heritage. We find both the openness of change and stricter regularities. The challenge is to see them combined and working together.

2

Societal Effects:
From Vacuum to Tropical Jungle

2.1 Introduction

The following saying is attributed to Charles V (1500–1558), emperor of the 'Holy Roman Empire of the German Nation' and of Spain in the Middle Ages, and in the latter capacity also ruler over the Spanish colonies in America: 'I speak German to my dog, French with my mistress, and Spanish with my God.' This was first related to me, with great pride, by a Spanish Jesuit. This emperor's mother tongue and favourite language was Dutch, but hardly anyone in his entourage understood it. Evidently, the empire of Charles V was unusually expansive and diverse and, by that token, an incredible patchwork of principalities, languages, cultures, and institutions. It was a system of rule and domination, although not one that would given its make-up last long, but was it a *society*, riven as it was by political, religious, linguistic, ethnic, and cultural divisions? We would hesitate to say that it was. However, that empire was part of an even larger European realm constituted by the Christian religion, occidental world-views and feudal subordination, alliances and warfare. Did some sort of European or West European society exist at the time? How hesitant should we be to call it a society?

Such baffling problems give rise to the more general questions of what constitutes society, how it is created, structured, extended, and possibly destroyed, and how internationalized action relates to societal integration and coherence. Such questions are addressed by social theory and general sociology, and history offers us a number of lessons on this topic.

2.2 An action theory of society

2.2.1 The constitution of society

The notion of 'society' is bewilderingly complex. On the one hand, there are the rather analytical definitions used in sociology or cultural anthropology, while on the other, there are the rather vague uses of the term. Let us attempt to define it on a scholarly basis, which will lead to an analytical and descriptively useful differentiation of terms deriving from it. Following in the footsteps of prominent classic authors, Esser suggests that the hallmark of society is a specific 'constitution', meaning specific institutions and not only a constitution in the political sense, in connection with relative social 'self-sufficiency'.[45] Self-sufficiency is a strong claim. It means that there are no other principles to guide acting individuals. This loads the operational definition of society towards closure, and that may be a problem. However, economic closure (autarky) is decidedly not what Esser and the classics mean. Instead, society is merely thought to be the sole purveyor of fundamental meaning for the action of individuals. This is also the classic point of departure for a legal constitution of a country. Witness the beginning of the Declaration of Independence of the United States of America: 'We hold these truths to be self-evident . . .'[46] Fundamentals are of course always taken for granted, or self-evident. For if they were evident by derivation from something else, this would itself be self-evident and fundamental.

The analytical definition presented by Esser has the advantage of pointing out, by use of the word 'constitution', that societies are distinctive for bringing about coherence across a larger and identifiable population, based on what may be a dauntingly huge set of meanings that are held together by principles necessarily taken to be self-evident. But in order for even basic human and civil rights, which are introduced at the beginning of many constitutional texts, to be considered valid principles, they must be interpreted in a way that society will accept as uniform. They therefore point towards that which can never be written down in a text: shared understandings. A written constitution thus presupposes a tacit constitution, and this is what shared understandings are. Acting individuals are united and can meaningfully interact on the basis of articulate or intuitive, principled or pragmatic knowledge. This enables them to interact in such a way that they 'understand what is going on' and pursue a purpose, even when they have conflicting views. Furthermore, the understandings include value-laden interpretations of what is ethically responsible, morally good, useful, or appropriate. There may be a religious side to the understandings and interpretations, or it may be cast within common-law or statute-law norms. But it is not necessary that the larger apparatus of norms, convictions, preferences, or other understandings be free of conflict, contradiction, or ambiguity. In fact, these are more or less inherent not only to any one norm but particularly to any set of norms intending to be complete and fundamental. A law may prevent me from bribing an official, but if there is a shared understanding that corruption may be appropriate in a specific situation, then we have a shared understanding and, by that token, societal coherence.

The implication is that societal coherence is established by acting and interacting individuals. It is not constituted by the existence of a legal constitution, laws, or tangible doctrines alone, for these are themselves in need of interpretation. This takes us back to shared understandings, which are upheld by the day-to-day interaction of people. Rather than being given, they have to be reproduced continually by the actors involved. Through their involvement, these actors are continually changing the understandings they share. This makes it difficult to specify such understandings in a formal way. Actors who cease being involved in a society and engage in another one will tend to lose the understanding that they initially acquired by having been brought up within this society. In 1975, I met the bursar of the college I worked in at Oxford. This man had just returned to England after working in Swaziland for about twenty years. In a way, he was lost, and said a number of times that 'this is not the country I have known and cherished'. In the end, he went back to Africa.

2.2.2   *Societal continuity and change*

If we say that society implies continuity, then this can only be construed to mean that society is rooted in continuous change. Society will appear to maintain its continuity, to stay the same over time, only to individuals who are continuously involved in it. To this extent, a society's identity over time is not defined only by an unchanging core of understandings inherent to laws or other norms. Even marginal but cumulative changes may alienate people who have no part in under-going, performing, or interpreting them on a daily basis. The identity of society therefore is an artefact of the imagination which people experience as valid when they participate in its continual change. It is thus self-evident in a pragmatic way.[47]

A similar point applies to internal diversity in a society. In different regions or population groups, people share different understandings. Behaviour that in Upper Bavaria would be understood as an attempt to loosen up social interaction, as an invitation to someone else to reciprocate, and an encouragement to put personal considerations on the agenda, runs the risk of seeming obtrusive in East Friesland. To this extent, there is a societal rift. However, once Upper Bavarians and East Frisians understand these differences and are able to interpret them correctly, societal integration is achieved because they have, in turn, created a shared understanding about the differences between them. They do not even have to change their own temperaments in order to achieve societal integration. It is quite enough simply not to misinterpret the other person's behaviour and to use this insight as the basis for a common understanding of differences between sets of people.

On this basis, we can see that change over time and internal differences in no way run counter to the identity of society.[48] The latter is not fundamentally constituted by the stability of precise norms over time or by uniformity across the population. Instead, it is a very pragmatic affair. It may have a strongly symbolic side that is manifested in flags, fundamental legal texts, national football team uniforms, or even more trivial but evocative symbols. But all this would be meaningless if it were not being continually interpreted and taken to heart by actors. It is pragmatic action that creates the very foundations of societal identity. It allows actors to gloss over the rifts, changes, inconsistencies, and contradictions that appear on closer scrutiny in the wider totality of societal knowledge, including 'moral sentiments', as Adam Smith could still call them in his first major work.[49] Rooted in Scottish moral philosophy and notably that of his colleague Adam Ferguson, the view propagated by Adam Smith considers the impulse of moral sentiments to be, metaphorically speaking, no less of an 'invisible hand' than is the guiding and ordering principle of free trade and competition. Certainly Smith did not envisage competition as directly constitutive of societal coherence. Although he emphasized the role of competition for the utilitarian achievements of society, he was equally clear about the importance of moral sentiments in making society possible.

Taken together, these views imply that the constitution and facilitating of society is different from and potentially in conflict with the facilitating of utilitarian achievements by societal institutions. Therefore we do have a dilemma. And this indicates the dialectics behind the conflict. A society that poorly facilitates the pursuit of utilitarian purposes or, as Marx would have said, generates a severe mismatch between productive forces and productive relations, will be subject to more generic or radical change. As later theorists would argue, dilemmas do not simply vanish when a body of theory is constructed that either bypasses them or integrates them into a unitary framework. They have to be taken for what they are: this is the task of pragmatism. Pragmatic human action, including what Weick later called 'sense-making', achieves a stable orientation for actors and the consistency of societal arrangements as a cultural artefact.[50] The pragmatic foundation of society follows from the Chicago School of social sciences, notably George Herbert Mead, which has brought in to being action theory and social interactionism as distinctive sociological approaches.[51] Injecting this dose of pragmatism into Smith, we can say that even free competition and free trade will only produce their beneficial effects to the extent that they are enacted and legitimated in line with moral sentiments that attribute a positive value to free competition and free trade. This, of course, is exactly what proponents of competition and trade do: they aim to advance the legitimacy of free trade and competition by invoking moral sentiments and by helping to create societal institutions favourable to their interests.

2.2.3   Cognitive and functional interdependence

This then is the theoretical foundation of the treatment presented here. It does not assume society to be a level of social aggregation that ranks above more individual or intermediate levels, one with separate variables to describe its characteristics. Instead, society is present in the everyday enactment by actors, and their personal knowledge and orientation always implies a measure of societal references. While I have found it convenient to develop a theory based on that of the Chicago School and of Berger and Luckmann, a similar argument could have been derived from Giddens.[52] Societal references can be divided into two major aspects.

1. The behaviour of people rests on knowledge; this knowledge may be articulate or tacit, factual or evaluative. This knowledge is typically brought about within a societal horizon. A *horizon* bounds all those 'facts of life' that actors 'see' and can interpret; it indicates the range of and limits to their *knowledge*. By further developing the ideas originating from the Chicago School (of philosophy and the social sciences, not economics) and from some central

European phenomenologists and interpretivists (A. A. Schütz, Wilhelm Dilthey, Hans-Georg Gadamer, and related authors), Berger and Luckmann posit that human behaviour is necessarily rooted in diverse sorts of knowledge, as something that arises within social interaction. Societal structures and human behaviour are, in fact, enactments of knowledge, and by that token they are interpretive performances.[53] The very foundations of social life in modern society are therefore no less mythical, when made explicit, than the foundations of any other pre-modern and even archaic societies. We pragmatically adhere to human rights, for instance, although people around the world and even in specific societies do not unequivocally share such understandings. We therefore evoke them as powerful myths in principally the same way that other people enact an animistic world-view. Even our concept of factual truth is founded on myth, to the extent that we see it as an unending challenge which we can only approximately fulfil at best. Let me call this the *cognitive* aspect of societal interdependence: we are interdependent in society by way of the sharing of knowledge, which always borders on the mythical. The qualitative nature or properties of the interdependence we experience is a consequence of perceptions and interpretive performances. If we do not pretend to share some understandings and knowledge, the existential foundation on which we stand more or less crumbles underneath us— a dangerous development for a species dependent as no other on creative cooperation.

2. However, we cannot claim to know the effects and repercussions of our action at all times. We do try to take these into consideration as much as possible, and they therefore enter into the codified or tacit knowledge that we acquire. To this extent, point (1) above applies to knowledge about interdependencies between humans and between the phenomena they encounter: we are dealing with enacted knowledge, which means that 'facts' acquire this quality through the collective sharing of an understanding that underlies their classification. However, since we can never anticipate all or even most of the things that ensue from our action, we are also subject to what I propose to call the *functional* aspect of interdependence. This means that we are factually dependent on having other people not only perceive or think something but also on having them do something, whether it is for us or someone else, for pay or out of moral conviction. There is much we do not know, we pretend not to know, we find too cumbersome to find out, or we find more comfortable to ignore. Then we wait for things to happen. But even then, we take note of events and try to relate them meaningfully to previous action, notably our own. So the border between the cognitive and the functional aspect of interdependence is not fixed around types of events or sequences. Again, it is enacted by the conjunction of cognition and the world around it. Hard-headed interpretivists would say that there is no world we can meaningfully discuss beyond our enacted or constructed cognition. Yet, our mind enacts it in this way at least some of the time, when it is open and curious.

Functional and cognitive interdependencies relate to the 'facts' and imagination, respectively. Crudely speaking, we can divide social sciences and, notably, organization studies into two categories, depending on how they interpret social facts. There are those who believe that social facts are indeed that—facts—so we had better not distort them or try to wriggle our way out of them. Others believe that social facts are what specific people make them out to be, so we had better not impose a meaning on them which would be alien to the prevailing understanding of those who enact them.[54] I propose to call, in a totally value-neutral way, the first class of scholars 'positivists' and the second class 'interpretivists'. I argue that we need both of them. We can see that the positivist tradition was closely linked to the drive to explain what Merton had called the 'latent functions' of behaviour, i.e. those that actors were not aware of and did not deliberately intend to happen, although they may indeed accept or welcome them.[55] Some sociologists even consider the analysis of latent functions to be the very heart of the discipline. Interpretivists, on the contrary, have been concerned with doing justice to the meaning imputed to behaviour.

Who could argue with either of these aims? Still, they tend to encroach one upon another in an erratic fashion because our knowledge is divided into manifold types and is never wholly stable with respect to what it claims to consider and deal with competently, meaning that which we feel confident to classify as facts. On closer inspection, we also have to acknowledge that the engineering of some functions may have been deliberate at some point, at least on the part of some of those who wield power in society. Later, these functions turn into latent ones by becoming habitual to the extent that they can even dispense with deliberate volition or manifest support in order to take effect and can rely instead on passive compliance. It may also be that habitual or normatively ordained patterns are manifestly and deliberately supported later because the function they fulfil was not one originally intended, at least not by their new supporters. Thus, we see that a combination of interpretivism and positivism is inevitable, especially if we pay attention to history and historical change in society.

To recapitulate, societal interdependence between actors, on the one hand, and between actors and the phenomena they encounter, on the other, can be divided into functional and cognitive aspects, and neither of these aspects can claim a stable substantive domain. There is a contingent relationship between knowledge and functional interdependencies in society. We are familiar with some of the latter, but others develop in unpredictable ways, so that we learn about them. Therefore, according to Berger and Luckmann, knowledge is vitally important to the functioning of societies. It is essential for us to know, learn, and interpret. Tacit and mythical knowledge are perfectly respectable forms of knowledge: even mythical knowledge does not at all fundamentally obstruct enlightened discourse.[56] Such forms of knowledge are fundamentally complementary. Even the concept of the Enlightenment, founded on self-grounded reflection, or any other proposition defined as self-evident, is the enactment of a myth.[57] It assumes a universal and harmonious reasoning that does not in fact exist because it is necessarily dilemmatic.

By assuming it to be a given, we construct a myth for a pragmatic reason. This is so that the quest for truth may be better accommodated by the idea of truth being one and indivisible. To some extent, substantiated knowledge can be substituted for more mythical knowledge, and it would be a shame if we did not use the opportunity to do so whenever it presents itself. However, experiential, scientific knowledge, constructed according to general and reasonable norms of enquiry and discourse, is itself an enactment of a particular myth.

2.2.4 Typifications, culture, and institutions

In the world of human relations and artefacts, knowledge is engineered to be an orientation grid that is at least temporarily self-evident and self-sufficient within a particular society. It is clustered around what Berger and Luckmann have soberly described as 'a reciprocal typification of habitualized actions by types of actors'.[58] Informed by the knowledge that they have come to share, actors construct typifications in a pragmatic way. These enable meaning and orientation to be attributed and shared by several actors. Pragmatism means that we explicitly or implicitly negotiate the meaning of behaviour. When we think that we have reached a 'deal', that we have come to a mutual understanding, then we force it into a sense-making container called 'typification'. To this extent, each typification exhibits a high degree of fluidity during its creation and throughout its marginal ongoing modification, because it is a stake in negotiations towards more certain understanding; therefore it is perennially at risk.

Consider this example: the spouse of an Israeli colleague whom I knew well once called me 'a nice Jewish boy'. In fact, I was neither a boy (I was 31) nor am I Jewish, and both of them knew this, of course. This was not an attempt to convert me to the Jewish faith, for Jews are not in the habit of converting Christians anyway. We had never discussed religion, and the only time I have ever been to a synagogue was when this couple's older son celebrated his bar mitzvah. Yet, they thought it fitting to apply this typification. And I could not help but concur. Moreover, we all probably shared the same understanding of what it implied. Such a tacitly negotiated understanding that pragmatically exceeds established definitions is part and parcel of how typifications fluctuate, and they are none the worse for that, as far as shared meaning is concerned. Their tacit construction even helps the understanding take root effectively by evoking self-evidence.

Now let us look at what Berger and Luckmann meant the definition in the quotation above to define. They provided the definition for an '*institution*'. Their definition runs contrary to the many uses of the term by political scientists, positivist sociologists, or those working in the economics of institutions. Such scholars typically use it to refer to arrangements that are not subject to negotiation in every transaction or decision. They would emphasize the relative inertia, the unchangeableness, and the binding and restrictive character of the arrangement they term an institution. In this terminology, institutions are typifications that are unhooked from the perennial negotiation that underlies their emergence and modification. This use of the term is positivist, for it takes institutions 'to be what they are' instead of what people make them out to be in a specific situation.

This is not to argue exclusively in favour of or against one of these definitions. Both positivism and interpretivism have a point, and we cannot dispense with either. Yet it is important to be aware of the double-edged nature of institutions. They are perennially rooted in the interactive negotiation of actors, and are therefore fluctuating and being pragmatically adjusted. At the same time, they tend to congeal into rigid patterns. In this respect, they can be metaphorically likened to water, which may also take on different aggregate states: fluid, rigid, or slushy. Eskimos can undoubtedly supply more distinct and finely tuned typifications. Likewise, institutions are more fluid or more rigid depending on the temperature, as it were, to which they happen to be exposed at a given moment. The upshot is that we should take care not to neglect either aggregate state, although there is nothing easier when we become immersed in particular paradigms, be they the paradigms of economics or political institutionalism, or an interpretive theory of action.

The awareness that institutions have both rigid and soft states of aggregation and can alternate from one to the other has been revived by Christine Oliver in the organization and management literature.[59] This is useful for correcting a fundamental misunderstanding that emerged in the wake of work by authors such as DiMaggio and Powell,[60] who suggest that institutions are about isomorphism and behaviour converging upon a standard of practice. Isomorphism is only one aspect of institutions. They are also about de-institutionalization (softening of institutions) and dialectical institutionalization, i.e. the institutionalized reaction against another institution.

If the analysis of institutions is founded in the sociology of knowledge, it does not mean that the intention is to create a reductionist framework which considers everything fundamentally to be due to knowledge and understanding. Political scientists will argue that power has an influence on institutions; economists will say (as Oliver Williamson has been saying) that relative costs and benefits are important and that, faced with competition, efficient institutions will prevail. Interactionists like Berger and Luckmann are the last to relegate power and prices to the class of less important phenomena.[61] The logic of interactionism can be used to argue that such factors take effect by way of knowledge. If I do not valorize the expertise, money, or other resources which a power-holder may grant me or withhold from me—resources on which his power therefore rests—that power collapses. In the conceptual world of interactionism, anything of importance becomes so by being 'reciprocally typified' as such. This is an approach that builds on the mutual constitution of meaning, even if it is dilemmatic. This also means that the action of understanding and interpreting brings in power or relative prices, even though such considerations are dilemmatic with regard to non-utilitarian and unpolitical ones. The diligent actor does not neglect them; he enacts them.

From this analysis, we can also easily predict when and how institutions become rigid or fluid. To the extent that actors are competent at understanding more extended chains of action and are more capable of integrating complex interdependencies into their tacit or explicit knowledge, they will be better able to enact institutions in their fluid aggregate state. They will be able to negotiate any arrangement by paying close attention to the possibilities, to the attribution of meaning, and to ways of changing them. But to the extent that actors, in their perception, extended chains of action into small self-contained pieces, they will find themselves faced with a world populated by rigid institutions which they cannot soften by negotiation. Such states of fluidity or rigidity relate to actors' cognitive frames. They change as horizons of action are extended or reduced. Therefore, they are related to the reconstruction of societal complexity and social relations. As a result of implicit or explicit negotiation about meaning, these states are also related to the power that actors have and the force that existing patterns exert in this negotiation. In this way, power, rule, and domination enter the picture via cognitive and functional interdependencies, and these will often be enacted dependencies.

This is where the analysis of institutions links up with the structure of knowledge in society. On the one hand, societies that are not overly complex will be better able to enact interdependencies in people's cognition, to fluidize institutions, and to juggle and negotiate possibilities and attribution of meaning. Such societies will expand the cognitive aspect of interdependencies. On the other hand, societies that are very complex will interpret *ceteris paribus* interdependencies as being based on rigid institutions that link black boxes supposedly containing stable internal characteristics. Such societies will therefore enact functional interdependencies, thereby minimizing the absorption and internalization of far-flung institutions within the mindsets of actors. However, it is important to note that rigid institutions can be treated as black boxes even if they do not inherently have this quality. Fluidity and rigidity are attributed by actors, and we become aware of any attribution only in a specific behavioural act.

2.2.5   *The propinquity of rigid and soft institutions*

Specific societies as we know them are not strictly rigidifiers or strictly fluidifiers. It all depends on the organization and transmission of knowledge. And societies have a habit of suddenly changing the aggregate state of knowledge organization and of having different aggregate states exist next to each other. As an over-stylized but appropriate example, let us consider present-day Germany, where the workflow organization of an enterprise is distinguished by great fluidity. At the same time, the coordination between the national government and the state governments, between both levels of government and the health insurance system, the social security apparatus, the pharmaceutical industry, the trade union federation, and the employers, respectively, is a marvel of rigidity. Although a cause for practical concern in Germany, this juxtaposition of extremes is a normal societal phenomenon. There is nothing that allows us safely to predict which areas will remain rigid or which will stay fluid, or where rigidity or fluidity will occur in the longer term.

As far as the juxtaposition of rigid and fluid institutions is concerned, societies resemble Kamchatka. Kamchatka is a large, geographically unique peninsula protruding south from eastern Siberia. Normally, we tend to associate volcanoes with warmer climates and glaciers with cold mountain regions such as the Himalayas or the Alps. But on Kamchatka, the volcanoes have glaciers, and it is only a short walk from hot springs or a volcano to a glacier. The fact that these geographical features exist side by side is not due to a quirk of nature, but to a chain of multiple causalities; these are of general or possibly universal import, but their time- and place-specific constellation and effect in Kamchatka is unique. I will describe later how this happened and use it to explain not the geology and topography of Kamchatka but German social history. The 'Kamchatka effect' denotes the linked, not accidental, propinquity of opposite things. Such things are diametrically opposed to each other in a conceptual dimension but close to each other in social or other spaces.

It is also important to note that the fluidity of institutions is not at all incompatible with their institutional quality, but it does establish this quality within interpretivist frameworks. Thus, visible change in the more rigid institutional typifications (through a succession of unfreezing, change, and refreezing which Kurt Lewin made popular in organization theory[62]), can only be viewed as counting against institutional quality as seen from a positivist perspective. Interpretivists would counter that the change that occurs between the unfreezing and the refreezing is inevitably related to pre-existing typifications, at least soft typifications. To this extent, there is always institutional continuity, even in the midst of more radical changes. It is again the continuous, practical, and pragmatic involvement of actors that generates both institutional stability and change at the same time.

2.2.6 The propinquity of opposite institutional and cultural patterns

To stylize pervasive institutions as covering an entire society across multiple actors, situations, and subsets has very limited value. Institutions differ greatly between domains and situations. They may be a good first approximation, but on closer inspection we find that they are subject to the Kamchatka effect: the societal landscape reveals a structured connivance of very distinct and even opposing patterns existing in close proximity. This will be analysed below as a partitioning of institutional spaces.[63] Thus, fundamental values are only an initial approximation used to provide meaning for the complete range of behavioural repertoires of different types of people in one society. Such generalized tools are used a great deal in the social sciences and by the general population: Germans are bureaucratic and humourless, Italians light-hearted and flexible, Swedes serious and compassionate, Americans pushy and pragmatic. The idea of institutions and values as universally activated schemes in a given society leads to a nightmare of obfuscation. This is certainly not what Geert Hofstede wished for when he pioneered the systematic mapping of work-related values across societies.[64] For this reason, he has often said, he is more afraid of his admirers than his enemies.

Of course, societies do have to share certain understandings, allow institutions to congeal into something rather rigid, and inculcate sets of values. But the important thing is that different types of actors activate different and opposing values in different types of encounters. They also enact different institutions depending on the context of an encounter, and they subtly or radically change the nature of institutions. Consider a simple example. Foreign managers and commentators are prone to characterize German workers and managers as being formal and stiff. This is indeed how they act during first encounters and as long as they feel that they do not really know someone, especially if the others are foreigners. One reason is that it takes more time to be properly understood by foreigners, and the other is that a special effort has therefore to be made in order to put foreigners or other new business partners at ease.

How do you put other people at ease during initial and often more superficial encounters in a work context? This is quite relative to the specific cultural knowledge generated and activated for this type of encounter in the respective society. Englishmen will put people at ease by using amicable humour. For the most part, Germans still believe that people will relax when you demonstrate serious concern for and dedication to the task in hand. They assume that new partners have every right to be initially apprehensive about your competence and reliability. Once you have satisfied yourself that both of the parties have good reason to relax in light of the concern and efficiency demonstrated, then the time may be ripe for humour. However, should humour be used immediately, it might be interpreted as a demonstration of flippant neglect of obligation. In this framework, humour and even boisterous merriment have a definite and secure place—be it after work, at the conclusion of a contract, or on an outing—according to the cherished formula that 'work is one thing and pleasure another'.[65] English culture is radically different, which often leads to ineradicable misunderstanding in first encounters: the Germans think the English are flippant and negligent, while the English think the Germans are humourless and stiff. A proper understanding of the time and place in which norms and values are activated in each respective society, which would be standard practice according to sound interpretive theory, would help avoid such misunderstanding and the perpetuation of facile clichés at the outset.

Cultural orientations, such as fundamental values, and institutions are really two sides of the same theoretical coin, according to the interactionist approach central to the present analysis. Still, the relation between the two is very often misconstrued, which is why it is briefly elucidated here. We can assume that differences between societies are located in the mentalities of people, in the way they think, and in the values and preferences to which they adhere; or we can focus on normative or strongly rooted habitual regularities, as institutions which are situated above the purely individual level. The first option leads to a culturalist approach to researching and explaining differences in organization and human resources. They are rooted in strong values and preferences; a practice is sustained because people find it repulsive, unethical, or unappealing to do otherwise. The second option leads to an institutionalist approach. People comply with norms because a wider formal machinery of laws, agreements, standards, or codes exists; people are often coerced, strongly or subtly, to follow such standards. Social sanctions can thus uphold and enforce regularities within both an institutionalist and a culturalist perspective. Actors need regularities, for in a world where everything is unpredict-able and in constant need of specification and negotiation, purposeful behaviour either ends in a total muddle or requires despotism.

Culturalism and institutionalism are thus linked through interactionist theory, which points out that institutions have a fluid state and are being constantly negotiated by knowing (imbued with cognitive programmes and knowledge) and learning individuals. In the end, the predispositions of actors and institutional typifications thus reciprocally condition each other.[66] Theory specialists will still argue about whether or not culture and institutions can, despite this reciprocal conditioning, be considered as separate phenomena. I do not propose to go much further into this, in a categorical way, except to propose that rigid institu-tions require a strong and specific cultural understanding, whereas fluid institutions require ingenious actors striving towards an understanding which is far from immediately self-evident; but it can be construed to be thus. Reciprocal constitu-tion, as a concept which is pertinent over the long run, therefore means that culture and institutions are not separate. Even rigid institutions become endowed over time with cultural ramifications that are quite different from those prevailing in an earlier state. Where fluid institutions are concerned, institutions and culture clearly over-lap because their very nature points to culture. Generally, they are always bracketed one upon the other in the sense that we cannot grasp one without seeing its background in terms of the other. Keeping the reciprocal constitution of actors and societal spaces in mind, we can use them as conjoined tools in societal analysis.[67]

2.3 Societal aggregation, integration, and internationalization

2.3.1 Societal coherence

A fundamental question is how to distinguish societies from other entities and how they stand in regard to other entities. One clue in this respect is provided by the keywords 'self-sufficiency', 'constitution of meaning', and 'interdependencies'. Together these indicate that society is a space, imagined yet no less real, in which individuals and groups are firmly fixed in relationships. In turn, these relationships are simultaneously constraining and enabling, and they have a quasi-monopoly in making sense of what happens within them and outside of them in the larger natural or social world. If societies are understood as such, it is not surprising that they should evoke and claim collective solidarity, since they are powerful providers of identity to people, not only or not even primarily by reference to themselves but through the many differentiated affiliations they constitute or legitimate. Solidarity results from the encompassing range of this societal horizon: since everything meaningful is contained within it or passes through it, its totality is diffuse—rather than functionally specific as Talcott Parsons would have said—and diffuse and encompassing attachment tends to go together with collective solidarity.[68]

To this extent, societies are analytically different from more specific alliances, treaties, or associations. Some occidental doctrines have suggested that societies began with a 'social contract', at least those societies in which the fictional 'war of all against all' was brought to a close. Many similar rational choice analyses have followed this tradition. However, as René König never tired of pointing out when summarizing earlier literature, this is not sociology, and it is unrealistic to impute a modern contractual choice to societal origins when the idea of contract in this form could not exist. In principle, sociology has developed in opposition to this specific rational choice tradition and has pointed out that the constitution of society has always occurred as a non-contractual enactment of a community of fate, one which may initially have experienced conquest and subjugation, but was always accompanied by the imaginary social construction of a societal entity. This social entity was seen as a quasi-body, sacrosanct, untouchable, and in earlier doctrines manifested corporeally in the person of the king.

This then is the root of a sociological theory of society as it began in the medieval Anglo-French doctrine of royalty, and was reinterpreted in the eyes of Scottish moral philosophers, including Adam Ferguson and Adam Smith. In a nutshell, their conclusion is that competition may be fine for the welfare of nations but if societies are to originate and function, they require moral sentiments based on collective solidarity and shared understandings.[69] Competition needs to be embedded, in order to be complementary to and supported by moral sentiments and differently constructed institutions. If it is not, it will be deprived of both its beneficial economic effects and its legitimacy. This is a more general example of the Kamchatka effect: solidarity and competition, while at opposite ends of a spectrum, are interdependent and coexist at close quarters.

As König pointed out with regard to European history, there are indeed processes of societal aggregation that have a strong social contract background. However, in reality these were not contracts between individuals but pre-existing societal communities. Switzerland is the most prominent example, having originated from an oath of mutual allegiance sworn by the representatives of the founding cantons. Confederation may thus start with a treaty, which is a contract of sorts, but as it endures, it is strengthened by an oath sworn for unlimited or 'eternal' solidarity that binds successive generations, who are thus deprived of the contractual choice exercised by the 'founding fathers'. Other *Eidgenossenschaften* (confederations, *foedus* = *Eid* = oath) that might be considered as hybrid phenomena were established within the territorial realm of the medieval Holy Roman Empire, as something between an alliance sworn by 'estates of the realm' (*Reichsstände*, i.e. principalities, monasteries, and towns directly subordinate to the king or emperor) and firmer societal aggregation. How should we classify the *Hanse*, for instance? Was it the beginning of societal integration and aggregation or was it merely a free trade area? After all, the *Hanse* was able to coordinate its members' belligerent activities more successfully than the present-day European Union. And how should we classify the *Lausitzer Städtebund* and many other grass-roots alliances?

Except in the case of Switzerland, history has made the decision purely academic, for alliances that might have evolved into proto-societies of an order higher than that of very local societal communities were aborted by larger territorial states imposed by princely rulers. Thus, the confederations started from 'below' were mostly annihilated before they had the chance to begin any 'nation-building', i.e. before they achieved societal integration with a more permanent degree of imagined and enacted community of fate, shared understandings, and collective solidarity.

2.3.2 *Coherence through solidarity*

Collective solidarity is not best ascertained by measuring verbally expressed sentiments. It is observed whenever the community asks individuals to contribute to a common cause. Whenever it demands that they should be prepared to give up life or limb to defend the independence, internal order, and territorial integrity of a society, and when people enthusiastically or grudgingly do this, we observe a high amount of societal integration. Do we have an integrated society in Germany across the East–West divide? Consider for a moment what happened in 2002 when the Elbe and its tributaries flooded large expanses, primarily in eastern Germany. Massive numbers of military troops, professional civilian relief personnel, and volunteers were deployed to lay sandbags in communities and to rescue the stranded; the chancellor donned Wellington boots and braved the rain to promise publicly that generous relief funds would be provided and that reconstruction would be paid for by shelving the plans for tax cuts; all across Germany benefit concerts and theatre performances were held to raise money, and the public donated large sums to the flood relief funds.

Of course, it helped that Germany was preparing for elections in just over a month's time. But when elections spur on the commitment of resources, they act as a catalyst of collective solidarity. Similar catastrophes in the Czech Republic or in Poland did not receive such generous help from Germany. If a catastrophe happens on an even worse scale in the Third World, professional services or agencies send a planeload of tents and medicine and some nurses and doctors. In other words, catastrophes quickly point out what a salient entity of societal integration is. When catastrophe strikes a society, that society turns existing policies inside out and makes a great effort to combat the catastrophe without asking any major questions.

Thus, society proves it exists and is salient by responses that, as it were, reverberate throughout its entire fabric in a short span of time. This is particularly so when catastrophes occur and external danger threatens. At these moments, collective solidarity, shared understandings, and institutional commonalities quickly materialize. If they do not do so, societal rifts may occur. It may be argued that a lack of solidarity is conditional on pre-existing cracks in societal architecture. Less dramatic instances are the ritualized, civilized, domesticated, and more playful enactments of solidarity, which represent a kind of war with only minor bloodshed, such as important national football matches. At such moments, national society experiences itself as a single entity with which to identify, even if the substantive core of the identity is highly blurred. This opacity indicates that the roots of societal effects lie in the vague and mythical marshlands of collective sentiments. Societal effects are notoriously strong, notoriously quick to emerge, and become visible under threat; interdependencies are more acutely felt, experienced, and enacted by rallying around a common purpose and coordinating disparate activities to address it. In this submerged mythical terrain of collective sentiments, societal effects become visible in a coherence that reveals itself in the rapid reverberation of action and meaning throughout the broader fabric of society.

It is in response to threat that cognitive interdependencies become most conspicuous. But in a less dramatic way, they are also present in everyday life. One element of this is the existence of shared understandings; another is the cognitive knowledge of the implications (requirements and consequences) that action in the specific domain of an actor has in domains which are not bracketed in the action itself, or which lie outside the domain under the actor's control.

2.3.3 *Coherence through practical learning*

Suppose the board of a German corporation decides to register and trade shares on the New York Stock Exchange. This particular action carries the enterprise far beyond the ambit of its country of origin. The management will therefore weigh the conditions at the NYSE and on the world financial markets and consider their implications for the company's domestic functioning. How does the generation of shareholder value for the benefit of NYSE investors affect strategy, organization, technology, and industrial relations implemented at home? Investors at the NYSE notoriously reward downsizing with higher share prices. This reduces the costs of capital procurement when new shares are issued. What if the downsizing at home then destabilizes the human resources that are needed to generate added value? What if the accounting practices (by business divisions or units) demanded by US investors are such that they impose an entrepreneurial organization that tears apart internal networks of synergetic cooperation across organizational units to an extent detrimental to value generation?

It is immediately clear that such considerations activate knowledge that actors have about the conditions under which workers are trained and socialized, about the conditions needed to establish and maintain loyalty and motivation, about the material and intrinsic rewards and incentives that make them productive, and so on. This knowledge is necessarily specific to the society in the country of origin. Furthermore, it is not set in stone, but is open to at least marginal negotiation with highly interested actors, such as works councils, trade unions, representatives of management, workers and outside interests on the supervisory board, chamber of industry and commerce vocational training committees, internal and external education and training establishments, and many more. In addition, the interests of existing and potentially dominant investors have to be taken into account. What if they strongly object to letting control over the enterprise slip into the hands of new investors who may have shorter-term interests and will be happy to sell their shares when the price drops (as long as they can take their cut) rather than aim at stable revenue over a longer time span?

These contingencies are so broad and diverse that our company's board of directors cannot simultaneously attend to them and control them in one conjoint operation. To a large extent, the board has to accept such institutional conditions and behavioural predispositions and operate in a diligent and knowledgeable rather than a wholly revolutionary manner. In this respect, the internationalization of the company prompts its management to activate local, societal knowledge. It may do this in anticipation of possible repercussions resulting from NYSE trading, but it may also launch itself into this financial market without extensive planning, and try to muddle through as experience reveals the consequences. The latter case is one of learning by trial and error, the former by pro-active learning. Whatever happens, the consequences and requirements of the company's course of internationalization will increasingly be experienced as local or national ones.

If internationalization addresses primarily finance but leaves operations, human resources, and other policies aside, it is partial. If that is the case, the need for operational implementation focuses the attention of actors more acutely on domestic conditions. Actually, internationalization cannot help but be partial, since investors already have varying interests, according to societal financial settings. This diversity is even more pronounced when we look at patterns of institutional organization, human resources, education, industrial relations, and government regulation. It is even likely that a more urgent focus on shareholder value makes it even more imperative to evaluate and utilize domestic resources that are institutionally and culturally specific. Generation of value requires a diligent utilization and cultivation of resources, for it cannot for ever rely on the speculative increase of capital value, as events in recent years have clearly shown when developments on the stock market sent share values tumbling back to the levels of about seven years ago.

2.3.4   Internationalization and domestic institutions

The foregoing experience can be formulated in the provocative form of a theorem-like statement: internationalizing action is highly partial, according to experience to date and by necessity. People striving towards purposeful change, such as the internationalization of capital markets, focus their attention on a restricted range of parameters. Now, human action can only be focused if a number of circumstances relating to such parameters are taken as stable or constant. Internationalization thus requires a number of things to be stable and predictable in order to establish a successful policy with regard to those action parameters that are assumed to be open to reconstruction. Internationalization thus sharply evokes societal effects. When actors take this into account, the effects work on the basis of cognitive interdependencies. If actors do not take this into account, the effects will emerge through functional interdependencies that carry them from segmental international involvement to domestic considerations.

This notion of societal effects is firmly grounded in action theory, specifically the view that focused actors require certain given circumstances. Action theory does use collective attachment to societal myths or fundamental values, but it considers the link between circumstances affecting focused policies and fundamental societal characteristics to be indirect and non-deterministic. Notably, links are non-deterministic in view of the perennial conflictuality and indexicality (specificity of culture and institutions invoked by time, place, and other situational contingencies) of more fundamental orientations. But there is a link with societal coherence that can be stated as follows: generation of economic value is itself a cultured and institutional phenomenon that works through the interdependency of institutions in different spheres of society; such institutions are always specific, within a societal order, and their interdependence is activated by cross-cutting action systems, which are analysed below.

Interdependence implies adaptation, and since exposure to external influences is always highly partial, interdependence will lead to a more or less biased or balanced adjustment between the external influence and domestic culture and institutions. Specifically, interpretive approaches rightly maintain that the external influence 'is not simply what it is', but what it turns out to be when filtered through the domestic understanding of local actors. In this view, there is no such thing as global understanding. This view has been put forward programmatically by Geert Hofstede in the German title of one of his books: 'Think Local, Act Global'.[70] This reverses the famous slogan 'Think global, act local.' From an interpretivist point of view anything else would be foolish, but this standpoint is supported by a number-crunching positivist such as Hofstede. We may indeed 'think' of global functional interdependencies, but the action that results from this awareness is framed by a culture in our mind, which we cannot consciously think away, and by local institutions, which we cannot reconstruct, intentionally or consciously, in all their ramifications.[71]

A more interpretivist rendering of the essence of the theorem-like statement proposed above would be: any typification taken out of its original context—in other words, decontextualized—and brought to bear on a different context will only take effect following a translation into the new context which changes and adjusts its meaning. Translation in this sense presents a more radical dilemma than the translation from one language into another, such as the translation of Shakespearian drama from English into German. Translation in interpretivist terms may nearly obliterate the meaning initially intended in the original context. Problems of translating artefacts from their context of invention into a new context of application often leads to complete change or reinvention.

That transfer implies translation is quite familiar from technology studies and the experience of transfer of organizational recipes from one case to another, and relates especially to the transfer of technology or organization across borders.[72] This insight is often neglected in the stylization of supposedly global typifications: for instance, as Saka shows, in the diffusion of 'Japanese' work and organizational practice in multinationals. Diffusion of practice in multinationals is often analysed as being subject to an 'organization' rather than a societal effect; however, it entails the translation of the practice into local situations and meanings.[73] It is hard enough for people in the same society to reach a large amount of general and binding understanding. On a global scale, this is much harder, and only a small number of people around the globe may achieve this. But then the penetration of this understanding within a local society will be severely restricted. Widespread penetration requires translation into a local understanding, and translation always changes meaning. Thus, from both a positivist and an interpretivist viewpoint, the exposure to external influences leads to consequences that vary according to the societal context into which they are absorbed; the more powerful this external influence is, the larger its impact will be on the society it penetrates and the greater the differences will be in the consequences for each society.

In cultural anthropology and culturalist organization studies, there is a related discussion about the difference between 'etic' and 'emic' implications of type. Etic implications are those which are posited by a cultural type, such as 'the nuclear family' or 'matrilineal societies'. The etic aspect of the type is that phenomena are basically the same. The emic aspect is the precise meaning that a particular practice (e.g. the nuclear family, or work within groups and teams) has within a society. For example, we find semi-autonomous work groups in many countries, and the etic type is increasingly prevalent, but the meaning it has within factory organization, industrial relations, and the sociability of group members may be quite different. This warning becomes even more urgent when similarities are superficial because they often exist in name only and dwindle as we dig deeper into the meaning of the phenomenon within the context in which it is applied. According to our definition, action systems can never be identified as etic typifications, for they are defined by the meaning they carry. Etic types are thus more like the more rigid end of institutions, whereas we see emic aspects emerging when we decompose such institutions into the action spaces of which they are a part.

2.4   The differentiation and integration of societal spaces and domains

2.4.1   *Action systems, institutional domains, and entities*

Societies are always divided into components with varying degrees of autonomy, interdependencies notwithstanding, and which evolve their own rationale of thinking and action contrary to or in addition to more widely shared understandings and institutions. This acknowledged fact is all the more evident the more societies have—as the classic authors used to say—a more intricate division of labour between different occupations, the private and the public sphere, family and organizations, and functions of rule or government. It is therefore necessary to explain how the internal diversity of society links up with the analysis of coherences.

To recall our point of departure, society is thought to be self-sufficient because there is nothing meaningful outside it. This is less dogmatic than it sounds, for society even translates and suggests transcendental meanings, i.e. those which extend beyond its own scope. But this does not mean that meaning is available in an easily understandable menu of choices. Just as there exists a division of labour, so too is there a division of meanings. Meanings creep into individual minds in so many ways that it may even be more difficult to control them than the division of labour. To that extent, society is like the tropical jungle mentioned in the title of this chapter; it is a habitat rich in diverse species that exist interdependently. Likewise, the plethora of shared and specific meanings, institutions, and cultural knowledge in human society is so great that it is not only impossible to list and categorize it all reliably, it is also beyond the control of single actors. Like the jungle, society may be easy to destroy, but it is much more difficult to create and to subject to purposeful change.

What are the main species into which we can subdivide this jungle of society? Let us replace the term 'species' with 'subsystems', society being the largest and most encompassing system. There are different sorts of 'groups' or 'quasi-groups', which we will leave aside for the moment. Social theorists suggest that there are two main kinds of subsystemic species: there are what I propose to call *action systems*, and there are *institutional domains and entities*. The elements of action systems are actions that are the same type, and these are of the same type if they have the same meaning across all those individuals who perform this action. Such action systems are central to the analysis of theorists like Niklas Luhmann,[74] and in French they are usually referred to as *espaces*, spaces with a clear reference point or dimensionality in terms of specific meaning(s). Of course, they are difficult to pinpoint empirically, because their foundation is phenomenological, and, by that token, we are not far from interpretivism and interactionism,[75] approaches that are averse to standard operationalizations

Analytically, every time that we see people applying the same meaning, we see them as part of an action system. This need not be very philosophically intricate. Crude distinctions work quite well. Whenever you make a transaction out of economic motives, you are part of the economic action system. Whenever or wherever you comfort someone, share with them an informal and friendly moment over a cup of tea, you are part of an action system with no good standard designation, one you may call a 'personal reassurance and comfort system'. If, upon closer inspection, we distinguish even more differentiated and specific meanings, then we differentiate the species further into subcategories. The main thing is that action systems are defined as being crystallized around an identical meaning.

Where societal analysis differs from Luhmann is in the view of coherence across and between action systems. Whereas Luhmann considered modernization as implying increasingly differentiated action systems, each endowed with an autonomous logic, societal analysis considers action systems to be tightly interlinked and eminently capable of transmitting meaning from one system to the other. The concrete and behaviourally instructive meanings with which action systems are 'loaded', as it were, do not follow from the abstract meaning that serves to define an action system. Concrete meanings emerge through action types cross-referring to one another across differentiated action systems. In other words, the 'division of meaning', in the differentiation of action systems, is concurrent with the relatively instantaneous integration of meanings through interpretative understanding or experiential learning or both across their systemic boundaries. This corresponds to the distinction Lockwood has made between what he calls 'social integration' and 'systems integration',[76] meaning another set of differentiation and integration mechanisms, to be discussed below.

It is important always to keep the differentiation and integration of *action systems* strictly separate from those of *institutional entities*. Such entities are collective 'bodies' (such as agencies, enterprises, churches, army divisions, Elvis Presley commemoration associations, trade unions, secret societies, mafia-like gangs, trade unions, Freemason lodges, parties, fast-food chains, football clubs) bound together by membership, governance (despotic or anarchic), goals, and action programmes. Many institutional entities are organizations in one form or another, but they may also be extended families, clans, or any other more archaic body with a recognizable membership, a common purpose, and a certain amount of social closure or exclusion. The major difference between action systems and institutional entities is that action systems have precisely the same meaning in mind although they do not have people who actually belong to them, whilst institutional entities are coordinated, governed, and endowed with people who are clearly members. Thus, we each belong only to a small number of institutional entities, but to a large number of action systems, although we are not consciously aware of these. This number may be unlimited, depending on the degree of refinement we use to differentiate action systems.

The main implication of this distinction is crucial: it is impossible to organize people collectively who have precisely the same meaning in mind; when we do group people in institutional collectivities, we can be sure that they have many diverse meanings in mind that are above and beyond a common purpose; and we should never underestimate the power of meanings which people share and follow even though they are totally unorganized and uncoordinated. In other words, we could explain a lot about the life of a society if we just knew how differentiated action systems and institutional entities were, and how they stood *vis-à-vis* each other. The distinction is also important for the methodology of comparison across or between societies. This will be discussed in Chapter 5, where it will also become clear that, in the last resort, the distinction between institutional and action systems is paradoxical rather than absolutely tenable. It is nevertheless a highly fruitful conceptual tool that helps avoid a mountain of theoretical muddle and generates salient research questions and explanations.

2.4.2 Societal spaces and domains in evolution

The classic theorist Talcott Parsons argued that societies become more and more functionally specific and differentiate subsystems accordingly. Thus, he thought that the division of labour in society went hand in hand with the division of meaning, such that differentiated institutional entities, in their respective subsystems, were becoming more and more single-minded in their concern with singular meanings specific to entities. That would mean increasing the overlap between the way institutional entities are divided up and the way action systems are differentiated.

In response, action theorists maintained instead that sets of meaning are evolving and becoming more and more refined and that they cut across the division of labour both between and within institutional entities. Thus, it would be silly to assume, for example, that schools and universities can ever absorb all the action with educational or socializing meaning in society. Socialization and education will also be developed, and not only to a minor degree, within other institutional entities, even those whose main purpose has nothing to do with education, such as rowing clubs, street gangs, businesses, and other organizations. Structural functionalists such as Parsons at first thought that we were steadily progressing towards conflating the division of labour with the division of meaning, as something that went hand in hand with 'modernization'. However, action theorists and interpretivists continued to emphasize that the ongoing differentiation and sophistication of meanings in institutional entities was always larger than suspected, such that the distinction between the division of labour and the division of meaning was eternally alive and kicking. Then, according to Münch, who came right to the point, Parsons met action theorists and interpretivists half way by proposing that subsystems not only crystallize but interpenetrate.[77] This means that institutional entities with a dominant function or meaning will also have action or institutional subsystems or both which belong—in the terminology I use here—to other action systems. In this way, evolutionary decoupling between action systems and institutional entities was re-envisaged, but the treatment still differed between interpretivist and positivist—such as neo-functionalist—authors.

It is not helpful to explore this difference further; the point is to use positivism and interpretivism in conjunction. However, the distinction between action systems and institutional entities and the importance of trying to find out how they stand *vis-à-vis* each other are quite crucial. Action systems are inherently 'blank' outside the meaning that serves as a reference point. In other words, they are a bit like an empty room, flat, or house. They become furnished and comfortable by receiving furniture, which in this analogy are institutions. Thus, the meaningful subdivision of action space occurs when institutions are put in a place, moved about, repaired, and redecorated. Likewise, the meaning of a 'room' or action system, although it is initially 'empty' or blank, does control the selection and fashion of the 'furniture' or institutions with which it will be filled. The analogy has its limits because human behaviour is more self-referential and emergent in evolution than is the architectural and interior design of flats, and it is difficult to imagine action systems as being physically partitioned. But specific and practically instructive meanings always result from the interpenetration of action systems and institutional sets. Action systems and their interrelations make institutional sets come alive, and institutions fill up what are otherwise blank action spaces.[78]

Distinguishable but reciprocally bracketed action and institutional systems also figure in other literature, not only in esoteric social theory but also in a praxeo-logically oriented systems approach meant to benefit business and management students. To my mind, the most lucid and handy conceptualization of this distinc-tion was developed by Ton de Leeuw. He distinguished between 'partial' (*partiële*) subsystems and 'aspect' subsystems within a systems theory of enterprise manage-ment. In my terminology, aspect systems are action systems and partial subsystems are institutional entities or subentities.[79] In both management and general social theory, this implies that the way aspect systems and structural system differentiation relate to each other tells us a great deal about how an enterprise functions. Thus, organic organization, which is better adjusted to more volatile or shifting task environments, can be described as one in which the division of labour cuts across the division of meaning, so that people who are separated by the division of labour are allied by being in the same 'box' within the division of meaning.

This conceptualization supersedes an earlier one about the importance of the 'extent' of the division of labour. Now it is possible to see that the quality of the division of labour is expressed by the extent to which it overlaps with or cuts across the division of meaning. This is also more useful in the sociology of work and technology.[80] We need to be concerned about the 'quality' rather than the extent of the division of labour, as was already made clear in the earlier distinction suggested by Durkheim about the need to distinguish between 'anomic' and socially integrative divisions of labour. In the present treatment, the quality of the division of labour is expressed by its relation to the division of meaning. A division of labour thus becomes anomic when its components have very singular meanings, and this may be called alienating because it removes other meanings from the scene of an organizational entity.

2.4.3   Societal effects versus institutional autonomy

From this excursion into society as a tropical jungle with its manifold species belonging to one of two major types, let us return to think about how these relate to societal effects. Do they upset coherence or do they maintain it? Let us look first at institutional entities as one of the major types. What the literature and research overwhelmingly point out is that institutional entities require autonomy of action and a freedom from manifest constraint in order to specialize. This argument is very liberal, in the European sense, and it goes back to classic Durkheimian theory: more intense specialization of institutional entities and their proliferation alongside each other make central coordination (the imposition of mechanical solidarity) unwieldy and unnecessary, because such entities become interdependent to such an extent that they will engage in peaceful cooperation or co-existence, at least across the boundaries of the niches involving goals, product markets, or technology, niches that distinguish the various subtypes of institutional entities from one another.

For example, when the division of labour is more extensive and functional specialization of institutional entities intense, these entities will deploy their autonomy without going against their general interdependencies with other specialized entities. In such a state of affairs, governments will refrain from licensing enterprises or exerting directive control. Granted, societies sometimes take detours via developments like Stalinism in their process of learning. But again, this depends on the institutions and culture already existing in a society. The fact that Stalinist socialism evolved in the Soviet Union therefore has to be explained against the backdrop of a long-standing absence of private property with regard both to land and productive capital in the Russian Empire, an absence dating back to the Asiatic mode of production according to Marx. Tartar and Mongol rule had introduced this, and the struggle against Tartar rule had aggravated it.[81] It boiled down to greater overlap between action systems and institutional entities, and to restrictions on the autonomy of institutional entities.

The autonomy of differentiated institutional entities thus makes the tropical jungle of society so rich and diverse that we are in danger of losing sight of the woods for the trees, not to speak of the multitude of other plants, insects, and animals. This, I submit, is what makes it so difficult for observers to diagnose and analyse societal effects. Indeed, how can we argue that the reason why a certain type of snake, for example, feeds on particular types of animals or lives in synergy with certain plants is the result of being conditioned by the characteristics of the jungle as a whole? How can we define integrated and general characteristics in light of the multitude of species living in the jungle and the fact that most of them are of no concern at all to snakes? Often, institutionalist scholars are inclined to look at the specific feeding and breeding requirements and policies of types of organizational species and how they change. This does factor in their environment, but only a part of the entire jungle or society. Naturally, they point out with some justification that only specific conditions matter and not the whole jungle of society.

It seems that the 'actor-centred institutionalism' that has emerged at the Max Planck Institute for the Study of Societies might be such an example. This also interprets institutions and actors' interests or predispositions as being interacting or mutually constitutive, and in this way the approach is similar to the theory put forward here. This approach also takes into consideration the interaction between different spheres of society. However, most of the research conducted with this approach can dispense with a notion of societal effects reverberating throughout all societal spheres in a rather systematic fashion. This would then allow us to attribute concrete and stable characteristics to a specific society because the approach analyses institutions as games within which actors make their moves, and games are themselves designed or produced by actors. Although it is a theory of 'rational choice' (of moves or of games), actors' choices are seen to be relative to institutional conditions, but again only those conditions that can be fully ascertained by considering what actors themselves take for granted or are prepared to negotiate as a basic understanding.[82]

In this perspective, which I do not propose to discard, societal effects are first and foremost vacuous. Specific conditions matter, but the entire jungle and the larger opportunities and threats it contains fade into the background. This is quite understandable. A tropical forest rich with institutions implies that we can only give a parsimonious explanation of the emergence and survival of a particular species if we concentrate on its direct predators, food, shelter, and other existential conditions. It is specific institutional conditions that actors evoke and influence when making their moves. However, in doing so, they also contribute to the manifestation, development, or ruin of the tropical forest as an ecological system, and to the coherence, development, or decline of a society. They may not be aware of this, but cross-societal comparison brings it out.

2.4.4   Loose and tight coupling in systems

Action systems are the neuronal circuitry that makes effects reverberate throughout society. Furthermore, they are interconnected to such an extent that they can be considered as an integrated whole. This does not mean that they can be controlled from a central node, such as a central switchboard. But they do ensure that the enactment of meaning in the specific action systems we choose to distinguish reverberates around all the other action systems. In organizational theory, this postulate may be framed in this way: in action systems and their linkages, *tight coupling* abounds; in institutional subsystems, however, *loose coupling* is developed to the extent that institutional entities have relative autonomy.[83] Nevertheless, tightly coupled action systems ensure that institutional and cultural adaptation and evolution are cross-referenced across institutional domains. The relative autonomy or loose coupling of institutional entities then means that diligent actors use their discretion, in a rational-choice way if you like, to absorb and generate societal patterns.

Action systems thus ensure that meanings connect across actors and institutional entities. Action systems can do this because they are a priori blank, which translates the 'world-openness' of human behaviour into a systems-theoretical term. Moreover, societal effects are not based primarily on concrete characteristics pervasive in society, but on the tight coupling of action systems. This implies that the changing institutional and cultural furnishing of action spaces is also tightly coupled. Institutional entities may be more loosely coupled, but the institutional furniture of action systems is more tightly coupled. This distinction reflects the idea that institutional entities make policies in regard only to a very specific set of conditions, but the tacit world of shared understandings and of soft and rigid institutions subjects such actors to a learning process, specifically when they are concerned with the implementation of policies. The learning process targets the ongoing institutional furnishing of action systems.

The concrete institutional and cultural characteristics that enable us to tell one society from another are the result of the ongoing fashioning of institutions and culture. The reciprocal conditioning of actors and cultural and institutional furniture has brought about 'constructed' actors and sets of conditions in the process. Because of their joint evolutionary origin and coherence, these combine to form a more or less concrete ensemble of tangible societal characteristics. But this ensemble is neither deterministically constituted nor inert. One reason is that both culture and institutions always feature conflict between norms; the other is that norms are inherently ambiguous. As interactionists emphasize, action is always built on the selective interpretation and activation of norms and other knowledge. This reasserts itself even in the smallest act, at least marginally, and it reminds us again of the a priori blankness of action spaces. This blankness does not mean ongoing emptiness, because the first thing that actors do in a blank space is to fill it with cultural and institutional furniture. This is transmitted or made coherent across societal space by tightly coupled action systems.

2.4.5   *Differentiation and integration of action spaces and institutional subsystems*

With regard to the specifics of systems differentiation, it is difficult to derive a neat scheme of action systems. For institutional subsystems, categorizations like the economy, the polity, the educational system, security apparatus, etc. come to mind, and within such subsystems, we can readily distinguish organizational entities or sets. We have much greater difficulty in putting forward such an array for action systems, for they have a pernicious tendency to be abstract. Postmodern theorists would metaphorically liken them to rhizomatic structures, i.e. a network of highly intertwined fungi that connect an array of more distinct trees underground.[84]

In principle, it is possible to imagine both action and institutional systems in cross- or supra-societal settings. Financial speculation or highly specialized research would be examples of action systems with an international extension, and the International Civil Aviation Organization is a thoroughly international institutional entity. However, societal space is not defined in the first place as being situated 'below' the international order. Above all, it is that space in which all the action systems that we have cared to differentiate combine into an ensemble that facilitates tight coupling between all aspects of human life in society. This societal horizon could exist at different levels of social aggregation; where it actually occurs is an empirical question to be dealt with in the next chapter. Since the emphasis is put on the distinction between horizons of action and societal horizons, the implication clearly must be that some conceivable action systems transcend societal space. Where this is the case, action systems have international exclaves, as it were. Furthermore, what happens in such exclaves does not reverberate across society through tight coupling. But by way of communication, the exclaves will nevertheless have some effect on that part of the action system that is not extra-societal.

In societal analysis, societal space is analytically divided into tightly coupled subspaces, or subsystems, as they are called in the terminology of action theory. The typology of subspaces is far from complete, and because of their rhizomatic nature, it must be conceded that it is not possible to present a definitive array.[85] However, some types are more established than others. In the tradition of the sociology of work, many explanations are based on the tight coupling between the space of organizing and the space of socialization, for instance. We can also distinguish a space of careers and internal and external labour markets, as defined by the employment relationship. In the tradition of socio-technical theory, a space of social relations was distinguished from a space of engineering (technology and operating principles of the technical means of production). The socio-technical school likewise insisted that, although analytically distinct, these spaces had to be seen as tightly coupled, for a change in one of the action spaces immediately effected a change in the other; thus, optimization of any production system— what I propose to call an institutional entity here—had to be conceived as an interlinked design problem tying together aspects in both spaces (or action systems or aspect systems).

Connected action systems thus make for integrative effects at different levels. According to the socio-technical school, they do that at the plant or enterprise level to the extent that a change in organization will be tightly coupled to others in, for example, socialization, careers, and industrial relations. They also connect and have a similar effect within the ambit of society. Much as action systems are useful concepts at different levels, we must not jump between levels in the analysis. For instance, a change in the organization of one plant may have a sizeable effect in other action systems at the plant level, but it does not imply an equally sizeable and immediate change within broader societal spaces.

Action systems are thus exemplary integrators. By attributing meaning, they channel institutional and cultural development, which evolves quietly first at the soft end and then has a tendency to harden. They work through the knowledge that individuals presume, establish, and enact. Action systems achieve a tighter coupling across institutional entities than these possess among themselves on the basis of their functional interdependency alone. Action systems work through cognitive inter-relationships, and, in turn, they predicate the interpretation of functional interrela-tionships. The reverberation of cognitive interrelationships around analytically distinct action systems leaves an emic impact on etically apprehended interrelation-ships and typifications. It fills them with specific meaning, both for themselves and between them and others. It thus ties the functioning of disparate entities together, giving them a societal pattern. This cannot be easily summarized in a typology, but it does exist. In this sense, a societal effect is inevitable whenever action systems come into play. Where human beings act, action systems are not only inevitable but crucial for the sense-making that pushes people to seek to 'put things in perspec-tive', or to gain a more rounded understanding that helps the disparate parts of the puzzle of life fall into place.

2.5   The dialectics and dynamics of societal reconstruction

2.5.1   *The partitioning of institutional domains and situations*

The tight coupling of action systems allows institutional sets to be decoupled and to engage in a division of labour. Yet they remain integrated through cross-cutting action systems. Action systems are like a network of communicating tubes, where an increase of pressure or quantity of a fluid immediately passes through the whole system. Conversely, institutional systems are like the hydraulic landscape of Holland: full of dams, locks, pumps, dikes, and other features that are geared to keeping water in autonomous reservoirs or streams and preventing a rise in the level of water from communicating itself across the system. Going from action theory to the harder language of institutionalism, we find that *institutional* landscapes are characterized chiefly by *partitioning*.[86] Although meaning (like water) tends to communicate through the system, institutions are typified by the variation of the specialized meanings they produce, much like the variation of water levels in the landscape of Holland. Therefore, the coherence of society is not only pragmatically tolerant of variation in meanings according to their institutional place, it almost requires it. Partitioning means that particular meanings are specified according to institutionalized collectivities and to the situations they confront. Different meanings may thus exist in close proximity, and actors understand such contrasts to be meaningful. This is the most general version of the Kamchatka effect as far as the structuring of societies is concerned.

Institutional partitioning is an artefact that societal actors have crafted, usually through intense conflict in the course of historical processes. An institutional space that was previously not partitioned and therefore governed by uniform meaning is broken up into smaller pieces that are governed by different sets of particular meanings. What used to be accepted as a straightforward and pervasive norm is contested, and the new set is less straightforward and pragmatically links previously opposing or contradicting meanings through institutional partitioning. At the outset, actors find this difficult to stomach as a rational design, but they do make their pragmatic peace with it later, extolling the functional or ethical beauty of the new artefact, and interpreting it as a 'tradition' or a 'model'. This is when myths are created. However, on closer historical inspection, any such tradition or model inevitably reveals itself to be a concoction of opposites. In a framework of non-identical reproduction of institutions, both rigid and fluid, institutional partitioning is therefore a pervasive ingredient. It means an increase in the complexity of societal order, thereby requiring more diligent and knowledgeable efforts at interpretation.

2.5.2 Societal complexity and horizons

The crunch is that this tends to work to the advantage of retrenched societal horizons, because more complex and differentiated systems are easier to understand and master at a less aggregated level, much like a complex hydraulic system is easier to master when dealing with an area the size of Holland, compared to the coastal region of Bangladesh or the Mississippi Delta. Curious and venturesome human beings do extend their horizon of action. But knowledgeable actors like their societal horizon to remain close by and circumscribed, not far off or expansive. This is a fundamental dilemma. For extension of horizons of action will be linked with greater institutional complexity, via the division of labour, which then separates horizons of action from societal horizons. Human beings while living pragmatically with this dilemma, also tend to overcome it by softening the contradiction. One way of doing this is to provide for different layers of societal aggregation.

Societal coherence is thus a pragmatic endeavour, subject to institutional partitioning and evolutionary dialectics but, in light of the latter, also firmly rooted in a myth about comprehensive understanding. Since comprehensive understanding cannot be unlimited in time and space, it tends to establish itself within the confines of a societal horizon. This will always be more specific and narrower in range than our minds will explicitly concede in their expansive and ambitious moments when we conceive the universe, the world, or universalistic principles. Comprehensive understanding may be unlimited within the terms set down by a universalistic religion, another form of knowledge firmly grounded in myth.[87] But it is subject to the division and integration of meaning being furnished by institutions and to institutional partitioning. For a long time, religion and its deities were specific to societies, so that religious knowledge was firmly linked with other knowledge in society and deliberately restricted within this horizon. Therefore, useful, practical, and realist knowledge was not separated from religion. As Frisians used to say at the time of Christianization: who cares about the god of the Franks? That god might exist, but this was of no concern to them.

Such local differences tend to continue in different forms, since societal complexity works in favour of the retrenchment of horizons, even though the Frisians have since learnt to pray to a universal God. This brings us back to a basic point: to partition institutions according to meanings that vary depending on the situation introduces dialectically a more abstract commonality or makes such commonality more apparent in an abstract form. The increasing complexity of institutional space thus implies a matching degree of complexity in action systems, even though these two sets can only partially overlap, since fundamental action systems must cut across partitioned institutional space.

Religious pragmatism used to blur the distinction between the sacred and the profane, but that did not mean that the sacred was immutable. Germanic tribes used to swap one deity for another rather pragmatically if a new god could be proven to work better than a previous one. If their enemies won a battle, that god was thereby proven to be stronger, and there were sound practical reasons for swapping gods. Thus, the relative differentiation between religion and knowledge, including their mythical foundations, has meant that realist and practical knowledge specific to a society had to give up pretensions of conflating what is true and useful inside a society with what applies more generally and outside of it. The consequence is that more comprehensive understanding becomes more realistic and practical, is profane but also rooted in myth, and remains confined within societal bounds. Therefore, acquired universalistic insights, regardless whether they pertain to the Christian faith or to shareholder value theory, may still not result in any direct consequences for the specific values-in-use and practical knowledge in society. We must always consider the intermediation that occurs when translating a general doctrine into a specific context, which usually implies the syncretization of a rather universal and a rather particular belief.

2.5.3 Horizons of action and societal horizons

Comprehensive understanding is bounded by a *societal horizon*, within which the puzzle pieces that comprise the full range of action systems fall into place, or at least do so more easily. A societal horizon is not the same as a horizon that encompasses the action and perception of actors. Human beings have typically gone beyond the established confines of the societal communities in which they have been raised. They have therefore tended to expand their *horizon of action* beyond societal bounds. As a result, their perception and action become decontextualized and unable to function on the basis of a more comprehensive understanding. Their comprehensive understanding therefore has to become more segmental and evaluate what it encounters as pieces of a puzzle with unfamiliar contours that do not fall into place. Or, when it is presumed that they do fall into place, the knowledge thereby activated is likely to be alien to the context in which it is applied and therefore inappropriate. Horizons of action have an inevitable tendency of outpacing societal horizons, and the consequence is that the understanding we achieve of action beyond societal horizons is much more curtailed and segmental, much less comprehensive, and therefore much more deficient than our knowledge already is within the bounds of our native society. It may be exciting and refreshing, but it is puzzling because the jigsaw pieces do not make up an integrated picture.

The consequences may vary greatly when the horizons of action are expanded beyond the accustomed societal horizons, regardless whether we are talking about Phoenician and Greek traders who sailed along the coasts of the Mediterranean in antiquity, or German Hanseatic merchants who operated under royal Norwegian licence in Norway during the Middle Ages, or American managers in recent years who set up a subsidiary of their business in Asia. One possibility is that expatriates 'go native', meaning they become integrated into the fabric of both the societal action systems and the institutional entities prevailing in their new environment. Another possibility is that they impose their own fabric upon the society they entered through rule and domination. More balanced amalgamations of culture and institutions may also occur.

Either way, we know that the construction of larger societies is a very pragmatic process, full of syncretism (the amalgamation of different beliefs), cultural and institutional compromise, and tinkering. Over the long run the pragmatics of action creates a new synthesis out of what formerly were opposing elements. Yet such pragmatism in no way excludes ferocious conflict and even atrocities at the onset. It may resort to subtle conversion or genocide, liberal association or enslavement. But when a new societal concoction does finally emerge, it exhibits a most astounding synthesis. This has been observed over time in every corner of the world. The aggregation of previously distinct societies into larger aggregates often occurs from a beginning marked by the superposition of a conquering and henceforth ruling elite, which eventually intermingle with their subjects, socially, culturally, and physically, and form new institutions with them.[88]

Very often, aristocracies in Europe were originally conquerors who subjected a populace to their rule and then found a new institutional shell as governing and protective intermediary institutions within a widening societal horizon, in which they protected society against the same incursions that they themselves initially made. Of course, not every conquest has resulted in greater societal aggregation, but even when foreign conquerors have been driven back or deposed, as in the case of the Tartars in Russia, they have tended to leave an imprint on culture and institutions; in the case of the Tartars, this imprint was called 'the Asiatic mode of production' by Marx and has proved resilient centuries after the decline of Mongol and Tartar rule, having blended more easily into state socialism after a total massive revolution than did liberal-bourgeois institutions in western Europe.

Therefore, larger societal aggregates may or may not result from the extension of a horizon of action and the subsequent expansion of a societal horizon. When complete societies are on the move, or when their migration is a collectively organized endeavour and supported by force, then the chances are apparently greater that an amalgamation of societies will occur. When it is only individuals or specific groups who migrate, then the chance is greater that they will become absorbed or that the new synthesis they create remains a local phenomenon. For instance, integration in the medieval Hanseatic League was based on alliances, on a more individual and contractual expansion of horizons of action that stopped short of societal amalgamation and left many people of German origin in Norway and other places to be absorbed into the native population. It may be that new and even conquering migrants may form distinct subsocieties side by side with the native population. The latter is demonstrated by a number of colonial ventures in Africa, but again it appears to be dependent on previous societal patterns. In this regard, the Portuguese probably stand out as the keenest amalgamators in Africa and South America and the northern Europeans as the greatest perpetrators of subsocietal seclusion through constructions approaching or achieving apartheid.

2.5.4   Amalgamation versus division

Even though migration and international contact may turn out in specific instances to be an abortive project of societal amalgamation, amalgamation does take place and it is noteworthy. It is not a foregone conclusion as horizons of action are expanded, but there are interesting intermediate solutions between the poles of complete amalgamation and the simple integration of individuals into a different horizon. In addition, we have to consider societal division, the splitting up of societal communities that were once more integrated. Current discussion is pre-occupied with the topic of societal amalgamation and its problems, and is neglect-ing the topic of societal division. These two phenomena may even coexist in close proximity, making them another variant of the Kamchatka effect. The Roman Empire, for instance, was marked by increasing societal integration as far as full citizenship was concerned. Whereas there had once been a sharp distinction between a Roman citizen (*civis*) and subjects of the empire, after the *constitutio antoniniana* in the beginning of the third century AD this status was extended to all free male subjects.[89]

While this clearly was an increase in societal integration, the growing importance thus obtained by the periphery of Roman society only set the agenda for civil war around the imperial succession and for increasing disunity among the various parts of the empire. Max Weber suggested that the decline and fall of the Roman Empire was a consequence of local elites in the provinces turning inwards, identifying with a province and its development rather than with the empire as a whole and its governing node, the *urbs* of which they were citizens.[90] Political and military disunity then enabled invading Germanic or other tribes to conquer large areas of the empire. Other prominent processes of societal disintegration occurred when European settlers in both North and South America severed the solidarity and rule that tied them to their societies of origin. Societal amalgamation may therefore be abortive. Following a process of integration, societal disintegration may also occur.

What we see are processes of societal integration and disintegration occurring, either parallel to one another or in succession. More massive attempts at societal integration such as in the Roman Empire may actually initiate disintegration rapidly, within a century or so. By the use of such terms, I seek to forge a link to the more dynamic concept of society, that of *Vergesellschaftung* as presented by Georg Simmel, another pioneering action and interaction theorist. *Vergesellschaftung* is probably best translated as 'societal integration'. At the same time, it immediately suggests the opposite, disintegration. This points to the necessity to envision clear limits to cumulative societal integration.

Apparently, the human capacity to amalgamate into ever larger societies is limited. A tentative generalization would be that societal expansion first implies a patchwork of complex and differentiated solidarities, culture, and institutions. Attempts to consolidate such patchworks are then likely to strengthen forces of disintegration and lead to a retrenchment of societal horizons within more restricted bounds. The Roman Empire is a good example. The fact that Germanic invaders had an important part to play in its division does not mean that external forces were dominant in this process. Even before the Germanic onslaught, the centrifugal tendencies within the empire had divided it into an eastern and a western part.

Naturally, much of this is due to power politics, quarrels over succession, and warlordism. But factional divisions would not assert themselves if they could not rely on important material and moral resources of support, at least passive support. Even the abandonment of a moral sentiment is relevant to the constitution of society. Resources and support would not be available if horizons of societal solidarity were not retrenched and divided up. Evidently, despite the observable troits of the jungle present in all societies, they cannot persist as mere patchworks, deprived of an encompassing coherence. Intricate social patchworks of institutions and specific functional interrelationships are able to fulfil many more

sober functional requirements, but they apparently fall short of something fundamental: the need to facilitate society–specific meaning through dense action systems. This suggests that human beings will always try to construct societies which
do this, and when overextended societal horizons fall short of this need, human
conflict will initiate a retrenchment of societal horizons. In other words, it would
be too easy to assume that societal complexity initiates integration more likely than
not within a larger and more aggregated society, which is better able to internalize
extended action chains within its ambit. This is because a decoupling of extended
horizons of action from societal horizons is one of the most frequent phenomena
that we can observe.

2.5.5   Layered and national societies

Once we have understood that the degree and nature of societal integration
changes dynamically, we must also acknowledge that, at any given moment,
societies are characterized internally by certain action systems and institutional
domains and entities, but also by subsocieties. The need for encompassing and
dense action systems and solidarity does not mean that this always has to be set up
within a single horizon alone. Indeed, it is rare in human experience for a
monopoly over a specific societal horizon to be sustainable. This is what the idea
of the nation state implies: that the most modern societal arrangement, one which
supposedly makes coordination of society unambiguous and therefore more rational to carry out, is the 'coextensive nation state', in which the range and
boundaries of government, the economy, language, culture, and central institutions
coincide in various domains.[91]

   This idea of the nation state has served as a normative or descriptive model in
both political tracts and scholarly writings. It is probably incontestable that for
much of modern history, many countries in Europe have moved in the direction of
establishing a sovereign nation state that corresponds territorially to the existence
of national society. Yet, it would be worth our while to inspect more critically
the extent to which this model has been realized. When examining individual
countries closely to see whether such a link has occurred, we find that the existence
and performance of the nation state turn out to be more of a societal myth, a
myth that people have been at pains to enact. However, it is dubious that the nation
state is that resilient when we examine its performance in the coordination of
society.

   In theory, it is rather simple: if a government is sovereign and legitimate, which it
can become with the help of democracy, it is able to accomplish much that is
beneficial for society while remaining free from outside interference and possibly
only somewhat disturbed by the presence of international economic relations and
markets which escape its control. As long as trade is not very important, it can be
kept under control by customs and excise duties, by fixed exchange rates or
currency fluctuation, and by agencies and institutions that are more or less international. In principle, the nation state is thought to do better than any other the job

of coordinating a democratic society, by holding in its grasp all the important strings tying society together.

Oddly enough, in empirical reality, we have no evidence that the sovereign nation state, the best conceivable model to date of a structure established to facilitate the development of generally valid institutions and culture, can cut through the underbrush of the tropical jungle, tidy it up, and do a better job of co-ordination.[92] Germany, of course, has often been berated as a latecomer to nation-building and therefore plagued with teething problems, such as a lack of self-assurance that metamorphosed into aggressiveness in the past century. It is undeniable that Germany has suffered some problematic consequences because it was late to begin its nation-building process. Yet Germany was somewhat similar to the prototypical inter-nation. The question raised here is the degree to which that belated nation-building implied problems of internal coordination. Since the emergence of Germany as a nation state in 1872, the country has been comparatively free from internal division or very forceful attempts against the unity of the federal nation state. Despite its history as a muddled inter-nation, which eventually influenced its federal structure, Germany became a stable nation despite its unprecedented involvement in territorial shifts and war between 1914 and 1945.

By comparison, the much acclaimed advantage of a relatively early consolidation of society in the form of a national polity, for which France is usually cited as a front runner, is questionable. The present territorial configuration of France has only existed since the end of the 1950s, when Algeria became independent and France lost the northern part of that country, which had been governed as three North African *départements*, i.e. an integral part of the nation since around 1880. Even in the 1960s, the bombing of public facilities by separatists in Brittany occurred with unsettling regularity. At present, Corsica appears set on pursuing a policy of semi-independence that exceeds the general regionalization of French politics. The historically greater sovereignty of the polity in France, accompanied by centralization and linguistic and institutional homogenization, has not meant that there has been less internal conflict between classes and political factions than elsewhere. If anything, the record would seem to prove that the advancement of the nation state in France, the imposition of uniform institutions and culture, has generated substantial class-based, regional, and local reactions. Thus, France may indeed have come rather far and been rather early in establishing a nation state, and this may have been beneficial in a number of ways, but it would be difficult to use France as the outstanding example of the mastery of problems of internal coordination.[93]

Likewise, another front-runner in nation-building, the United Kingdom, has never had a firmly established and demarcated nation state without civil or sectarian war, due in great part—at least since the Easter Uprising in Dublin in 1917—to the problems in Ireland. Even if the Irish question is close to being settled in Northern Ireland, the UK still faces what has become an increasing push for independence and diversity from the regional governments of Wales and Scotland. National unity and the quality of internal conflict management are thus far from a foregone conclusion, and much of the literature has failed to distinguish the consolidation of a core of national integration from stable, lasting, and encompassing integration. Early unification may unlash centrifugal forces with a vengeance. It is true that both France and the United Kingdom had a core consisting of a large, dominant societal segment very early on and that this core initiated the process of national unity (England and the Île-de France, including adjacent territories). But there has also been a marked distinction between their core or centre and their periphery. In both countries, the peripheries have recently become more assertive, leading to a renaissance of layering, including layering in government. Germany, however, has been more or less layered throughout, such that it only had a core–periphery problem from 1872 until 1932 or at the latest 1945, a period when Prussia held a dominant position. However, the core–periphery distinction has only been salient in Germany at a regional level. Germany has had other striking problems, which will be discussed later. Its present state of national unity now does appear to be final. There may be grave problems of policy coordination between the federal government and the governments of a number of states, and the country lacks a definite core, but it has neither muddled, contestable borders nor ongoing bloodshed over the issue of where its borders should lie.

A looser federal structure is, however, no guarantee that societal integration will work. The division of the Austro-Hungarian Empire into two major states (Austria and Hungary) with separate and almost equally important capitals (Vienna and Budapest) could not sustain this attempt at societal integration. Even after the division, both Austria and Hungary could be referred to as empires in the sense that ruling ethnic or cultural groups (German and Hungarian, respectively) were established who were more influential than others (Slovenes, Italians, Poles, White Ruthenians, and Czechs in the 'Austrian' part; Croats, Slovakians, Serbs, Romanians, etc. in the 'Hungarian' part). Democratization would have jeopardized Austria-Hungary, for it would have meant the end not only of the larger empire but also of its two halves. The rudimentary federation that existed did not define these entities along ethnic or cultural lines, and a regional layering was also precarious since regions were often no more than a patchwork of different local populations whose cultural centre of gravity lay outside the region.

Probably the best and most convincing example of an early and persistent consolidation of society upon a template of a national state in Europe is the Netherlands. It has persisted in its present territorial configuration since the Treaty of London (1839), when Belgium became independent. The country has generally managed to conduct its internal affairs without major and violent conflict such as the shooting of demonstrators, terrorism against national rule, the toleration or conduct of civil war, direct military rule over parts of the territory, and military revolt—all of which has occurred in the United Kingdom and France not only since the Second World War but even after accession to the European Community, and which are apparently often ignored in a collective memory keen on interpreting these countries as model nation states. In the Netherlands, the national language is not in dispute, institutions are spread out across its territory, its culture is national despite a great deal of regional diversity, and it has been free of bloody internal conflict, with the exception of some disturbances created by exiled Moluccans in the 1970s. In most of the rest of Europe, particularly in eastern Europe to date, nation-building has involved a turmoil of unification and partition, bloodshed and dictatorial peace. It has not given any nation much time to prove the worthiness and effectiveness of social coordination in the nation state. Driven by their own internal problems and expanding or retrenching international horizons of action, societies have more or less hurried through the historical episode of the nation state, engaging in both supra- and sub-national societal integration.

2.5.6 *The historical normality of layering*

In light of the developments described above, I propose that we consider a kind of historically normal state of affairs in which societal integration is focused on different levels of aggregation at the same time. In societal space, there is no necessary and inherent competition between different collectivities and levels of integration. Pragmatic human beings are, in principle, eminently able and willing to develop multiple societal attachments, so that they do not see one of these as fundamentally conflicting with another. Societal space may therefore be layered: societies form subsocieties, or smaller societies federate into larger ones. Of course, the historical evidence about federations is that they are slow at establishing firm governmental control and do not perform very well against competing systems that are more centralized and combative. But in a larger territory where war in the region is not a viable choice any more, except in the name of a supranational community and in order to establish peace or subdue aggression, the federation of societies is a natural, slow-moving, but fairly sustainable option.

This would be the present-day scenario for layered societal integration, such that societal collectivities within different layers (European, national, regional) do not fundamentally conflict with one another. In this situation, people would not be worried about the fact that they are implicated in Bavarian, German, and European culture, institutions, and solidarities all at the same time. Such a situation would only be radically different from societal integration in the Roman Empire to the extent that the latter originated from a dominant centre and expanded through conquest, not federation. But for hundreds of years, most people in the empire belonged to their respective tribe or local and ethnically specific community, featuring its own deity, language, culture, institutions, and solidarity, while at the same time being subservient to a larger Roman society with its own language, culture, institutions, and deity. The viability of Roman societal integration was built on this tension between the tolerance of subsocieties in their own domain of responsibility and an insistence on religious respect for the person of the emperor and obedience to his rule.

Layered societal integration was not a second-best solution that people found laden with ambiguity and therefore tried to avoid. Along the Rhine and the

Danube, rivers which more or less marked the border between the Roman Empire and Germanic territories for centuries, the people along both sides of these rivers were not very ethnically diverse. The major difference was that those on the western or southern border had, voluntarily or involuntarily, slipped under Roman control without having to sacrifice their language, culture, and customs. They became sedentary farmers and supplied a civil and military service class for the Romans. Those 'beyond the pale' of the Roman Empire continued to roam about their habitat in a more traditional Germanic way, refusing to be subordinate to more central authorities and to succumb to the more decadent urban habits beyond the border. What the Romanized tribes traded for their independence, however, were public baths and hygiene, a more regular supply of bread and wine, and a great many more comforts of civilization.

Throughout the existence of the empire, a stream of Germanic tribes travelled westwards or southwards, knocking on the Roman door in the hopes of finding a place to settle within the bounds of the empire, to become subservient to Rome but then enjoy greater protection from foul weather, failing crops, and intrusive neighbours. The ambition of many Germanic tribes was to insert themselves into a wider Roman societal horizon. At first, they tried to smash their way in after they had been refused entry. They battled ferociously in pursuit of the sun. The most prominent examples were the well-known Cimbri and Teutones, who desperately sought a residence permit whilst beating many legions sent to stop them before they were finally slaughtered at Aquae Sextiae and Vercellae in 101 and 102 AD.

There were also Roman incursions into Germanic territories. But as the empire became larger, more and more of the soldiers it sent to fight off the new arrivals or inhabitants across the Rhine and the Danube were (Romanized) Germanic soldiers. Even the leader of the most successful Germanic revolt against Rome to occur east of the Rhine was a man named Hermann, or Arminius, who, as the second version of his name indicates, had been trained as an officer in the Roman army.[94] In the later stages of the Roman Empire, Germanic soldiers formed the mainstay of the army, together with other peripheral populations, and many of them achieved a high rank.

Likewise, a layered societal integration that differentiated between local communities and the institutions and culture of the larger domain worked without major problems in the Danish realm up until the middle of the nineteenth century. Denmark had lost Norway earlier, not through revolt but because it had allied itself with Napoleon. Its rule over Schleswig (as half-German) and Holstein (as a German territory) was uncontested until the Danish king proposed to impose central Danish statute law on both Holstein and Schleswig, in an attempt to consolidate the realm in the form of a national state. It is probably not far-fetched to suggest that today's Danish monarch would still be ruling over these regions had Bismarck not used the occasion to mobilize an otherwise sleepy German confederation into action and wrest control over both Schleswig and Holstein from Denmark.[95] The present settlement has left German minorities in Denmark and Danish minorities in

Germany. Each group has been able to maintain their cultural identity in a protective institutional niche, whereas in other cases, such problems have been resolved by coercion, extinction, or territorial ethnic cleansing.

Nation states are thus highly artificial constructions. When they emerge, they are often a patchwork of different societal communities, each containing different institutions and culture. However, this in no way prevents nation states from establishing more pervasive culture and institutions that superimpose themselves on a rather circumscribed regional layer. In this respect, there is not a radical difference between societal integration in the Roman Empire and in later European societies. It is not even necessary that they share the same language. Switzerland is a case in point. This nation state is a highly artificial construction in which no one language dominates nationally and the cantonal governments are highly independent. Yet Switzerland represents probably one of the highest expressions of community and solidarity found in Europe. The twist in multilayer societal integration is that it is precisely local autonomy that sets it apart from neighbouring societies, institutionally marking national society in a very distinctive way. In other words, even a strong layering of society into subsocieties can be a national institution. The enactment of institutional and cultural diversity may therefore happen as a complementary counterpoint to national homogeneity in a different institutional domain.

Even a patchwork of societal integration can thus amount to more than this alone. It may be a meaningful purpose of a larger societal order with consequences that reverberate through every action system to uphold and facilitate decentralized coordination in subsocieties in such a way that differences between such subsocieties are experienced as meaningful and understandable, rather than obstructing the movement of people, goods, and information in the larger society. In this case, even fairly strong layering does not conflict with comprehensive integration. Layering will then even reinforce a sense of greater solidarity.[96] The patchwork of our tropical jungle may therefore also be more coherent than appears at first sight, because it is meaningfully divided into subsocieties. These are functionally dependent on a higher layer of integration. Dependencies and interdependencies will always present an occasion for friction. But as long as dependence is experienced as meaningful support in all spheres of life, it will not be seen as encroaching on societal integration in a lower layer.

Thus, even in layered societal space and very complex arrangements, societal effects can be very strong. Risks and the danger of failure are inherent when broadening the horizons of action so extensively that they become societal horizons. Societal integration may thus be retrenched to more reduced horizons. And it may happen that a favourable solution to the problem of peaceful social coordination entails the layering of societies while conserving restricted horizons at the same time that a more expanded one is imposed. In all of these real or imagined situations, societal effects are present, and the differences among them lie more in their quality than their strength; they extend across layers as they do across institutional domains.

2.6 Summary

In the present chapter a theory of societal aggregation, identity, and change has been outlined that underlines dialectical effects in three respects. First, societies are phenomena in need of constant enactment by social actors and are therefore very pragmatic affairs. Although society is experienced as a 'constraint' by actors, that which is societal is always constituted by actors themselves. Through open action systems, actors even in relatively autonomous institutional entities make specific cultural and institutional considerations (whether they are experienced as constraints or as facilitating resources) reverberate through societal space and across different institutional domains. Society and actors thus constitute each other reciprocally; one cannot be properly conceived without the other, so that they are mutually paradoxical. Second, societal aggregation is restricted by the dilemma that actors like to expand horizons of action but also like their societal horizon to be within close reach. The dialectics unfolding from this dilemma imply cycles and interdependencies between societal aggregation and disaggregation, and a solution is to layer society in such a way that the various societal levels are differentiated from one another. Such a solution avoids the obvious societal rifts that occur in the midst of overextended societal aggregation. Good cases of such a solution are all the present-day states that have German as a national language, as well as others in different ways, such as Belgium and Canada.

Last but not least, increasing societal complexity (more institutional differentiation as a phenomenon of modernization) is potentially a corollary not only of aggregation but also of disaggregation and layering. The expansion of a horizon of action implies internationalization; the way this affects societal identity will be analysed in greater detail in the next chapter.

3
Emergent National Distinctiveness through International Exposure

3.1 Introduction

Most of us are familiar with the international traffic sign requiring drivers to stop: it is a bright red octagon with the word 'STOP' on it. One notable exception to the international use of this sign is found in the Canadian province of Quebec, where the word 'ARRET'—the French word for 'stop'—is used instead. This deviation from the international norm is evidently non-functional, i.e. it has nothing to do with the inability of the local population either to read or understand the word 'stop'. Note that 'ARRET' is not used on traffic signs in France, Luxembourg, French-speaking areas of Switzerland or Belgium, or any other country which has French as an official language. Note also that inhabitants of Canada whose mother tongue is French are certainly not reluctant to speak English to foreigners. Visitors to Quebec from France even report that as soon as a waiter or shop assistant notices they are foreigners from their different accent, he may address them in English, even though they are French.[97]

This is no quirk. For instance, the inclination to use Dutch words as opposed to French words is weaker in the Netherlands than in the Dutch-speaking parts of Belgium, although the two major national languages of Belgium are French and Dutch and one would otherwise think the Belgians would mingle the two rather comfortably. But that does not appear to be the case. For instance, the Dutch would use *centrifuge* for what the Flemish denote as a *droogzwierder* (literally 'dry-spinner', but of course this is a spin dryer). How can we account for this paradoxical world in which immediate neighbours are much keener to separate themselves from one another and do things differently than are more distant neighbours?

This chapter analyses this particular paradox step by step. It explains how international exposure is formative for distinctive societal culture and institutions, often in more retrenched societal space (provincialization). Internationalization and domestic societal distinctiveness are subject to questioning and change in a process of internationalization, which does imply convergence upon some trans-societal templates. But convergent internationalization is also paradoxical in the sense that it implies its opposites: divergence, retrenchment, and provincialization. This dialectical balance of convergence and divergence is eminently evident in the case of

Germany. By the end of the Middle Ages, internationalization had led to the emergence of a cultural and institutional bedrock that gave the label 'German' a somewhat precise meaning. A similar dialectic involving the interdependence of internationalization and national distinctiveness can also be applied to other societies. The cultural and institutional heritage, periodizations, and dialectics will vary qualitatively depending on the societies being investigated, but the basic mechanism generating societal distinctiveness through international exposure is widely found.

3.2   A rhythm of societal expansion and retrenchment

3.2.1   *Convergence and divergence*

Let us first examine why we should consider it odd to use an idiosyncratic traffic sign in a highly internationalized context in which people are very familiar with English. One of the first reactions would be that Quebeckers are known to rebel against the English language and cultural domination and do anything, however crazy, to protect the status of French as an official language. But merely to classify the Quebeckers as mad is not a satisfactory explanation. It invites the question why such madness should occur under these particular conditions, where a people are prepared and capable to an unprecedented degree of using English when dealing with foreigners, including those foreigners whose mother tongue they share. We probably expect the propensity to use more international cultural artefacts, of which traffic signs are one example and English is another, to be higher when the size of a national group is small in relation to that of others, notably to the numbers of visitors and guests passing through or in regular contact and communication with a more distinctive society such as Quebec. This, in fact, is what we can observe over time, in all manner of societies. In western Europe, the country whose population has mastered the greatest number of languages is Luxembourg. A pervasive feature of opening horizons of action is that new words and other symbols enter society from the outside, are assimilated, and at some stage used as if they were of domestic origin. So far, the idea that international exposure leads to cultural or institutional convergence is confirmed.

Yet this idea also has elements which do not explain very plausibly the origins, persistence, and decline of societal specificities. An expansion of societal horizons and an expansion of horizons of action can have totally opposite effects. Let us explore which factors might help to explain why they may work out one way in one case and another way in a different case. Basically, as a species, we appear to have originated somewhere in or near the East African Rift Valley and then spread out across the globe. As our very distant ancestors migrated to many different places, they probably formed new types of societies, not only with developed language, culture, and institutions, but also with adapted physiognomy and other biological characteristics. While migrating, *homo sapiens* seems to have wiped out with particular effectiveness precisely those species that were biologically the closest, possibly because they were seen to claim similar environmental niches for their sustenance. This appears to eliminate mixing with other species as a significant reason for differentiated societal evolution.

To make a long story short—the story about the differential influences of society, the environment, and biology—it is the adaptation to and the selection of a new niche in which to live that plays the most important role in explaining emerging particularities. These will persist as long as the society which evolves from this remains relatively isolated from others developing elsewhere. Some traits will be retained, but many others will be changed. So, the particularity or divergence of a society is explained by its detachment from others, while its convergence with regard to the culture and institutions of other societies is explained by societal contact, communication, and integration: detachment breeds divergence while contact, communication, and integration breed convergence.[98]

This appears to work well as an explanation in two major cases. First, when a part of society splits off and migrates into new, uninhabited territories, then settlement in a new niche and separation from others explain divergence. Second, when migration leads instead into inhabited territories and when contact and communication are individual, convergence probably has to and does occur, because otherwise individuals cannot meaningfully connect, except in a senseless drive to annihilate each other. For example, as more and more Germanic immigrants settled in the territories east of the Elbe that were mainly inhabited by western Slavs, after about AD 1000 the two peoples began to intermingle despite initial societal segmentation by villages or settlements. After several centuries, a homogeneous society emerged from this melting-pot in many regions.[99] Even war, the opposite of peaceful assimilation, can have the effect of building up social relations if there are survivors on the losing side. When the losers were turned into slaves, as happened so often in antiquity, this also eventually resulted in a build-up of societal community. Enslavement, let alone the mingling or intercourse of people on equal terms, requires a pragmatic redefinition of roles. The fluidity of institutions makes this pragmatic convergence possible. Individual human beings, in principle, have every interest in establishing pragmatic commonalities with those in a different society with whom they connect and cooperate.

When individuals lose their societal horizon, they may have some difficulty in adapting and settling somewhere else, but they tend to overcome such difficulties. Despite some social and personal uprooting that goes with losing their societal horizon, people *as individuals* generally and in the medium and long term take to new societal environments like fish to water. One of the best-known classic studies in sociology on former Polish peasants who had emigrated to Chicago clearly showed that those who continued to socialize within Polish circles kept their Polish societal horizon within view more tenaciously, whereas those who restructured their friendship groups and patterns of interaction to include other immigrants or Americans in their circles of acquaintance rapidly adopted a more dominant and exclusive American horizon.[100]

People do not migrate and strike up new societal relationships only in a purely individual way, even when the culture and institutions of the society that are new to them strongly encourage them to do so. This is the decisive difference between a foreigner entering a bank in Luxembourg or a bar in Montreal, and a group of typical foreigners, who behave or are expected to behave accordingly. In the latter case, the foreigners are not socializing with local people within fluid culture and institutions; the locals and the outsiders are more likely to be separated by divergent and rigid institutions. Let us therefore examine what happens if humans migrate into non-virgin territories as social or societal groupings, i.e. as bearers of culture and institutions they presume to be legitimate and not in any need of fundamental change. Thorny issues arise about compatibility and inferiority versus superiority of the societies that come into contact. As population density has increased over the course of human evolution, the chances of finding uninhabited territory in which to settle have declined drastically. Where such chances do still exist, as in Antarctica or Kamchatka, the locations are probably unattractive. In any case, the clashing, coming together, or intermingling of societal orders is a creative process and produces an order that is not simply the sum of its parts, because a meaningful order requires integration; it does not come about through juxtaposition of distinct societal segments.

3.2.2   *Societal unification, division, and layering*

When people emigrate from societies that consider themselves superior and are able to impose this view on others, this typically triggers the construction of a new society in which the immigrants form a new ruling class. This imposition from outside, whether or not we find it palatable, has historically been the major mechanism of aggregating societies into larger entities, which has also often meant authoritarian rule and domination. The classic researchers and theorists working in this vein, studying various parts of the world, have been Ibn Khaldun, Ludwig Gumplowicz, Lester F. Ward, Franz Oppenheimer, Richard Thurnwald, Alfred Weber, and Marc Bloch.[101] Societal aggregation, social stratification, and the structures of political rule are greatly influenced by the act of a conquering society imposing itself on another. Naturally, immigration from other societies also exerts an influence, but in a more piecemeal and less belligerent way that occurs across a broad range of strata beneath the ruling echelons and the other elite groups. New conquerors tend to arrive armed with their own forms of organization and a strong belief in their own superiority, so that they are more likely to maintain their own societal horizons. New immigrants tend to originate from the lower end of the social ladder and, conversely, may be encouraged to consider their origins as inferior. Still, immigrants may react negatively to such an evaluation of the culture of origin and posit it instead as a counterculture, in need of rediscovery and greater appreciation.

Even fairly integrated societal orders, ones with social inequality as a distinctive feature, have arisen as a result of such clashes of culture and institutions. We must not be blind to the fact that there are societies we consider as integrated or even homogeneous that have come about in this way. Germany and its historical, ethnic, and territorial predecessors have both received and produced new conquering groups but also massive non-conquering mobility. Although this is not well recognized in sociology, Germany has been an exemplary melting pot[102] from its earliest days to the present. But although Germany has federalism as a principle of organization in society, a bit like the United States, another melting pot of sorts, there are great differences in the historical construction of society which have had long-term consequences for organizing social relations in the economy and around work. These need to be sorted out here.

Throughout history, conquerors have often come from warrior societies that have cultivated skills in horseback riding and fighting, or other more advanced techniques of killing people or exerting physical force. Although farming societies have been considered an evolutionary improvement on hunting, gathering, and herding societies, the development of hunting and herding techniques into human combat skills may have given less advanced societies the upper hand as far as conquest is concerned. This was clearly the case when Arabs and Turks were building their empires and also when Germanic tribes imposed themselves on the older Roman Empire while Huns and Mongols established control over central and eastern Europe and successively invaded the Indian subcontinent. While Roman rule had established a fairly rational, bureaucratically sophisticated, and technically advanced civilization for sedentary colonist farmers and town dwellers in its territories, the advent of Germanic rulers caused a regression into personalized relations rather than orderly formal schemes, oral rather than written communication, primitivism on most fronts rather than aqueducts, public baths, and other previous comforts.[103]

After conquest, the challenge facing the new rulers is whether they are able to consolidate rule in the long run, acquire legitimacy in the eyes of the ruled, and become recognized as part of local society. By and large, Germanic invaders appear to have achieved this, with some exceptions which will be mentioned later. But this was because they had proven pragmatic and even negligent in handling the relations that bound them together in their larger empire. They split up into more local or regional allegiances as they integrated with the people over whom they ruled. Basically, this is also what helped cause Roman rule to fall apart: local elites became provincial in their societal horizon, rather than firmly fixed on Rome. Germanic aristocracies appear to have been predisposed, by the societal context from which they came, to suspend any arrangement of rule in an uneasy balance of loyalty and treason, harmony and quarrelling, collective and individual interests.

One is tempted to formulate another theorem-like statement meant to be applicable in every corner of the globe and throughout history: the creation of societal integration through empire-building produces an inevitable backlash since it invariably entails an overextension of societal horizons which stands in the way of deeper societal integration. Either the elites fall out with each other and integrate with the locals, or the elites stick together and are ousted by domestic or external contestants. In either case, societal integration thus tends to swing like a pendulum, such that every noticeable movement toward increasing integration (imposition of a ruling societal stratum on previously diverse societies) is met with a corresponding movement toward decreasing it (retrenchment of societal horizons through societal division, or strengthening of entities at intermediate or lower layers of societal integration).

We can therefore visualize the clash of societies as having quite different outcomes. On the one hand, it may be possible to maintain for a while a very extended society established by conquest. Yet if it is being coherently maintained, this tends to imply an allegiance to a central authority (a ruler, myth, belief, or tradition) that acts against local integration and promotes integration within a larger society. On the other hand, it may be that the new rulers split up—dynastically or into other factions—so that the horizon of societal integration again becomes retrenched. Furthermore, every process in which previously 'international' elites integrate with more disparate populations is likely to generate interaction effects, so that what had previously been the internationally coherent elite becomes so internally differentiated by 'going local' that their nexus is not societal any more.

The integrative performance of empires that have been created in a short span of time has thus been rather mixed. Most of the societies we know have not evolved in seclusion in a smooth, traditional way. They have originated from massive and successive processes of immigration and conquest. They have been amalgamated superficially or thoroughly, and disintegrated by reverse processes of division. The extension and the retrenchment of horizons appear to alternate regularly. Yet this need not only occur like the swing of a pendulum over time, a continual oscillation between the two. The extension and retrenchment of horizons may also become interdependent and occur concurrently. The Mongols and Tartars left many traces in Russia, for instance, that can be found in anything from the physiognomy of the population to public law, but societal integration in the larger Mongol Empire was stopped dead in its tracks after the conquerors were defeated. This is a case of the pendulum swinging back from integration to disintegration.

The history of Germany and its predecessors differs from such stark cases of imperial overextension and collapse. In a way, Germany never became completely unified and autonomous and, although it was often severely threatened as a societal layer in this respect, it never collapsed. Let us look closer at each historical episode. The Franks (another sort of tribe that appears to have been more like a selective amalgamation of people from neighbouring tribes[104] who were good with horses, but this time more Germanic) established an empire in western Europe (called the empire of the 'Franks and the Lombards' in northern Italy[105]) that stretched from the English Channel and the North Sea to the Pyrenees and northern Italy, and eastwards to the River Elbe.[106] This empire also disintegrated rather rapidly because of dynastic division, change of rule, and the integration of elites into the local population. But the intensity of successive historical rearrangements of the fragmented societal puzzle was such that the larger territorial entity brought forth the initial European Communities in roughly the same area, this time as an attempt at societal integration through federation rather than through empire-building.[107]

In the paradoxical way that is distinctive for the formation of extended societal aggregation, the soil that produced societal integration by way of the peaceful federation in the original core of the EU (Benelux, France, Germany, Italy) was thus fertilized by the bloodshed and rubble of centuries of wilful and conflicting attempts at redrawing societal boundaries and layering.

The societal architectures that have originated over time are more likely to be layered ones that express the paradox of extended societal integration. This is particularly visible in all of the societies that at one time or another belonged to the Roman Empire or that of Charlemagne between AD 800 (his coronation as emperor) and 843 (the division of the empire by the Treaty of Verdun). Upper layers of integration may have been maintained, weakened, or strengthened. Lower—more local—layers may have been annihilated, strengthened, or continued. This depends very much on specific societies and their history. In European history, non-layered societal integration seems conspicuous by its absence. If we look at the present-day nation states in Europe and compare them to maps of the past, it becomes abundantly clear that societal integration has not only been layered but layered in different fashions than are visible now.

3.2.3 *The paradox of universalization and provincialization*

One of the first important questions to ask is what causes modern society to differ from others. The first answer provided by social science was that some sort of nation-building occurred. Such theory has been focused mainly on two major questions: first, how it came about that nations, as societies emerging from more disparate entities, were demarcated in a certain way; and second, what characteristics a society took on to facilitate its process of nation-building. Political scientists and historians have dealt with these questions. Thus, smaller societies were integrated into larger ones and social integration was promoted by particular nation-building elites. Salient social cleavages (religious, estate, class, regional, cultural, etc.) also played a role at particularly critical junctures in history and thereby helped set into motion particular processes of institution-building and cultural stylization. Stein Rokkan, Perry Anderson, and others have pioneered this type of theory, each with a different focus; for Rokkan it was on party systems and political structures, and for Anderson, types of state formation.[108]

It has also always been clear that external relations of emerging nations or states have a lot to do with the settlement of internal conflicts and the choice of institutional types. One of the best-known factors is the type of external conflict facing nations: England, as part of an island, maintained a large navy and did not have such great need for a standing army on its own territory. This is evident for the period following the War of the Roses until the Glorious Revolution in 1688 effectively put an end to major civil upheaval in Britain. Violent conflict in the United Kingdom did erupt again, as we know, in the Easter Uprising in Dublin in 1916. Yet, even when this kingdom needed ample land forces to fight battles in Europe (such as the Battle of Waterloo against Napoleon), it relied mainly on forces raised in Germany. About two-thirds of the soldiers at Waterloo under Wellington's command were from Hanover, Brunswick (Braunschweig), or other German territories, accompanied by some Dutch allied troops. The British monarch was also ruler of Hanover, one of the larger principalities in the German federation. When the British needed a war to be fought on the Continent, they usually used German troops, as did the Dutch. Likewise, the Swedes used Finns and the Austrians used Croats, Hungarians, and Spaniards whenever they could in order to avoid sacrificing their own countrymen.

On the Continent, however, monarchs needed the aristocracy in order to finance and maintain a large standing army. Consequently, monarchs were more likely to side with the aristocracy and strengthen it. This eventually led Prussia towards a process of modernization from above, and towards the establishment of a corporatist state and a bureaucracy, whereas in Britain, it led to the formation of a more liberally minded middle class which became a central nation-builder. Granted, this is a rather simplified version of centuries of historical development, but the central purpose of this mere sketch of a historical depiction is simply to remind us that external threats and opportunities have always been part of the comparative picture of nation- and society-building.

This interpretation has tended, however, to bias perspectives unduly in the direction of universalism. The formation of societies into more aggregate nation states has been depicted as a march from greater division and segmental societies towards larger and more integrated societies. Supporting this is the older Parsonian idea that we can view the evolution of society as moving from particularism to universalism, from diffuseness to functional specificity, from ascription to achievement, and from affectivity to affective neutrality. Recently, more and more doubt has been expressed about the viability of such an evolutionary scheme. On the basis of more detailed evidence, we have been led to conceptualize societal evolution as *paradoxical*. This means that it is propelled in the direction of universalism, functional specificity, achievement orientation, and affective neutrality by a renaissance of counter-forces, by a resurgence of particularism, diffuseness, ascription, and affectivity. Paradox does not imply the absence of logical coherence, but this coherence originates from dialectical evolution and is linked with the partitioning of institutional space. This does imply that opposing institutional principles occupy more restricted and specific niches or aspects of the larger institutional set. In this way, societies pragmatically enact coherence, based on the 'self-evident' understanding that 'there is a time and a place' for everything: affective neutrality and affectivity, achievement and ascription, and also cosmopolitanism and provincialism.

Modernization has thus been conceived as a paradoxical enterprise over the long run, while in the shorter run, either of the poles of the pattern variables may predominate. However, we are not dealing with a simple oscillation between the poles of the space in which the pendulum swings; it is more accurate to picture this as an upward spiralling movement. Van de Loo and van Reijen have discussed this at greater length.[109] With regard to the 'globalization' discussion, a similar point has been made by Robertson and Khondker:

What is involved in globalization is a complex process involving the interpenetration of sameness and difference—or, in somewhat different terms, the interpenetration of universalism and particularism. . . . In sociology we have grown used to thinking in terms of a temporal, diachronic transition from particularism to universalism. But we now need to bring spatial, synchronic considerations firmly into our thinking and consider fully the spatiality of particularisms and differences.[110]

The implications for our notion of society are considerable. For societal specificity and identity are not only the result of aggregation of more disparate societies into more aggregate and integrated ones, which implies movement toward relative *universalization*. In the midst of universalization, and indeed because of it, there is movement in the direction of particularism, which can be called *provincialization*. The conjunction of universalization and provincialization is made compatible by the layering of societies.

This can be traced step by step. First, consider the implications of a population extending its horizon of action more broadly and systematically in the direction of another society. This may have a variety of causes, from migration of a friendly or unfriendly nature to the intensification of trade and other exchange and increased social contact. The extension of the horizon of action does not necessarily lead to a sharing of societal horizons, as we have seen. As populations come closer together, it may well be that they demarcate the boundaries between them even more clearly. Indeed, this takes us back to the examples mentioned initially. It was social inequality and the domination of one segment of society over another that turned the encounter of English-speaking Canadians with Franco-Canadians, of dour Scottish Calvinists with the Catholic Frenchmen who arrived in Canada first, into a clash rather than a process of smooth integration. The resulting acrimony has produced a situation in which one of the possible solutions, the only integrative one, sees Quebec as 'a society that is part of Canadian society', while the other considers Quebec to be 'a society different from the rest of Canada which should strive towards independence'.[111]

This example clearly illustrates that the interdependencies evolving among the various populations during the process of modernization only make societal differences all the more acute, even to the point of determining the design of traffic signs. One powerful motive appears to be revenge for inequalities suffered in the past.[112] This can also be ascertained in Belgium. The segment of society which was subject in the past to attempts at assimilation, thus blurring its identity somewhat, may come back even more strongly to reassert its identity. It is likely to do this when economic, demographic, or political resources give it a stronger hand in the political struggle for the power to create rigid institutions or gradually change soft ones. Hence, when the new industries of the 1960s were being established in the Flemish parts of Belgium at the same time that heavy industry was declining in Wallonia, Flanders pushed for a greater political division of the country. When the oil industry developed in Scotland, this was used to bolster claims for Scottish independence and ultimately led to the development of Scotland into something resembling a German federal state. This also occurred in Wales and will happen some day, one hopes, in Northern Ireland. As part of this process, the societal segments that had receded during the process of nation-building re-emerge as stronger entities on a lower layer of aggregation.[113]

But the strength of more retrenched layers need not only come from acrimonious resentment of inequalities endured, subjectively or objectively, in the course of nation-building. Switzerland has, more or less, four officially acknowledged languages and cultural communities, crystallized in cantons. Local self-government (the power invested in cantons and the role of local or national referenda) and the cross-cutting of cultural cleavages by religious ones and by status distinctions (social inequality not being conflated with cultural differences) have made the encounter of cultures with one another more peaceful. That peace is relative, of course, because the Swiss did have a civil war in the nineteenth century, and cantons were formerly divided into two sorts: more sovereign cantons and 'subject cantons' (*Untertanenlande*). Nevertheless, the Swiss have not found it helpful or necessary to erect ARRET signs in the French-speaking cantons as a gesture of emancipation, and they have kept in place retrenched societal layers that are instruments of societal demarcation as effective as those in Belgium or Canada.

Now the subdivision of Switzerland is not a case in which various populations emigrated to a greater extent than elsewhere. The different populations have been able to unite themselves politically by devolving power to the cantons, which was an important factor in uniting the cantons located around 'the lake of the four forest towns' (*Vierwaldstädter See*) and in accommodating new cantons into the confederation. Thus, politically and in terms of hard institutions, Geneva opted for Switzerland, although it had had much more important links with Savoy, which eventually became part of France. The Swiss option allowed Geneva to remain solidly Protestant, which would have been impossible in France, and it could be combined perfectly with other cantons opting to stay resolutely Catholic. Regional self-government also applied to the legitimation of religion and thus became a powerful integrative force in Swiss society for Catholics and Protestants, Romanic and Germanic speakers alike, notwithstanding unbroken cultural and trade links with Germany, France, and Italy. It is not the factor of seclusion that explains why Switzerland acquired independence by the end of the Thirty Years' War in 1648. On the contrary, Switzerland sat astride major trade routes from Germany to Italy and to the River Rhône. Even the Habsburg dynasty, which provided the emperors for the German Empire or federation for four hundred years until 1866, originally came from a region that became part of Switzerland (the canton of Aargau).

It was a combination of the relative weakness of infeudation and aristocratic rule, the devolution of power to cantons and town assemblies and meetings, and the substantial power to wreak havoc in international trade that enabled Switzerland to rise as a nation conscious of its identity to a degree few others have ever been. Thus, this country is also an illustration of how power can be accrued in the international division of labour and used to retrench societal horizons, while expanding horizons of action at the same time. Even in pre-industrial times, Switzerland developed into an international financial centre and was a major recruitment ground for mercenaries serving foreign countries. Reputable Continental states, not only the Vatican, had Swiss guards, raised by cantons always willing to supply their sons as soldiers for a fair sum of money. While this type of phenomenon is often remembered as typical of supposedly retrograde potentates such as the prince of Hesse, who sold local regiments to the king of England to fight American rebels in the War of Independence after 1776, the rulers that practised it to perfection were the republican, grassroots, and popularly elected local authorities in democratic Switzerland. The soldiers who had to suffer the brunt of the attack when the Bastille was stormed in Paris in 1789 were mainly Swiss, and Swiss guards were also slaughtered when the Tuileries were stormed later.[114] Even Prussia had a battalion consisting of a sort of Swiss guard until 1866.[115] For Swiss men keen to make a fortune by soldiering abroad, rather than eking out a precarious existence on inhospitable mountains, this was apparently an attractive option.

This did not at all result in societal integration into larger external aggregates, except for individual migrants who decided to settle where they had fought. Not even the foundation of a 'Helvetic Republic' under temporary Napoleonic tutelage in 1803 disturbed the national separateness of Switzerland; it only seems to have augmented its internal coherence. This country is a clear example of how societal identity is produced and maintained by introducing extended and international action. Curiously enough, the identity that Switzerland has maintained is the one that generally prevailed in the Holy Roman Empire before the advent of modernity, i.e. one of considerable devolution of power to local entities in a patchwork of rule. While this local patchwork was gradually being consolidated within larger territorial entities under more absolute rule in the rest of Germany, the Swiss paradoxically succeeded in remaining more Germanic in their form of government by resisting absorption into Germany, although ethnically they are probably as Celtic as Ireland. It did not matter that there was little cultural, religious, and linguistic homogeneity and interdependencies with neighbouring societies existed. What counted was a favourable position in trade, weak feudalization, and a clear, single common denominator (the principle of local independence and rule guaranteed by larger society) put forward by political movements.

3.2.4 The expansion and retrenchment of horizons

An intermediate conclusion is that retrenchment of societal horizons is a pervasive feature of processes of internationalization. In Switzerland, this has led to a marked preoccupation with external independence, which goes so far as to reject membership of international alliances, the European Union, and even the United Nations. A politically pious explanation is that Switzerland wanted to stay out of the vile and vicious scheming and warmongering of unelected potentates. A realistic explanation is that it wanted its citizens to take part in war for good wages, without the country itself being affected by the ravages to which others had to submit. Despite its separation from the Holy Roman Empire in 1648 and its modest size, the layering of society and the regional segmentation of government remained a part of this domestic phenomenon. While the conservation of local autonomy was the motive for constituting Switzerland in the first place, layered rule and domination appears to be characteristic of almost every entity that the former Holy Roman Empire brought forth. Even Austria, a linguistically homogeneous society with only six million people, was divided into federal states after 1945. One almost wonders why Liechtenstein did not do so. In Belgium and Canada, greater societal integration was achieved beyond local cultures and institutions, and a more forceful imposition of rule was part of this, but that has not prevented retrenched layers from holding their own or resurfacing. This effect is also appearing in other countries, such as Spain and Italy, as are similar tendencies of devolution, such as in the UK and France.

This is not to argue that regionalization works against the nation state. There are different types of nation states; some may even thrive upon the paradoxical interdependency of societal integration processes in different layers. Federal nation states are supported by lower layers of societal integration and political rule. Clearly, there are several possible directions societal integration can take as a result of an internationalization of the horizons of action. On the one hand, such horizons may become societal when expanded. On the other, the unending quest for tangible coherence and identity of action systems pushes towards provincialization. Actors like their societal horizons close by, even when horizons of action become very extended. When the extension of horizons of action becomes societal and extended and retrenched horizons merge or clash, then either layering or societal rifts occur, respectively. If Belgium and Canada had not been divided into distinct regions and communities, they might have broken apart as nation states, as many others have, notwithstanding substantial commonalities and substantial societal integration through political unification, social mobility, and sharing of institutions.

The evidence presents a more complex picture, of course. Not every type of layering and segmentation stabilizes a larger societal aggregate. The empire of the Russian tsars was rather stable as long as Finland, Poland, and the Baltic States had greater autonomy, whereas the autonomy of the Baltic States in the Soviet Union was apparently more superficial. Yugoslavia collapsed despite the strong federalism practised under Tito and the favourable treatment of non-Serbian nations, possibly because Serbian nationalism fomented other nationalisms after Tito's death. Czechoslovakia is another case; the unity between the Czechs and the Slovaks appears to have been at the breaking point following the pressure of centuries of societal integration with other nations, specifically with Germany and Austria for the Czechs[116] and with Hungary for the Slovakians.

Larger-scale societal integration can thus turn out to be interdependent with layering. The same interdependency between societal integration into a European Union and demarcation of nation states might exist, but this need not be the case everywhere and always. Whether or not it exists might depend on specificities involved in the construction of the layering and whether the act of repressing societal retrenchment makes a population opt for severing relations. This option is frequently used, as Ireland and recent examples in Eastern Europe demonstrate, even when it means severing long-standing societal links. For example, it was the link joining Moscow and Kiev that became the genesis of Tsarist Russia, but this centuries-old association did not prevent the recent split between Russia and the Ukraine. The question is whether the split would have occurred without the Stalinist repression of Ukrainian culture and institutions. Therefore, layering can be hypothesized to depend on a number of contingencies. Whether and how it occurs, and whether it is sustainable, become questions of social and political action, preconditions, and options.

Generally, it seems that both the extension of horizons of action through trade and migration and expansion of societal horizons, mainly through the imposition of a new ruling class and institutions, bring about ambivalent results. Either the existing societies may react defensively against extended horizons, or an over-extension of societal horizons leads to provincialization. Possibly, the complexity of extended societies becomes so great that it inhibits societal integration. If the latter is promoted effectively, this may very well imply provincialization as a way of integrating new rulers and systems of rule with their subjects. The history of both the Roman and the Frankish empires suggests this. This leads to the hypothesis that the increasing complexity of a society is not just one of many factors but, in fact, the main factor causing societal identity and meaning to evolve through provincialization. This then is an inevitable, eclectic, and innovative construction under a retrenched horizon. In other words, the quest for wider societal community notwithstanding, institutional differentiation and complexity push towards provincialization.

This analysis is generally pertinent for the build-up and restructuring of societal community. Social actors like their societal community to be on a small scale, because this permits transparency and smoothly working action systems and nurtures an identity that counteracts anonymity in large and complex aggregates. But the drift of historical development favours large-scale integration. These are two conflicting aspects of one and the same phenomenon: 'social action' implies both the extension and the retrenchment of horizons and interdependencies in order to keep action systems tightly coupled in complex institutional landscapes. In conjunction, the two lead to layering as a way of combining retrenched and extended societal horizons. However, the process of combining them has occurred in very different ways in various places throughout the ages. German empires and confederations are known for their strong degree of layering and an unending balance between centralized and decentralized authority, of national harmonization and local provincialization. This has allowed Germany and its predecessors to avert the massive collapse of overextended empires that we otherwise frequently find. The difficult balance between collapse and integration that has evolved and been maintained over centuries has had very long-term consequences. In what follows, our analysis will pursue two aspects: one is more generally theoretical, the other is the reconstruction of a particular pattern of societal aggregation that we need to understand because it leads to modern economic institutions that are societally specific.

3.3   Societal expansion and retrenchment in pre- and proto-German epochs

3.3.1   Varying shades of Germanness

The process of achieving the societal integration of Germany is exemplary in zigzagging between attempts at expansion and internationalization and periods of provincialization. Because Germany, with its 83 million inhabitants, has come to be the largest nation in the EU and at earlier points in history also included present-day Austria, Bohemia, and Slovenia (until 1866) and Switzerland (until 1648), in addition to other regions with non-German-speaking populations, its aggregation cannot be explained by strong provincialization alone, despite the common language and national unity it presently enjoys. Germany has also been involved in one of the most powerful drives towards universalization; in view of the historical deal achieved with the Pope, its emperors long maintained a claim and pursued the aim of expanding and integrating Christianity by politics (including aristocratic intermarriage) and conquest. The resulting layering is one of the factors that explains why Germany is commonly thought of as being not only a 'latecomer to nation-building' in Europe, but also a precocious inter-nation.

One of the greatest ironies in the history of ideas is the association between Germanic ethnicity or culture and Germany. This association is suggested in part by a confusion of terms in the English language but also by German romanticism, as it developed at the beginning of the nineteenth century. This romanticism was instrumental in constructing an interpretation of what present-day Germany came to be as a nation. The term 'Germany' is originally Latin, certainly not Germanic. Germanic peoples had no generic name for themselves, only tribal ones. 'Germany' worked its way into the English language from Latin. After it was romanticized, it also crept into Germanic languages. *Germani* was the name the Romans gave two groups of people: first, a tribe they encountered on their northern border, more or less along the lower part of the Rhine; and second, all manner of tribes they encountered in the region at large that had similar languages, cultures, and institutions. They thus took *pars pro toto*, which is quite common for people to do when typifying foreign populations, such as when the French call Germans *les Allemands* (these being originally a group of tribes found predominantly along the upper Rhine in the early Middle Ages), or when Finns call Germans 'Saxons'.

These two groups known as *Germani* in Latin were actually a mixture of peoples with Celtic and Germanic origins, who had evolved through the westward migration of some Germanic populations into the larger and older habitat of the Celts, roughly in an area bordered by the River Weser, the Alps, the River Scheldt (Escaut) up to its estuary near Antwerp, and along the North Sea coast. This area of Celtic inhabitation had thus been subject to the immigration of Germanic people from the east and the north, and Celtic tribes had extended their own habitat westwards to cover much of what today is France.[117] When the Romans approached the Rhine in the century before the birth of Jesus Christ, what they encountered were mixtures of Celtic-Germanic ethnicities and peoples, the predominant language in most groups apparently being Germanic, but the predominant artisan skills, cultural artefacts, and other aspects being Celtic. This is what any historical atlas found in German schools will show.[118] Thus, the Romans did not, for the most part, encounter truly 'pure' Germanic peoples but a Celtic-Germanic mixture. The purer Germanic tribes were further to the east and the north. Whilst the mixed Celtic-Germanic tribes west of the Rhine and south of the Danube gradually turned into cooperative service tribes, the others were much more recalcitrant and aggressive; they resisted Roman incursions. But they were also prepared to negotiate or smash their way into the Roman Empire when they expected this would improve their well-being.

These two groups of *Germani* were first taken note of in a systematic and written form by Tacitus, the Roman historian. His description was also applied to Anglo-Saxons, a group of Germanic tribes then living in the very north of Germany who later left their habitat to conquer England, as did Norman populations after them. So, Tacitus' description was meant to apply to many Germanic tribes, whether they had intermingled with Celts or not.[119] In the main, Tacitus suggested the following characteristics:[120]

Society was rather egalitarian, at least much more so than was Roman society.

Cooperation was generated more voluntarily by individuals, rather than through servitude and stable rule. Lateral social coordination was predominant, and it was based on discussion held in the assembly of all the free men in a tribe or in a smaller entity. Collective decisions originated here.

The nuclear family was important, whereas extended familial relationships were weaker except in matters of inheritance; peer groups cut across familial structures and were entered into voluntarily, or established by social constraint quite regularly.

Stable rule and domination over larger societal entities were only accepted with difficulty under certain conditions and for the duration of a collectively agreed campaign of war, when campaign leaders (*duces*, *Herzöge*, *hertogen* in Latin and some Germanic languages) were chosen by popular acclaim.[121]

People alternated between hunting and farming and had a social structure that was weakly or barely differentiated.

Differences attached to gender were much smaller than those common in Rome.

Great importance was given to valour in battle, and warriors' wives supported and admonished them behind the lines, for example by cheering the men on in battle and vilifying them when they were not fighting hard enough. The women also killed themselves when a battle was lost and there was a risk of being taken into slavery.

Loyalty to an in-group of comrades and to their own wives was a central virtue that Tacitus propagandistically contrasted with the urban treachery and degeneracy of Romans.

Throughout the course of history, themes reminiscent of Tacitus' writings have been instrumental in kindling German national pride, the terms (German/Germanic) have been repeatedly equivocated upon, and the virtues of 'Germanic freedom and loyalty' have been cloaked in romantic stylization and held up as a model for Germans to emulate since 1800.[122] As we have seen, Tacitus' writings were probably slanted towards peoples of a Celtic-Germanic mixture.

The characteristics of the purer Germanic people may have been different from those Tacitus noted, although they may also have exhibited the characteristics listed above with even greater emphasis. Yet, the greatest propagation of misunderstanding probably came through the English language. A prominent political scientist, Harry Eckstein, has pointed out in his book on Norway that '[Norwegian] political commentaries are large and meticulous to a Germanic extent', the supposition being that Norwegians are not expected to be as Germanic as Germans.[123] However, quite to the contrary, they are much more Germanic than Germans. All would agree that what Tacitus said, including the emphasis on belligerence, relates much better to past and present-day Norwegians or Scandinavians than Germans. The absence of gender differences, social equality, accommodation of individual rights and collective constraints, and the difficulty of central rule are traits much more characteristic of Norwegians than Germans. Belligerence, which Scandinavians have come to pretend was not so important after all, had been epitomized by Nordic Germanic tribes more strongly than by the southern Germanic ones until the end of the great Nordic war(s) in 1721 when Sweden—then including Finland—stopped warring with its neighbours, exhausted from its efforts to become a world power.

Characteristically, Germanic people found it extremely difficult to erect impersonal proto-state collectivities on a larger scale due to their penchant for personal and peer-group freedom and independence. The only way out of this problem was to use personalized bonding, in this case feudalism, to establish control over larger aggregates. The epitome of this conundrum was the emperor of the Holy Roman Empire, until the emperorship slipped under more or less durable control of the Habsburg dynasty. Although invested with considerable charisma and religious mystique, the emperor was a wretched soul when we look at the way he had to conduct his official and personal life: deprived of a stable residence and material comforts, he had to tour the realm continually, going from one frugal 'palace' (*Pfalz*) to another, pacifying restless vassals and helping to solve problems on the spot. This was vastly different from the comforts and stability enjoyed by emperors in Byzantium (Constantinople) and later in Vienna, when it served *de facto* as the capital of the Holy Roman Empire after the Middle Ages.

Eckstein's book has served to make this clear, involuntarily but effectively, and countless comparative social science findings support it: it is the Norwegians that epitomize traditional Germanic virtues (and vices), including the characteristic bravery and cruelty manifested in multiple Norman forays into other parts of Europe until the advent of modern history. The legalistic fussiness and concern with procedure, very visible in Norway, has been constructed to overcome problems of justice that arise with the inherent jealousness of egalitarian individualists who, on top of that, also require the state to recognize as a prime mission the meticulous preservation of regional diversity, influence, and allocation of resources and benefits. They have preserved a purer Germanic culture and institutions than Germans have. German romantics, from the reflective poets to the lunatic fringe, have always greatly appreciated them for doing so and have welcomed cultural products from Norway, from old sagas down to Gulbrandson, as a reminder of a Nordic past they regrettably left behind.[124] Germans have obviously forgotten that the old Germanic peoples accepted higher authority only with difficulty and would have been very sceptical of any generalized *Führerprinzip* In Germany, much as in France until the end of the Hundred Years' War and in England until the end of the War of the Roses, feudalism was linked with perennial strife within the apparatus for domination, and with strong drives to differentiate society into semi-autonomous segments.

3.3.2   Enter the Wild Bunch

What Germanic tribes shared, whether they exhibited Celtic influences or were purer or had adapted to Roman rule or had fought their way through its empire from the fourth century on, was an unwillingness to refer to themselves under a more generic name or consider themselves as united across tribal affiliations by birth, descent, language, or culture. When in doubt, they considered other Germanic tribes as competitors or as dubious rather than natural potential allies. Many of them, in fact, sided with Rome, notably the more Celticized factions along the Rhine. The major push in the large-scale turbulence of the great migration that brought Rome to its knees came from those Germanic tribes in territories not or not firmly occupied by Rome, regardless whether they had been located in central or northern Europe for some time or had arrived on the scene more recently over diverse paths that had brought them to Europe from Asia or the eastern fringe of Europe. Again, any school atlas can be used to verify such vast movements.[125]

In addition to pervasive societal disintegration in the wake of this migration into the Roman Empire, a ripple of movement began that would eventually lead to another wave of large-scale societal integration. Again, this was characteristically devoid of any reference to Germanic attributes or Germanness. From their home on the eastern shores of the Rhine came the Franks, whose name, associated with the more gung-ho types found in residence, meant, more or less, 'the Wild Bunch'. With the characteristic ambivalence of Germanic invaders vacillating between forceful intrusion and cooperation, they came into the late Roman Empire as upholders of governmental order in the northern centre of Roman Gallia[126] and then battled in every direction to establish the above-mentioned empire of Charlemagne. The resulting realm was called that of 'the Franks and the Lombards'. Again, the word 'German' did not figure, either in Latin—except for the clumsy reference to the *Teutones*, a tribe that had been annihilated by an army under Marius centuries before—or in the local vernacular languages, where the term 'German' did not even exist. This Frankish Wild Bunch demonstrated a perennial capacity of the less-Celticized and romanized Germanic tribes to generate new belligerent subsocieties that sought their fortune elsewhere. The same was true of the Normans or Norsemen. Besides being territorially very extended, the expansion of the Wild Bunch brought forth European feudalism as a personalized way of assuring domination over a large expanse, by reciprocal interdependency of rulers and both individual vassals and confederations or brotherhoods.

In true Germanic fashion, Frankish rule was subject to reccurring egalitarian jealousy, bickering over inheritance rights, dependence, and accumulation of power. Still, the ambition of the empire, especially under the reign of Charlemagne, was firmly universalistic and in this sense imbued with Roman heritage, including the Latin language as the only one which permitted written communication and the recording and archiving of information. It struck a major universalizing deal by giving the Christian bishop of Rome a territory of his own (Pippin's donation) that became the Vatican and a monopoly over religion. Charlemagne reinforced this deal by having himself enthroned as an emperor, in keeping with Roman tradition and endowed with religious charisma. The enlargement of the Frankish and Lombardic empire by and large corresponded, at least in the long run, with the ascent of papal authority, despite continued rivalry: At its height in AD 800, the Frankish Empire was an eclectic mixture of Frankish rule, the Christian religion, Roman civilization, and local cultures. Far from being generically Germanic, the empire considered its major enemy and target of conquest to be the Saxons, another term used *pars pro toto* to refer to those peoples living further north and east of the Rhine river, and north of Thuringia and Hesse.

3.3.3   The origins of the South Germanic bedrock

Although the Franks did not constitute the beginning of a German nation and are not recognized as having done so by present-day history books, the Franks did lay the cornerstone of what I propose to call the South Germanic bedrock. This is distinguished from its northern Germanic counterpart in Scandinavia by being more Celticized and Romanized and by implying the imposition of foreign rule and domination through conquest and subsequent, continuous intermingling of feudal rulers and the local population. Although both the ruling class and the ruled were Germanic in culture and institutions, the imposition of rule implied a deviation from Germanic social structure. This happened on the South Germanic bedrock but not in Scandinavia where the influences of feudalism remained weak, either held in check by a strong king or the plague. Egalitarian Scandinavian countries had strong kings and a weak aristocracy, whereas thoroughly feudal Germany had a strong aristocracy and weak kings or emperors. Again we see that institutional practices in different societies do not only or mainly differ in their measure of, in this case, authoritarianism and egalitarianism. They are different in the way they combine authoritarian and egalitarian practices and allocate them places in the societal order. While the plague is mentioned as having wiped out the already rather sparse feudal aristocracy in Norway, such natural causes were far from singularly responsible for the demise of feudalization. In the Holy Roman Empire of the Franks and subsequent dynasties, feudal posts were awarded by the emperor to upwardly or laterally mobile individuals whenever such posts became vacant for whatever reason. These vacancies caused by the plague, wars, and other phenomena were the main impetus to upward social mobility in medieval Germany and thereby helped to stabilize feudalism and the power of the emperor as a promoter of up-and-coming warriors and ruling talent.

The South Germanic bedrock was henceforth composed of opposing but linked tendencies of expansion and division, large-scale societal integration and provincialization. Political scientists discuss systems of checks and balances, and these are thought to consist either of the division of governmental functions (legislative, executive, and judiciary) or the rivalry between a ruling party and its political opposition. Clearly, the checks and balances instituted in the South Germanic bedrock consisted of the rivalry between central rulers and their more or less independent vassals and other subordinate powers, such as bishops, monasteries, and knightly orders. It was a feudal system of checks and balances along the vertical lines of feudal bonding. In English history, it became a system of checks and balances primarily between the head of government (the king) and the representation of vassals and other dependants, before a balance between government and opposition in Parliament superseded it. Although the German territories were composed of exactly the same ethnic and cultural ingredients (Celts, Germanic and Roman invaders), the comparatively greater degree of independence enjoyed by vassals in German territories led to an initially strong but increasingly feeble estate parliament that all but disappeared in early modernity (the Reichstag). This was a balance of power in which the centre (the emperor) gradually became weaker inside the empire or federation, and it was counterbalanced by independent principalities and other estates.

The eastern Frankish Empire still did not even remotely approach the embodiment of a German identity. German historians identify the beginning of that embodiment with the coronation of Otto I as emperor in 936, the first Saxon sovereign over an empire now called that 'of the Franks and Saxons'.[127] There was still no reference to anything Germanic or German. Otto was a Saxon and thus came from a territory and ethnicity that had been violently conquered, ruled, and Christianized by the Franks during their period of expansion. The designation of Otto's empire was somewhat ambitious, since the western Frankish realm was now outside its ambit, having congealed into a kingdom of France after undergoing several divisions of Charlemagne's empire. However, Otto's coronation signalled that the subject Saxons had finally achieved equality with the Franks. In contrast to the western Frankish rulers who henceforth became 'French', Otto succeeded in maintaining the historical accord with the Pope to become an emperor endowed with universalistic aspirations and sanctioned by a similarly universalistic religious monopoly.

The king of France entered into a continuous rivalry with the emperor 'of the Franks and Saxons', also maintaining similarly universalistic ambitions and insisting that France be 'la fille ainée de l'Église' (the elder daughter of the Church, on the basis of Pippin's donation to the bishop of Rome, which was made when the Frankish realm had its centre of gravity in the Île-de-France). This started a competition for universalistic legitimacy that achieved just the opposite:

particularization of societies, Romanic, and Germanic languages; distinctive institutions and culture. Once again we find that a new societal aggregation was instrumental in deepening a societal rift that had already opened between one provincializing people and another. Nevertheless, there was no mention of Germanness in the way realms or segments of society were designated.

Some time after the coronation of Otto and the firmer positioning of a South Germanic bedrock, a striking reversal of migration trends occurred. Until then, migration across the Continent had moved from east to west and had involved both Celtic and Germanic tribes attracted by fertile land or the spoils of battle for or against Rome. By the eighth century, territories east of the Elbe had been, by all accounts, almost completely emptied of Germanic inhabitants. Slavs also migrated west, and by the turn of the millennium, this area was more or less exclusively inhabited by western Slavic populations. However, under the Frankish-Saxon empire, the major direction of migration now turned eastward, with colonists from all over the South Germanic bedrock founding new villages and towns amidst a local population that was predominantly Slav. To some extent they were attracted by Slav rulers; to some extent they conquered territory. This boiled down to a Germanization (in language and institutions) of much of central Europe and the Baltic shore, but it also created a patchwork of different communities living side by side. Germany thus became ethnically replenished with western Slavic ingredients to the same extent that Germanic and Celtic ones were present. It is no exaggeration to regard the ethnic contribution of the Slavs to the German population as just as substantial as the Germanic one.

On the whole, this integration progressed much more smoothly than often assumed in light of the more recent period of rivalry and aggressiveness after the beginning of German nationalism in the nineteenth century. Over the centuries, a number of western Slavic populations living alongside the Poles and Czechs all but disappeared in the melting pot of central European and Baltic Germanization. These people undoubtedly left indelible traces in the mental and cultural heritage of what is now considered German—despite the paucity of truly Germanic roots—such as in the romantic penchant for forests, in the cuisine, and in Easter and Christmas rituals. Yet they traded their autonomous identity for a thoroughgoing integration of languages and institutions. Thus Polish, Czech, and other Slav family names are common currency in German telephone books, just as Poles, Czechs, and Slovakians often have names such as Miller, Gottwald, Klaus, Schuster, and Dienstbier, to mention some of the more prominent ones. At least within the territory of the Holy Roman Empire and, in some respects, on the Baltic seafront, the Slavs 'melted into' a Frankish-Saxon order through an integration process that occurred no less peacefully than in other and better-known melting pots.

Even the co-existence of separate but neighbouring German and Czech settlements in Bohemia remained relatively unproblematic until the Habsburg emperor set out to integrate the kingdom into his own realm against the wishes of the estates, who wanted a Protestant prince from the Palatinate as king of Bohemia rather than the Catholic emperor from nearby Austria. The touch paper of the Thirty Years'

War was lit when envoys of the emperor were thrown out the window in Prague. Until the Habsburgs intervened heavy-handedly in Bohemia, it had not experienced any major conflicts of national integration. The melting pot in the east of the empire was comparatively free of the problems incurred where populations mixed less and retained separate communities, which appears to hold true more for territories further east and south. The Slavic-Germanic melting pot underscores the necessity of defining the South Germanic bedrock in terms more independent of the ethnic and cultural origins of its peoples.

3.3.4 *Ambiguous Germanness and the meaning of the South Germanic bedrock*

The thorny question thus arises as to what 'German' actually means in terms of an identity that is more unified then the Germanic people have been and that neither overlaps with other Germanic derivations nor with the imposition of Germanic rule. The adjective used in German is the word *Deutsch*, and it originally means 'of the people'. This root is also visible in other languages: a representation of 'the people' is sometimes called 'diet' in English or 'la diète' in French. Oddly enough, Germans are thus understood in German to be the people 'of the people', which does not tell us much. Yet it is not uncommon for other ethnic groups to call themselves 'the people' in their own language. In Germany, this usage dates back to the split within the Frankish empire and its aristocracy into those who adopted a more Latinized language and those who opted to stick with 'the language of the people', meaning the more Germanic dialects. This already included a wide range of languages. As the Dutch national anthem, composed in the sixteenth century, puts it, the founding father of the country (William of the Nassau-Orange dynasty, a sort of Spanish viceroy or *stadhouder*) extolled his descent *van duitsen bloed*, from 'popular', non-Latinized roots. Thus, the notion of German culture and heritage arose in connection with the vernacular of non-Latin languages, not as something coherent but as a loose category of languages that were anything but Latinized (*Welsch* or *waals*).

The definition of what is German is as broad and unspecific as that, and yet this qualification excluded sizeable cultural and linguistic groups in the west (Walloon, Lorraine, Savoy, Franche-Comté, Provence), northern Italy, Bohemia, and Moravia, as well as other western Slavs who did not speak Germanic dialects, much as they were an integral part of the empire as it existed then. For this reason, it is a distortion to call the empire 'German' in the sense of *Deutsch*, as a hodgepodge of mainly Germanic dialects in the territory of the realm. For the border of the realm did not coincide with language borders but extended far beyond them. By this token, even in the South Germanic bedrock, layering was present not only (albeit on a somewhat reduced scale) in the checks and balances of central rulers and differentiated vassals but also in cultural and institutional rifts. It was a patchwork from the start, and became more of a patchwork over time. In turn, its patchwork quality was necessarily linked to the process of stabilizing an overextended empire, in the same way that the Roman Empire—once it had extended itself to include all manner of cultural and institutional differences—was stabilized by a layering that made use of 'indirect rule' and ethnic, cultural, and institutional entities.

Therefore, the South Germanic bedrock of feudal institutions of government is larger than the one featuring Germanic dialects as popular languages. The point here is not to debate what present-day Germany can claim to be part of its unique historical heritage. Any such heritage can be claimed with equal justification by different nation states. It is important to acknowledge first that there is a need to differentiate carefully the spectrum of terms ranging from Germanicness, South Germanic feudal rule and domination, and South Germanic feudal rule and domination plus mainly Germanic language. I will use 'South Germanic bedrock' henceforth only in the last sense. It is therefore twice removed from Germanicness, contrary to the English language and romantic German nationalists, both of which tend to link them.[128] The link between 'pure' Germanicness or archaic tribes such as the Goths and Germany (in the sense of a more restricted version of the South Germanic bedrock) is very tenuous indeed. If anyone can claim a more direct link, it is the Scandinavians.

Following the coronation of Emperor Otto I, the South Germanic bedrock was composed of the following major elements:

1. It implied an overextension of a system of rule and domination beyond cultural boundaries, such that rulers or elites in the western, southern, and eastern parts of the empire often spoke a language different from many of the subject peoples, although in most of the territories rulers and their subjects had shared at least a similar language and culture when rule was imposed. The internal heterogeneity of interests was also great in other respects and interacted with the division of rule and domination, often by creating new, independent imperial towns, monasteries, fiefdoms, etc.

2. Rule and domination were feudal throughout. Such feudalism was a Frankish and, by that token, 'rather' Germanic invention, which is demonstrated in the perennial feuding over monarchical and aristocratic succession and other specific rights and entitlements and in the characterization of feudal relationships as reciprocal rights and obligations that can be severed or differentiated, as opposed to relationships implying unilateral submission. Until the advent of modernity, there was continuous competition for rule and domination, either by lobbying at the imperial court—the emperor having the ultimate say in feudal allegiance disputes and appointments—or by war and conquest. Straightforward dynastic succession by inheritance was often contested and contestable in view of complex and conflicting dependency and dynastic-familial relations.

3. Feudal rule however, did include, older mechanisms of social coordination, such as peer control through guilds, which acted as cooperative associations on all levels of society. The Germanic word for 'peer' (*Genosse*, *genoot*) has been used or revived a number of times throughout history, such as in the

word for cooperative enterprises (*Genossenschaften*). Much more recently, it has been used as a form of address (*Genosse*) between members of the Social Democratic and Communist parties, or in the Nazi terms for citizens (*Volksgenosse*) and party members (*Parteigenosse*).[129] Peerage was conferred through a collective oath (*foedus* in Latin, i.e. oaths were sworn laterally as well as hierarchically between masters and their vassals) and a communal dinner. It reflected the Germanic tendency to achieve coordination by lateral but constraining association between 'peers', rather than by fiat from above. Extended families or other clan or kinship groups exerted little or only indirect influence. This is how semi-independent or independent social formations were set up; a ruling guild of regents or patricians were sworn into power, and guilds were sworn in as associations set up by the founding rulers to govern the gradual urbanization of the territory and the internal institutionalization of towns. These, in turn, set up guilds of urban occupations. Rulers were present at such ceremonies, conferred legitimacy on them, and approved charters for towns or other associations.[130] Even urban self-government, which was to some extent different from that found in 'the countryside', was thereby integrated into a thoroughgoing feudal scheme of things.

Feudalism thus did not simply imply autocracy but also lateral control exercised within peer groups, as well as mutual although not necessarily equally distributed control between rulers and their subjects. Personalized coordination was closely intertwined with formal organization, since any type of guild meant not only the creation of a corporation with its own statutes, membership, rules, and procedures, but also that a person 'belonged' to the guild in all respects, including being 'governed' by it. Even after the advent of more centralized and bureaucratic rule in the sixteenth century, this blend of restricted autocracy and guild control was exemplified in the counterpart and partner role that estates committees played with regard to princes. As Ulrich Lange notes:

Committees formed by estates act in a way as the counterpart to the sovereign's [*Landesherr*] central authorities and are a decisive organizational requirement for maintaining political participation [*Mitwirkung*] by estates, in the face of the expanding bureaucracy of the sovereign. Basically against their will, they supported the advance of early modern bureaucracy. However, their co-determination [*Mitbestimmung*] had the effect of instituting a division of power that protected established liberties and, to a great extent, accounts for the moderation of princely rule in early modernity.[131]

Probably the best example of high-level guilds were confederations of independent territories or knights, such as the one which is known in English as the Order of the Teutonic Knights, which was both a religious and knightly order founded to conquer and Christianize the eastern shore of the Baltic Sea. Examples of 'lower'-level guilds were those of craftsmen, traders, or other professionals in towns. In addition, history is rich with examples of confraternities and entire segments of society devoted to a particular and important job, such as setting sail and conquering new territory. Monastic communities also fitted into this pattern; numerous areas of the countryside were governed by monasteries or other religious guilds (*Stifte*) consisting of unmarried male or female aristocratic members. The problem was whether a new guild or fraternity was instituted with the blessing of higher authorities, which might be anything from royal assent to that of a local meeting of all free men, or whether it was considered a conspiracy against the public, the faith, or a legitimate ruler. This was a large grey area with respect to jurisdiction. Despite thorough feudalization, or rather because of it and because of unsettled questions of jurisdiction, medieval society in the South Germanic bedrock in the Middle Ages naturally felt that such ambiguity could be resolved through warfare. Feudalism means feuding, and open, visceral conflict between competing authorities was thus an endemic feature of both societal splits and societal integration.

3.3.5   *Extension and division of rule and domination*

In compliance with terminological conventions, I have applied the term 'empire' to a number of different empires, such as that of the Romans, Mongols, Franks, and Franks and Saxons. However, as we move on through German history, the term becomes increasingly differentiated in meaning. In German, it is mostly translated as *Reich*. More recently, with the experience of the Third Reich (Nazism) behind us, the term has become almost taboo for present-day neo-German political correctness, except when used to designate a historic building such as the Reichstag in Berlin. But its historical connotations are highly diverse. The Latin word *imperium* means that the ruling elite of one societal community (Rome, the Franks and Lombards, the Franks and Saxons) also rule over other societal communities. This is indeed what the empires in question looked like when they were established. But the German term *Reich* also has another meaning, and this is equivalent to the Latin word *regnum* or the English word 'realm': an institutional and geographical entity defined by an integrated system of rule and domination. Linguistically, *Reich* is a derivative of *regnum*, not *imperium*. It is widely used to refer to the nation state in all Germanic languages, even in the smallest—and with regard to empire-building, least pretentious—countries (*rijk, rik, rige*, etc., in Dutch, Swedish, Norwegian, and Danish). In historic texts, it was also customary to refer to a smaller principality as the *Reich* of the ruler in question, even if it was only that of a minor duke. Note also that Austria calls itself Österreich, i.e. 'the realm in the east'. This is the rather mundane and non-imperial aspect of *Reich*. Austria got away with retaining this name, though it had been an outstanding empire-builder in European history.

The question now is whether each German empire should be labelled an *imperium* or a *regnum*. The simple answer is that it depends on the case in question, and typically, the nature of the empire changed as layering intensified and the elites became more and more 'local'. An overextension of rule implied an *imperium*, but social integration implied a *regnum*. The empire under Otto I and his successors clearly evolved to the point where it was not possible to say any more that one societal community ruled over another, and the same happened in other parts of the old Frankish Empire. More recently, the Weimar Republic was also called 'Deutsches Reich' although it was totally devoid of any *imperium*. Had the republic had one, it would have been revealed when the League of Nations organized referenda in some border regions to determine whether the people of these regions wanted to remain within the *Reich*. As in the Netherlands and Scandinavia, a more relaxed use of the term would have established itself in Germany had Hitler not built a *Großdeutsches Reich* that included quasi-colonial territories as dependencies (Poland and the central Czech regions), as well as other countries conquered and occupied during the war.

These events caused the term to be replaced by the word *Bund* (federation), which had previously been predominantly used between the early nineteenth century and 1872. *Bund* was less ideologically laden and emphasized the lateral bonding and peer control typical of earlier Germanic autonomy and the social control exercised by guilds. It had also inspired youth protest against conservatism, bureaucracy, bourgeois rigidity, and superficiality, in associations of the *bündische Jugend*, in the first half of the twentieth century. What a later age came to term as a 'third way' (between the market economy and socialism, and across different social strata and classes) was very often linked between 1920 and 1960 to the notion of *Bund* in various movements: socialist, communist, Christian, free-thinking, and Nazi.

The conversion of an *imperium* into what was, in fact, a collection of *regna* meant that the complexity of political differentiation and subordination arrangements increased, at least until the Thirty Years' War (1618–48) and even somewhat beyond. In 1648, the emperor was as far from being an *imperator* as one could get. The patchwork exhibited in historic atlases becomes more and more intricate as time progressed.[132] There was an increasing plethora of duchies, earldoms, free imperial cities, bishoprics (territories governed by bishops), monasteries, and fiefdoms, such that the increasing institutional differentiation of society—along with the urbanization and modernization of the economy—was translated into a fragmentation of rule and domination. Fragmentation of rule, notably the frequency of imperial free cities, was more intense in southern Germany (primarily south of the River Main) than in the north. The south was more highly developed since it was located closer to Italy and important metals and salt mining areas, and to important routes of long-distance trade.

Urbanization, economic and technical advancement, and modernity were thus clearly translated into political fragmentation, in stark contrast to our more recent association of progress with large-scale societal integration. The same is quite evident for the Low Countries and northern Italy, the standard-bearers of civilization in the empire of the late Middle Ages. However, a series of attempts were made by princes to extend their realms by taking part in the marital, courtly, and belligerent competition for rule and domination. As stable as the overall feudal system was, this did not in any way guarantee the stability of every specific territory or population. Feudalism, in the non-autocratic form it assumed in the

Germany of the late Middle Ages, defined a competitive market for amiable or aggressive takeover bids and invitations to merge in the wider market of territorial governance.

With the advent of modernity and notably as a result of the Napoleonic Wars, efforts were made to 'tidy up' the landscape, to aggregate territories and remove very localized sovereignties. Such efforts broke with the principle of exerting peer control through various sorts of guilds, fraternities, and confederacies. But on the whole, these efforts did not do away with either sovereign rule or peer control. In the pre-modern settlement, there was no clear distinction between policy fields: towns and their dominant guilds felt as free to control access to occupations as they did to pursue diplomatic relations, conclude alliances, or establish trade links. The latter is what territorial princes fought against with greater vigour. The modern settlement represented a clearer division of labour: princes took care of external relations but left peer control intact with respect to internal economic governance, especially in towns. Thus, for instance, after quelling by force an urban revolt in the town of Münster, the prince-bishop had a motto fastened to the town hall: 'Shoemaker, stick to your last'—meaning, get on with your job and see to its governance, rather than pursuing greater political schemes. A distinctive trait of societal order in the South Germanic bedrock was that hierarchical rule was never far away, but it also intimately incorporated the countervailing and older principle of self-government through guilds. The two were also linked to some extent by estate-based representation in princely territories, with the estates (*Landstände*) usually being divided into urban, landed and aristocratic, and ecclesiastical benches or chambers.

What we witness here is a partitioning of institutional space, in the course of non-identical reproduction of culture and institutions. This theme will resurface time and again in later chapters. It means that a previously integrated institutional space (in this case political and economic authority, including external relations) is partitioned[133] into differentiated domains: the domain of general politics and external relations, on the one hand, and that of economic institutions of self-government, on the other. Local guilds and estates focused on the latter domain, while the sovereign focused on the former, the link which still existed through estate assemblies and their committees. Peer control was thus continued in a novel arrangement and configuration by being recombined with what was 'in principle' considered its diametrical opposite, namely sovereign rule.

Whereas societal integration had a fairly authoritarian aspect, certainly with regard to relations between rulers and those subjects who were neither vassals nor peers in an ordained corporation, the larger scheme of society was unsystematic and shifting. Although vassalage implied subservience to a feudal lord to the point of death, this relation was neither one-sidedly hierarchical nor stable. Furthermore, the exercise of imperial prerogative appears to have been increasingly restrained by the importance of the imperial assembly of all the estates (Reichstag) and above all by the increasing influence of an intermediate stratum of rulers situated between the monarch and the lower aristocracy. In England, the dukes and other members of the higher aristocracy gradually grew more ceremonial and the gentry more important as a class, while the monarch consolidated the power of sovereign rule. In medieval Germany, exactly the opposite occurred: to take control of the increasingly intricate patchwork of societal inclusion and political rule, the stratum of vassals directly subordinate to the emperor became more important, as did the electorships (seven princes entitled to take part in electing the emperor in the late Middle Ages), duchies, and larger earldoms.

3.3.6 Layers, competences, and power

The overextension of societal integration across an unusually large and diverse expanse of territory, including non-German-speaking cultures and many institutional differences, and over time thus meant mainly two things. One was institutional fragmentation into increasingly self-assertive and functionally important towns and other, smaller entities, which acquired privileges from the king or emperor in return for strengthening the country through economic development. Another was a shift in power that granted the aforementioned intermediate stratum of rulers a greater degree of control. These princes became increasingly absolutist in their reign, reduced the power of the emperor, integrated church territories and free towns, and focused their territorial estates on more specific themes. The peace treaties concluding the Thirty Years' War in 1648 were a major step towards strengthening this medium stratum of territories and princes at the expense of the emperor. These princes consistently discovered foreign princes to be more useful allies than domestic ones, certainly more than the Catholic emperor when they themselves were Protestant.

The religious split that followed the Reformation in Germany further increased the heterogeneity of the empire and made it very hard for the emperor to achieve a consistent policy, particularly in upholding his historical commitment to the Pope to promote the Catholic faith. This weakened the position of the emperor in his rivalry with the kings of France, who succeeded in keeping their country much more in line with Catholicism and in a much better position to suppress local revolt and deviation, as they demonstrated with great ferocity in the early thirteenth century by crushing the Cathars, a gnostic Christian movement in the south. Central authority in the empire was therefore considerably weakened. The ascendant princes found foreign rulers to be attractive partners—whether they were Protestant, such as the king of Sweden, or Catholic, such as the king of France. Foreign sovereigns always supported opponents of the emperor keen on greater independence, and even Catholic kings of France were usually willing to support Protestant princes in Germany or the Netherlands if this helped divide the empire.

All this worked to bring about a societal construction in which the regional layers of the polity gained more and more political power, and policies were increasingly established and enforced by such regional authorities. At the same time, something resembling a German national language was evolving, and German culture was becoming a more tangible concept, particularly after Luther's translation of the Bible into German established the first standard for High German as a written and codified language.[134] It is a bit daring to make such a historical generalization, but during the late medieval period the empire underwent, by and large, a fragmentation of both rule and institutional competence—although not necessarily institutional forms—that coincided with the advance of German culture, meaning the language became more than merely a haphazard assemblage of overlapping dialects. This play of forces brought about a unique type of layering: politics and policies were being increasingly dominated by intermediate rulers in their pursuit of a semblance of absolutism, while culture was being conceived in an increasingly national framework. Language instruction, schools, universities, music, and theatre, as well as other useful, performing, or decorative arts, were being perceived as matters to be handled at national and international level, so as to protect them from control by emerging states. This is the very particular constellation of forces behind the concept that Germany first emerged as a *Kulturnation*, invented or constructed by writers, scholars, and composers, each in their own domain. Governmentally, Germany was an inter-nation segmented into rather autonomous entities, but culturally and in a different territorial ambit, it started to arise as a nation.

This indicates that the extension of horizons brought on by urbanization and international trade was linked, first, with a very intense process of decentralization of political power, notably in the more developed south of Germany, and second, with a concentration of power at an intermediate level of aggregation. There existed absolutely no parallelism between the extension of horizons of action and the movement of power or relative sovereignty across levels of societal aggregation.

3.4 The South Germanic bedrock and internationalization in early modernity

3.4.1 The emergence of a metatradition

The structures emerging from evolution in the South Germanic bedrock were the result of a distinctive fusion of what sociological theory and political science tend to classify as opposites, of autocratic rule with peer control, of 'democratic' or republican legitimation with the 'divine right to rule'. This articulation of opposites was possible at the time thanks to estate-based representation and the fragmentation of an overextended society into more independent entities. Eventually this led to a dominance of rule at an intermediate level in the accidental aggregations that resulted from interminable feuding, war, and more civilized forms of competing in the market for power and domination.

The tradition of having estate-based representation incorporated into a system of guilds is a particular and fairly concrete one. Traditions may last for a long time; but more concrete and specific traditions do not. The more concretely we define a tradition, the shorter-lived it is. To this extent, concrete traditions come and go. It is easy and banal to demonstrate their demise. But this is not all there is to tradition, its effects, and how it is involved in intertemporal societal effects. An abstract essence of a concrete tradition may persist after the concrete form has vanished, as it normally does. The abstraction will then be linked to a new concrete tradition, which means there will be continuity within change. The continuity of tradition, however, is dialectical since it involves the partitioning and recombining of opposites.

Continuity has two angles. One is the presence of an abstract characteristic that remains detached from the eclectic to-and-fro of partitioning and recombining. An example of such an abstraction of tradition would be the unbroken continuity of common law, custom, and practice in England that persists despite the rise of statute law and many other changes in institutional norms and practices. The other angle of continuity, in which dialectics is very evident, is the regularity with which opposite phenomena are linked over time and are recombined in various, typical ways despite their inherent contrariety. An example would be the oscillation between legal and bureaucratic order imposed from above, on the one hand, and the highly spontaneous and forceful eruptions occurring in France, on the other.[135] A 'meta-tradition' embodies the dialectical continuity inherent to a heritage and posits that this continuity consists of typical, alternating, and recombined opposites. Institutional reconstruction within society means, as we saw in the last chapter, a non-identical reproduction over time. It results from the pragmatic consideration given by competent and diligent actors to constellations of forces, existing coalitions, and contradicting interests, behavioural predispositions, and inhibitions. However, once different practices have reacted with one another and congealed into a new substance, we then observe that its coherence is stylized by the social construction of myth.

When embodied in the form of a metatradition, tradition is never an unreflecting act of 'doing things the way they have been done'. Metatradition implies that rational consideration and the weighing of opportunities govern the selection and development of the institutional and cultural toolbox offered by the 'garbage can'[136] of history, within a society and beyond. It is therefore different from that notion of tradition that has become simplistic common currency in sociology. Max Weber distinguished action types by predominant orientations, and he suggested that we should distinguish mainly between affective, traditional, value-rational, and instrumentally rational orientations of social action.[137] This places tradition in a pigeonhole separate from rationality. It is indisputable that unreflective tradition exists. Weber firmly located 'traditional' behaviour in a category filled with most of 'everyday behaviour'. Apparently disregarding for a moment his famous plea for neutrality in the social sciences, Weber used strong words to disparage such behaviour: it was 'dull' and even 'at the border of what may be called meaningful behaviour'.[138]

Weber would certainly not have excluded the possibility that the compilation of tradition may well be founded on the rational redesign of institutions. Upon closer reflection, he also would probably not have denied that 'everyday behaviour' was, before modernity, permeated with perfectly rational behaviour. After all, it is modernity that brought about the single-minded quest for 'romantic love', as

William Goode has called it, in the selection of marriage partners. This motive is of course affective, whereas in the Middle Ages, it was perfectly natural for a marriage partner to be selected on the rational basis of the size of a dowry, the status of the family, and the possibilities of merging or inheriting farms, firms, or territories. People in medieval society made rational decisions all the time, but it may be that the institutional isolation of rational decisions from traditional or affective ones became empirically more tangible in modernity. That would concur more closely with a Parsonian understanding of the classics. In interactionism, any rational decision implies the enactment of affect and tradition, just as traditional behaviour, upon closer inspection, not only borders on the 'dull' but, often half-consciously, instils a measure of rationality into a problem. Interactionism, this time entirely faithful to Weber's programme of a *verstehende* social science, emphasizes the need to consider the motives for action not only to be distinct, but to be bracketed one upon another in every act and to be linked in the evolution of culture and institutions.

We must distinguish carefully between 'simple' and unreflecting traditionalism, as an action orientation prevalent in an actor with respect to specific problems, and more reflective and thereby rational action. A different reflective traditionalism is present when actors reflect upon a number of circumstances. Rationality could hardly be seen as very important if it was not constituted as a tradition and thereby able to 'come naturally' to actors. Tradition and rational design are thus dialectically linked in a manner typical for the interactionist approaches mentioned in the previous chapter. Metatradition acknowledges that traditional, affective, and rational modes are interwoven. It consists of a stream of divergent and changing institutional forms and practices, a stream exhibiting continuity on the basis of two things:

- commonalities in terms of abstract and intertemporally valid characteristics;
- serial linkages of old and new practices through non–identical reproduction and the search for constructive recipes in the 'garbage can' of historical experience.

One person who has insisted on the continuity of long-running soft institutions and culture is d'Iribarne.[139] In addition to internal paradox, this is one aspect that constitutes the metatradition with regard to pervasive change through partitioning and recombining. The subsequent chapters will show how the South Germanic bedrock works as a metatradition within modernity and recent history. Over the centuries, it developed in a highly distinctive manner for one particular, over-extended, aggregate society. Its large geographical and cultural core is due to three factors: the imposition of one kind of ruling tribe on other mainly Germanic tribes, the balance of power in the overextended aggregate, and the way this influenced the institutional partitioning of rule and domination. The conjoined effect

- strengthened an intermediate layer of societal community,
- imposed a systematic order onto the patchwork of entities comprising this intermediate layer, despite the instability of the arrangements that determined which entities these were,

- created a layering that facilitated the definition of language and culture within an emerging or potentially national level, while sovereignty, competence over external relations, and a monopoly over the use of force were concentrated at the intermediate level,
- closely intertwined two opposing forms of control, namely autocratic rule and peer groups, within a more partitioned institutional space.

Major checks and balances appeared as part of the close intertwining of autocratic rule and peer group control and of the play of forces between central, intermediate, and local authority. Critical observers would say that Germany has always had a strong autocratic metatradition. That may well be so. But this metatradition has not worked because autocracy has been more absolute than elsewhere, or more passively or willingly accepted by people. On the contrary, the metatraditional logic seems to have been that autocracy would always be checked by responsible peer groups and would be implemented in a manner attuned to the fundamental interests of subjects or citizens by a government which would remain in close touch with them. This meant that the government had to be reachable by the people and had to keep its finger on the pulse of popular sentiment, rather than distance itself from the populace. For a very long time, this provided stability in the complexity of the patchwork, despite drives to establish absolute rule.

Let us return to the example of particularism in Quebec noted at the beginning of the chapter. Although the German metatradition includes a strong layering of society, it is also quite different from Quebec's situation in Canada or federalism in the United States. In the United States, the union followed a clearly national pattern in creating new states. In Germany, however, the national community remained dubious and was contested for centuries. But both Canada and Germany demonstrate that the creation of societal community exhibits an emerging prevalence of what is locally more specific, as a reaction to an extension of horizons and particularly to a societal community begun by expansive rule and domination. The eventual division of the Frankish Empire into a western and an eastern part also resembles Quebec-in-Canada in so far as linguistic-cultural diversity was related to the split, although it did not at all occur along the same lines. The evolving layering in the South Germanic bedrock was decidedly different in nature. It was related to the outcome of a constant conflict over the localization of rule and domination and a quasi-monopoly over the use of external and internal force, a Weberian requirement for creating a state. While the identity of Quebec was thus linguistically and culturally distinctive, the identity of German states became detached from culturally stable identities through an almost accidental allocation of territories (with specific dialects or other cultural repertoires) to rulers and emerging states.

Most parts of Germany have at one time or another been combined with any one of the others under a government that was later replaced by a different one.[140] Curiously enough, had territories and states been grouped together differently at crucial moments in history, this probably would have had very little effect on the degree of difficulty experienced during integration. One is tempted to say that the metatradition has attributed a great deal of significance to federal states, as is evident in the smaller states of present-day Austria or in Switzerland, but that ultimately it does not matter much where their borders are drawn. Such federalism is quite different from Italian or Spanish provincial organization, which has always been hotly contested throughout history and has revolved around much clearer cultural and institutional identities and—in part—distinctive languages. None of the arrangements that have historically occurred in Germany can be explained by dynamics within the country alone; foreign relations and the interests of foreign actors have always played an important part in the way the country has been divided up into states. The most prominent example is the Treaty of Westphalia, which was drawn up not only by established estates of the realm but also by Sweden and France.

After that, the outstanding rationalizers and unifiers of an earlier, much more complex patchwork of states were Napoleon in 1806, the Congress of Vienna in 1814–15, and the Allied Powers (the United States, France, Britain, and the Soviet Union) in 1945 and again in 1990. Significantly, all of these rearrangements of rule, domination, and sovereignty were international settlements. Societal integration and subdivision in Germany have thus been international throughout its history. Bismarck, who represented the pursuit of internal merger, primarily provided 'only' a forceful consolidation and unification of existing states outside of Austria, in addition to the outright annexation of Hanover, Hesse-Nassau, Schleswig, and Holstein into Prussia in 1866. Even this was an international affair, conducted under the close scrutiny or participation of tsarist Russia, the United Kingdom, France, and the emerging nation state of Italy.

3.4.2   *Novel forms of international expansion and a new trauma*

The creation of domestic traditions contributing to societal layering and segmentation was triggered by the way society was constructed, in this case by the decidedly expansive, universalistic, and international aspects of its history. As a result, German domestic traditions were inevitably affected by foreign powers throughout. It is an inherent part of the metatradition that an overextended society should have collapsed into a patchwork of sovereignties and societal layering. Let us return shortly to Europe after about 1500. At the time, the realm of the Holy Roman Empire was more or less shrinking, the power of the emperor diminishing, and the universalistic claims receding. Whereas previously, the emperor was in the powerful position of being able to imprison a king of England (specifically, Richard the Lionhearted) for having supposedly neglected his feudal obligations to the emperor to too great an extent, since 1648 there have been only a few major redefinitions of German state entities that have not been based on an international agreement. To the outside world, the size and composition of a German nation has mostly been a question of maintaining or creating equilibrium in the centre of Europe. That experience is not unique because Poland has also been treated harshly by its neighbours, after its demise as an overextended system of rule (as a kingdom including Poland, Lithuania, and some regions increasingly populated by German-speaking subjects, as well as Russian and Ukrainian territories), in the interest of what they proclaimed to be a need to prevent chaos and anarchy.

Of course, an expansion of German states continued throughout the High Middle Ages and beyond, but this occurred outside the borders of the empire and involved the territories of some rulers (technically held as an *allodium* outside the feudal relations with the emperor), but not the empire itself. The main beneficiaries were the emperor as the ruler of Austria (expanding east and south, the main portion of the expansion being the inheritance of the Hungarian Empire) and the Elector of Brandenburg (by gaining territories previously in feudal allegiance to the Polish king and inheriting East Prussia from the last Master of the Order of the Teutonic Knights, thus creating the kingdom of Brandenburg-Prussia). Quite understandably, Habsburg emperors found it useful to keep new acquisitions outside the boundaries of the empire; their largest peaceful acquisition by far was Hungary, which would not have accepted integration into a German empire. Likewise, other princes preferred acquiring an *allodium* outside the bond with the emperor because this, by virtue of the sovereign rule it permitted, made the respective prince eligible for royal status. This is the way the elector of Brandenburg-Prussia became a king, as did the elector of Saxony (by being elected king of Poland for a limited term).

After the end of the Thirty Years' War, the empire itself shrank, while some of its territories expanded independently outside of it. Ironically, it was the Habsburg emperors themselves who profited most from the undermining of the emperorship by turning their interest to new pastures outside the empire and gaining a realm that greatly exceeded their possessions within it. A great deal of the modern state formation that originated from within Germany was thus international, adding further to the complexity of the patchwork and its inherent dilemma of divergent nationality and state formation.

Furthermore, it is useful to remember that the Thirty Years' War was a time of death and devastation to a degree probably unrivalled to date in the population of a large country. Through war and its related phenomena such as starvation and the plague, the population living within the empire decreased from 16 to 10 million people. Particularly hard-hit were territories in the north-east (Mecklenburg, Pomerania, Brandenburg), the centre-west (Thuringia, Hesse), the Palatinate and Franconia in the west, as well as Silesia in the east.[141] This war definitely changed the trend from expansion of the empire to the experience of foreign incursions, which most of the time meant foreign troops ravaging the country (usually Spanish or Swedish, in addition to the habitual and ubiquitous Swiss mercenaries and a range of ethnicities under Austrian rule). It created a trauma over war and destruction, but those who profited specially from the trauma were again princes seeking more absolute rule.

One consistent feature in the long-term development of the empire in this era was that the intermediate level of government benefited from this, which only continued a pervasive tendency of overextension of societal community leading to stronger intermediate layers, whichever way the entities in the intermediate layers were demarcated. Why more absolute government benefited is well explained by a case that proved decisive over centuries, until 1945. Brandenburg was one of the areas whose population was ravaged the most, even though its ruler (the elector) had tried to stay neutral during the Thirty Years' War in a vain attempt to walk the tightrope between the country's adherence to Lutheranism and its loyalty to the emperor. The aim was to keep this rather sleepy and territorially divided country out of the war, a country full of sand, placid Slavic-Germanic lake fishermen in the centre and the east, plus some richer agriculture in the Altmark and near Magdeburg, as well as regionally detached and smaller craft regions in the west (Jülich, Kleve, Mark, etc.). This realm was difficult to hold together, and it had very few troops. In popular parlance, Brandenburg was ironically called 'the sandbox of the Empire'.[142] Neutrality was to no avail; one of the starker episodes of indiscriminate viciousness in the war was the sacking of Magdeburg by Tilly, a general in the service of the emperor. To be killed, ransacked, and razed to the ground by Catholic forces was, however, still more comprehensible than to suffer this fate at the hands of the Swedish army, which was supposedly there to help fellow Lutherans.[143]

The successor of this elector (who was unfairly punished, as pacifists tend to be) was the Great Elector, Friedrich Wilhelm, a man who was not only a Calvinist but took government as seriously as his faith prescribed.[144] It may seem accidental, but it is also a dialectical twist within a metatradition that the seeds of rational government and militarism were sown in the particularly fertile soil of a country that had been relatively sleepy and peaceful; because of that they were traumatized far more than many others. In an attempt effectively to counter this trauma, the rulers of this country undertook its redevelopment (through immigration and promotion of new industries and agriculture) and exhibited greater assertiveness abroad. In doing so, the Brandenburg-Prussian dynasty (the Hohenzollern) attained a position of power that became difficult to rival in Germany.

Prussia also developed into a state and society that was prone to sharper dialectics; revolutions were promoted from above. Gorski has compared the 'disciplinary revolution and state formation' in the early Netherlands and in Brandenburg-Prussia, two states that were unique in having Calvinist rulers or ruling strata. He characterizes disciplinary revolution in the Netherlands as having arisen 'from below' while it originated 'from above' in Brandenburg-Prussia.[145] Undoubtedly the Great Elector and later kings in Brandenburg-Prussia possessed much greater authority than did the stadtholders (*stadhouders*) in the Netherlands. But the seed of disciplinary revolution lay in the same social position, namely the higher urban strata that in Holland could not really be thought of as located 'below' since the greatest segment of society at the time were farmers; in Brandenburg this revolution was instigated by French refugee Calvinists (Huguenots) and Lutheran pietists in Halle, a centre of the early Enlightenment. To this extent, disciplinary revolution 'came' from below in both cases, if urban elites can be considered as 'below' in rural society, and it was imposed from above in both states, too. In the Netherlands, this happened through one of the most protracted wars ever witnessed in Europe, the Eighty Years' War against Spanish rule which established the Netherlands as a nation consisting, at the time, of an initial core in Holland and Zeeland. In Prussia, a revolution emerging from a few urban pockets would not have gained such general importance had strong rulers not championed the cause.

Even imposition from above depends on pioneers from below. A rapid oscillation between influences from below—mainly from immigrants and some indigenous populist rigorists—and from above appears to have become the main engine of developmental dialectics in Prussia and later Germany. As we shall see, modernization in the south-west and in Saxony was more 'piecemeal' and continuous, while Prussia incorporated sharper discontinuities and more striking recombinations of absolutism and liberalism, stratification and equality, liberalism and corporatism. Institutional partitioning of societal space and the recombination of distinct principles in close proximity is pervasive in any society. But it is particularly perilous to downplay it with regard to Germany, particularly when we aim to explain its internationalization.

3.5 Summary

As Djelic and Quack show, the recombination of distinct and even somewhat opposing institutional elements within a novel synthesis is an important and neglected feature of social innovation.[146] It is particularly noteworthy in the course of internationalization: institutional features that at first appear 'alien' and strange are 'socialized' and recombined with features that appear more 'domestic'. Yet, even these may have originated by an earlier recombination of domestic and alien culture and institutions. Rather than being quirks, such recombinations are part and parcel of normal historical evolution. They need to be integrated into any concept of societal change. They make for pervasive continuity in the midst of a change which may even be radical.

This continuity was shown to be vested in metatraditions, as dialectical and pragmatic amalgamations of culture and institutions of different types. Metatraditions encapsulate contrasts, the pendulum movements between them, and also interdependencies between contrasted patterns. The emerging metatradition in the South Germanic bedrock has featured an amalgamation of princely rule in a highly layered society with peer group control in numerous guild-type bodies that increasingly concentrated on economic governance and government. This configuration will be considered more closely in the following chapters, as one which was formative for more recent institutions in the governance of work, management, organization, business, and industrial relations.

The emergence of this configuration needs to be related to the great amount of internationalization that has permeated German society from its medieval beginnings, in characteristic swings between overextension and provincialization. These have given the dialectics of convergence and divergence a particular form in Germany. The character of the internationalization has shifted, from more 'active' or expansive modes to more 'passive' ones (as the recipient of foreign influence). In the following chapters, we will continue to examine this line of development throughout modernity.

4

The South Germanic bedrock under foreign incursions

4.1 Introduction

The city of Cologne is known, at home and abroad, for its majestic Gothic cathedral, one of the most magnificent examples of medieval church architecture. The historical background and significance of the cathedral is very interesting. The Gothic style originated in 12 c. France. Although there are many churches in the historic old city of Cologne, none other is Gothic.[147] The cathedral was planned and construction started in the Middle Ages. During this time, however, Cologne's power was waning, as was that of many other cities and members of the Hanseatic League, leaving the city without the finances necessary to finish more than about half of the cathedral. For centuries, the building remained unfinished, an ugly testimony to the decline of the Hanseatic League and the power of free imperial cities. At the time that Napoleon annexed the left bank of the Rhineland to France, the archbishop of Cologne even suggested that the unsightly building site be closed and the rubble removed.

The cathedral was finally completed in the middle of the nineteenth century, but only because the new ruler of the Rhineland after 1813, the king of Prussia, was a gentle, romantic soul. He sought to win the hearts and minds of Rhinelanders, who resented having Protestant Prussians from the east as their new rulers. He thus committed himself to the completion of the cathedral and donated half of the money needed for its construction. It is therefore nearly as new as Chicago, despite the style, and it came about as a symbolic gesture of pacification after what the people of Cologne thought was a foreign incursion. Today, it is wrongly remembered as a manifestation of the greatness of one of Germany's most important medieval cities. Instead, it is actually the manifestation of the benevolent side of a very modern foreign incursion, in this instance brought about by a Protestant Prussian king.[148]

Oblivious to the historic nature of the artefact, tourists take it for granted that they are seeing an age-old landmark that represents local power and tradition. This chapter seeks to help correct an error that occurs in both social science and popular texts when stylizing traditions. Any stylized tradition or 'model' has to be deconstructed as a step-by-step, continuous, and dialectical elaboration of a metatradition, which incorporates institutional partitioning, the recombination of opposites, their harmonization through pragmatic interpretation within action systems, and newly emerging functional interdependencies within a societal order. Germany shows how much this evolution has been prompted by internationalization throughout modern history, which has sustained the elaboration of institutions specific for this society. The analysis here moves from general history to the socio-economics of economic institutions and their closest corollaries. This takes us to the keynote in the build-up of modern and contemporary institutions pertaining to economics and work organization: the institutionally partitioned recombination of liberal and non-liberal principles. This is a metatradition with strong roots in Prussian history; it has informed more recent tendencies in the governance of work, management, and enterprises, i.e. the topics of the next two chapters. The metatradition is as astounding a case of forgotten eclecticism as is the modern and romantic promotion of a Roman Catholic cathedral left half-finished in the Middle Ages and completed centuries later by a Protestant king.

4.2 Proto-industries and the French incursion into the homeland of the Franks

The South Germanic bedrock acquired a particular configuration that was historically interdependent on internationalization. This is shown particularly by the shift from expansion of the empire to its segmentation and by the greater influence exerted by foreign powers after 1648. As far as war and occupation are concerned, the next historically major episode in the same vein was the Napoleonic Wars and the occupation of parts of Germany from the beginning of the nineteenth century until 1813; but these wars also produced a more lasting, peaceful, and constructive after-effect. I do not use the term 'incursion' with any sort of negative connotation. It denotes the influx of outside information, culture, institutional patterns, or people, often in combination. Such incursions may be aggressive or peaceful, destructive or constructive. The Napoleonic incursions from post-revolutionary France were a characteristic mixture of all of this.

Let us consider the example of a region in the old homeland of the Franks, that wild bunch who founded a vast empire and bequeathed a variant of its name to the new France and to Franconia, the northern part of Bavaria known in German as Franken. The earldom (*Grafschaft*) of Berg stretched over the mountainous eastern bank of the Rhine, roughly from the western end of the Ruhr area down to where the River Sieg joins the Rhine. Berg had been governed by the counts of Berg, some of whom are commemorated in street names in Düsseldorf, which has served for all practical purposes as the region's capital roughly since 1288 (the Battle of Worringen). In a way typical for Germany, rule had shifted to the Wittelsbach dynasty (from the Palatinate) after the Thirty Years' War. This dynasty had also come to rule over Bavaria and held the electorship of Brandenburg for a short while. There had been rivalry between the Wittelsbach and Brandenburg for rule over Berg, during which there was even an episode of joint government. Later

Wittelsbach rulers spent most of their time in Bavaria or the Palatinate. But in the late Middle Ages and early modern era, this did not yet mean that institutions and policies were centralized and standardized; Berg retained its own estates, laws, and customs for the most part.

Berg was an exemplary case of proto-industrialization in early modernity and one of the seedbeds of modern industrialization in the Ruhr area, the western end of which included Essen and its vicinity and extended into the flatlands of the lower Rhine valley. Located here were the towns of Solingen, an early and well-known industrial centre producing scissors, knives, and other cutting or household implements, and Elberfeld and Barmen[149] with their textile manufacturing. Near Bergisch-Gladbach, paper was produced, and manifold cottage industries grew up around the large number of fast-flowing streams that enabled the construction of mills to generate energy.[150] Being a rural rather than urban area, Berg also had the advantages of weaker incorporation, meaning less restriction of practices and more open access to occupations. In short, Berg enjoyed a location that offered natural and socio-economic advantages and significant capacities, both actual and potential, in a number of industries.

Furthermore, the region magnificently exemplified the Protestant work ethic linked with a spirit of capitalism, as analysed by Weber: there was a profusion of 'non-conformist' Protestant denominations,[151] and many villages and towns were more Reformed than Lutheran or Catholic. Artisan and industrial entrepreneurship was perfectly correlated with fundamentalist variants of Protestantism, and the assertion of local specificity was dependent on or instrumental for the foundation of locally idiosyncratic and intolerant religious communities. Throwing bricks through the windows of the homes of members of other denominations in another village under cover of darkness was endemic following the Reformation.[152] In religious segmentation and fervency, the country was almost Dutch in character.[153]

After being occupied by France, Berg became part of the Confederation of the Rhine, an alliance into which Napoleon forced neighbouring German states when he did not integrate them into France directly. Territorially, Berg profited from this; it was expanded to incorporate smaller territories and former church lands. It was styled, as was the new kingdom of Westphalia (ruled by a brother of Napoleon from the new capital of Kassel) to become a new model state outside France but closely related to it and following Napoleonic doctrines.[154] The new ruler of Berg became Murat, Napoleon's best-known cavalry general and his brother-in-law. The intention was to use Berg's industrial potential to turn it into a modernizing principality. To that extent, it was given unusually generous attention, and it was even honoured by a visit of Napoleon to Düsseldorf.[155]

Although such new territories were formally independent, Napoleon made sure that policies would not differ significantly from what was done in France. He did this by enthroning new rulers both in Germany and Italy who were invariably a part of his extended family. On the whole, many princes in the Confederation of the Rhine which now had French rulers or tutelage—Bavaria, Württemberg, Baden, and above all Berg and Westphalia (at the time also including Hesse and large parts of the northern German plain)—proclaimed and established formal legal equality of citizens. Moreover, the Code Napoléon was introduced in civil law, and many feudal privileges, public office monopolies, economically restrictive rules, and exemptions from taxation and military service were abolished.[156] This was a radical change from older German traditions of rule and societal order, which had been based on rights and obligations specific to the various estates (*Stände*). Distinctions were made between town dwellers and country folk, nobles and commoners, clergy and laity, with many more distinctions for specific entitlements and obligations. Also not to be forgotten were estateless pariahs such as resident non-Christians and those in stigmatised but necessary occupations, such as undertakers. This refined patchwork was replaced by a more modern concept of societal inclusion, one governed by general rights and duties, a public administration different from private life, and a greatly reduced tolerance of guild-like organizations mediating between the state or ruler and subjects or citizens.[157] For practical purposes, Berg and Westphalia were French colonies, and the rest of the Rhenish confederation was what a later age would call 'protectorates', a euphemism for less intensive colonization.

4.3   Transformation of French legacies through and after war

Berg thus experienced a mixture of forceful liberalization in economic relations, political liberalization in the sense of standardization and formalization of rights and obligations, and governmental centralization at the level of territorial government in Düsseldorf if not de facto directly in Paris. In executing such policies, new civil servants, who originally came from outside the country, often met with resistance. Whether this was more extensive than in France is difficult to tell. No comparisons appear to have been made which would corroborate such a statement. In principle, the new order did find supporters among the urban citizenry and manufacturers, although many inhabitants found the new rules and systems as hard to stomach as many Englishmen have recently when forced to change their measurement units from yards to metres and pounds to kilos, and otherwise adapt to new directives from Brussels. Back in Berg, there was open revolt against the new rules, but it was quelled by force. However, modernization and abolition of feudal distinctions did make the life of merchants, artisans, and industrialists easier and held out promises of more predictable legally and uniformly ensured operations. Also, the access of the citizenry to the higher echelons of the social order (officer rank in the military, the courts, and other highly responsible government offices) was improved; specifically it was made independent of being or becoming part of the aristocracy. More than Murat in Berg, Napoleon's brother Jérôme lived a life of excessive consumption and luxury in Kassel that eventually sent Westphalia into bankruptcy.[158] This was definitely not what Westphalians and Hessians were used to.

But although the balance sheet of Napoleonic modernization was mixed, there was nothing that led the populace to reject the new internal order more ferociously than Frenchmen. It is anyone's guess how nation-building on German soil would have evolved had Napoleon left it as it had been, softening the Continental blockade against Britain and leaving Russia alone. However, the modernizing impact of the Confederation of the Rhine, which stretched about as far east and north into Germany as the Frankish Empire had at its greatest extent under Charlemagne, was dramatically counter-balanced by its military impact. The main purpose of the Confederation was to guarantee France allies and military manpower. Since Napoleon could somehow never manage to conclude a lasting peace, the human and material resources of the Confederation were thus used up in a war of attrition. The famous Grande Armée which was sent off on the fateful campaign against Moscow was only half French. One-third of the army cosisted of German troops from both the Rhenish Confederation and other areas, and there were also substantial Polish and Italian contingents.[159]

How did this affect Berg? During the time that it was part of the Confederation until the battle of Leipzig in 1813, Berg fulfilled its treaty obligations imposed upon it by Napoleon and raised 60,000 soldiers for service, out of a total population estimated to be roughly 900,000 at the start of the Confederation.[160] Two-thirds of these soldiers were killed. Such a rate of attrition was small compared to the phenomenal loss of life during the Thirty Years' War more than one hundred and fifty years earlier. But this was only because civilians were no longer systematically tortured and killed. One had to wait until the First World War for Germany to experience similar large-scale military bloodshed: the proportion of the population killed in World War I was, at roughly 3.5 per cent, above that for Berg in the Napoleonic Wars; the death rate in the latter case was similar to the one Britain experienced in World War I, which is still called 'the Great War' in that country because, in terms of loss of life, it exceeded World War II.[161]

The fate of one of Berg's regiments illustrates what war meant in practice. Following the treaty with France, Berg was obliged to put up two cavalry regiments, one of which was the Régiment de lanciers du Grand-Duché de Berg. The military terminology and language of command were mainly French, even in German official documents. Once training was completed, this regiment was integrated into a brigade with a Polish regiment and dispatched to Spain, where it had to fight a gruelling war against the guerrilla forces resisting Napoleonic occupation forces, a war which was fought with a level of atrocity on both sides that staggers the imagination. By the time the regiment finally returned to Berg, it had lost the greater part of its soldiers through combat, disease, and malnutrition.[162] After being replenished with new recruits and retrained, it then had to leave with the Grande Armée for Russia. Like most of the army, it returned vastly reduced by cold, starvation, and Cossacks. Once again its ranks were replenished without delay in preparation for what was to be the great battle of Leipzig, in which the Confederation of the Rhine was pitted against Prussia, Austria, Russia, Sweden, Hanover, and Saxony (which changed sides just prior to the battle). On both sides, there were a great many soldiers from Germany. In a skirmish leading up to the main confrontation, the regiment suddenly found itself in an unfavourable position, was attacked by a Prussian cavalry regiment from a superior vantage point, and was again decimated.

Typical of other forces from Berg, this regiment had sacrificed—without any revolt or disobedience reported but with repeated praise by superiors and eventual integration into Napoleon's imperial guard—two-thirds of the personnel that passed through its ranks. After the Rhineland became part of Prussia in 1813, the regiment was integrated into the Prussian army and henceforth called the '2. Westfälisches Husarenregiment no. 11' until it was disbanded in 1919. Again its ranks were filled with new recruits, who were trained within the new military set-up and in due course mobilized in the run-up to the Battle of Waterloo. But, allocated to a reserve corps, it was mercifully spared a battle against its former comrades-in-arms.[163] In addition to military losses, Berg and other Rhenish Confederation territories, but also more loosely allied states such as Prussia, also had to suffer the requisitioning and plundering among the civilian population that habitually accompanied any Napoleonic army on the move, undersupplied as they were by an *intendance* that, as the French have a habit of saying, *ne suit pas* (does not keep up), particularly when a war turned against them. In short, when the war was finished, so were Berg and many other areas of Germany.

My reason for describing all this is only to underscore a very central point: what sympathies the new modern Napoleonic order acquired in the Rhenish Confederation were savagely and recklessly destroyed by the conduct of futile wars at a greater cost in lives and materials than the populace had ever been forced to sustain in the earlier absolutist cabinet wars. There, at least, princes had sought to spare civilian life, lest nothing should remain after a war that made it worth the trouble. Napoleonic warfare was much more 'total' than anything Germans had experienced since 1648. While the US civil war of 1861–5 is rightly remembered as a stunningly cruel one that left the nation in lasting trauma, it pales in comparison to the Napoleonic Wars in central Europe. These were to a large extent wars fought within Germany and its close neighbours, conducted by German forces on both sides, at the service of domestic or foreign rulers. There is also an aspect of assertive German nationalism towards the end of the century that is linked to a compulsion to exorcise this trauma.

Much as some authors have lamented the 'restoration' of the 'old forces' of feudal rule after Napoleon was sent off to St Helena for good, the dilemma is that no one did more to re-establish the credibility of earlier princes and their rule than Napoleon. A frightened and impoverished population often sought refuge in the arms of the princes with whom they had become familiar. When the Elector of Hesse returned to 'his' country in a coach to succeed Jérôme at Kassel, jubilant locals even replaced the horses drawing the coach, pulling it themselves.[164] However, the effect of Napoleonic rule and that of the Rhenish Confederation with France on German society was unique; it linked the attractions of modernization with repulsive brutality, extortion, and bloodshed. It meant the legitimacy of intermediate-level sovereigns was enhanced and what little power the emperor still had dwindled correspondingly. But it also put liberalization irrevocably on the agenda. A combination of the two inevitably meant a strong dose of 'modernization from above', as it also did in Sardinia-Piedmont, the seedbed of nation-building in Italy.

Above all, liberalization amounted to establishing legal equality of citizens, granting them greater personal liberties and the country a written constitution, standardizing and centralizing rational-legal rule, guaranteeing more codified instruments and fewer personal ones for doing trade and running companies, and granting political participation through less differentiated parliamentary assemblies, rather than through estate-based (*altständische*) participation. Since the German principalities were infused with French ideas and practices, the rulers decided that it was in their interest not to dismiss this inheritance, at least not wholly, but to use it to augment the functioning of their own government. Some of them had been more willing supporters of Napoleon and owed their promotion in aristocratic rank to him, such as the kings of Bavaria and Württemberg, and the Grand Duke of Baden. To the extent that they were geographically closer to France, they were less likely to dispose of the new French heritage anyway. Others had been constrained to help Napoleon, such as the king of Prussia. As a result of the Congress of Vienna and of being head of a country that had devoted more troops and lives to the war against Napoleon than any other, the Prussian king was allocated the whole of the Rhineland and Westphalia, where the Code civil had been established, and also northern parts of Saxony.

4.4 Partitioning space for liberalism and corporatism

At this stage, we can identify the following partitioning of societal space and the partitioned recombination of distinct and initially opposing institutions: intermediate-level sovereign rule was decisively affirmed, and although it continued to be linked to older estates-based (*altständische*) forms of representation and guild corporatism in many places, the definition of the nature of citizens or subjects advanced considerably towards a more universal scheme and an integrated parliamentary assembly. It was not without tensions that these contrary schemes of societal order co-developed and coexisted. But the dynamics of their integration fuelled the development of German society for far more than a century. This institutional partitioning modified the earlier one discussed in the last chapter, in which economic and occupational governance was mainly an affair of guilds and the estates, whereas general politics and justice, diplomacy and war, were mainly affairs of the sovereign.

As republican and democratic ideas increasingly addressed the wider field of politics, it first appeared as if the power and importance of estates and guilds were diminishing. In France, this conflict had been resolutely resolved by abolishing corporatism in the private economy. But intermediate-level princes in Germany, whom no one else had helped to legitimate once again as much as Napoleon, often saw corporatism as an alternative or complement to unified parliaments, i.e. assemblies undivided by estates. So did many citizens who thought bread-and-butter interests would be better served in a corporatist scheme, in which everyone was delegated a social standing with the corresponding corporative rights and no one had to concern themselves with diplomatic and other general matters since these were the proper responsibility of the prince and professional administrators. To them, the recent tribulations of war and oppressive government were linked to a societal order that had established unified parliaments, strengthened central government and a less layered conception of society, and put forward a coherent democratic framework. Unsurprisingly, the alternative to Napoleonic centralist and liberal policies was somewhat attractive to a broad sector of the German public. This gave particularism, local and dynastic allegiance, a powerful impetus. The shift to a new partitioning of an evolved institutional space can therefore be described as being analogous to a see-saw: one side goes up as the other goes down.

This is a dialectical movement, i.e. one which not only featured competition between the two sides for relative height, but an elevation of the entire see-saw such that corporatist and republican tendencies caused each other to escalate over the long run. Societies are most intensively marked by specific contrasts which are never definitely resolved; these contrasts keep coming back in ever new forms within a metatradition. They keep society moving along a roughly defined track constituted by such a metatradition. The dialectical interplay between republicanism or liberalism and corporatism has proved to be central to a German metatradition. Different societies probably have different core dialectics around which their emergence and functioning closely revolves. This dynamic interplay can be discussed by using the example of Prussia, which became the dominant state and the motor of national unity in Germany in the nineteenth century. The interplay was particularly intense here, and therefore the resulting metatradition in Prussia had a greater influence on institutions than did the more piecemeal co-evolution,[165] or cushioned movement of the see-saw, found in the south-west and Saxony.

4.5   Prussia on a see-saw of liberalization and revival of corporatism

In an improved Weberian scheme, as we have seen in the two previous chapters, societal institutions and culture are influenced by a conjunction of motives for action: affect, tradition (in the sense of doing things the way they have always been done without reflecting on this), and rational consideration. These motives and the action that results from them then congeal into a more complex heritage, one which includes traditions resulting from the interaction of unreflectively traditional, affective, and rational motives. That heritage includes complex but temporary (reflected) traditions. It also includes a metatradition that is stable despite changes over time; oscillation between opposite poles is central to a metatradition. Prussian social history is a good example of this dialectical interplay of continuity and change.

Before the Napoleonic incursions, Prussia was a model of a state strictly divided by estates, in a way almost incomparable to any other German state, with the exception of Mecklenburg.[166] Military obligations fell upon the shoulders of the landed estates, both noblemen and farmers; towns and also some artisan occupations such as miners and church ministers were exempt from conscription. Access to occupations occurred on the basis of corporative decisions and royal decree.

Whereas towns were self-governing in the restricted manner of medieval corpor-atism, the countryside was ruled by lords in manorial and larger governmental districts (*Kreise*), the latter usually by a nobleman appointed by the king as a *Landrat*. There were also a number of royal domains directly run by royal administration, in which farmers were more independent than in manors. The ruling class were the Junker[167] or gentry as they would be called in England, i.e. the nobility in charge of manors and local church and civil administration. There were very few high feudal lords, such as dukes.

The king effectively harnessed the gentry to become an unusually dedicated service class, a recruitment pool for the officer corps and the higher civil and diplomatic services, by striking a simple bargain: the gentry became independent of royal attribution of a fief and could simply inherit their estates; this meant a break with feudal tradition. In return, no aristocratic family could escape the obligation to send a sufficient number of sons into military service; this meant a regularization of feudal obligations. Already here we see the recurrent Prussian phenomenon of successive or interdependent liberalization and absolutism combined with corpor-atism. Outside town limits, the more traditional principle of peer control was severely curtailed; the differences between more self-governing towns and the gentry-run countryside were considerable. But the administrative and military set-up was also governed by peer control through corporatism, at least in the case of the nobility's choice of profession. For example, in order to enter the officer corps by being appointed second lieutenant, even in the days of the 1872 *Reich*, candidates not only had to pass a series of examinations but be co-opted by a collective vote held in the officer corps of the regiment they sought to enter.[168] Appointment by the king was conditional on this co-optation. It was precisely the peer rather than hierarchical control over officer appointments in the army that enabled an increasing 're-feudalization' (aristocratic appointments) in the infantry and cavalry regiments even in the nineteenth century, even though the artillery and engineers, as the technical branches of the military, had become bourgeois.

The Prussian tradition had become a systematic fusion of rational-legal govern-ment by royal administration and personalized social control in the countryside. The gentry figured as the central element in both, although non-aristocrats were prominent in the professional bureaucracy. Prussia's societal institutions were thus both very modern and very antiquated. But Prussia was not known for strong urban corporatism, despite its strongly feudal structures. There were probably few princes who attacked urban self-government as successfully as the Great Elector. Prussia emerged from the eighteenth century as a country successful in both its peaceful and its military endeavours. Then Prussia's distinctive combination of feudalism and professional bureaucracy suffered a historic shock, when Napoleon entered the scene in a way that proved particularly humiliating to the Prussians. The Prussian king, Friedrich Wilhelm III, who is generally described as having been shy, hesitant, and awkward, tried at first to keep his country out of the war instead of unilaterally taking sides with France, the UK, or Russia and Austria-Hungary. There was, however, a faction at court that was in favour of an alliance with France, rather than siding with the emperor at Vienna. The dynasty and the elite had developed a profound mistrust of the Habsburgs, whom they considered as adroit in mobilizing Prussian allegiance when Austria needed troops but deceitful when compensation was on the agenda.[169]

Napoleon's first move against Prussia was to take central Franconia and the Bayreuth area, although there had been no justification for war with Prussia at all. Central Franconia was not excessively large but was the oldest territory belonging to the dynasty, dating back to a time before the Hohenzollern were allocated Brandenburg.[170] Napoleon needed central Franconia and Bayreuth as a gift to bestow on Bavaria, which had helped him in his campaign against Austria. This territorial gift helped tie together the very intricate patchwork of local rule in southern Germany. But Napoleon did not turn his back on Prussia altogether. He offered the Prussians Hanover as compensation, a principality held by the king of England, who was also a prince within Germany. Hanover happened to be a larger territory than central Franconia, but it was a poisoned chalice. The English king and prince of Hanover was, of course, France's main enemy, overseas and on the northern German plain.

Thus corrupted by the gift of Hanover, the Prussian king promptly received a declaration of war from the English king, who had been robbed of what was not just any possession, but the home of the English Hanoverian dynasty. Now, instead of siding with Napoleon unequivocally, the Prussian king became fearful of the Frenchman's further intentions and challenged him to pull his troops out of southern Germany. Napoleon was not daunted, and the Prussian declaration of war against France promptly brought about the defeat of Prussia at Jena and Auerstedt. This led to the next humiliation, the peace treaty at Tilsit in which Prussia lost every territory west of the Elbe, was forced to cut its army substantially, was occupied by French troops, and was obliged to assist France militarily upon request, as well as to pay substantial contributions.[171] It reduced Prussia from a major political entity and leading military power in Europe to a second-rate territory with few troops and little sovereignty.

Like the smaller principality of Brandenburg during the Thirty Years' War, Brandenburg-Prussia paid a heavy price because its ruler had manoeuvred inconsistently in an effort to keep the peace. As Churchill said about Britain in the years before 1939, Friedrich Wilhelm III had accepted disgrace to maintain peace; but what his country got was disgrace *and* a war, as well as a humiliating peace treaty providing for continued extraction of resources and political surveillance by France. Inevitably, this touched a chord in the Brandenburg-Prussian collective memory; it reawakened traumatic feelings and led to a degree of mobilization and assertiveness that resembled the rallying of forces behind the Great Elector. This time, however, the ruler himself was not the main instigator of the mobilization; the movement was spurred on by a coalition of modernizers in government and the military, as well as by spontaneous formations of militias and volunteer forces, including the urban strata that had been exempt from military conscription. The reform think-tanks, planners, and leading politicians now guiding the country into a new era were very often immigrants from outside Prussia (Stein, Hardenberg, Scharnhorst, Gneisenau).

Within a relatively short time, Prussia had what was unheard of in a strict feudal regime: general conscription, a concept of military duty as a patriotic obligation and privilege, the disappearance of estate differences, at least in the military. All this was voluntarily offered by the citizenry in a spirit similar to that of the volunteers in the French revolutionary national guards.[172] In an extraordinary dialectical twist, Prussia thus obtained virtually French-style universalistic military institutions, although the society remained feudal and authoritarian in structure. In the 'War of Liberation', Prussia became egalitarian in spirit and in human sacrifice.[173] It learnt a more important institutional lesson from its military defeat than any lesson from allies in time of peace.

Characteristically, defeat and the popular discontent with French occupation, plundering, and requisitioning initiated a 'revolution from above'. The king himself gave power to a modernizing faction, much to the discontent of many conservative gentry. In addition to the changes in the recruitment and set-up of the army, there was a parallel drive during the war against France to reform public administration, grant towns greater autonomy, liberalize entrepreneurship and trade, do away with feudal privileges, introduce generalized citizenship, and abolish the serfdom of peasants and turn them into full citizens. In other words, both the military and the civil side of the reform programme were as Napoleonic as any Rhenish Confederation state could make them. In view of the connection between military and civil reform, military reformers (Boyen as minister of war; Clausewitz, Scharnhorst, and Gneisenau as leading staff officers) were referred to as 'the Jacobins' in more traditional court circles. It is also remarkable that probably the best disciple that Napoleon had in matters of strategy was his adversary Neidhart von Gneisenau, the mastermind assisting Field Marshal Blücher, who was decisive in setting the scene for the battle of Leipzig in 1813 and in securing victory at Waterloo by joining forces with the Hanoverian–British–Dutch army, a move that tipped the balance in their favour. Thus, the remarkably effective deployment of forces against Napoleon was accompanied by hostilities between the new and the old military leadership.

Prussia thus became infused with French institutions in the process of fighting against France in a war that Prussia remembered as one of the most heroic in its history.[174] It was influenced far more by the experiences brought on through war, first in defeat and later in victory, than it would have been had peace prevailed. This war was one of assimilation; it triggered the most profound process of institutional influence from France, including the importation of general civil rights and duties and commercial freedom. It was the Prussian War of Assimilation. Although the assimilation was radical, it was specific and related to certain other areas of divergence that continued to exist or were subsequently strengthened. Napoleon consistently exerted pressure to have the reformist ministers and generals dismissed for he feared they might implement so many lessons from France that they could become dangerous to French interests.

4.6   A comparative picture of economic liberalism

The prominent names behind the reform of state administration and civilian society
are Stein and Hardenberg, both of whom—like many military reformers—were
from territories outside Brandenburg-Prussia.[175] With regard to economic social
institutions, Hardenberg's reforms were economically liberal to the core, while
Stein was the advocate of local municipal responsibility (*Gemeinden*). Hardenberg's
reforms were more powerful and attracted far less opposition from the gentry: the
instituted the freedom of trade and contractual liberty, did away with guild
privileges (*Zunftzwang*) and monopolies, and introduced differentiated but general
taxation. These reforms were probably even more economically liberal than those
of France, which had retained some monopolies. Once an antiquated state as far as
liberal economic institutions were concerned, Prussia had now moved to the
forefront alongside of England. Needless to say, liberalization was not as forthcom-
ing in the area of political participation and parliamentary rule.

   This turnabout in policies and public order is clearly dialectical. A measure of
continuity of royal rule and government was instrumental for a dialectical swing
towards liberalism to occur effectively. Radical change and continuity are therefore
combined dialectically, and at that time and in that place this meant a combination
of economic liberalism with relatively absolutist rule compared to the western and
south-western states in Prussia's neighbourhood. As we shall see later, a metatradition was emerging to the extent that swings between liberalization and the reassertion of the corporatist order have become a recurrent phenomenon, first in Prussia
and then in Germany. After institutions see-saw, so to speak, between liberalism
and non-liberalism and between internationalization and the assertion of domestic
specificity, temporary orders are enacted that show a 'balance' has been reached
between such opposing principles, recombined as they are in temporarily unique
ensembles. The construction of such ensembles changes, but the see-sawing may be
similar over time, which means that a metatradition exists.

   When Germany's economic institutions are discussed and compared, scholars
often label German capitalism as 'non-liberal'.[176] But at the outset, the origins of
German capitalism, as evolved through the Prussian reforms, certainly were as
liberal in the English and French sense as could be with regard to contractual
freedom and the abolition of guilds. Later, a pervasive programme to privatize
mines was also enacted; this ran contrary to the Continental tradition that mining
was the prerogative of rulers and that the property 'below the soil' belonged
primarily to them and was not available for private transactions or acquisition.
Prussian economic liberalization was indeed embedded in a state which remained
'fairly' absolutist, although provincial estates had been established throughout the
kingdom. But the political side of liberalism is not the issue in discussion about
economic institutions, and the latter were thoroughly liberalized. It is not correct or
at least not the complete story to state that 'liberal alternatives were historically
suppressed and non-liberal patterns were institutionalized' during this formative
period.[177] Institutionalization started off on a track that was definitely economically

liberal. Lehmbruch has made this quite clear in line with socio-historical research.[178]

Institutionalization could be radically liberal because it came as a revolution from above, rather than emerging gradually through 'disincorporation' (local abolition of guild privileges) as it did in English towns at their own discretion and in a country that had almost no effective constraints on incorporating economic activities outside of the towns. Whereas in Britain, economic liberalization was advanced by traders and manufacturers and was thereby connected to political liberalization, in Prussia it was enacted from above by a more absolutist state and therefore divested of potential for political liberalization. The urban strata that had volunteered for military service in the War of Assimilation would certainly not have put full-blown economic liberalism on the political agenda. It took an admirer of Adam Smith who was serving as the king's prime minister to do that. Therefore, institutionalization was non-liberal only in its political implications, which is not part of the definition. The partitioning phenomenon in this case is that in the Prussian reforms, economic liberalism was instituted by non-liberal rulers.

Interestingly, Lehmbruch mentions that 'southern' states in Germany (Baden, Württemberg, Bavaria, Hesse, and Saxony) limited contractual freedom more than Prussia did after the reforms. These were states that had felt the impact of Napoleonic law to a greater extent. In particular the south-western corner of Germany (Baden and Württemberg) developed a reputation for liberal constitutionalism and economic-institutional modernity at an early stage; yet it was these states, rather than more autocratic and politically less liberal Prussia, who did more to preserve traditional guild functions.[179] Also, Saxony, the state which at the time was probably the most economically advanced in Germany, exhibited a characteristic mix of technical advancement and commercial ingenuity, on the one hand, and arrestingly conservative corporatism, on the other.[180] Again, this helps to indicate that economic liberalism was not necessarily tied to political liberalism. A corporatist tinge to economic institutions co-evolved with more generic liberalization in some places, whereas in Prussia, the state that became dominant in Germany, economic liberalism greatly reduced the space of corporatism.

One has to be careful to distinguish different traditions: whereas in the south-west and in Saxony, economic liberalization co-evolved rather smoothly with a tradition of corporatism, in Prussia, economic liberalization became more pervasive because it depended on more autocratic modernization. Within this period at least, it is doubtful whether the epithet 'non-liberal' is appropriate for the institutions that emerged. Likewise, we should carefully question whether the full range of economic liberalization was related to economic and technical advancement as systematically as is often claimed.

Our notion of economic liberalism is apparently focused excessively on Anglo-American conceptions, in so far as we consider the freedom to engage in contracts to be by definition more hamstrung by corporatist institutions than by custom and practices, as is the case in the English common law tradition of contract. Under English law, contracting was more market-driven and respectful of individual entrepreneurs and enterprises. At the same time, it was also de facto bound to common law or informally effective conventions. These may have been as effective as more formal or statutory rules on the European continent at the time. The entire history of industrial relations in England proves this point:[181] it may have been liberal in terms of statute law, but this did not mean the absence of effective constraints. There was a resurgence of regulation or other constraints, and we do not have any methodologically sound historical comparison which allows us to state whether de facto liberalization was more or less intensive over a longer time when we compare, for example, Prussia and England at the beginning of the nineteenth century. Moreover, if corporatism facilitated contracting, it cannot be construed as working against it without closer empirical examination. In a world in which the partitioning of institutional space in history commonly results in the creative recombination of theoretical opposites, entire institutional sets can only be labelled as being predominantly liberal or non-liberal in the context of a specific historical period. This is because partitioning and recombining alters the balance of liberalism over time, and, at least in Germany, such changes in the balance resemble pendulum swings; developments first move closer to liberalism, then away from it. Furthermore, it is important to discuss not only where the balance is found, but also the make-up of such a combination of opposites.

This reinforces doubts about the viability of attaching the labels of 'liberal' and 'non-liberal' to forms of capitalism, to entire societies, and to extended periods in history. In the characteristic Whiggishness of social science, the oscillation between, or the combination of, corporatism and liberalism has come to be considered 'schizophrenic', to use a term Rokkan feels is appropriate.[182] Unfortunately, this casts aside the dialectical-evolutionary perspective Rokkan himself sought to develop. History is always schizophrenic in the sense of not being governed according to one and the same mindset, and so are major movements and the practical implementation of their fundamental ideas. Of course, they are always schizophrenic in societally distinctive ways.

Streeck and Yamamura posit Germany and Japan as having non-liberal forms of capitalism, and Streeck mentions a German *Sonderweg* as a particular path of developing capitalism.[183] He rightly points out that every country develops its own special path, which fortunately liberates the German term from the isolationist connotations it has acquired.[184] In view of the overwhelming evidence that corporatism, governmental regulation, or other traditional conventions have been found to persist for lengthy periods of time in non-Anglo-American countries, it may be more appropriate to call Anglo-American capitalism a *Sonderweg*, to the extent that it has avoided or curtailed such traditions more than others. Even this is questionable, given that systematically comparative and properly periodized historical research on effective limitations to free contracting does not exist. Furthermore, Japan and Germany do not have more in common in this area and in other respects than, say, Germany and France.

There is a tendency, probably going back to Anderson,[185] to classify Japan and Germany as having the same type of capitalism for reasons of supposedly similar paths of historical development that suggest an association between non-liberal modernization and totalitarianism. This is not something that Streeck and Yamamura evoke in their analysis, but Anderson has done. Japan, of course, has used Germany as a model a number of times, but it has also adopted things from other countries in a very eclectic manner. More systematic scrutiny casts decisive doubt on claims that Germany and Japan are close on typology. The criteria of relative similarity that researchers have used, such as a strong state and weaker markets, apply to many societies outside the Anglo-American ambit. But the pertinence of those criteria is limited when historical oscillations and institutional partitioning between the non-liberalization and liberalization of markets and between the strengthening and the collapse of the state are taken into account. My suspicion is that Japan and Germany tend to be associated because in relatively recent history they were allies in a military coalition confronting the Anglo-American world. However, as the Franco–Prussian and Anglo–German episodes described here show, societies may develop greater similarity by being enemies than by being allies. It is for precisely this reason that Germany and Japan also diverge in other respects.

Now that 'varieties of capitalism' have been studied, our attention should evidently be directed toward investigating 'varieties of economic liberalism' and, even more important, those of non-liberalism. There are at least two economic liberalisms: traditional liberalism, embedded in common-law norms, as exemplified by English institutions; and revolutionary liberalism, constituted by statute law after a revolution 'from below' (such as France in 1798) or 'from above' (Prussia at the beginning of the nineteenth century). There are equally diverse varieties of political liberalism, and it is surprising how no thought has been given to the way the term 'liberal' or 'liberals' came about to describe a political movement. The origins of that are not found in an Anglo-American context, but in Spain at the beginning of the nineteenth century.[186] Regardless of where that use of the word was pioneered, whether in Spain or subsequently in Germany, political liberalism very much came 'from above' and was first instituted by Napoleon's occupation army and even its bitterest Prussian opponents who, nevertheless, became involved in emulating France as far as general statute law, commercial freedom, and citizenship were concerned. It is a variant of liberalism that shades into mercantilism in the typical way that historical opposites tend to come together.

German economic liberalism has come to be a less individualistic liberalism than the Anglo-American one, to be sure. This has had negative effects on the freedom of competition in some markets, but the opposite effect in others. And whereas German states have often been strong internally, they have not come close to achieving the strength abroad that Anglo-American states have achieved as leading colonialists.

This is another kind of mercantilism that is surprisingly disregarded when authors describe Germany or France as mercantilist and the United Kingdom as liberal. Especially in the formative phases of capitalism and worldwide trade, the societies and economies described as liberal have practised mercantilist protection of those industries on which their own 'take-off' depended.[187] In this, they were no different from the so-called non-liberal economies. We must not confuse liberal doctrines with what in fact happened in those societies that have come to extol and claim them for themselves. Their factual historical practice was limited in time and domain. The appeal here is to give much greater weight to qualitative differentiation and the recombination of types. Societies and economies are liberal and non-liberal in their own distinctive ways, and these have changed over time. The following sections seek to demonstrate this for the German case.

4.7 Liberalism, absolutism, and corporatism: co-evolution and conflict

In addition to economic liberalization from above, another distinguishing feature shaping Prussian development was the increased importance of the western territories it had gained from the defeat of Napoleon. These were the Rhineland (including Berg and adjacent territories to the south, and the western bank of the river, which France had annexed) and Westphalia, plus some territories that had been lost in the Treaty of Tilsit (Minden, Ravensberg, Tecklenburg). Once primarily an eastern power with rather rigid, feudal institutions, Prussia now became a power straddling the landmass of northern Germany, with centres of gravity on both its eastern and western ends. It extended deep into the Baltic region and Poland, which was divided between Austria, Russia, and Prussia, and lay outside the bounds of the 'old' empire.

The western centre of gravity was characterized by modern manufacture and trade, French civil law, and a greater amount of social modernity. It was also, in northern Berg and adjacent areas in Westphalia, the region that had Germany's most substantial concentration of coal-mining, steelmaking, and heavy engineering. These areas were also the ones that were particularly good at advancing liberalization, both economically and politically, thanks to the legal provisions and indigenous interests acquired through the Rhenish Confederation or directly from France. Thus, grassroots liberalism in western Prussia was combined with absolutist and possibly more rigorous economic liberalism from above.

Once again, it is important to visualize this evolution within a metatradition that brings new institutions, even radically new institutions, but which also has a distinctive leitmotiv. For Prussia, this leitmotiv is the trauma of a somewhat antiquated country falling prey to devastation and degradation at the hands of external invaders, after reluctant or inept manoeuvring on the part of its ruler. The counterpoint to trauma is to escape the devastation and degradation through forceful and rationally considered rule, the adoption of foreign institutions to a considerable extent, with the support and utilization of the coherence of a very committed service class. This constituted the characteristic mixture of affective foundations with rational-legal absolutism, which was reinforced. In a way, what Joan of Arc or the *levée en masse* organized by Carnot did to inspire and rally France's inevitable response to trauma was perpetuated in Prussia in an institutional shell that permitted the partitioning of societal space in a way that made it possible for economic liberalism to coexist with an absolutist rule of law. Even after Napoleon had disappeared from the stage of history, this mixture remained fairly distinctive, although Sweden is clearly similar so far as the strength of the king and a loyal civil service bound by rules are concerned.[188]

A more specific impetus to consider for the period at the beginning of the nineteenth century, which originated in the Prussian War of Assimilation, is the trauma which resulted from the division of Germany into rather independent territories and which became the seedbed for unpredictable coalitions and resulting instability, and at worst devastation and degradation. Whereas the Great Elector came to the conclusion that a strong and independent realm of Brandenburg had to be achieved, some of the Prussian elite now drew a different conclusion. On the basis of experience both before and during the Prussian War of Assimilation, Prussians generally considered Austria to be an unreliable ally, prone to diplomatic scheming, pursuing interests outside the empire, and working against unity of command in any military coalition.[189] Although Prussia's territory was divided into eastern and western provinces and although important eastern lands (West Prussia, East Prussia, Posen, and much of Silesia) were located outside the old German Empire, Prussia had now become the largest territorial state within Germany. Therefore, some members of the elite concluded that Prussia had a strong interest in achieving greater unity within Germany. This conclusion was most clearly drawn and pursued by Bismarck.[190] It was the impetus behind the drive of 'Prussian *Realpolitik*' to achieve national integration.

There were also other motivations, propounded by completely different people. A number of merchants and industrialists interested in a larger market pleaded for unification. There were also citizens who were more generally dismayed about the loss of national unity in government, which had increased with and even after Napoleon, although Germany had become a more coherent unit culturally and through mobility. Such coherence, however, left out a 'Slav fringe' from the old empire in parts of eastern Brandenburg, Silesia, eastern Saxony, Bohemia and Slovenia, who had not dissolved in the melting pot and were not likely to do so. There were also new romantics in the younger intelligentsia who rekindled the memory of the Middle Ages, when the emperor enjoyed uncontested rule, mores were uncorrupted, and the empire was supposedly more united and invincible against foreign hordes.[191]

Before dealing with the stage of national integration, we need to note that economic liberalization in the first half of the nineteenth century was not wholly triumphant. Just as England experienced an ebb and flow of regulation and a resurgence of constraints on contracting by custom, practice, and law, so too did Prussia undergo a resurgence of corporatism. Of course, these are different phenomena resurging within a metatradition and recombining with dialectical opposites. Within the English heritage, we would not expect to find a corporatist resurgence as long as the country was undisturbed by massive military invasion and defeat. Yet if such a resurgence did occur, it would be expected to remain weak or to be abortive. One result of consequential, Prussian-style liberalization was a complaint about shortcomings in training and a lack of manpower. It was business, then, that prompted the government to pass a law (in 1845) to bolster guilds and preserve compulsory apprenticeships in forty trades.[192] Despite a general political turn towards more conservative inspiration after 1820, liberalism was predominant in economic policies.[193]

More generally, pendulum or see-saw movements appear to be characteristic. We observe them just about everywhere; human beings need trial and error. Since society is a rather complex thing that creates traditions and routines and needs time to learn, it would be amazing if we did not find see-saw movements. It is inevitable that periods of narrowed focus will occur in the process of structured learning. The see-saw movement which appears to be characteristic in Prussia is one of sharp descent and resurgence, in which an estate society was forcefully moving into economic liberalism but also pulling out of it in order to reintroduce corporatism. According to the authors cited, the see-saw effect was not as great in other German states as in Prussia, particularly not in the south-west and in Saxony. However, an eventual combination of liberalism with corporatism is found just about everywhere. As Prussia became the dominant German state, the rise of corporatism after 1845 can only be explained as a reaction against absolutist liberalism, because corporatism had not been a strong enough element of its own historic feudalism to prevail against other forces simply because it had existed and had been indispensable.

4.8   Dynastic feuding in aid of national unity

The path to national unity in Germany was complicated and need not concern us here in detail. In short, the confluence of forces that tried to achieve it (liberal merchants and industrialists, romantic students, revolutionaries against a Holy Alliance *ancien régime*, educated middle classes, groups within the ruling elites) was so heterogeneous that it was extremely difficult to give Germany a clear direction without losing essential players. Important players were, of course, those sovereigns imbued with a sense of duty to work always for the best interests of their own country. As a Prussian delegate to the Bundestag, the assembly of rulers forming the loose German Confederation after 1815, Bismarck had watched the conundrum from all angles. Without doing too much injustice to the intellectual refinement of which he was capable, we might say that his experience convinced him that the process took up too much ink and not enough 'iron and blood', as he called it in a parliamentary speech.

The only question for him was how to deploy the blood and iron as intelligently and sparingly as possible so as to be able to justify it to 'the lowliest Pomeranian grenadier'[194] but also to the princes who needed to be persuaded to unite 'their' territories into a tighter confederation. Problems of dynastic interests and feudal legitimacy had to be overcome in order to unite diverse states into a nation; this was bound to upset the 'Holy Alliance' from the Vienna Congress—Russia,

Austria-Hungary, and Prussia—as well as the alliance between Hanover and England. Moreover, it would conflict with the interests of France and Denmark, a stable ally of Napoleon until his defeat. Vienna was conceived as a lasting peaceful solution for Europe, and it aggravated German disunity, one of the few things that most of the participants on both sides of the Napoleonic Wars could agree on, including the emperor. He now considered himself to be first and foremost emperor of Austria-Hungary; he harboured little interest in Germany except to repress German nationalism and maintain the status quo.

It was Bismarck's conviction, not devoid of plausibility, that German unity could only be realized under threat and through deftly crafted cabinet wars. The best way to make this happen was to create an external threat so that others would have to take the blame for the aggression. Yet, if Prussia needed to posit a threat internally in the German Confederation, then this was also an option to be diligently pursued. The Bismarckian road to unity, which was the only one that worked, used foreign policy at least as much as it did integration from within Germany. The first steps had been executed, before Bismarck became prime minister, by the reformist ministers of finance and trade, who had established a customs union (the Zollverein) that gradually included all German states except Austria. The latter was unable to join in view of commitments to the integrated lands outside the old imperial heartlands reaching deep into Poland and the Balkans.

The fact that Austria failed to qualify for the customs union in Germany (the Zollverein was started in 1833/4 and gradually extended) and opposed national political integration had decisive consequences. After 1850, the Prussian government increasingly strove to exclude Austria from Germany in order to build a confederation. This was made abundantly clear by Bismarck, who, in another revolution from above, demanded unlimited male adult suffrage for a German national parliament. Austria could not accept this for fear that Slav and other nationalist movements would thereby be able to break up the empire. This ploy helped to achieve a gradual fusion of interests as divergent as those of liberal parliamentarians and conservative gentry.

Bismarck then exploited a quarrel with Denmark, which was both a foreign state ruling over Schleswig and a domestic state within the Confederation ruling over Holstein. Following the war with Denmark, Prussia ended up annexing both lands after using the Schleswig and Holstein issue as an opportunity to have a 'federal execution' declared upon it by the Confederation. This led to a swift war and a peace treaty in which Prussia annexed Hanover, locked out Austria, ended the loose confederation that had emerged from the Congress of Vienna, and established a new North German Confederation, as well as secret treaties of protection and defence with southern German states.[195]

This was Bismarck in a nutshell: a series of swift wars—not declared by Prussia but by others foolish enough to do so—to build alliances rather than subdue an enemy; it worked surprisingly well. Napoleon would not only have approved but been envious of this most successful emulation of his own type of statecraft, which caused much less harm.[196] Again, the policy had been learnt from France.

The conservative Prussian gentry quickly realized this when Bismarck, without any respect for princely legitimacy, simply had the king of Hanover deposed for being in the way territorially and for being generally obnoxious. Just as the Prussian reformers were called Jacobins, so now Bismarck was called a Bonapartist. He represented a manhandling of legitimacy and princes that they thought could be prevented by the Holy Alliance of the Congress of Vienna, since Bonapartism was supposedly at the root of all the evil that had befallen European societies.

Once Austria was excluded, an external aggressor had to be found to force the protection and defence treaties to take effect and to lay the foundation for a German Confederation embracing both the north and the south. France promptly obliged, by a declaration of war in 1870. Her motive was a mixture of perceived insult and threat. After Spain had enquired whether a Catholic member of a branch of the Hohenzollern family was interested in becoming its new king, and the Prussian king had, upon Bismarck's advice, allowed the discussion to carry on for a while, the old French trauma of Habsburg encirclement, dating back to the time of Charles V, was reawakened.[197] At the time, Bismarck seems to have been reasonably sure about being able to get France to declare war on Prussia at any time. It was not a problem to arouse French sensitivities to the necessary pitch; the problem was to organize a declaration of war from France to coincide with an optimal state of preparedness of the army, to rally the rest of Germany around Prussia,[198] and to discourage foreign powers from siding with France.

France was beaten by this new German coalition and, after some hectic negotiation about state privileges and the arrangement of slush money for the Bavarian king, the new German Empire was established in 1872, with the Prussian king as the new emperor, acclaimed by the ruling princes.[199] More than half of the territory and the population of the new German Empire was now Prussian, and the template for the constitution was provided by the North German Confederation, concluded in 1867. Thus, while Prussia and other parts of Germany had successfully repressed the trauma they had sustained back in 1648 and which had been re-evoked on subsequent occasions, France suffered from the re-opening of an old wound[200] after the Germans annexed Alsace and parts of Lorraine. This annexation proved to be much more controversial in the eyes of those annexed, although the majority of them spoke a German dialect as their mother tongue. All European countries appear to harbour some sort of trauma; Germany is not unique in this. But there does tend to be a difference between them with regard to the specific nature of their traumas, their origins, and the ways each country overcomes them.

At the time, the German resolve to rid itself of its trauma initiated a fever of nationalism, but also an incredibly productive period of institution-building. Policies could be conceived and interpreted as being domestic in origin, even if in fact they were not. But this only meant that the nexus between international diplomacy, wars, or alliance formation, on the one hand, and domestic events on the other, became mediated. Again, at the outset, the nation-building that led to this empire and developed it was decidedly liberal. In this respect, the impetus defined by the Prussian reformers was still powerful. From the Zollverein to the Trades and

Industry Statute (Gewerbeordnung) of the North German Confederation, the emphasis of regulation was clearly liberal, geared to institute free trade and give people free access to both occupations and markets.[201] Political liberalism had also made substantial inroads with regard to universal suffrage for all male adults. Especially during the boom phase after the empire was founded in 1872, there was a heyday of industrial start-ups and trade intensification, which occurred without restriction by guild privileges, customs, or governmental domineering.

4.9 Towards non-liberal coordination

As a reaction to an abundantly liberal keynote, there was a resurgence of corporatism that originated from the grassroots of business (artisan shops or small industrial firms) more than liberalism had. As early as 1848, a proto-national convention of artisans and tradesmen—master artisans rather than journeymen or other employees—at Frankfurt on Main had demanded a return to an economic order which gave guilds and other corporative economic associations more important roles. The event took place during a period of economic downturn, and the plea for a return to corporatism has to be understood as a search for defensive mechanisms to prevent the oversupply of labour in each trade, as well as to protect against price-slashing and bankruptcies during a crisis. At the same time, it was also geared to stabilize human resource development and employment in small firms.[202] Interestingly, it was the journeymen who pleaded for liberalization at the time, apparently in the hope of benefiting from their quickly achieved independence as producers. The prevailing reassertion of corporatist interests was a continuation of the currents that had also led to the earlier minor renaissance of guilds and crafts in Prussia in 1845. In a significant dialectical twist, the reassertion of corporatist interests therefore followed strong waves of liberalization in both Prussia and the whole of Germany. This continued the peculiar Prussian dialectic of having liberalism imposed from above, to which the strata of artisans and small industry reacted by conducting grassroots drives back to corporatism, particularly when the economy took a turn for the worse.

The reaction was not limited to the context of small artisan shops and firms. For corporatism was not abandoned by the new capitalists and financiers of the new empire, as they might have done initially as devout liberals or paternalists who preferred to focus solely on the well-being of 'their' enterprise rather than that of the larger economy. Of course, the make-up of firms prevalent in Germany during the boom period (*Gründerjahre*) after 1872 were vastly different from those of 1848, which would have made cumulative liberalism all the more plausible: there was substantial investment in the public infrastructure, and more concentrated mechanical, electrical, and chemical industries had either started a process of company growth and concentration or were preparing for it. However, the boom phase after unification was short-lived and led to a relative economic decline in the 1870s. Again, it is far from a foregone conclusion that enterprises should try to escape a downturn by resorting to forms of collective solidarity, rather than to those of liberal enterprise individualism. What they do will be influenced by the heritage of their society's institutions and culture.

From then on, corporatism emerged mainly on two fronts, and it was also connected to the emergence of collective bargaining between unions and employers' associations. One front was the revival of guild corporatism in the artisan sector of the economy, where it had been strong before the onset of liberalism, and the other front was cartelization, primarily in the more concentrated industries and in bulk or large-scale manufacturers. With regard to cartelization, Kocka observed: 'The disruptions to growth, and the fall in prices from 1873 to the mid-1890s, led to a rapid increase in the number of concerns cooperating in cartels, beginning in the 1880s... The agreements reached in these contracts were at first usually aimed purely at a common price policy; the cartel gained stability when it also regulated the quantities of production for each firm and conditions of distribution'. In addition to American firms but probably earlier than in the United States, German enterprises became the record-holders in cartel-building. Cartelization might also have developed in America, but legislators moved against it more rapidly; whereas in Germany, another fifty years had to pass before such legislation existed. From the literature, it is clear that cartels were first and foremost a defensive mechanism to assure survival in a time of recession.[203]

Recession alone does not make it self-evident that firms should engage in cartelization as spontaneously and promptly as they did in Germany. Other equally plausible explanatory scenarios would be the continual increase in concentration of ownership and in bankruptcy, even to the point of being wrapped up in an 'end game' in which presumably only the 'fittest' survived. Competition law would not have precluded this at the time. What must have emerged once again was an institutional and cultural memory, perhaps an entrepreneurial concept, of a 'community of fate', as Weber would have called it, consisting of a limited number of producers who had to confront whatever challenges the markets might throw up in the present or the uncertain future.

If a cartel was only to be a means of defence, it should have quickly disbanded with the onset of an economic upswing. But nothing of the sort happened in Germany: 'cartels continued to develop in the upswing conditions prevailing after the mid-1890s; they even increased thereafter. They served to limit competition, stabilize prices and profits, and they tended towards a monopoly control of the market'.[204] Having initially and thoroughly embedded themselves in economic liberalism during the first half of the century or beyond, businesses now rediscovered the advantages of corporatism. What businesses did was to take important instruments from the toolbox of the old guilds, namely price-fixing and the stabilization of supply and profits, and to enact them by formal agreement or contract, rather than on the basis of statutory privileges. Although there was something inherent to the idea of corporatism through cartelization, of exploiting the customer and consumer, the re-inventers of corporatism were also thinking of what J. M. Clark later called 'workable competition',[205] that is, competition which assured returns sufficient to invest in new products and channels of distribution. Now, if we define economic liberalism to be a market order that avoids collusion between actual or latent competitors, then we are surely right in calling it non-liberal.[206]

However, it has to be pointed out that this non-liberal reaction was not a 'simple' tradition. Especially in Prussia and the larger North German Confederation, cartelization was a reaction to 'cut-throat' liberalism. In a curious way, it perpetuated a medieval concept in which 'work' needed to 'nourish' a limited collectivity of firms by fixing a 'fair price' (*pretium iustum*). Such a non-liberal concept had, incidentally, influenced the English trade unions even more profoundly, and these enforced it at least as effectively as did German artisans, at least until Margaret Thatcher reformed industrial relations. Now, cartels also became endowed with more modern ideas, namely the facilitation of investment on the basis of sufficient and stable returns and margins and the necessity of innovation and expansion. While cartels were becoming more dynamic in this way, capitalism and markets were also becoming truly international. As a reaction to internationalization, however, the second German *Reich* also started to pursue a policy of imposing customs duties on imported goods, clearly in order mainly to defend the static domestic market order.[207]

However, at the very beginning of the twentieth century, internationalization reached an unprecedented level, at least in Europe and North America, as far as foreign trade was concerned. Moreover, main currencies were convertible against each other and were fixed to a gold standard. Cartelization was a policy used to achieve not only domestic distribution of demand but also dynamic effectiveness in an international market. Some cartels were already international. Even if German firms applied cartelization only domestically, where presumably the possibility of transacting and enforcing such agreements was greater, they pursued this policy in order to generate funds for expansion and product development abroad, thus giving the cartel more than a purely static role.

Also characteristic of this period was the emergence of German multinational companies, mainly in electrical engineering, chemicals and pharmaceuticals, and some other concentrated industries. Lane has shown that post-World War II German multinationals were at first very reluctant to set up producing subsidiaries abroad.[208] At the turn of the century, however, attitudes were quite different and— for a country with relatively few colonies—Germany was an active promoter of multinational enterprise. It was much more 'natural' for British or American companies to become multinationals, for instance by establishing a subsidiary in Canada or India. German companies had to overcome more local resistance from established interests in order to set up subsidiaries abroad. The subsequent experience, in which foreign investments were expropriated after each of the world wars, also put a damper on the proclivity to venture forth into direct investment abroad.[209]

From the end of the nineteenth century until well into the 1950s, it was typical for German firms to differentiate between 'export' and 'standard' products or models. Export models or products were of better quality and more expensive, and they targeted a more demanding or munificent slice of the market. For example, the Volkswagen Beetle was initially sold in two versions, one called Standard and the other Export. The implication was not, of course, that domestic consumers were not able to buy the Export model as readily. It meant that they had to pay more for quality and 'luxury'. Even for beer, it was customary to differentiate between *Helles* (simple lager beer) and *Export*. Undoubtedly, most of the export beer was drunk in Germany, and one wonders whether many of the brands proclaimed as 'export' ever crossed the border. Still, the labelling was accepted without question, and the dim view that Germans have taken of foreign tastes in beer has made it quite immaterial whether it was actually exported. This expressed the importance given to exports as a general mark of quality, and to the mobilization of resources for 'differentiated quality' production as a selling point for customers in labelling and production.[210]

The other front of resurgent corporatism was public organization and governance in the artisanal sector. In Germany, this sector had always been conceived as large, including the 'nobler' tradesmen such as goldsmiths, watchmakers, and other producers of more luxurious goods, but also plumbers, bricklayers, sawyers, cartwrights, carpenters, decorator painters, shoemakers, and all other suppliers of more mundane products and services. Artisan trades were also quick to make technological advances in new areas, such as electrical and electro-mechanical applications. Even when production itself was taken over by new industrial firms, artisan trades held their own by shifting from original production to maintenance, repair, installation, and service, often combined with retail functions.

Furthermore, training in artisan apprenticeship was by far the most important pool of human resources for the emerging industrial firms: 'The most significant contribution of the artisan sector lay in the supply of skills to industry . . . There was, then, no dual economy in the quality of labour . . . The craftsman's contribution has tended to be disparaged because of the presumed anachronistic influence of guilds on economic growth. . . . But guild regulations interfered more with personal convenience than with economic development.'[211] In 1886, it was revealed that about 43 per cent of all journeymen trained in artisan trades had switched to employment in manufacturing.[212] It is therefore not surprising that artisans had a solid lobby, for not only did they defend vested interests but they were also a convenient producer of a large reserve army of skilled manpower that industry could tap into. They also belonged, typically, to an occupational category that was, by virtue of its social position, close to 'the common man' or an important sector in both the working and middle classes, an ideal target for populist policies and politics.

When the economic tide turned and the 1872–3 boom went bust, politics on the whole became more conservative. At the time, this included an effective appeal to populist sentiments. Such sentiments were decidedly in favour of securing social positions and of a return to guild responsibility. In a way, this was part of the older heritage of channelling Germanic freedom and participation into the domain of occupational and economic self-government by means of peer control.

During the economic downturn, the parties in power in the Second Reich therefore sought to appeal to popular strata that were open to and interested in corporatist formation. In a reversal of the guidelines of the Trades and Industry Statute of the North German Confederation, which had been continued into the new *Reich*, the government in 1897 thus introduced legislation that provided for obligatory incorporation of artisan trades and obligatory apprenticeship and examination, as well as further training and examination for master craftsmen (*großer Befähigungsnachweis*).[213]

Heinrich August Winkler has called this legislation a 're-feudalization' against the interests of the Social Democrats.[214] Analytically, this is precisely what it was, though the term 're-feudalization' is pejorative. But Winkler did not know at the time that the Social Democrats would, in the 1979–80 electoral campaign, stylize the dualist vocational education and training thus set in motion and introduced against their wishes more than fifty years before, as part of a 'German model' (1980 version) that they thought they were entitled to sell. There were many institutions in Germany that started off as vilified 'neo-feudalism' or 'reactionary policy' only to end up as valued elements of the Social Democratic *Modell Deutschland* in 1980, just as the radical Social Democratic or union demands of 1890 subsequently became treasured and indispensable parts of the Weimar Republic, Nazi, or social market economies. As usual, the recombination of opposing principles within partitioned institutional space creates a new common sense out of conflict and schizophrenia.

This change was part of a larger populist-conservative current, which also led to pioneering social security legislation initiated by Bismarck. Bismarck needed new allies in addition to the 'national liberals'. Like many other representatives of the older Prussian establishment, he had the gut feeling that, in a pinch, the common people, including farmers and workers, were more loyal and trustworthy than over-educated and socially uprooted progressives and liberals. This even led Bismarck to make tentative overtures toward collaboration with a Social Democrat leader, Ferdinand Lassalle, a politically important step in a nation that had unlimited and free male suffrage at the national level, the first larger country to achieve this in Europe.[215] In so far as the policies of the time were non-liberal, they were populist-conservative. But it is equally true that they contained a strong emphasis on human resource creation and its reward by status, and this in turn fitted the interests of modern industry in creating a plentiful reserve of skilled workers.

What we witness here, in terms of partitioning of institutional space, is a division of meaning such that a more incorporated artisan class was governed by different institutions than were industry and non-artisanal services. Yet the logic of this partitioning within an action-system perspective is that human resource generation and utilization meant a steady and remarkable flow of labour from the crafts to industry. In this, there has been no fundamental change until the present day. In this respect, the internal diversity of an institutional order is not simply random variance, it is systematically structured in a way that makes things 'fall into place'. It is the institutional partitioning that helps to define working careers, not obstruct them. Rather than the retrograde and inflexible residue of a world long vanished, which some of the literature has made it out to be, the artisan crafts have remained a means of socialization and a talent pool from which careers typically headed in the direction of more modern industry have been started, not as a convenient escape but as a continuation of individual evolution. J. J. Lee writes: 'The vociferous disputes about the privileges of artisan organization can too easily distract attention . . . from the fact that on balance, the achievement of the guilds—in fostering commercial honesty, in adapting rapidly to the unprecedented demands for skill in the course of industrialization, and above all in encouraging high educational levels—entitles them to be considered positive rather than negative influences on the supply of skilled labour'.[216]

By the turn of the century, an institutional order had thus been established that can be termed non-liberal on the fronts of cartelization (and industry-level collective bargaining) and neo-corporatist organization of artisanal occupations. Possibly, this also occurred because of an early and rapidly advancing build-up of obligatory social insurance. But this non-liberalism was a response to earlier experience with pervasive liberalism. It drew lessons from this experience, rather than suppressing alternatives to liberalization. Societies do typically learn in this way, by recombining things from the 'garbage can' of history in order to respond to new stimuli. In this case, the process eventually led to a new synthesis of capitalism, corporatism, and mercantilism, to the point that capitalism not only competed with (the older form of) corporatism that had been pushed into the background, but co-evolved with a modernized corporatism. So too did liberalism (large contractual freedom in industry and commerce) co-evolve with segmental corporatism in the crafts and with 'cartel corporatism' in concentrated industries. Furthermore, the whole evolution not only contained domestic aspects but strong international overtones or motives, and it altered its strategy from maintaining a rather defensive posture to undertaking a more aggressive one of penetrating international markets. If someone had been asked to define the components of a 'German model' in 1900, the answer would have been economic coordination by cartels, nascent collective bargaining for the purpose of keeping industrial peace, segmental corporatism complementing more liberal contracting, and governmentally ordained, compulsory social security.

4.10   The development, perversion, and crisis of non-liberal governance

This 1900 version of the 'German model' continued to exist to a large extent, except that in the Weimar Republic in 1922, a dualist system of vocational education and training (linking apprenticeship with instruction at *Berufsschulen*, technical colleges) was instituted to cover not only handicrafts but industry, commerce, and other services. In this system, local chambers (of industry and commerce, handicrafts, etc.) set training schedules according to national guidelines and provided examination and certification. What had been an artisanal model of education and training thus spread throughout the entire economy. To this extent, institutional partitioning was reduced. Artisanal education and training continued to provide a major pool of industrial labour. What helped were efforts to bestow a good measure of parallelism on the definition of the crafts and industrial trades (particularly in construction, mechanics, and electrical engineering). Whereas collective bargaining and cartels had initially focused on different industries, the 'model' of the time gradually combined and strengthened cartelization, collective bargaining, tripartite social security, and corporatism.

In the Weimar era, the names of many political parties included either of the two epithets '*Volk*' or 'socialist'. Very few of them were devoid of populist traits; populism was one of the major heritages of the 'equality in the trenches' resulting from World War I, and no movement could escape it. The crudest form of populism was, of course, enacted by the Nazis, and their rule therefore also meant an even more thorough enforcement of corporatism. I will not go into the less palatable aspects of this 'innovation', in which a panorama of corporatist associations were used for dictatorial purposes. However, lasting elements from this heritage are the compulsory membership of firms in chambers of one sort or another and the more extensive and intensive education and examination required to obtain the occupational title of master craftsman (*Meister*). This has served to institute a pervasive system of further vocational education and training by building upon earlier apprenticeship and occupational practices. The populist logic[217] of this is, simply speaking, that each common man or woman deserves to start with a good practical education and training and to have the chance to advance up the occupational ladder, depending on motivation and opportunity, by way of advanced training in preparation for greater responsibilities.

In the imagery of the time, this system of practical training was preferable to a more academic approach, which ran the risk of being impractical as well as conducive to a 'free-floating intelligentsia'. Free-floaters were very hard to control, likely to be excessive in their pursuit of individualism, and were thought to be out of touch with what came to be called 'sound popular instincts' (*gesundes Volksemp-finden*). The resulting scheme of things thus combined a great deal of career opportunity and industrial development with a high degree of social control. With regard to cartelization, Nazi policies also greatly furthered this development by harnessing conglomerates and industrial associations to a central scheme of economic planning and development, including price controls and rationing. All this was contrived to make economic institutions more non-liberal than they had ever been. The see-saw reached a position diametrically opposite to that of one hundred years previously. But we can also see that during this period, liberal, corporatist, and mercantilist institutions were conflicting at certain times and in certain situations, while at other times they were complementary.

In light of these see-saw movements, we witness the trailblazing of a path towards modernization in the South Germanic bedrock (including Germany and Austria) that combined a more universal concept of citizenship and political rights with corporatism in a populist scheme, regardless of changes in regime and government. Part of the process of developing universal citizenship was to integrate most people into one corporation or another and to link the polity and corporations by a devolution of responsibilities from the state to associations.[218] This neo-corporatist form of populism in the South Germanic bedrock is different from the corporatism found in the North Germanic bedrock in the Nordic countries. The latter was focused to a greater extent on establishing inclusive trade union and social democratic associations and drawing up a 'contract' between them and employers that defined economic citizenship and 'status rights'. Whereas Germany and Austria anchored corporatism in statute law and emphasized the role of employers' associations and chambers, the Nordic countries laid the foundation for fundamental collective agreements to a greater extent on trade unions and on their link to politics via social democratic parties, the new standard bearers of Scandinavian-style populism.[219]

4.11 Recombining liberalism and non-liberalism during and after occupation

The total defeat of Germany in 1945 ushered in a new order, which—much like at the beginning of the nineteenth century—was marked by influences radically different to those prevailing in the heyday of non-liberalism between the end of that century and 1945, culminating in 1933–45. Before we turn to the development of institutions in societal space, we should look at the political and demographic heritage of the war. While World War II was not as devastating as the Thirty Years' War, it was horrifying by more recent standards of civilization, particularly the perverse recombination of rational organization with atavistic ideology and brutality. The worst victim was Poland (14 per cent of the population killed), followed by Yugoslavia (11 per cent) and the Soviet Union (about 9.5 per cent), which demonstrates that the atrocities of this war were most intensive in eastern Europe, a great deal of which has to be blamed on Germany. Germany itself follows in 'only' fourth place (8.5 per cent). Depressingly, the nation which suffered most, Poland, was one of the official 'winners' of the war, as were the other two most afflicted countries.[220]

As a result of war and ethnic cleansing (whether or not this was agreed upon at the Allied conferences in Yalta and Potsdam), more than 12 million German citizens or ethnic Germans were expelled or fled, mainly from the eastern territories of the 1937 *Reich* that had to be 'evacuated' even though the population living within the 1937 borders was solidly German, never mind its ethnically diverse roots. In addition, about 2 million civilians were killed or died in the course of the occupation or on the trek westwards. Poland had to 'move west' and received the land east of the Rivers Oder and Neisse in return for being deprived of what Stalin had occupied on the basis of his alliance with Hitler until 1942.[221] Accordingly, it was decided that Germany also 'had to move west'. The massive migration of more than 12 million refugees and expellees into Germany remains the greatest displacement of population in human history. Even when British India was divided into India and Pakistan at the time of independence, the 'religious cleansing' that happened 'only' affected around ten million people, either Muslims who moved to Pakistan or Hindus to India. At the same time, Germany was experiencing the pervasive destruction of housing, infrastructure, and businesses by air bombardment, inflicted on civilians sometimes inadvertently ('collateral damage') and very often deliberately. This combination of mass migration and widespread destruction gave the populace a grim determination to reconstruct the country, a determination that translated the earlier populist sentiment evoking 'equality in the trenches' into a new 'equality on the national building site'.

On both sides of the divided Germany, reconstruction was based on models that were both domestic and external. The two Germanys that emerged from the war were thus greatly influenced by foreign incursion, much more so than in 1648 or at the beginning of the nineteenth century. For the first time, Germany had to surrender unconditionally and submit to foreign military government without even a peace treaty. The trauma was even more intense because at probably no other moment in the country's history did the people feel as shattered over what had happened at their own instigation and what they had inflicted on other human beings, politically, militarily, and through unprecedented genocide. This only came fully to the fore after the war, after dictatorial control over both media and personal communication was lifted. With unconditional surrender, the two Germanys that emerged ceased being sovereign states. This has not changed radically even since re-unification in 1990, for the country has become so fully integrated into international treaties and a 'federation'[222] (e.g. NATO, the European Union) that the next best but still rather distant approximation to a semblance of sovereignty to which it can aspire is a new style of *entente cordiale* with France.

In view of the total deflation of national pride before and after 1945, foreign incursion was very often welcomed by the population. Rarely in German history was the opportunity to implant foreign institutions and culture as great as then. But the large bag of tools from which a selection could be made was an assortment including extensive liberalism, communism, and other instruments from the German past that fit somewhere in between. One important starting point, however, was as German as could be although it was imposed upon Germany by the occupation powers, namely the division of the country into American, British, French, and Soviet occupation zones, each with its own military government. This laid a cornerstone for decentralized government. Before the Federal Republic was constituted out of the merger of the American, British, and French zones in 1949, the federal states or their smaller predecessors had already been established. Historically, the federal states preceded the federation (*Bund* is a term pertaining to the German Confederation following the Congress of Vienna in 1815, to the North German Confederation of 1869, and also to some extent to the 1872 *Reich*, and for centuries in Switzerland).

Major decisions faced the new Federal Republic in selecting an alternative on which to establish its socio-economic institutions. First, it had to be decided how liberal its institutions would be. The purely domestic and more recent tradition, as outlined above, tended to favour a non-liberal 'German model' that consisted of a mixture of elements from the 1890, 1922, or even 1934 versions, featuring cartels, macro-economic planning, collective agreements, and the nationalization of 'key industries', notably coal and steel. The varying degrees of emphasis which Germans placed on each of these elements depended on their political persuasions. Yet there was a very strong consensus that an economy as destitute and in need of reconstruction as Germany's needed precisely such a non-liberal model, not only for this reason but also because its neighbours were more likely to strengthen their borders than relax them. Therefore, both those whose opinions were shaped by what they had learned from the misuse of capitalist power and those who sought to establish a new legitimacy for capitalism were initially very sympathetic to the idea of coordinated regulation and planning. Employers and entrepreneurs favoured cartels and corporatist regulation, while the trade unions, Social Democrats, and some groups among the Christian Democrats opted for nationalization and national economic and social planning.

The heritage of economic concentration, corporatism, and Nazi central planning suggested to many that, since a modern economy was being visibly run by a well-organized and restricted circle, one might as well subject this to public control to make it serve the general interest rather than very specific private ones. After all, private interests had recently succumbed to the temptation to cooperate with one of the most pernicious political movements the world had ever seen. Public control of the economy had already been predicted by Joseph Schumpeter, since organized capitalism[223] had shown that it was viable. German communists and socialists inevitably took up the cue. So did the forces of occupation, including the Western ones.

All this has been described by Djelic, based on a thorough inspection of documents. This was the scene that awaited the occupation powers when they sought to do what Djelic terms 'exporting the American model', i.e. a much more liberal slant to economic institutions than recent non-liberal domestic models allowed.[224] The 'American model', favoured by military administration in the American zone of occupation (Bavaria, Hesse, southern Baden-Württemberg, and the American sector of Berlin) was emphatic about dissolving cartels and large monopolies, such as IG Farben, in chemicals, pharmaceuticals, coal, steel, and banking; it put free entrepreneurship and checks against the 'restriction of competition' in place, while keeping economic planning and price controls to a minimum and doing away with much of the existing corporatist apparatus.[225] The only coherent domestic support the American policy had was among the 'ordo-liberal' factions in political economy, the Free Democratic Party, and—last but not least—Ludwig Erhard, as the first minister of economic affairs in the Federal Republic, who would stay in office for more than a decade and a half. It was the conjoined influence of the American military government and Erhard that tipped the balance within the CDU in favour of 'importing the American model': 'Without American support and active involvement throughout the 1950s... Ludwig Erhard and his team would certainly not have been able to push for a restrictive cartel act. By providing material and intellectual support to a small group of West Germans ready to fight cartels, by helping to ground their institutional power, the Americans had in the end a significant impact on the West German anticartel debate.'[226]

By that token, the building of socio-economic institutions came to constitute a systematic break with the recent past. But as we have seen, it was not the first one in German social history. To this extent, it can be compared with the Napoleonic influence and the Prussian reforms at the beginning of the nineteenth century. As Djelic's analysis shows, nowhere in the rebuilding of western Europe was this foreign influence as great as in Germany. Interestingly enough, what was later styled a 'German model' in 1978 was formatively subject to an influence radically opposed to recent German institutions to a degree unlike any other except for the Napoleonic period and the Prussian reforms. At the same time that the French were increasing national planning and nationalizing all banks and enterprises that had collaborated with wartime Germany, Germany was becoming more profoundly Americanized than any other country in Europe. How could a supposedly 'German model' originate in such a period? If one had asked observers at the end of the 1950s whether they could see the beginnings of a 'German model' being put together, they would certainly have taken this question to be a political joke.

Once again, it is essential to look at the partitioning of institutional spaces and the recombination of distinct institutional principles under new auspices. First, it is true that not only in the economic order but also in enterprise management, the post-war period in Germany was one of the most extensive Americanizations to occur anywhere. Suddenly, Germany again became a model pupil of liberalism, this time including political liberalism by assuring the thorough protection of human rights and parliamentary responsibility of any government. It abolished price controls and rationing more quickly and de-nationalized public enterprises more systematically than Britain, the standard-bearer of economic liberalism in Europe according to the literature on the varieties of capitalism. At the time, Britain was far above the German level of ruin, destitution, and poverty. Before Thatcher came to power, it was Britain that publicly owned enterprises to a large extent and in a less economically liberal fashion, whereas Germany had become the shining example of denationalization in Europe. Germany abolished cartels, split up industrial groups even before the Federal Republic was founded in 1949, and instituted in 1957 the most elaborate watchdog over the practice of competition and avoidance of monopolistic behaviour in Europe (the Bundeskartellamt). But this liberalization focused on the order of markets, specifically commodity rather than labour markets, and the behaviour of firms within them. Characteristically and in line with the approach of the ordo-liberal school, it thus both enhanced and restricted contractual freedom; its restrictions served to prevent contracts from limiting competition.

4.12 Continuities or discontinuities in management and organization?

Another piece of institutional furniture affected by Americanization was business and management behaviour. In his work on managers and management in West Germany, Peter Lawrence observed a general reaction during company visits: managers were pleased to learn from the United States, which can be described as having offered a pragmatic but purposeful, unconventional, sober, and analytical approach. Status distinctions in the enterprise lost their legitimacy, social conventions were more critically examined and adapted to help solve problems, and unreflective practices were changed to comply with a perceived functional rationale. Social relations and business practices became less personalized and more matter-of-fact.[227] Lawrence himself has rightly wondered whether this fascination with American practices was not related to the urge to do two things at once: first, sincerely to leave behind the vestigial constraints of older conventional methods and of the Nazi *Führerprinzip*, which had been strengthened within companies; second, to legitimate in a new way some populist and more egalitarian codes that had evolved continuously under the auspices of non-liberal populism, culminating under the Nazis. It will not have been easy for social actors to distinguish these two motives, for egalitarian populism was laden with connotations of both American and Nazi types of modernization.

In the drive to forget their shameful past and get things done that needed doing which typified much of the post-war period, Germans found enthusiasm for American solutions ideal for enacting what appeared to be 'sensible' and avoiding any entanglement in 'ideological' reflections. Also, the interest in America was not radically new. There had already been close relations between German and US industrial groups, even beyond the moment when Germany declared war on the United States, and the populism that had built up in Germany viewed energetic American business practices as familiar if not a model to emulate in its combination of ruthlessness and opportunities to get ahead, even for the 'common man' if he proved himself effective and forceful. It would be worth investigating the extent to which Americanization in business and management behaviour was thus a convenient way of developing and adapting solutions which also had domestic roots. Interestingly, one of the major post-war normative conceptualizations of 'sound business and management practice', which at the time engrossed prominent American gurus such as Austrian-born Peter Drucker, was the *Harzburger Modell*. This was certainly not presented as a 'German model' but as a universalistic doctrine. The 'model' was developed under the leadership of a former SS officer from the war economy management (Reinhard Höhn). A continuity of personnel was also maintained in business for the most part.

With regard to business and management tools, much of European post-war reconstruction was, of course, inspired by the Marshall Plan (European Recovery Program). This implied not only direct relief and loans but also a large-scale drive to upgrade productivity in Europe. In all of the participating countries, consultancies were set up to act as mediators between American methods of productivity increase and local firms in Europe. There was thus a systemic drive to align European firms with more American methods of management and production in the expectation that this would lead to an economic growth that fed on both latent or suppressed consumption needs and more efficient production. Later, this pattern was called the 'Fordist mode of regulation' and stipulated that efficient production in a competitive economy can be used to reduce or reverse price increases and increase wages at the same time, so that latent demand is always there to buy what efficient production can manufacture on a grand scale.[228] Productivity increase on the supply side and latent demand and ability-to-pay on the demand side are key conditions for this to occur.

In the Marshall Plan countries, this gave a new impetus to productivity development and generally promoted the growth of consultancies.[229] Djelic's analysis for France reads as if productivity development was indeed more of an 'imported' toolbox.[230] For Germany, she shows that from 1950 the RKW (*Rationalisierungs-kuratorium der Wirtschaft*) was active as an official promoter of productivity thinking in the economy and as an agency aiding the Marshall Plan effort.[231] However, the RKW was far from new; it had already existed before the war under the same acronym but a slightly different title: *Reichskuratorium für Wirtschaftlichkeit*. For both Weimar industrialists and the Nazis had also thought of productivity development. Next to the RKW, there were a host of other national institutions (REFA for work study and industrial engineering; DATSCH and DINTA for technical education in colleges and within industry). Corresponding to productivity promotion, Nazi economic and social policy strove for consumerism and large-scale production. However, consumerism also conflicted with wage and price controls and particularly with massive rearmament. Mass-production consumerism was epitomized by package holidays, the 'people's radio' (*Volksempfänger*) and the 'people's car' (*Volks-wagen*) which, however, had to wait until after the war to enter civilian mass production. Before US multinationals invested more heavily in Europe, there was clearly no other place in Europe that could match Germany in the emulation of macro-regulation and productivity-enhancing Fordism.

A part of Nazi corporate architecture in the past, the rebaptized RKW now figured as a massive countrywide consultancy jointly supervised by employers and trade unions. It is difficult to tell whether productivity measures promoted by the RKW before and after the war differed greatly. Undoubtedly, anyone expressing an opinion on it after the war would have been led to suggest that there were important differences, for the Marshall Plan provided for study trips to the United States that constituted one of the greatest 'perks' to be awarded to anyone. It also enabled one to learn directly about advanced mechanization and sophisticated mass-production operations, which at that time were few and far between in Europe. We still need to ask about the extent to which advanced American methods could be transferred to Europe without substantial adaptation and change. This is not to suggest that the RKW continued doing precisely what it had done before. In all likelihood, it was a gradual change from Nazi productivity policies to Marshall Plan ones, and Germans will have found it easy and convenient to extol their enthusiasm for things American. This required little actual behavioural re-orientation and was rewarded with approval by the new powers, because it was visibly consequential for successful practice.

West Germany was full of similar cases of the piecemeal adaptation of established practices combined with an enthusiastic conversion to an Anglo-American programme. 'Normal' German collaborators and activists in the war effort could thus smoothly 'reinvent' and clean up their practices, providing that they reinvented them as American-style management. Once the former ideology was cast aside, the populist instincts and institutions that had already been instilled could still function very well. The same thing happened in East Germany, where former Nazi activists were likewise welcome to forsake, with strong disdain, the regime that had 'misled and betrayed' them, and swear allegiance to communism. The apparatus of mass mobilization and control that emerged owed as much to the Soviet Union as it did to the populism of Nazi Germany in lessons learnt about the techniques of mass rallies via the control of industries to obligatory all-inclusive social welfare.

4.13　Partitioning, domestic institutions, and internationalization

In the process of maintaining the balance between international influence and the assertion of domestic culture and institutions, intricate interrelationships become evident. At times and with regards to some aspects, the scales are tipped clearly in favour of domestic assertion, whereas at other times and in other respects, internationalization weighs heavier in the balance. More recently, the line that partitions societal space and specifies a new division of meaning across different institutions has lain between regulation of markets for goods and regulation governing production factors, both capital and labour. In the older non-liberal regime, cartelization, collective bargaining, and corporatism could be seen as adhering to the same principle: restriction of competition was meaningful everywhere, for it helped to steady economic cycles, protect economic and social resources from being swamped in business downturns, and maintain workable competition in a world that required long-term stability for investment and development. Now, the regulation of product markets has become separated from that governing the production of human and capital resources, including productive interrelationships between the public and the business world and between different businesses. Thus, on the front of corporatism and industrial relations, we see a thorough renovation and intensification of domestic models.

The elements and logic of recent corporatist capitalism in Germany have been summarized extremely well by Streeck.[232] They include:

- collective bargaining over wages and other conditions by unions and employers' associations that represent and de facto encompass the entire industry; bargaining takes place mainly above the plant and company levels to achieve something approaching comparable wages for comparable work in all companies.
- an economy-wide and compulsory system of chambers acting as quasi-governmental institutions but based on membership in both voluntary and compulsory associations. These regulate a number of specific tasks, notably the administration of vocational education and training, both at entry levels (apprenticeship) and at intermediate levels (technical shop-floor supervision and management, *Meister*; commercial and administrative specialists; *Fachwirte*).
- pervasive tripartite co-responsibility of employers, unions, and the government in regulating and managing vocational education and training, social security, general health insurance, and national employment services.

- co-determination and joint consultation in enterprises by comparatively strong and unified works councils and employee-elected supervisory board members ('nearly' half of the board members in large joint-stock companies, one-third in smaller ones).

In addition, it must be noted that there exists a network of cross-holdings of shares among large industrial groups, meant to stabilize ownership interests in view of the possibility of an aggressive, unfriendly takeover by outside interests via the stock market.[233] Bank participation in the share capital of those companies that it services with loans (house bank, *Hausbank*) is also part of this pattern, as is the practice of financing investments out of bank loans as far as possible, without incurring the risk of undercapitalization.

Altogether, the type of institutional order that sums up such characteristics is the 'socially coordinated market economy' as set out by Whitley.[234] In this type of order, Whitley combines two sorts of business systems, one found mainly in the South Germanic bedrock, the other in Scandinavia. The German business system clearly shows the effects of its feudal history, which has produced a corporatist structure rich with derivatives of guilds and legal linkages between government and organizations representing business interests. In Scandinavia, weak feudalism has led to a prevalence of regulation in industrial relations on the basis of voluntary, fundamental collective agreements.

So, is what we find for Germany after 1945 an intermediate order, situated between radical liberalization and neo-corporatism while including and integrating unions and employee representatives even more than in the past and shedding the dictatorial vestiges of Nazism and the non-liberal heritage of the Second Reich and the Weimar Republic? On average and across the board, Germany holds an intermediate position. However, such a general analysis does not contribute much towards explaining what the business system means or how its division of meaning is significant and perceived to be such by actors.

At this point, the partitioning of institutional spaces becomes very important because the co-determined neo-corporatism involved in the generation and allocation of all types of productive resources has come to be a non-liberal or less liberal complement to a new and very liberal order of product markets. It is complementary, rather than being merely different in form and governing principles, with regard to the sphere of economic competition in product markets. Evidently, actors set the institutional scene to generate human and capital resources in a non-liberal way, in order to confront heightened competition in goods markets. The world of non-market social coordination was thus enacted as a backdrop from which to launch into free competition more securely. The logic binding such opposite and complementary forces together into a meaningful ensemble is again set within the long-term metatradition indicated earlier: the visibly wide swings in the see-sawing between liberalization and corporatist quasi-government achieves partitioned articulation of distinct principles and thereby elevates the whole economy and society to a higher level of functioning. It does this on the basis of an innovative partitioning and recombination, which again turns out to be a central mechanism of societal differentiation.

This differentiation does not simply imply a partitioning into institutional spheres, occupations, strata, etc. It is a more creative and refined division of meaning, such that different meanings are allocated to parts of partitioned institutional domains but are nevertheless complementary and thus contribute to an overarching meaning. When actors intuitively or explicitly acknowledge this coherence and take it for granted, they enact societal community and identity. In practice, actors are not always consciously aware of such partitioning and divided meanings, and this is one of the most prevalent sources of intersocietal prejudice based on misunderstandings. The consumption and sale of alcohol in public places has been highly partitioned in time and space in Britain, just as humour and irony have been in Germany. The biggest mistake a foreign visitor can make is to generalize a contrast that is specific to a time and place.

Note also that international forces are again inextricably bound up with domestic ones in Germany and are more identity-enhancing over the medium and long run than is admitted in the habitually short-term discussion of the striking changes that have taken place within a 'German model' regardless of the version. The overlap between American and German variants of populism and approaches to mass society is a case in point. The 1950s and 1960s are a time best characterized as one in which the German population displayed an extremely weak conscious identification with Germanness. The importance of German tradition and symbols and the degree of national consciousness and pride reached an all-time low, and most people concurred that the country was becoming Americanized. Marx would have called this 'false consciousness'. Tacitly, actors still contrived to re-enact societal identity through a process of trial and error, and they only became fully aware of its new meaning explicitly and consensually when the post-war 'German model' was becoming mature. Despite the programmatic designs about a 'social market economy' earlier on, the creation of this model implied a great amount of pragmatic tinkering, painful compromise, and heated debate. The partitioning and its logic had no visionary advocate to foresee and achieve it.

4.14   Catastrophe, the quest for stability, and 'unitary federalism' in division and unity

The process just analysed is marked by a catastrophic point of departure, as processes of societal innovation have been on several occasions. In Germany this was particularly evident as the start of the Thirty Years' War brought the Middle Ages to a definite end. It may even be that the extent of the catastrophe spurs on the mechanism of partitioning and recombination and the close intertwining of international incursion and domestic assertion to the point where they are hard to distinguish in places. It is again significant that this has helped rather than prevented the development of German identity in institutions and culture, with the recombination of strong variants of both liberalism and corporatism. We can take this as further attestation of the impossibility of adhering to 'models' that overstate the generic pervasiveness and concrete stability of institutional arrangements.

Germans are often attributed or attribute to themselves—with pride, self-flagellation, or a measure of both—a penchant for order and stability. While this is undeniable, it also has to be appreciated as a safeguard against the chaos to which the nation has been subjected and which it has helped to produce much more than any other nation in Western Europe. In this part of Europe during the previous century, Germany experienced the greatest degree of forced and voluntary migration, civilian and military loss of life, destruction and reconstruction. Precisely because it has been uprooted like no other West European society since the late Middle Ages, one finds a compulsion to seek refuge in more stable arrangements or in the illusion of their presence. What is more, the heritage in the South Germanic bedrock, with its close intertwining of hierarchical governance and lateral peer-group coordination, and of governance mechanisms linking aggregate society and entities at lower layers, has equipped this society with the cultural and institutional tools to launch itself out of chaos and into a socially accepted order.

By the end of the 1950s, the new apparatus of German economic and social institutions was reasonably complete. It was two-pronged, with one prong pointing towards liberalism to an extent unparalleled in Europe, and the other towards corporatism, collective bargaining, co-determination, and the welfare state to a degree comparable only to Sweden at the time. The 'Janus-Faced' new West German societal order was, as chance would have it, probably ideal for entering the European Economic Community, which started to become a reality just as the two-pronged institutional apparatus was being completed. West Germany was prepared for free competition, and it had a system for generating human and other resources that emphasized concerted regularity and abundant supply. Although this interpretation is overly stylized, it helps make sense of the cliché about the founding of the EEC: German manufacturing needed a larger free market, and French agriculture needed a larger market accompanied by protection and subsidies.

For the sake of simplicity I have left to one side the conceptual challenge of the division of Germany and its reunification. The German Democratic Republic has surely left behind a layering of elements of culture and some soft institutions. But in a society in which division of rule and domination has been pervasive throughout its history and was even aggravated as modernity developed, despite increasing unification of the language and other cultural domains, the division of Germany was not a radically new phenomenon, nor did it last long. Although the Iron Curtain was nearly impenetrable, more than four million East German citizens did migrate to the West, and cultural and economic links were never completely severed. As state socialism experienced more and more difficulty and became increasingly dependent on West German subsidies, loans, and demands for importable goods, communication between East and West even intensified. This makes it possible to pinpoint precisely the demise of the GDR, namely at the moment in 1990 when the penultimate government (under Modrow as prime minister) did not obtain an urgently needed loan from West Germany.[235] From then on, a conjunction of financial constraints and popular demands left no choice but to reunify. In 1990, Germany was again a consolidated nation state with uncontroversial borders. That has come about not in spite of the fact that, but because, it is solidly embedded in international treaties and the EU. Again, this interdependency of national consolidation and international networks of alliances is not new to Germany. Its topical manifestation is unification through international integration, which incidentally also appears to have solved for good what I dare to call 'the Austrian question'.[236]

Another line of continuity has been the complexity of German federal states. The dominant position of Prussia has disappeared, since Prussia itself vanished by order of the Allied Military Government.[237] Arguably, Germany is now more federal than it was in 1932 when the *Reich* government—a conservative one— deposed the Prussian government, which had been a Social Democratic one. The sixteen states remaining or newly formed after 1945 are more similar in size, although a couple of very small and possibly unviable states remain. Here too, we witness institutional partitioning and recombination, for what Germany received concurrently was the greater importance of federal states and greater centralization: the 'unitary federation'.[238]

4.15 Summary

The German metatradition has been described and analysed here as a successive combination of economic liberalism with mercantilism and corporatism. Emphases on the respective elements have shifted over time, such that corporatism had its heyday between 1880 and 1945, and liberalism between about 1820 and 1870 and then again after 1945. In addition to oscillations between them, it is striking that they have entered into combinations specific to certain periods and then escalated each other. Similar to the recombination of corporatism with liberalism and rooted in the same historical configuration analysed in the last chapter is the ongoing theme of a lateral peer control that is closely articulated with hierarchical control within a societal space subject to layering and the retrenchment of societal horizons. Layering and retrenchment have alternated and been interdependent as horizons of action have expanded internationally.

Like earlier periods in German history, the nineteenth century was one of systematic interrelations between domestic influences and foreign incursions to an extent that it often is difficult to tell them apart. Much as the end of the nineteenth century was a period of great nationalism, the culture and institutions it brought forth were the unmistakeable products of foreign (notably French and English) models mingling with the domestic heritage. Similarly, the institutions arising after 1945 were equally pervasive products of domestic populist corporatism and American models. Furthermore, if we do not consider the embeddedness of institutional origins in international conflict, war, and its aftermath, it is difficult to explain how the development of institutions could be biased by social and political coalitions in particular ways. This also means that learning, convergence, and subsequent or parallel divergence occur between former or bitter enemies as much as or possibly more than between allies.

This dialectical evolution in the South Germanic bedrock has set the scene for the culture and institutions that we find in the worlds of work, management and organization, and industrial relations. The latter worlds can be visualized and explained as being subject to the same but continually reconstructed metatradition. It is continually reconstructed in the precise way that action spaces are partitioned and filled with new institutional combinations. More recently in history, the liberalization of markets has increasingly focused on product markets whereas corporatism and national regulation have become more extensive with regard to the construction of productive assets: human resources in particular, but also capital generation.

5
The Governance of Work Systems

5.1 Introduction

Work systems are related to larger political and social structures and processes. One of the most highly regarded texts positing alternatives in the design of work systems, written by Michael Piore and Charles Sabel, traces patterns of 'flexible specialization' back to the Jeffersonian ideal of 'yeoman democracy'. This is a democracy for a population of small and independent farmers who, as citizens, not only have their individual interests at heart but also those of both the local community and the society as a whole.[239] Let us trace the full historical meaning of 'yeomanry'. It is an old English term for independent farmers living outside manorial estates. It is also a term for certain cavalry regiments in the British army, recruited from yeomanry circles, since this was a population known to be loyal to the king and voluntarily receptive to military discipline and leadership. In the countryside, they were the royalists, and they volunteered for service in the cavalry, which afforded a great deal of freedom of movement and glamour but also demanded more individual responsibility and commitment. Even after World War II, the British army had tank regiments (former cavalry regiments) called yeomanries.

By their appeal to yeomanry, Piore and Sabel intend to champion a more egalitarian distribution of knowledge, responsibilities, and rewards. However, they fail to realize that the yeomanry ideal was already a romantic one when Jefferson used it. As for the historical reality of yeomanry, recognition of royal authority was combined with civic, social, and economic freedom; a more authoritarian pattern was thus linked to a more egalitarian one. My grandfather was a Prussian yeoman, from a village in the Altmark where, surprisingly, fertile soil existed alongside independent farming. Here, too, existed the same pattern of loyalty to the monarchy and military service in the cavalry, as part of a commitment to the community. Respect and obedience each had their institutional and cultural domain, and so did collective deliberation and power. However, Jeffersonian yeoman democracy would have been considered an illusion, as it would have been in the English yeomanries, because the authoritarian pattern was complementary to the egalitarian one, and these were linked through partitioning of societal space, as I have explained in the previous chapters.

Work systems are subject to this regularity, too, and their own partitioning is closely related to the institutional landscape of other action systems. In a realistic perspective on work systems, yeomanry stands for a striking co-evolution of hierarchical and peer control, which we find in parts of England as much as in Scandinavia or Prussia. It will have qualitatively different forms in different societies. Still, it is a particularly suitable point of departure for the analysis of work systems in Germany, a society which is easiest to misunderstand if one is focused on the contrast between hierarchical and peer control. This then is the purpose of this chapter: to link the analysis of work systems with governance and show that German work systems are governed by a metatradition with strong interrelations between hierarchical, peer group, and professional coordination, and to show what this has implied for work systems ever since German work systems have been systematically compared with others.

5.2   The meaning and structures of work systems

Work systems are, on the one hand, action systems. They hinge on the differentiation of jobs and tasks in structures and processes, and on their integration into a larger meaningful ensemble. The term 'work systems' is also used in the literature with regard to institutional entities such as factories, plants, companies, and service establishments. Such institutional entities *have* or *share* work systems, in addition to other action systems. Work systems also extend across institutional entities. This is not primarily because workflow links institutional entities or subentities with one another. Instead, it is meaning, as constitutive of action systems, which cuts across the institutional 'containers of people' and capital that are organizational entities.[240]

To speak of work systems may imply a somewhat artificial distinction between the world of work and other spheres of society, its economy and polity. This is not what is intended. Specific meanings connect in a way that is different from, say, communication lines or electronic circuitry. They do not run through isolated lines but, to adopt another metaphor, spread like waves. Specific action systems are therefore not separable from one another. To that extent, a term like 'work system' might falsely be taken to imply more isolation or separability than is intended. However, work is the essence of human existence, as Marx would have said; according to his definition of work, it is a process that generates value and constitutes both individual identity and social relations for human beings, who both playfully and purposefully engage with the natural and social environment. This is why it is pragmatically convenient to unravel meaningful action systems from this end. It does not imply any primacy a priori. One could just as well start from another focal point of action systems. One example would be social stratification, i.e. the differential distribution of material and other resources such as generalized status. Stratification has consequences for the division of labour, and vice versa.

While the organization and work sciences (in management, sociology, psychology, and industrial engineering) generously use the term 'work systems' to designate a field of enquiry and theory from the perspective sketched out here, the term is highly ambiguous. On the one hand, work systems are institutional entities: work groups, departments, plants, enterprises, public agencies, firms of professionals, and many more. They are concrete and well-defined entities that transform input into output, and are subdivided into smaller entities. On the other hand, socio-technical theory has considered work systems to be decomposable into, say, a technical and a sentient subsystem. These are clearly aspect or action subsystems: technical subsystems are not subunits but consist of technical equipment and work functions, whereas the sentient subsystem consists of the social relations and identity of the participants.[241] Even minute acts of work thus simultaneously have both a technical and a sentient aspect.

As action systems, work systems are not bounded as rigidly as are organizational and institutional entities. Since the literature treats them as both action systems and entities, they are systemically ambivalent, meaning they are open and closed at the same time, as one of the classics has expressed it.[242] In organization theory, the implications have not been appreciated as much as they ought to be, except by authors such as de Leeuw.[243] We need to distinguish two sides much more rigorously. As action systems, bounded by a reference point in terms of meaning, work systems extend across institutional boundaries into the wider fabric of society. Indeed, socio-technical systems theory, as exemplified in the work of the Tavistock Institute or experiments in Norway, has always had an interest in larger societal challenges or demands that aim towards reorganization and upgrading of skills and knowledge. For this reason, it is inevitable to look at work systems as societal action systems. They overlap with institutional work systems, which are social entities. However, overlap means that work systems as social entities are not confined to work action systems, and that work action systems are not confined to social entities.

Work systems are subject to 'governance' like any other systemic construction in society since, as pointed out in Chapter 2, action systems need to be 'furnished' by institutions. They are governed by government and quasi-governmental entities, by associated groups of employers and employees; they are subject to soft or hard institutional norms. Even when their configuration results from ideal-typical individual bargaining between contracting parties, it is embedded within an institutional framework that may be legitimate or contestable, but is in any case tangible and understandable. Work systems are thus best understood if we follow the general heuristic explained in Chapter 2: we understand social, economic, and political phenomena much better if we trace how action systems relate to an institutional order by mapping out the division of labour in society with regard to the division of meaning. This gives the chapter a focus that allows us to control the ambiguity inherent in the notion of work systems.

With regard to the action-systemic side of work, there are, in principle, no limits to decomposition into subsystems or subspaces. As long as a meaningful enactment of a subsystemic reference can be ascertained, there are grounds for putting forward a subspace. To visualize how institutional domains, institutional entities, and action systems or spaces are distinct and interrelated, it is convenient to refer to Figure 5.1.[244] It originated in a text focused on innovation; hence the centrality of the innovation space. This is the only graphical representation of societal analysis that shows how spaces, domains, and levels of aggregation, such as the enterprise and society, should be conceived. Of course, a different space can shift to the centre and innovation to the periphery. 'The outer triangle depicts the societal context of the enterprise; the enterprise figures as the inner triangle which in its centre figures the space of innovation; this latter comes about through interdependencies between technical professionalization and "organized creativity"'.[245]

Note that every one of the terms in the inner triangle could be visualized as being split up into an action space and an institutional domain, in the same way as are the ellipses in the corners of the outer triangle. As noted earlier, societal analysis is pragmatic about the typology of spaces and domains and its variation depending on

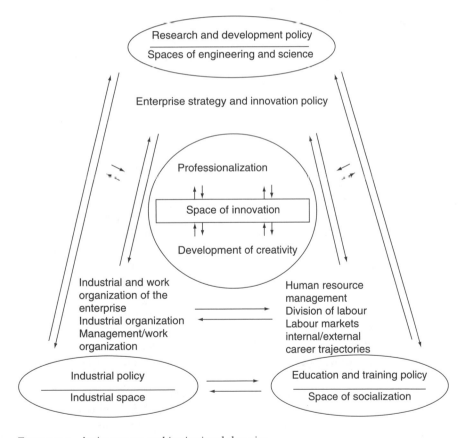

FIGURE 5.1. Action spaces and institutional domains

a specific explanatory task. The main thing is to bear in mind reciprocal interactions between spaces and across levels of aggregation. There follows a simple explanation of work systems as societal action subsystems or spaces.[246] This does not take into consideration institutional domains and entities, whereas Figure 5.1 does.

The action subsystem or space of *organizing* denotes both process and structure, i.e. principles underlying the subdivision of work into jobs, groups, departments, or other subsets, and their integration. These may vary between being vertical or horizontal, more or less differentiated, segmented or overlapping, or may vary in the way they are controlled (mutual adjustment, standardization of rules, standardization of skills, direct supervision, decentralization of responsibility, standardization of culture). These are different pieces of furniture filling the organizing space, and they always possess an institutional quality that is rigid or soft or both.

The space of *socialization* combines all practices that are meaningfully geared to socializing individuals into the successive roles they adopt in their biographical trajectory. Socialization occurs with regard to familial roles, political roles, work roles, leisure roles, and others. We can imagine socialization being divided into more subsystems. The aims of socialization can also be short-term or long-term, ranging from preparation for another job just one level higher on the salary scale that does not require special training, to participation in an extensive course outside a work entity in preparation for a wider occupational field. Again, socialization spaces have to be seen as being furnished with a wide variety of institutional practices, ranging from informal help and sanctions by parents, colleagues, and superiors, to formal curricula, entry and exit exams, diplomas, and entitlements.

Labour market and employment relations denote the spaces defined by the differentiated allocation of work tasks, compensation, and other working conditions to working persons. It includes both self-employment and salaried work and internal and external labour markets, as well as all procedures to include joint consultation, co-determination, and bargaining within working conditions. Accordingly, it stretches from the more confined space of a work group to the extended space of the economic and social order. John Dunlop first conceived of labour market and employment relations as an action system, which he called an industrial relations system.[247] Dunlop saw this action system, in the functionalist spirit of the time, as increasingly congealing into an institutional system. The present analysis, as explained in Chapter 2, stresses that the action system always transcends the institutional system. Institutional entities are closed and more autonomous whereas action systems are open and bind all action to far-flung interdependencies.

The *technical or engineering space* consists of anything that contributes to the development, design, operation, and maintenance of technical artefacts, and can be extended to include science spaces. According to Woodward's definition of technology, this space dovetails with technical artefacts themselves and with the logic and knowledge underlying their design, operation, production, and maintenance.[248] It should also be conceived as dovetailing with a more static aspect involving the maintenance of a given state of technology and innovation, i.e. the continued change of technical artefacts and routines. Although it is difficult to conceive of technical artefacts themselves as a type of human action, Woodward's concept makes it clear that, at least through their constructed logic, technical artefacts do imply meaningful human action and are, in a way, their visible substrate, but one whose constructed nature imposes restrictions on action. This takes us into the institutional system of technology, one which provides the action system with furniture by positing restricting and facilitating conditions. These are not only 'natural' but vested in technical norms, heuristics, standards, and conventions.

There are no limits to imagining other action systems beyond those indicated in Figure 5.1. *Social stratification* would be one, to the extent that societies have a meaningful conception of allocating status and rewards to positions. This subsystem is close to socialization and labour and employment relations, but it is also cross-related to all the others. There is also a *financial action system* within which funds are generated and distributed within and across organized entities and other econom-ically active subjects. Although neglected in the literature of societal analysis, it has very much come to the fore in studies on the varieties of capitalism and on business systems. There is an *industrial system* of coordinating activities, by markets, alliances, ownership relations, other corporate governance, integration or disintegration in the industrial chain of activities; this is already included in the lower left corner of Figure 5.1.

All of these systems should be understood first as action systems that are distinct from related institutional domains, such as organized classes, financial institutions, and industrial sector associations. This distinction is not made in the bulk of literature on business systems and varieties of capitalism. This is a weakness, because the position on institutional stability and change, path dependency and path independency, thereby remains vague. Societal analysis is categorical about the distinction between action spaces and institutional domains. This distinction dia-lectically resolves the ambiguities found in the literature on the varieties of capit-alism and business systems; as we have seen, this design is necessary if we are properly to conceive partitioning and recombination as mechanisms that generate non-identical reproduction, which enables us to define paradoxical combinations of continuity and change within a metatradition.

Aspects relating to financial and industrial systems are covered in the next chapter, on corporate governance. These also imply action systems and institutional entities (industries, sectors, supervisory boards and boards of management, regula-tory agencies) but are analytically distinct. What was said above applies here, too: an action space that is in principle blank is furnished with institutions. Despite their loose coupling, such institutions become meaningful and evolve conjointly by being attached to action spaces that are more tightly coupled. Such ties make even revolutionary decoupling possible in an evolutionary trajectory, because they ensure the meaningful coherence of disparate furniture in different institu-tional domains. This happens when meaning is rapidly reverberated across action systems, thus giving institutions an emic 'slant'. This slant makes them coherent with other institutions across domains. This coherence includes the dialectical coherence occasioned by partitioning and recombination, when according to the Kamchatka effect, opposites are located close together.

5.3 Societally specific work systems: comparing the incomparable

To identify, explain, and track the development of societal work systems or any other construction requires an adequate comparative methodology and research design. These are anything but easy to obtain. Comparison implies a logic stating why certain kinds of supposed facts are to be compared with certain others in order to generate certain kinds of statements. The point to be made here is that such a logic is unavoidably paradoxical, a point which has been forcefully made by Maurice.[249] Paradox in this case means that implementation of a clear and consistent methodology leads to a revision of the methodological foundations originally posited because of the insights that arise and the further research that is thereby stimulated. The paradox results from the dilemma that we basically have to compare the incomparable and, in the beginning, to present these as being comparable.

How this works can be explained on the basis of the theoretical foundation provided in earlier chapters and by using the metaphor of interior architecture and furniture. In order to be lucid, any kind of comparison requires a statement about what the phenomena to be compared have in common. We can compare apples with oranges once we can classify both as 'fruit'; we can then compare their shape, colour, outer layer, sugars, acids, and other components. Comparison across societies makes it difficult to establish comparability on the basis of institutions, for these are different both by definition and empirically. We need something more abstract, something quasi-universal that does not discriminate between those societies which have it to a greater or lesser extent. Action systems provide, pragmatically and rather systematically, such an abstract definition as a point of departure. It is precisely their distinction from institutional entities that qualifies them as useful comparative angles. If we can legitimately define a space of socialization as an action system that all human societies have, then we have a grasp on selecting all the institutions and entities that have a bearing on socialization.

Likewise, we can establish other action systems as points of departure. The comparisons of societal analysis used in this study to understand the historical background started by homing in on the 'wage relation' (*rapport salarial*) as an abstract space permitting many institutional manifestations.[250] This excludes a comparison with societies that do not have wage labour, which did not pose a problem because the societies being compared (France and Germany in the 1970s) did have wage labour. On closer inspection, it may be found that an abstract and institutionally neutral action system (in this case, the wage and employment relation) does have an institutional foundation, in this case wage labour, which is not universally valid and thus eliminates some societies from the comparison. One does not have to venture deep into the Amazon jungle to find societies without wage labour coexisting with other, contemporaneous societies. The Athenians had

wage labour and money when they were fighting the Spartans during the Pelo-
ponnesian Wars, whereas the Spartans did not; this was something these societies
did not have in common, even though they shared a societal horizon with similar
languages, myths, deities, and ceremonies such as the Olympic 'games'.

In the 1970s both France and Germany did have wage labour, which made it
possible to classify the wage relation as an abstract space on which to base a
comparison of institutions. This is a bit like saying that flats have bedrooms, living
rooms, a kitchen, and a bathroom, which defines an abstract and supposedly
universal, functional purpose, so that we can then set about comparing how
differently they are furnished and decorated, from one building or society to
another. This is the way sound comparisons have often worked: you compare
different institutions and institutional entities on the basis of their being different
manifestations within the abstract space of one or more action systems. The latter
form a quasi-universal, comparative grid that assures the comparability of the
former. Now, how would we make Athenian and Spartan society comparable?
We would formulate a more abstract action space allowing for both moneyed and
other forms of exchange and attribution of compensation. Call it a 'space of
exchange and reciprocal obligations'. Such a phrase would have made it possible
to identify a more abstract action system.

On some occasions, it may be more appropriate to define action systems that
are quite obviously institutionally specific. For instance, we could choose to
compare 'metal-working' (the truly socio-technical problem of turning steel
and other metals into meaningful parts, components, and products, by various
techniques of cutting, turning, milling, grinding, processing, finishing, etc.) from
one society to another. This is quite acceptable once we pragmatically accept that
the comparison is not truly universal, but limited to those societies that do have
metal-working. More specifically, this is the logic used to define which comparisons are pertinent here. We can designate any action system to be a point of
departure—be it steel-making, the wage labour relationship, manufacturing,
the application of microelectronics, or anything else—provided it is institutionally
neutral.

Another problem is to make sure that the breadth of a comparison corresponds to
the coverage of culture and institutions in the societies being compared. It is
important to avoid anything that narrows the results of the comparison to too
specific a domain—for example, that which is shown to be valid for large firms but
not for small firms, or that which applies to the processing industries but is the
opposite of what applies to small-batch production. This problem is usually avoided
or diminished in importance by basically using two alternative research design
principles that can be combined. One is careful random sampling of all the
investigated units implied by an action system. Another is the matched-pair
technique of studying cases; the technique prescribes the selection of units in all
of the pertinent domains that are known or must be assumed to vary with regard to
the empirical facts to be established. The latter is suitable for more qualitative
methods of collecting information in depth, whereas the former is suitable for the

standardized collection of information. Comparisons of societal analyses have included the collection of standardized data and qualitative information.

By definition, such comparisons aim to identify and explain what is societal, rather than what is rooted in very specific conditions. If someone had shown in 1960 that Germany had a very small aircraft industry compared to Britain and France, then this would have been easily explained by the fact that Germany had been utterly defeated in World War II and consequently forbidden to engage in any aircraft production whatsoever. Therefore, the industry had been thoroughly dismantled, except where it could convert products to civilian use.[251] This allows us to pinpoint a precise cause for differences, but the question is whether it is a societal one. The cause is historical and specific, and the explanation is therefore not societal in the way theoretically presented here. However, such incidental events may certainly trigger societal effects. This means that their effect reverberates through all the action systems and their institutional furniture. This, and continuity over time, has to be demonstrated in order for a societal effect to be credible.

In this case, Germany's aircraft industry did experience a comeback given NATO's demand for German rearmament and the procurement policies of the Ministry of Defence and the mounting of the Airbus consortium in the late 1960s. So, the effect in this case may have been incidental and temporary. Yet incidental events may have enduring and pervasive effects. Germany had been stripped once before of large sectors of its aircraft industry, in 1918, but one industry not forbidden under the Treaty of Versailles was the building and operation of glider planes. This became an industry (first a cottage one, then a more technically advanced one) in which Germany has become increasingly dominant. It was an industry in which artisan experimentation was vital and closely linked to applied research. This has become characteristic of German work systems. Societal effects are involved here. They may well have historically unique roots in accidental events. But they are societal if such an event has pervasive consequences across the different action systems, leaves a sustained impact on their institutional furniture, and is influenced, in turn, by societal institutions.

5.4   Comparative methodology and types of theory

The explanations produced in societal analysis combine positivist and interpretivist ones, as explained in section 2.2 above. There is the dilemma that action systems and the division of meaning are universal grids on which a comparison can depend, while they are, in fact, historically constructed and, as such, far from universal. Consider this point in light of the rooms-and-furniture metaphor. A 'bathroom' as such is a very abstract space, which serves a purpose that can be described as all-round cleansing of the body. That can be achieved in many ways, and bathrooms are accordingly furnished and equipped with many different and alternative facilities and furniture. But even the purpose of bathrooms can vary; there may be a combination of the cleansing function not only with the function of discharging bodily waste, but also with that of sheer enjoyment and relaxation. In other words, there are no universally valid and stable action-systemic grids; these are themselves subject to social construction. For instance, it is easy to state that the economic space of society is geared to the procurement or production of scarce goods in a utilitarian way, i.e. subject to a rationally calculated ratio of results to effort. This type of economy is an ideal type. Real types deviate in many ways in their emphasis on short-term or long-term benefits, in their differential weighting of different costs and benefits, in preferences for risk-taking and risk avoidance, and also in the absorption of other than utilitarian motives. Therefore, economic action systems are themselves differently constructed, not only in their institutional furniture but in their meaning.

Since we cannot compare something with anything else without a standard, we fall back upon quasi-universal action systems to serve this purpose. They are theoretically postulated tools, ideal types rather than real types. The paradox of science is that it cannot realistically dispense with ideal types or abstractions, or that ideal types turn out to be real types when we apply them in research. Ideal types deliver a comparative logic to start with. They put us on the track of comparing the culture and institutions that furnish the space defined by the targeted action systems, and they help us explain the nature and change of culture and institutions. To give an example, let us define an action space of manufacturing as a grid of comparison, one tightly interrelated with action systems such as organizing and socialization (see above); then we can generate a number of insights into tightly coupled interdependencies and the way culture and institutions in different domains are related to one another.[252]

As we continue the detailed analysis of such relations and deepen the qualitative analysis of culture and institutions, however, we become aware that action systems are constructed differently. A frequently cited result and interpretation in the research of both societal analysis and varieties of capitalism is that shareholder interests are more enmeshed with other stakeholders' interests, and that expectations are rather long term, in what Whitley called the socially coordinated market economy, compared to the liberal 'arm's-length coordinated' Anglo-American economy. We can certainly explain this as being caused by institutional differences. Yet, on closer inspection, it is also hard to resist the interpretation that financial and industrial action systems are tangibly enmeshed more with other systems in socially coordinated market economies, something which applies less to arm's-length coordinated economies. The way and extent that actors themselves differentiate among action systems or bundle them together may vary. Such a diagnosis and explanation would be accepted by scholars of the varieties of capitalism.[253] It adds societally varying constructions of action systems to our list of what is different, for action systems can only be comparable or universal if actors enact them to be such. As we have seen, action systems have a habit of submitting to provincialization.

Actors thus ruin our beautiful point of departure. This happens all the time: we have tried to compare institutions as being 'functionally equivalent' with regard to some purpose or goal but find time and again that their meanings are different.

When the specific meanings attached are different, which on closer scruting they invariably are, then we are comparing the incomparable. Therefore, we cannot help but pretend that comparability is given 'somewhere', as long as we are aware that this is an inevitable postulate which only takes us part of the way, such as in the comparison of financial action systems in Athens and Sparta. During the course of our research, we may shift the concept of an action system in a more abstract direction in order to obtain more universal categories. It is an unendingly paradoxical quest, and it would be futile to pretend that we can proceed differently. With their focus on a singular meaning, action systems are ideal types, but institutional entities and domains are real types. When we use words to qualify action systems, the nature of language itself draws us to real types and this leads us further into a paradoxical quest to obtain more ideal-typical systems by using more abstract language.

Once this is understood and appreciated, readers can be more comfortable with systematic pragmatics. Some theories take pride in the fact that some axioms or theorem-like statements are fairly robust. Such theories are called 'nomothetic', and there definitely is a need for them. They belong to the positivist arm and are present in societal analysis, too. In scientific endeavour, the point is not just to have a thick and robust catalogue of empirically supported theorem-like statements. Alongside nomothetic theory, there is what Weick has called 'theorizing', a more pragmatic reflection based on somewhat ambiguous but evocative and general heuristics. Theorizing has a distinct lineage in management research, dating back to such authors as Roethlisberger, who posited 'clinical knowledge' alongside nomothetic theory. 'Critical theory' is also a variant of theorizing that has strong heuristic foundations and does not aim at unequivocal nomothetic statements. Arguably, it is in fields where the central focus is on human action that this kind of theorizing is an indispensable complement to nomothetic theory. Again, although there is conflict between nomothetic theory and heuristically oriented theorizing, they are dialectically complementary.[254]

Contrary to what is often claimed, nomothetic theory does not primarily produce direct causal knowledge. It mainly posits general functional interdependencies in the form of 'if . . . then . . . ' statements. Even if such a statement does make use of unidirectional causality, the question is where this form of theory is really meaningful. Causal understanding, certainly in the social sciences but also in the natural sciences, is mainly an affair of conjointly applying a set of nomothetic statements. Specific cases exhibit causality whereas generalized relationships are better conceived as interrelationships that express associations in which causality is unclear. The law of universal gravitation tells us nothing about why some objects fall downward in a certain situation and others do not; it merely explains the acceleration of a mobile object in an ideal space, neglecting its shape and the effect of air. Nor does Ohm's law tell us why an electrical fuse blows in one circuit whereas it does not in another. Likewise, organizational change may induce a change in training and competence distribution in one case whereas in another case it does not. If we then add further knowledge on why it is one way or the other, we combine different sorts of knowledge into a purpose-specific bundle to explain an occurrence. Even nomothetic interrelationships are highly contingent. Such contingencies, and the fact that lots of different nomothetic theories have to be combined, make ambiguous and evocative heuristics useful—although they may be fuzzy—in the search for the combination of specific theories and other types of knowledge needed for a specific explanatory task or practical purpose.

In the practice of societal analysis, nomothetic elements have alternated with heuristic theorizing, and the emphasis attributed to one or the other has not been the result of principled adherence, but to the experience that using one has led to results which make application of the other plausible. In short, the refinement of nomothetic research by multivariate analysis may, in practice, lead to highly contextualized (time- and space-dependent) statements about causality,[255] which may not be a bad thing at all. It takes us closer to history but far from the generalization that was intended. The latter may, however, be approximated by combining evocative general heuristics and general functional relationships. However, general theories are then so prolific that the explanation of a specific organization, industry, or society takes us into a specific analysis, which is properly historical.

5.5 The first systematic evidence: steelworks

Systematic comparisons of work systems using state-of-the-art social science methods do not have a long tradition. The first comparative study ever done involved Germany, and it was conducted by an international team that included a pioneer in the field, Frederick Harbison. This study methodologically and substantively set the scene for things to come. It was a comparison of two steel plants, one in the United States and one in Germany: the Indiana Harbor works of Inland Steel and the Dortmund plant of the Dortmund-Hörder Hüttenunion.[256] These were studied in the early 1950s, at a time when both countries had just emerged from the war, the Federal Republic of Germany had just been founded, and all manner of social arrangements were still very much governed by a culture and institutions that had not yet been subjected to the subsequent learning across borders that commenced with the diffusion of American managerial practices. There had, of course, been some reform of economic governance by the occupational powers in Germany, but co-determination of supervisory boards in the steel industry was brand-new, and work systems were presumably being governed to a great degree by the immediate past of the Weimar Republic and the Third Reich.

The plants had roughly the same size of labour force and made similar products, albeit with somewhat different technologies, the American plant being more 'modern' and automated. However, the authors took pains to control for technical diversity and to focus on those differences that would have existed even allowing for some technical differences. It helped a great deal that some of the authors were engineers. In this comparison, one can see in a nutshell the proto-typical implementation of the logic that came to prevail later. Plants were matched as rigorously as possible on the basis of similar products, technology, size, and social and task environments. This was a specification of an action system taken to constitute comparability, in which the selection of entities to be studied was standardized, in this case the making of a certain type of steel at a given scale of operation. The implication of the research design was that observable differences will relate to other action systems, their coupling with steelmaking as an action system, and the institutions that furnish the spaces concerned.

A more conjectural implication at the time was that observable differences could presumably be extended somewhat to other work systems, and possibly to more societal patterns, presumably because institutions were not only specific to steel-making but also related to the construction of culture and institutions beyond the plants and the industry being studied. However, it was uncertain at the time whether it would be possible to present the diagnosis and explanation as being truly societal, because there were no parallel studies of other work systems in other industries. I emphasize the societal aspect more than the authors did, which is not warranted by the study design and results per se but by the striking similarity with many results that were brought to light later on.

Work systems in the first instance imply workers, and at the time there were still a great many of them in evidence in manufacturing industries. The authors reported: 'It is generally conceded that the proportion of the highly skilled workers at DHHU (Dortmund-Hörder Hüttenunion) is much higher than that at Inland Steel, although we did not gather statistical data to support this view. This is explained by the greater investment in labor-saving and skill-saving machinery at Inland and also perhaps by the greater extent of supervision over workers at Inland. The DHHU management relies quite extensively on the all-round skills of trained craftsmen who can carry on their tasks with a minimum of supervision'.[257] In other words, work was regulated at DHHU by more pervasive training of workers, permitting greater scope of operation and more flexible use of labour in different jobs, whereas the predominant instrument of coordination at Inland was the pooling of expertise in specialist functions and more extensive management and supervision. Inland therefore had more management layers and significantly higher percentages of managerial, technical specialist, and clerical employees.

Although Germany had just emerged from the Nazi era, the social coordination of work was clearly more lateral and rooted in professional autonomy and mutual adjustment between skilled workers. Although it is very hard to imagine the social climate of a steel plant at the time in Germany as devoid of hierarchy and authoritarianism, it clearly had a smaller and less differentiated hierarchy than in the United States, which left more tasks to be regulated by the shop floor. The inference one can draw is that authoritarian behaviour in Germany is not necessarily the antidote to lateral coordination. These may instead have co-evolved, linked as they were by the figuration of the foremen (*Meister*) and chargehands (*Vorarbeiter*), emanating from the ranks of the workers and building a powerful bridge between their world and that of the management. The foremen and engineers at Inland had already become socially and educationally more detached from the workers.[258]

The US plant invested proportionately much more into the recruitment and education of managers, engineers, technicians, and foremen, i.e. those who also had a more important role in social coordination.[259] There were fewer highly educated engineers at DHHU, and managers and engineers often had received further education and training at technical college in addition to their earlier work experience and training.

One must not overestimate the role of rigid institutions, such as in education or vocational training, in these matters. At the time of the study, formal occupational training for steelworkers based on national regulation was just emerging. What the authors thus observed, with respect to the greater professionalization of work roles in directly productive functions at DHHU, was an emerging company policy, the culture of the factory, or soft institutions. Of course, even soft institutions always have a societal angle. It was only later in the 1950s that the occupation of steel-mill worker (*Hüttenwerker*) was instituted, complete with apprenticeships and technical school training corresponding to a national profile. The harder and more general institution was thus enacted on the basis of softer ones. Institutions do not usually arrive on the scene by the fiat of important decision-makers. They emerge subtly from the soft end of the institutional spectrum of rigidity. Institutionally more rigid patterns build upon soft emergent patterns. This is again demonstrated by the DHHU case. As they emerge, they reflect societal effects as much as they do the individual considerations of actors, as Chapter 2 noted with respect to the inter-relations between societal analysis and rational choice.

On a different topic, some results of the study probably had to be revised after a number of years had elapsed. The low level of investment in Germany into 'intermediate' occupations and training, which the study had noted, was probably reversed as continuing education and training for foremen became a much more widespread institutional practice. Today, it would be the exception for industrial foremen not to have had further education and training before being appointed. Although it is painful to remember, this is a practice that began to be widely established under the Nazi regime,[260] as part of a drive to combine authority with vocational training. However, that was not its only purpose. The intensified support for promoting advanced education and training, and the regularization of an increasing number of occupations based on earlier training and experience in more 'basic' occupations (*Weiterbildungsberufe*), became the policy pursued by governmental authorities, employers, and unions alike. It corresponded to an older historical motive to link expertise with authority tightly and to use profes-sional specialization to do this. This is an early example of a comparative study pointing to the importance of change over time, but a change which reinforces longer-running tendencies in a novel way.

At the time that Harbison *et al.* conducted their comparison, American foremen were better educated for their jobs, but this difference faded into the background later. Arguably, a course set up by chambers of industry and commerce or specialized colleges to prepare workers for foreman positions is no less solid than a course offered by an American community college or state university. However, the

qualitative differences between nationally specific types of courses are more important than the formalistic comparisons of how many types of employees hold college
or university degrees in different countries. Germany has since seen the proliferation
of further education and training, which has made the upward mobility of employees on the job ladder of their chosen occupation a regularly occurring phenomenon.
This boils down to a pervasive effort to keep employees in occupational fields by
promoting and elevating the quality and reputation of these fields, rather than by
enhancing the individual upward mobility of specific occupations.

In the late 1950s and early 1960s, Marc Maurice conducted a national study of
France as part of a European project studying steel plants on behalf of the European
Community of Coal and Steel. He was also struck by the fact that German plants
purposefully went about professionalizing the occupations of workers and foremen
by providing them with a generally ordained set of competences, functions, training courses, and diplomas, contrary to practices in the other countries. This was the
beginning of his interest in international comparison. Was this a truly societal
phenomenon? Obviously more studies in different industries were needed to
establish that.

5.6   Convergent technology and divergent organization and human resources in NATO

Another piece of comparative evidence, from the military, is half-anecdotal.
NATO offered one splendid opportunity. German rearmament was organized
under the auspices of NATO military doctrines, and it implied the massive adoption of equipment developed or produced elsewhere. Rearmament initiated one of
the first major drives to standardize weapons, technology, and strategy across
countries. Yet, it has gone almost completely unnoticed by students of the internationalization of work systems.

In the German army, much of the heavier equipment in the first half of the 1960s
was of American origin (artillery guns, battle tanks, helicopters). The air force did
not have any combat planes developed in Germany, only foreign ones (the F 84 F,
RF 84, F 86, and later the F 104 G from the United States as well as the Italian G 91).
Probably the most 'internationalized' segment of the army was rocket artillery. At
the time, NATO doctrine still emphasized a heavy nuclear response to an attack.
This not only implied nuclear bombs as standard armament for fighter-bombers but
also nuclear rockets for corps and divisional artillery, and even nuclear warheads for
20.3cm gun shells. Internationalization also included American control over nuclear warheads, to be delivered to German artillery batteries only when higher
NATO commanders ordered their release. The standard rocket for corps artillery at
the time was the Sergeant. Contact between the US and German armies within
NATO took place frequently to compare and adjust maintenance and field practice. In other words, German nuclear rocket artillery batteries functioned much like
the German subsidiary of an American multinational enterprise would, and the
name of this enterprise was NATO.

A close friend of mine happened to do military service in a Sergeant-equipped missile battery. Through regular contact with the US army, he was also able to compare operational practice in both armies with regard to one and the same weapons system. What he reported at the time was strikingly parallel with what could be ascertained in the article by Harbison *et al*. As he related to me in 1966, he was quite surprised to see that the Americans made much greater use of detailed written instructions in their batteries, subdivided jobs more minutely, and relied on a hierarchy of technical specialists and officers to coordinate and control operations. Although there was also a great amount of documentation on equipment in the German artillery batteries, the army trained artillerymen to be more versatile in their job and relied more on occupational competence and mutual adjustment to achieve control.

The experienced comparative scholar would immediately ask: even if technology was absolutely the same, could it be that labour resources used in the two armies were different by nature of recruitment and personnel policies? Interestingly at the time, conscription existed in the US army as it did in the German one. The length of conscript military service was two years in the United States and a year and a half in Germany. If anything, longer conscript service in the US army would have allowed or suggested more pervasive professionalization. But it was the other way round. On the other hand, more of the conscripts in the German batteries had probably done vocational apprenticeships in some kind of technically related occupation since, at the time, apprenticeship was clearly the dominant mode of entering employment. It is not appropriate to speculate further, but it was clear then that the expectation in the German batteries was that every soldier should be required to develop some measure of autonomy and should have already been equipped to do so by his previous civilian socialization.

We also notice similar contrasts in the area of tactical and strategic decision-making, and of the rules and principles governing this. Having experienced the influence and threat of Napoleonic warfare discussed in Chapter 4, Prussian military reformers introduced a practice of 'management by objectives', meaning that field commanders at all levels were given general goals to achieve and the freedom to choose the means at their disposal as long as they complied with general operating principles laid down in instructions. In addition, the career rotation between staff and line work and the co-responsibility of chiefs of staff[261] for command decisions facilitated a closer integration of hierarchical authority with military professionalism in arms (infantry, artillery, cavalry/reconnaissance, etc.) and tactics, as well as the operative, intelligence, logistics, personnel, and training specialities into which staff work became subdivided. We will encounter the tighter link between staff or specialist functions and line or command authority again in section 5.7. While the Prussian army became widely known for schematism and inflexibility, it was nevertheless the one that infused German and to some extent other military traditions with the delegation of responsibility and the flexible adaptation of tactics and strategy to situations; these were construed to be best and most rapidly understood by commanders on the spot.[262] In Germany,

'management by objectives' is actually quite traditional, dating back to the beginning of the nineteenth century. Whereas regular armies are probably unrivalled
exemplars of 'machine bureaucracy' everywhere, the Prussian and later German
army had become increasingly unlike the facile cliché often applied to them. The
relative superiority in both victory and defeat, with regard to any army encountered
in battle after 1813, was built upon a tactical, strategic, and organizational flexibility
that had increasingly emerged by learning from the trauma of defeat at Jena/
Austerlitz, and from the bitter and indecisive trench warfare of World War I.[263]
This was unique and influenced the flexibility of enterprises in a way radically
different from the clichés. In this respect, undeniable militarism in Prussian and
later German society had an effect which is very counter-intuitive: it supported the
build-up and operation of enterprises that, on the whole, proved to be more
flexible than elsewhere, just as the Prussian and German armies have tended to be.

Some authors have suggested that broader culture is built on certain manifestations within it. It has been proposed, for example, that American football tends to
predispose people to perfectionism in the skilful application of standardized set
pieces, while European soccer expresses a culture that tends to instil flexible
variation and combination of tactics and manoeuvres, with mutual adjustment
controlling the operation in addition to the hierarchical authority of a coach,
trainer, or manager in the world of sports and of a commander in the military.[264]
Following the post-Napoleonic reforms, the German military was able to moderate
its defeat and build its success on the professional autonomy of its commanders.
Over time, non-commissioned officers have also become included in this.[265] In the
present German army, courses for senior non-commissioned officers and platoon
leaders at a weapons school are considered equivalent in intensity and status to
the further education and training provided for artisanal and industrial master
craftsmen (*Meisters*).

The contrasts described again imply institutional partitioning. This means that
standardized set pieces and more individually crafted tactics occur in most armies. It
is the various ways they are distributed among functions, people, and situations that
indicates societal differences, in addition to and possibly even more than the relative
frequency of set pieces or individually crafted operations per se. German armies
have tended to use set pieces or standard modules as a stepping stone towards
achieving on-the-spot professional autonomy so that military operations become
adaptable and flexible in the face of changing situations.[266] Therefore, spaces in
work systems subtly alter the institutional and cultural furniture according to the
biography of the professional military personnel or the conscripts, but there is a
great deal of continuity of the furniture from one phase to another. Work systems in
other armies have more substantial gaps, such as between the professional autonomy of special forces and the precisely stipulated, standard operating procedure of
'normal' units. Since the demise of monarchy and the royal guards, Germany has
had few elite units and during the Weimar Republic there were none at all.
Germany has expected normal units to have a rather highly developed skill for
professionally adjusting and adapting to non-standardized contingencies.

In this way, we can see how work and socialization are very tightly coupled as action systems. We can also see how institutional practices in the two different institutional domains evolve through the coupling of action logics. In Germany, the coupling is rooted in the concept that recruits are potential if not actual skilled workers and, even if they have only been to grammar school, they should be trained and used as skilled labour. This responsible autonomy is a necessary complement to hierarchical authority, and the two can be articulated side by side when professional specialization is the basis for hierarchical authority as much as it is for responsible autonomy in ordinary work roles (e.g. gunners, turners, or clerks). Following this logic, continuity and contiguity of vertically ordered occupations govern the furniture of socialization space; in the organizational space, enrichment of roles and mutual adjustment complement hierarchical coordination and relieve it of an overload of centralization or the inertia of bureaucratization.

Such reasoning inevitably engages a societal argument, because the terms of reference address circumstances specific not only to some particular unit or army, but to further-flung expectations or solutions in society. As in the example of the steelworks, the micro-contingencies within the plant, company, combat unit, or army are neither necessary nor sufficient to explain how cultural and institutional arrangements have come about. They demonstrate the inevitability of needing to acknowledge the widespread reverberation of effects throughout broad action systems; these are already furnished with cultural and institutional patterns that actors take into account in the way they develop and change institutions. Thus, even in a case involving a very straightforward transfer of identical technology, such as the Sergeant missile and weapons system, the combination of such an action system with others immediately brings in domestic institutional furniture although the technical artefact and its documentation are unquestionably international.

These reflections link up with the results in the previous chapter. Just when Germany was experiencing internationalization in the form of Americanization as perhaps no other country in Europe, the institutions that actors helped bring about bore some semblance to American models but eventually came to be quite different. Also, note how social spaces were being partitioned and how new furniture was replacing the old: American missile technology was being combined with a German military order[267] which, when we control for the distinctiveness of the military as compared to civilian spheres, showed the effect of common societal action systems.

5.7 Comparative properties of work systems

Further systematic studies comparing German work systems with those of other societies were mainly carried out in the 1970s and 1980s. After some decades in which most students and observers concurred that Germany was well on the way to Americanization, there was a striking turn in the interpretation of results. Before the 1970s, few truly comparative studies existed. Yet we could see that work systems were being influenced by the diffusion of production concepts that appeared to be originally American, i.e. strong on achieving economies of scale, large-batch or mass production, and continuous processing production, mechanization, automatization, deskilling of direct production work, and greater polarization as it was called, meaning the drifting apart of characteristics of routinized production work and those of maintenance, work planning, production control, and engineering work.[268] This led to discussion about convergence, not only of work systems but possibly of the whole social order, on an international template.[269]

This diagnosis and interpretation changed from the mid-1970s onwards. Now that Americanization of work, organization, and management in Germany could be assumed to have been completed, more rigorously comparative studies showed exactly the opposite. It turned out that actors in German society had effectively counteracted, probably quite unprogrammatically but nevertheless consistently, an Americanized approach to designing work systems. This did not mean that technology or production concepts had not been influenced by the American experience. But in the way that partitioning of spaces happens, it had been combined with its near-opposite, a German craft production logic as far as the social order of organizing and socialization is concerned. More systematic comparisons at the time did not involve the United States but, in the main, European societies. Nevertheless, it was strongly reminiscent of the results reported by Harbison *et al.* twenty years earlier when looking only at steel plants. The work has been read and reviewed many times, which is why I choose only to repeat some essential points here.

The research was designed to compare institutions and cultural dispositions in strictly matched production units, in small-batch production, large-batch production, and continuous processing production. This made it possible to show general tendencies prevailing across distinct industrial production logics. There was also a great deal of attention given to more 'macro' statistics and studies, such as those on labour mobility and wages. On the basis of an originally Franco–German comparison carried out at Aix-en-Provence, I could add to that a limited British replication of the design.[270]

Table 5.1 summarizes results which applied to all of the matched pairs in the three production types covered.[271] Most of the variables are expressed as percentages, ratios, or index values.

The differences between the countries were usually in the order of 10 to 20 percentage points, which is a large range when we consider that we are dealing with organizations which operate in identical contexts (size, products, technology, urbanization). German sites came across as having laterally 'lean' and structurally simple designs, the hierarchy being strong but flat. There was a tendency to restrict the growth of any component separate from direct production and the line of authority. French organizations tended to have tall hierarchies with large numbers of people in managerial, supervisory, administrative, and specialist positions. British firms tended to rank in the middle on most counts, except that they had the smallest numbers of people specifically classified as having line authority.

Table 5.1. Overall view of administrative structures of production plants in the UK, Germany, and France

	Low	Medium	High
Height of hierarchy	G	UK	F
Proportion of white-collar employees	G	UK	F
Range of supervisory control	G	UK	F
Administrative workforce commercial personnel/workers	G	UK	F
Proportion of workforce in positions of authority	UK	G	F
Proportion of workforce in white-collar positions of authority	UK	F	G

F: France; G: Germany; UK: United Kingdom.

Organizational differences were related to striking contrasts in labour control, management control, payment systems, industrial relations, work careers, personnel policy, competence requirements for jobs, and vocational education and training.[272] German organizations put the emphasis on extensive vocational training for most employees and positions, continuous development of vertically differentiated qualifications (further education courses building on more basic courses and occupational practice), and job stability and autonomy, within a fairly tight and coherent overall scheme. French organizations emphasized learning by hierarchical advancement, qualification and career distinctions, upward mobility and restriction of autonomy, all within a complex and centralized scheme. British organizations were more loosely coupled amalgamations of components, each with its own identity and displaying a number of status, career, and qualification differences between them, but held together by generalist management.

Such differences have been observed whenever organizations in similar situations are compared in the three countries.[273] Of course, this does not mean that organization in concrete terms has not changed over time. However, the overall comparative picture with regard to Germany and other countries is remarkably resilient. In the wake of the post-1990 boom and the predicament of German reunification, there has been much clamour about change in the 'German model' and complaints that the 'model' was being dismantled.[274] Again, this does not mean that basic characteristics have changed in the way German organization, socialization, and industrial relations practices differ from those in other societies and in comparable organizations and industries. Rather than increasing the number and depth of methodologically controlled cross-societal comparisons, the critics of societal analysis may have thought them dispensable in view of institutional change. But that is a fallacy. The fact that institutional change happens all the time in several societies in no way implies that the way they differ compared to each other changes. To make a statement about change relative to another society requires comparison, and this is different from a statement about change in one society, which does not require cross-societal comparison. Therefore a statement about change in one society by no means implies that the comparative difference with regard to another one has been reduced.

Comparative studies have been remarkably consistent in their findings. The general picture of comparison has held up despite numerous changes in technology, industry structure, the international economic order, and many other things. Comparisons have also included the encultured perceptions about what kind of arrangement is 'natural', self-evident, or ideal. Germans seem to appreciate professional autonomy in a well-oiled, productive machine. British employees appear to strive for individual and group prerogatives and the possibility of negotiated compromise between different interests. The French invariably show a preference for detailed and complex schemes that permit, first, sizeable inequalities while allowing extensive upward mobility, and second, guaranteed individual rights while buttressing the exercise of authority.[275] Such encultured inclinations have always been part and parcel of societal analysis.[276]

5.8   The commonalities of institutional furniture across action systems

All of these contrasts are rooted in distinctive institutions, the logics of which reverberate around action systems and posit recognizable limitations and stimuli for actors. For Germany, these include the following:

1. A distinctive vocational education and training system that closely integrates school-bound education and practical training in courses and across career trajectories, as well as a more distinctly vocational system of higher education, particularly in engineering and business administration.

2. A quasi-normative concept of management and organization, which emphasizes the social integration of the workplace and a transparent and simple organizational structure, as well as the legitimation of leadership and management on the basis of professional and specialist competence—this being a competence that links superiors and inferiors, rather than separating them socially.

3. An integrated system of industrial relations, not subdivided to any great degree by unions or arenas of separate consultation and bargaining, so that the legal institutions of works council representation and supervisory board co-determination are enmeshed with collective bargaining between industrial unions and employer associations.

We can see the South Germanic roots of such a scheme: there is a pervasive tendency to articulate hierarchical control with more lateral coordination and to achieve a degree of social control of capitalist activities by a welter of intermediate associations (unions, employer associations, chambers, vocational training committees of chambers with union and employer representatives, tripartite man-agement of social security insurance, etc.). This ramified corporatist apparatus is a modernized version of medieval governance of work by guilds. Yet as we have seen, it has not been a smooth transition from this to the modern corporatist apparatus. The establishment of the latter was provoked by the countervailing establishment of liberal-capitalist enterprise to such an extent that, in the long run and despite significant struggles between liberal and non-liberal tendencies, they have become co-evolutionary within a metatradition. Hence we find that American influences, although strong, have also stimulated the emergence of work systems that are anything but American.

The image of German work systems that emerges from such studies may to some extent contradict more popular impressions of them as being bureaucratic. Allow-ing for the institutional partitioning of action spaces, it may well be that relations in enterprises are quite different from relations between the citizen and public authorities, relations within public authorities, etc. Still, one does not necessarily expect Germany to rank very low in bureaucracy when, on a macro-level of employment by occupational categories, the numbers for managerial and admin-istrative staff are counted as part of non-agrarian employment. This list is headed by the United States; Sweden and Germany are at the bottom. David Gordon has measured and demonstrated such differing extents of 'bureaucratic load'.[277] Statis-tical classifications are, of course, not necessarily comparable across countries. However, the widespread supposition of German governance by bureaucratic fiat is not sustainable across the board.

It has also become possible to distinguish institutions and culture in the South Germanic bedrock from North Germanic ones. Karl-Henrik Sivesind conducted a matched-pair comparison of two sorts of continuous processing plants between Norway and Germany.[278] This is the only methodologically ingenious organiza-tional comparison between a Scandinavian country and Germany of which I am aware. It shows that the main differences do not lie in the organization of work in direct production, although vocational education and training in Norway is school-based, whereas Germany makes greater use of apprenticeships. It seems that some sort of vague Germanic pattern applies, which amounts to job rotation and enrichment and the importance of lateral coordination. But the German factories concentrate expertise into more hierarchically defined positions, and skilled labour also expects superiors to legitimate their position by technical leadership. In Norway, however, the role of management is more one of facilitation and coord-ination, and technical expertise is left more to staff technicians and engineers. Also, wage differences are clearly greater in Germany.

We see here the difference between the South and the North Germanic bed-rocks, exemplified by Germany and Norway, respectively. Greater feudalization in the South also implied a greater role for medieval corporatism, an urban way of setting up feudal allegiance and bonding as described in Chapter 3. The greater weight of government in the South, however, also meant that guild-type, lateral coordination was, in the more provincial space of society and its government, closely combined with the hierarchical control exerted by superiors, who in turn were themselves tied into more lateral guild coordination.

To return to the topic raised at the beginning of the chapter: where in this scheme of things do we find the German yeoman, what kind of figure is this, and how can it be likened to someone like my grandfather? The yeoman now is a prototypical skilled craftsman, technician, or clerical employee, who comprises the recognized productive basis of the organization. This person is being provided with occupational competence according to a generally ordained occupational profile and training schedule, striving towards responsible autonomy, expecting superiors to provide professionally consistent and intelligible leadership, and hoping to advance in his or her career by upgrading competence in further education and occupational mobility chains, inside the organization or beyond. The social figurations involved here are quite different and more modern than in the case of Prussian yeomen recruited from the countryside, but they all share some similarities when it comes to action logic. Like the yeoman, my grandfather left a farm to seek his fortune in various cavalry regiments as a non-commissioned officer, serving in peacetime and in war.[279] By way of an officially sanctioned mobility track, he was able eventually to become a clerk in a public insurance company. Industrial work studies have shown how mobility tracks have been subject to governance by public institutions as a response that actors identified as adequate.

Actors have subsequently hardened such mobility tracks within a firmer institutional form. Confronted with more rigid institutions and enculturated predispositions, actors have thus contrived novel institutions by way of softer institutions, their adaptation, and their subsequent hardening. German yeomen closely combine lateral coordination in the peer group with hierarchical subordination governed by technically competent leadership. Scandinavian yeomen would be different in the latter respect, for they have experienced strong kings and royal administration, but little feudalism. This is what makes the difference.

5.9   Technical change in relation to other action systems

Since the beginning of the 1970s, countries in Europe have been subject to changes and have also produced changes that have upset the temporary post-war equilibrium of expanding and new mass markets, expansive mass consumerism, full employment and advancing social security, progressive and specialized automatization, and stable exchange rates against the US dollar against a gold standard. These years, which the French have called *les trente glorieuses* (the glorious thirty years of growth under a Fordist regulatory regime), petered out in a more muddled period of oil crises, flexible exchange rates, the increasing relocation of industrial production to less industrialized countries, and growing resentment against, and action to check or control, the excesses of massive industrialization, such as congestion, pollution, and other disturbances of the living and working environment. One of the technologies that the 'military-industrial complex' of the post-war period bequeathed to the new era was the rapidly increasing integration of electronic transistor functions into integrated circuits, which meant exponential growth in the capacity and speed of all manner of electronic control, measurement, communication, and computation equipment.

'Microelectronics' was one of the keynotes to the new era, as far as the technical response was concerned. It also led to an exponential growth of software development and application, and was the basis for another, more important wave of innovation, namely the networked information and communication techniques which spread rapidly in the 1990s. Microelectronics has now become a commonplace ingredient of most sophisticated office and household equipment. At the time, however, it was an innovation that appeared radical and potentially unsettling. It led to many studies about the supposed 'effect' of new technology.

In societal analysis, I and two colleagues took up the research challenge beginning in 1979, by addressing the way technical systems were developed and applied in different societies.[280] This led us to view technical systems as contextualized, influenced by societal culture and institutions as much as it offered new opportunities and constraints. In the previously cited example of how Sergeant missiles were handled in different armies, the technology itself is largely the same and can be taken as given. It is put in place but has different consequences for organization and human resources. Microelectronics embraced a continuous and increasingly complex network of developments. It was not identified with a single product or technical configuration. The hypothesis was that technical action systems and their results would exhibit the characteristic interplay of communicating action systems, with technology being an endogenous factor evolving from an interaction with institutions in other domains.

We conducted a series of investigations of the introduction and application of computer-numerically-controlled (CNC) metal-cutting machinery, as the major application of microelectronics in industrial processes at the time, in the three countries mentioned earlier. This made it easier to combine automation with productive flexibility, and to let shop-floor workers share in work planning and programming tasks more than had been possible under previous forms of automated metal-cutting. Yet the precise impact of such new machines depended less on the potential of the technology itself and more on the continuation of previously existing characteristics of the various dimensions. While user companies usually did not directly develop controls, there were still visible feedback loops to firms that did, and this influenced the development of variants of technology.

German companies accordingly exploited the potential for 'shop-floor programming' of machine tools more purposefully than did British companies, and this coincided with a renaissance of the skilled worker.[281] French companies continued their earlier patterns of generating rather hierarchically differentiated human resources, work organization, and internal labour markets.[282] Rather than encouraging the development of the skilled worker, they cultivated the 'shop-floor technician' and 'new foremanship' (*technicien d'atelier* and *nouvelle maîtrise*, respectively). Again, institutions proved to be robust, but there were also changes: French companies adopted a policy of recruiting and training a higher calibre of metal-worker, but these people were hired in addition to workers with less training, so that the established hierarchical patterns of differentiation as well as the fundamental distance between practical workplace experience and vocational education was preserved. Similarly, British companies invested more in training production workers, but the investment mainly targeted 'company skills', those needed immediately at work, rather than the broader apprenticeship skills needed to maintain the status of a craftsman.

To some extent, institutions were thus reproduced in the midst of change. In Germany, there was a clear renaissance of apprenticeship, valorization of shop-floor competence, and redesign of technology to permit more flexible forms of production. This was linked to the emphasis on features of work systems that were more traditional than the more recent influences of Taylorization and Fordism. Naturally they were metatraditional, but not in the sense of being unreflective reproductions. The skilled workers who now compiled or adjusted the computer programmes running the factory machinery were not the hard-graft, manual workers of the old school, whose skills required physical effort and manual dexterity. What was comparably metatraditional was their aspiration for control over the job and the importance given to decentralization in optimizing the workflow.

Another case in point is the differential evolution of the French and German machine-tools industries. Work-systemic institutions had better prepared German industry for developing and manufacturing universal, flexible CNC machines and control systems, giving them a better position in the machine-tool market and leading to better outcomes in terms of market share and employment. The French machine-tool industry entered a severe crisis and shed jobs on a larger scale after suffering a series of redundancies, bankruptcies, and takeovers by competitors from abroad. Interestingly, the French manufacturers that survived or did better were those that produced CNC machines designed for a specific, complex purpose. French industry already featured more manufacturers of single-purpose machines, whereas German industry had previously been stronger in the production of universal machines.[283] Users of universal machines tend to have small- or medium-sized batch production, whereas users of highly specialized machines tend to have large-batch or mass production, which makes dedicated, single-purpose machines a better option.

In Germany, success was attained through the manufacture of universal machines, while France achieved it by producing single-purpose machines of a more specialized kind. This was valid both for the period preceding and for the period after the rise of CNC as a major metal-cutting innovation. The differences point to the importance of customer and user requirements, depending on the types of institutional systems in place in the domestic economy. All this attests to the reproduction of institutions, even when the up-and-coming innovation is basically the same everywhere. Such changes are not quite the same in every society, even when they are technical. International state-of-the-art technology, managerial practices, and other novelties are adapted and internalized with regard to existing institutional patterns. They therefore exhibit change to the same extent as continuity.[284]

At this point, it is possible to see how the industrial space of industry structure and linkages in the supply chain comes into play. This space also has institutional furniture, in this case consisting of the types of customers, their interests, and their requirements, which are taken to be relatively inert and therefore institutional. This meaningfully interacts with the institutions in the work systems of manufacturers. The interaction is such that it also attaches to the design and development of technology.

Interaction involving all types of work systems and extending into development of technology and industrial systems was also demonstrated forcefully in another Anglo–German comparison of ours in the late 1980s on the application of micro-electronics to the products of companies in the mechanical engineering, electrical engineering and electronics, precision mechanics, aeronautical and defence, and automobile manufacturing industries. The way this happened differed in Britain and Germany. In Britain, there was an abrupt break with given structures, strat-egies, and products during the structural conversion from 'old' to 'new' industries. In Germany, the keynote was one of gradual conversion of existing firms and products to new techniques. The latter also implied a more widespread updating of existing occupations (workers, technicians, and engineers alike), as well as a tighter meshing of electronics, software activities, and competence with knowledge in the product- and industry-specific application of evolving products. British companies sought not to 'reinvent the wheel' but to use state-of-the-art technology, whereas German companies were more likely to consider such technology as potentially deficient and in need of further development, in tune with postulated requirements of the specific products at hand and their users.[285] The development of technology thus occurred 'in tune with' existing occupational institutions. British engineering occupations and education have historically exhibited greater segmentation, both lateral and vertical (between more academic and more practical occupations), whereas German technical occupations have been constructed to be less segmented and more overlapping in competence and careers, both laterally and vertically.[286]

Societal analysis tends to look at the operation of all kinds of effects as endogen-ous. But the endogeneity above all refers to action systems; their tight coupling in a societal horizon enables externally originating effects to become meaningful only when they are remodelled into the cultural and institutional furniture in place. This does not mean that the analysis excludes external effects. To be sure, microelectronics did not originate in Germany, nor did numerically controlled machine-tools, nor did the Maudsley hand-controlled lathe on which the machin-ing tool was carried on a fixed slide rest, which was one of the outstanding innovations in the nineteenth century. Like the Cologne cathedral, most of the technical appliances we take to be domestic and familiar products were unfamiliar foreign artefacts at the time of introduction. They came in as external effects. But their remodelling into domestic furniture in all domains boils down to thorough endogenization. This is assured by tightly coupled action systems; they transmit the style of institutional furniture from one action space and institutional domain to another.

5.10   The Kamchatka effect in work systems

The argument in this chapter so far may have given the impression that societal effects produce uniformity throughout society, ensuring similar culture and institutions in all domains. However, this is far from what is claimed by the theoretical foundation. As we have seen, the partitioning of spaces and domains generates striking differences in structure and meaning and enables them to exist side by side. One of the objections raised against societal analysis is that it stylizes the uniformity of characteristics across industries, sectors, and types of enterprises, gender, occupations, etc. In domains other than those for which these characteristics have been empirically established, things may be quite different. We have not only admitted this but demonstrated it ourselves. This is, in fact, what typically happens when institutional partitioning of societal spaces has occurred.

A clear example is machine-tool manufacturers in Germany as compared to those in France. While German mechanical engineering firms 'normally' have more skilled workers and fewer semi- or unskilled ones, this turned out to be the other way round among machine-tool manufacturers: the French firms had higher percentages of skilled workers than the German ones. A crude view of societal effects would lead one to claim that since, in this instance, the effect is the opposite of what it is in a different setting, the framework is therefore refuted. However, a refined view integrates this supposed deviation into the framework. As stated above, French machine-tool makers have faced or targeted a clientele of large-batch and mass producers and have therefore been more likely to make dedicated machinery. Such machinery differs in design from one customer to another. Hence, production systems feature very small batch sizes and frequent conversion of machines, which goes hand-in-hand with the use of skilled workers. The German machine-tool industry has been the near-opposite in all these respects, and it therefore has had more semi-skilled workers than the French.

The upshot of this comparison is that the interaction of work institutions with the industrial system in Germany results in larger batches and a greater propensity to use semi-skilled workers, although skilled workers have a dominant role. In France, it is the other way round. Here we see a particularly obvious partitioning of institutions: machine-tool firms are much more 'artisanal' than their client firms, as evidenced by the striking contrast in both production systems and the use of human labour in production. However, on the basis of partitioning, this contrast is systemically consistent rather than accidental. Above all, it is explained by societally different industrial systems implying different producer–client structures.

Probably the most prominent case in which societal analysis has been challenged is that of the gendered division of labour and work. It is true that, on the one hand, the Franco–German comparison that first gave rise to the formulation of a societal effect did not have any units of investigation in which sizeable numbers of women were employed. This led to the suspicion that its reasoning left out half of society. Catherine Marry raised this point and argued that the societal effect might be different in gender relations and, accordingly, its explanatory power might be limited.[287]

On the other hand, the earliest Franco–German comparison had already ascertained this contrast. In an earlier sample of firms, French female employees were less subject to wage inequality than men; in Germany, it was the men who were less subject to wage inequality.[288] This could be readily integrated into the framework. Female participation in employment is higher in France and also steadier, rather than being interrupted by pregnancy and the raising of children as they are in Germany and notably Japan. This is facilitated by various social policies.[289] In addition, some of the more feminized domains of work in enterprises—clerical and technical work in offices rather than on the shopfloor—are more highly esteemed and rewarded in France. The greater stability of women in their careers is related to the interests of employers and management in developing their competence and responsibility. Hence, in retail work and various clerical and administrative functions one finds that the gendered space, or the division of meaning between men and women and relevant institutions,[290] is constructed in such a way as to invert the differences between France and Germany that are observed when we focus on jobs mainly held by males. Once again, we see a partitioning phenomenon which implies the coexistence of contrasting institutions. This has to be understood as being caused by the differential gendering of institutions reverberating around different action systems and leaving its mark on work-systemic institutions.

A societal effect does help explain this, even though it does not affect everybody in the same way in all places. The way this works can be unravelled by straightforward nomothetic theory. Where work-systemic institutions contrive to bring about occupational stability by less differentiated job ladders in less segmented organization structures, wage differences will be smaller. When women have interrupted careers and less vocational training, as they do in Germany, they are underprivileged. Work systems that segment and differentiate job ladders and careers to a greater extent will feature greater wage inequality. But when women have uninterrupted careers and vocational education is focused on schools or colleges, they work under more favourable conditions, which is the case in France. When the incidence of either type of work-systemic arrangement coincides with gendering and societal location (the former type of work systems being more German and the latter more French) we get an inversion of societal differences at the gender line.

The qualitative side of this effect with regard to gender is that the central and interlinked institutions in German work systems and industrial relations are quite masculine. They are historically bound up with apprenticeship in handicrafts and other more masculine job territories of extraction and manufacturing; the emphasis on socialization in the workplace itself is strong and carries over into related occupational schools and even institutions of higher education; and males have been the major contracting and consulting agents in works councils, trade unions, and employer organizations. Governmental policies have strongly favoured the image of the male as the stable breadwinner and the distinction between male and female roles in the social order. In France, however, the greater importance given professional socialization in schools and policies which help to relieve women of the tasks of child-raising and family duties (nursery schools, full-day school attendance, and day-care facilities) have given many industrial and technical occupations a more gender-balanced flavour.

The point is therefore not that governmental policies or other actions by purposeful actors merely reproduce existing societal patterns. As we have seen, they may modify these patterns, and in particular they may introduce a partitioning of institutional domains such that a domain may be governed by a meaning in a given space which is the opposite from the meaning prevailing in another. But whatever actors do, they will take some specific institutional traits for granted and generate effects which reverberate through action systems. To some extent, institutions even have contrary effects, but this does not mean that the order to which they belong is incoherent. For example, German vocational education and training institutions prescribe, organize, or help execute training for most jobs in the economy; this happens by bundling jobs into occupations or occupational fields, for each of which the appropriate training, education, and diplomas are specified. This makes education and training rather uniform across firms, including training within industry. The expectation then is that the interfirm mobility of labour will be facilitated. Why else should occupations be so standardized? However, industrial relations specialists tell us that industrial collective bargaining in Germany has a tendency to set standard wages more effectively than elsewhere and thereby 'take wages out of the competition' between firms. We can see that both of these tendencies have clear historical roots in the corporatist toolbox of German trades and industries. These have produced interfirm labour markets fostering mobility, and have stemmed the competition that thereby arises by assimilating wages.

Without becoming overly functionalist, it is easy to conclude that the resulting balance, as an interdependency of opposite effects, explains why such patterns are being reproduced. Possibly in the interests of employers and employees alike, these patterns apparently form a quasi-equilibrium, in which, on the one hand, labour markets are contestable and competition possible, but on the other, interfirm mobility of labour is checked in the interest of safeguarding investments in human resources, such that inducements to leave a firm do not ruin internal labour markets. Even countervailing patterns in different domains, for example one promoting interfirm mobility and the other discouraging it, may thus form a meaningful ensemble. This is understandable if we conceive of a tight coupling between industrial relations and occupational socialization spaces. Indeed, it is the tight coupling which makes countervailing institutions viable over the long run, within the checks and balances that operate across action systems. Like many checks and balances, they should not be regarded as clever designs invented by such thoughtful systems designers as Thomas Jefferson undoubtedly was. In the case of Germany, this balance is probably due to a mixture of industrially coordinated regionalism, corporatism, and paternalism which, as we have seen, has historically become more pronounced under the successive onslaughts of economic liberalism.

The importance of the partitioning phenomenon is not only that it helps to explain deviations from a rule of societal homogeneity, which societal analysis has never posited in this form. It makes us aware that institutional contradictions, in which things are the other way round on the other side of any partitioning boundary, are as normal as straight similarities. To that extent, the 'exceptions to the rule' may reveal the limitations of some specific nomothetic theory, but not of the broader framework. Broader frameworks are heuristic and include dialectics, and dialectics have attachments with different and to some extent mutually contradicting theories of the middle range. So, in short, the construction of the overall theoretical framework amounts to a collection of specific nomothetic theories, coordinated and moderated within a broader framework that is mainly an abstract and heuristic set deliberately including dialectics.

5.11 Contextual and strategic affinities

Work systems emerging from the South Germanic bedrock have for centuries been subject to two kinds of opposing influences. On the one hand, there has been small-scale production for a local or regional market by firms, which in the close confines of a market has regulated the entry of firms, methods and standards of production, prices, and training methods. In the Middle Ages, they even controlled civic behavioural standards. This was the provincial guild context of work systems, which has been supported by the provincialization of societal horizons and political rule. This aspect of work systems is still visible today in the prerogatives of regional chambers, notably those of handicrafts, but also in the practice of regional collective bargaining in manufacturing industry and non-public services. The formation of national identity has not obliterated them, but processes, standards, and results have possibly become more similar as learning and regulation across regions has occurred. On the whole, this aspect of work systems and their regulation and governance has implied small-scale markets.

On the other hand, the types of firms have changed. Nowadays firms and regions engage in trade across greater distances, specialize in products tied into interregional and international labour markets, and cut across the regulation of product markets by regional or national governments. It has become fashionable in the literature to point out the respects in which Germany developed later than other countries, mainly in nation-building and industrialization. While this is true, it is unexciting and theoretically inconclusive. Compared to France in nation-building and England in industrialization, everyone was late. However, the other countries do not exhibit any of the characteristics attributed to the supposed influence of 'late development', except in methodologically inconclusive, one-to-one comparisons with England.[291] A theoretically and methodologically more suggestive question to ask would be: what was the first step a society took towards nation-building or industrialization?

What a society does first gives us clearer pointers about what factors have a formative influence on it. What it does with a delay is not formative. Formative factors affect the (re)construction of a metatradition and thereby continue to assert themselves even during the oscillation of social, economic, and political change. Germany and other parts of the South Germanic bedrock are pioneering and lasting examples of a layered construction of society and political rule. Particularly in the late Middle Ages and in modernity up to 1872, this has implied a co-evolution of provincialism and internationalism. Provincial and internationally oriented firms have coexisted side by side for a long time. While a tension or contradiction between the two principles is inevitable and never to be resolved, it is also a productive one which may undergird the movement of firms from one league to the other over time. They may grow from provincial traders and manufacturers into international ones, and they may also lapse from the latter to the former. As they undergo such change, they may evolve by adopting new products and shedding others, by specializing, expanding, or changing their product and service portfolio, by merging with or taking over other firms or being taken over by them, or by spawning new firms in the process.

Both the institutional order of the German economy and its export performance have been greatly influenced by medium-sized firms run by owner-managers, rather than by the well-known company names in concentrated manufacturing and services. This is an acknowledged and uncontroversial fact. Such influence is part of a metatradition linked to the aforementioned construction of the economy, polity, and society in the late Middle Ages and beyond. What it definitely caused was the creation of populations of small and medium-sized firms which were governed within a corporatist structure and, at the same time, exposed to the vagaries and opportunities of freer international trade. Through the propinquity of provincial and international leagues in confined provincial societal spaces, movement from one to the other has always been a possibility, one that is exemplified and to some extent supported by networks and institutions. Paradoxically, it has been the provincialization of governance that has promoted an extension of horizons of action as a more generic phenomenon.

The population of internationally active firms can again be decomposed into two distinct segments. Gary Herrigel has especially emphasized this point, showing that there were 'two kinds of Germany': one was the large population of specialized small and medium-sized firms, the other was that of emerging large firms and industrial conglomerates.[292] The latter were more prevalent in northern Germany, the former more prevalent in the south. This shows the formative influence of societal construction in the Middle Ages. As we have seen, it was in the south that local fragmentation of rule was most intensive, and internationalization co-evolved with this fragmentation. This was the context of 'flexible specialization', particularly of firms. However, my contention would be that the preponderance of such smaller and specialized firms is clearer in Germany and its weight implies greater overlap and transition between the two stylized populations. The large and concentrated firms are also distinctive for 'the product' as constitutive of identity, and this is supported by the construction of work systems. The craft nexus between employees and the firm, built around a strong technical orientation, vertical integration, overlapping skills and careers, and a rather flat hierarchy that is organized primarily on the basis of functional principles, has been translated into this context. It is the large firms that have been the strongest supporters of industrial collective bargaining to date,[293] because it helps to 'take wages out of the competition' or control wage drift. Although this phenomenon can, in principle, occur elsewhere, it is distinctive to Germany.

5.12 Characteristics of industrial relations

Discussion and recent findings on the decentralization of collective bargaining are far from unprecedented. An earlier review of findings came to the same conclusion thirty years ago.[294] At that time, there was an extension of regionally negotiated agreements at the company and plant level that improved conditions and salaries, rather than allowing for exceptions and undercutting. Of course, the interests of employers and trade unions are not identical. Unions and employees consider broad-based collective agreements as a way of assuring general standards, but they do not mind company-specific improvements. Employers are interested in 'taking wages out of competition', in order to check the rise of labour costs and not lose experienced workers; they do not mind company-specific reduction of standards as long they can retain labour they consider important. Employers and unions thus have different sets of interests, and the opportunities to realize one set and not the other have shifted over time.

Despite such changes of opportunity, both sides have concurred on the need to maintain two-pronged and articulated industrial relations with links between company and plant co-determination or bargaining and regional-industrial bargaining. Sellier observed earlier than many others that one of the major distinctions in German industrial relations was articulated in the interplay of works council co-determination with regional collective bargaining, which extended the complementarity of the two rather than playing on their contradictoriness.[295] Recent tendencies of decentralization notwithstanding, many German firms, particularly large ones, have remained staunch supporters of collective bargaining across individual firms. The conclusion is inevitable that this would not have occurred had less effort been exerted to create a community of practice that bridged the gap between large and small companies. Had common interests not been viably nurtured, the articulation would have collapsed rather than evolved into the higher level of differentiation and refinement that Streeck and Rehder suggest as an interpretation.

Work systems affecting German firms are thus comparatively distinctive in utilizing strategies that emphasize the particular nature of a product or service to help constitute a corporate identity and act as a central reference point in all company policies. Such strategies imply an interest in human labour, which acknowledges the importance of an interfirm labour market based on training standards and transferable skills; at the same time, they keep labour mobility from rising to a level that would deplete the internal supply of experienced workers who are focused on specific products or services. This has also been observed by foreign researchers.[296] Such a socially integrative focus on the product, the service, or the operation does not mean that these remain the same. Instead, a focus on the product or service may well be dynamic, meaning that they will be adapted, improved, and developed. German firms are eminently able to identify a primary process; this establishes a rallying point that controls and sometimes overshadows other processes. Hence, direct production is central and vertical integration is high.

5.13 The setting and character of innovation

Such firms are not radical innovators by way of enacted posture and knowledge; they are forceful piecemeal innovators and adapters. In the compulsion to safeguard the identity of the enterprise, they will understate innovation if consulted about it. While the Anglo-Saxon literature has played up the prevalence of radically innovative firms or 'hyper-competition', meaning the complete change of product and industry, German firms are less conspicuous in the dramatization of such heroic feats. This is what has come out of the varieties-of-capitalism studies comparing German with Anglo-American innovation. Over time, the industries in Germany that have held a comparative advantage and have been distinctive for gradual innovation have come out even stronger.[297] It is sometimes difficult to tell whether it is the real phenomena or just the interpretive constructions of innovation that are different, but both differences can be found, across the board. German companies thus tend to tackle innovation as a stream of continuous development and apply an innovation at the moment when they can treat it as such, whereas Anglo-American companies characteristically are divided into those that dive right into innovations with early-mover advantages and more radical shifts, on the one hand, and those with price competition in more standardized market segments, on the other.

The strategic and contextual characteristics of German enterprises compared to British ones were first described some time ago and have probably not changed very much despite neo-liberal transformations in Britain and post-unification rigidities in Germany. Germany exhibits larger plant size but smaller enterprise size. Germany favours more concentrated units of production in different sectors, whereas Britain favours looser amalgamations of smaller production units into more complex conglomerate structures.[298] Despite the higher concentration of output and employment in large enterprises in Britain, German firms have had better economies of scale, even in small firms. British companies in major industrial sectors have pursued strategies geared towards reaching the scale advantages they may or may not have had, and have competed over price rather than quality.[299] This picture has probably changed somewhat. However, Germany still comes across as a society in which concentrated industries more closely resemble a continuation of the broad spectrum of small and medium-sized firms, which is fairly homogeneous in its conception of work systems, more integrated with the world of large enterprises through collective bargaining and other industrial relations institutions, and more important in setting the institutional keynotes.

Whereas in other similarly large societies, the world of large enterprises strikes one as quite different from the world of small and medium-sized firms, in Germany there is a tendency to cover both worlds with rather similar institutions. Small German firms are more likely to look like miniature industrial companies, and large enterprises are infused with artisanal or craft principles. Some would rightly say that this is precisely the way British engineering used to look, certainly from its inception in the West Midlands[300] until the commencement of deindustrialization and reform by the Thatcher government in 1979. However, British enterprises have always been more loosely coupled amalgamations of sites, divisions, plants, crafts, and above all, work gangs. They have been beset by the perennial dilemmas inherent in the contrasts between lateral coordination and hierarchical control, the identity of the craft and that of the plant or firm. German enterprises, on the contrary, have closely intertwined these opposing factors.

These are the strategic and contextual properties of enterprises that one would expect from a population of firms that has become marked by the combination of a rather international horizon of action and a regional regulatory ambit. Wherever we go in provincial Germany, we are likely to stumble upon small and medium-sized enterprises which are the pride of local communities and happen to be the leading European or worldwide competitor for a very specialized product and market that most of us were probably not even aware existed. The situation is no different in Switzerland and not much different in Austria. The epitome of the phenomenon can be found in Liechtenstein, the smallest, independent remnant of the Holy Roman Empire of old, a kind of super-Switzerland thanks to its focus on both highly specialized manufacturing and legal and illegal money-laundering. Even East Germany, to the extent that it has well-performing companies that do not cater solely to a regional market, is quickly returning to this pattern, after an interlude in which a centrally planned, socialist economy built massive conglomerates and razed small firms to the ground.[301] The more established worlds of mechanical and electrical engineering, as well as new industries such as computer software, are full of such variegated products and specialties. With regard to GNP and export performance, such small and medium-sized industries comprise the mainstay of the German economy, rather than the well-known names of concentrated enterprises like BMW, VW, Bayer, Thyssen-Krupp, and Siemens. The latter are powerful, but in terms of employment and contribution to GNP they are peripheral.

The distinctiveness of such work systems is likely to have increased over time. Whereas there used to be a great deal of large-batch and mass production in the post-war era when the value of the currency was low and stable against the US dollar and wage and cost inflation were low compared to those of Germany's trading partners, such production systems have eroded since currencies started to fluctuate and the value of the Deutschmark steadily increased, more or less until the conversion to the Euro. After 1972, mass production that could accommodate a great deal of unskilled labour was to a large extent located in newly emerging industrial countries, or automated so that it did not need much labour in direct production, or converted to differentiated quality production. This tendency accelerated further in the 1990s as German multinationals chose to increase their foreign direct investment.[302] The landscape of both the industrial and service sectors thus became increasingly dominated by a more restricted typology of work systems, in the wake of this erosion of mass production.

The institutional corollary of such contextual and strategic implications is, of course, the interplay of liberalization and corporatist order and of extended horizons of action coinciding with provincialized societal horizons. This interplay has been shown to be an endemic feature of German social and economic history. The work systems observed beyond 1945 and their ramifications fit into this pattern, and it is quite probable that the post-1945 evolution of work systems did not bring anything that was radically new. Although the combination of free enterprise on an international scale and the reassertion of corporatism in the present form is new and would be highly surprising to anyone who had tried to predict Germany's economic future in 1950, it is, from a long-term perspective, yet another distinctive episode within the South Germanic metatradition.

5.14   Industrial districts?

Industrial districts are territories with a concentration of firms linked by relational contracting, i.e. long-term contracts to cooperate in business either across stages of a supply chain (suppliers and customers, possibly at different stages) or within a particular stage of a chain. Industrial districts also have supportive institutions, such as those dedicated to research, training, marketing, standards or label control, or industrial relations. Industrial districts thus combine relational contracting and supportive institutions, each with a different emphasis in their diverse world.[303] In recent modernity, industrial districts are endemic to provincialized horizons of society and governance where national government has not standardized or provided effective national institutions. Prominent examples usually cited are mainly located in Italy, but also in Spain. The earlier West Midlands in England, one of the seedbeds of industrialization in mechanical engineering industries with a multitude of small firms that had not yet been amalgamated into conglomerates, were one of the examples that Alfred Marshall must have had in mind when he coined the term 'industrial district'. Under the concept of 'flexible specialization' put forward by Piore and Sabel, one aspect is the Italian variation of industrial districts, and the other is diversified quality production within individual companies.[304]

The question now is whether Germany has industrial districts. By all accounts, it does have supportive institutions with a substantial amount of regional deconcentration. There are also historically persuasive examples of districts such as cutlery crafts and industry in and around Solingen. On the whole, it is difficult to come up with examples as numerous and straightforward as in Italy, except where local natural resources have been the determining factor. One such natural resource was the coal found in the Ruhr area, which led to a population of collieries and associated industries. This has been subject to amalgamation within industrial conglomerates, which makes the relational contracting between independent firms fade into the background and the district metaphor difficult to apply. Although supplier networks of larger firms have had a territorial aspect, such as the supplier network of VW in and around the Lüneburg Heath, they are not covered by a congruent institutional entity which supports and regulates them. Another example would be shipbuilding on the coasts, but this industry has also developed into a loose network of just a few firms, which to some extent has come under the control of entities outside the region or even the nation. It would seem that in Germany supportive institutions have become differentiated from relational contracting, such that regions may be distinctive in types of production systems but not in strongly institutionalized district links in or across particular supply chains. Interestingly, in the course of a recent DFG (Deutsche Forschungsgemeinschaft) research programme on 'globalization and regionalization', the search for industrial districts in the full sense led to few convincing results, apart from those in one study to be mentioned later and more recent networks in media services and industrial development.

What is an industrial district and what is not? Frankfurt am Main has the most significant concentration of banking headquarters and other financial services, including central banking, in the world apart from national capitals. Next to the City of London, it is an outstanding internationalized but regional industrial district. Likewise, there are networks of film and television firms regionally clustered in certain areas, such as in and around Munich. On other occasions, students of work and organization have been inclined to change the research focus from traditional manufacturing industry to services. There is therefore no reason why the headquarters of large service firms or regionally clustered networks of service firms should not be considered industrial districts, if they exemplify synergy by relational contracting and supportive institutions.

One might hypothesize that, compared to Italy, the relative weakness of industrial districts in Germany is a consequence of a high amount of uniformity in work-systemic institutions and the willingness of states to support the regional corporatist apparatus. This may be or may have been different in Italy, where the state is national and corporatism also regional. Whereas in Germany, regional states have instituted education and organized training to benefit regional industry, it would appear that Italian districts have, to some extent, evolved through the regional machinery of enterprises themselves doing what the state has not done as readily. In Germany, although local or regional responsibilities may be clear-cut, the form of institutions is not strikingly different within the nation. Vocational training falls under the authority of the national government and is co-governed by employers and unions at this level; it is not subject to the authority of provinces as in Italy. Much as Italian provinces can conduct autonomous policies in such matters, they are not states; and although German states preceed the nation state even after 1945, their autonomy lies in domains different to those that generate and sustain industrial districts. Furthermore, in matters of economic and regional policies, states in Germany have often copied each other while competing to attract and maintain industries, so that the decision to locate and develop an enterprise in a territory is probably less contingent on specific public goods created by regional governance and industrial districts. This conforms to the impression that German federalism has been subject to a sophisticated but at times tedious dialectical interplay of competition between states, on the one hand, and harmonization and solidarity, on the other.[305]

There is one convincing example of an industrial district with a long tradition; it is the manufacture of surgical instruments in and around Tuttlingen in Baden-Württemberg. I and my colleagues first came across this district by accident, in a comparison of the application of CNC machine tools in Britain and Germany. One of the German Firms studied also supplied machines for teaching purposes to a regional vocational training centre, which offered courses and modules for both apprenticeship training and advanced training programmes. This training centre was run by the regional chambers of handicrafts, industry, and commerce. Among others, the centre catered to a remarkable population of surgical instrument-makers in and around Tuttlingen. At the time of study in 1981, there were about 120 firms in the area, a few of them rather industrialized while others were only small workshops, some of them linked to larger manufacturers by relational contracting. This industrial district and population of firms was the first one to introduce CNC training modules as a requirement in the educational schedule of surgical instrument mechanics, an occupation governed by regionally specific regulations. Regional specificity of an occupation is allowed only in craft regulations, where it is legitimated by the existence of districts. Surgical instrument mechanics in Tuttlingen thereby became the first mechanical occupation in the world to include an obligatory module on the programming and operation of computer-numerically-controlled milling machines.[306]

The question in the present context, however, is how this highly specific population of firms came to establish and organize itself in the region. This may tell us something about how regionalization is related to wider societal and action horizons. Several years after our findings were published, Hans Maier again came across this district in a study of diversified quality production in Baden-Württemberg.[307] It was discovered that the district had been strengthened by the immigration of French Huguenot refugees forced to leave France to avoid religious persecution following the Edict of Fontainebleau in 1685. A French refugee community came into being in Tuttlingen and by concerted effort strongly cultivated the manufacture of all types of cutlery. The district had initially made general cutlery tools, including all kinds of knives and scissors.[308]

This type of phenomenon was not an exception in Germany at the time. French refugees formed sizeable communities, which developed new and specialized types of manufacturing, commerce, and learning in many Protestant German states. Under the Great Elector, Brandenburg offered Huguenots refuge in massive numbers, because they were considered as potentially more experienced specialists from a more developed country. Brandenburg's generosity toward the Huguenots was part of a deliberate policy of repopulation and commercial development after the catastrophic losses of the Thirty Years' War. They did not necessarily found sustainable districts but very often did establish privileged firms producing speciality and luxury goods.

The sales area covered by the Tuttlingen cutlery manufacturers was more regional, as often when customs and excise duties, privileges, and restrictions ordained by princes, estates, and guilds determined the size of a market in addition to transport costs. After 1806, policies in Baden, the state that Napoleon had created to unite a number of smaller territories, increasingly moved towards both economic and political liberalism. Baden was also very receptive to the German Free Trade Area (Zollverein), begun in 1833–4 and gradually expanded to most German states except Austria. This meant that the Tuttlingen knives and scissors producers were confronted with severe competition from the Solingen area. Solingen manufacturers, formerly of the Duchy of Berg (for all practical purposes a part of France through the Rhenish Confederation) and now of Prussia, had thereby already profited from a larger market and had advanced towards standardization of products, mechanization of production, and economies of scale. They enjoyed comparative advantages in cutlery manufacturing which were greater than in the rest of Germany. Accordingly, Solingen imposed itself as a cutlery district in Germany and crowded out other competitors as the free trade area increased in size. In a way, after Tuttlingen had become the Sheffield of Baden, Solingen became the Sheffield for all of Germany.

At a loss as to how to make a living with its market share shrinking, Tuttlingen cutlery makers took another coordinated step, which was to detect new and growing market niches. They agreed that surgical instruments should be the basis of a new and narrower specialization. This was rather remote from anything approaching large-batch production; surgeons tended to influence or approve the design of instruments in line with their operating experience. Furthermore, medicine and hospitals were an expanding industry with rapidly increasing skills and knowledge and demand for its services. In conjunction with the change from surgery as an experiential craft to a profession based on academic research, surgical tools also became increasingly refined. However, the artisan element remained in surgery, and it left intact the high degree of customization in tool design and manufacture. Accordingly, Tuttlingen manufacturers were able to continue the artisanal system of production they had long been developing, converting it as needed to the creation of new products.

Recently, the district has begun to change once more as a consequence of new tendencies of internationalization. New diagnostic and operating techniques have also been emerging. The coordination capacities of the district are again being put to the test, and it is difficult to predict how and in which form the district can be maintained. Links with firms and institutions outside the region are becoming more important. This has become evident in the most recent study done on the district, by Eichhorn, Hessinger, and others.[309] In Tuttlingen, a regional industrial district has managed to remain a regional node compatible with internationalized value chains, one that remains competitive as long as it is able to replenish its specific knowledge and competence. In the mean time, the Solingen district has also evolved and broadened its manufacturing from cutlery to assorted kitchen machinery, vacuum cleaners, and other household machines. This is in line with the earlier evolution of Solingen work systems towards large-batch production. Yet it has also become clear that the economic rationalization of production has led to the relocation of activities outside the district in newly emerging industrial societies—a fate shared by many large-batch and mass production activities established in Germany.

Work systems are apparently more stable than the products themselves. They may be easy to annihilate through competition but are difficult to change fundamentally overnight. The Solingen district has become much more industrial, but it could be argued that in the course of this development it has lost its characteristics as an industrial district: a vacuum cleaner manufacturer has less in common with cutlery firms. Most important of all, the evolution of districts appears strongly contingent upon their insertion into expanded horizons of action and upon the division of labour manifested or permitted by such insertion. In this, such evolution is as dependent on international events and tendencies as it is on the regional cultivation of expertise and institutions. In the evolution of Solingen and Tuttlingen, everything that has happened bears a strong international imprint, ranging from the religious settlement in France, via national and international customs regulation, to the international situation with regard to competition, alliances, and outsourcing. District institutions are sustainable to the extent that they can strategically be made to tally with, and address, international market orders.

5.15 Internationalization and domestic specificity

Work systems in the South Germanic bedrock have changed substantially over time. We are not quite able to ascertain and document this because systematic comparisons have only begun fairly recently. Yet, the international angle of all the developments that have taken place is, in a way, the corollary of the development of domestic specificity of culture and institutions. The work systems that have survived in Germany, or have continued to be subject to German corporate control, have converged on the aspect of diversified quality production. This means a sharpening of the societal effect, due to international exposure and insertion of work into an international division of labour. As Taylorized large-batch production has emigrated to newly industrializing countries or eastern Europe, not only the institutional but even the technical and strategic furniture of work systems has become more harmonious within society, rather than internationally.

Mass production using substantial labour has become rare in Germany. This is a substantial change from Germany just before and immediately after 1900. Then, it was a sort of Japan of Europe, a country combining standardized production with quality. Multinationals have increasingly sorted their production processes into domestic and foreign-located ones. Some industries have all but vanished, such as the manufacture of cameras and other consumer optical equipment. Likewise, a great deal of the manufacture of consumer electronics has left the country or been started up abroad. Manufacturing companies that have remained in Germany in this industry have come under the corporate ownership and control of foreign multinationals. Saba, Nordmende, and Grundig were German household names until the 1970s, after which they were taken over by Japanese, French, and Dutch multinationals, respectively. A comparative study by Geppert and others has demonstrated this sorting and allocation of different production concepts to different societies and has compared development and production policies of multinational manufacturers of lifts and escalators with headquarters in Finland, Germany, and the United States and with production subsidiaries in Britain and Germany.[310] However, subsidiaries in different countries continued to use nationally specific work systems and types of products, and the multinationals to some extent made use of such differences by allowing if not forcing the subsidiaries to specialize in associated products.[311] Various studies on the automobile industry also demonstrate similar phenomena.

The internationalization of work systems has been obvious for quite a while. It has not implied harmonization but specialization and institutional continuity. To a large extent, it has preceded the internationalization of corporate governance and ownership and has not been subject to strong convergence through supranational government in the European Union, although that was considered highly likely by some observers ten years ago.[312] Germany has learnt about rational agriculture and small-batch production in mechanized engineering from England; mass and continuous processing production as well as Taylorization and automated flow production (the industrial engineering side of Fordism) from the United States; continuous improvement and just-in-time production from Japan; outsourcing and co-makership from either America or Japan; and, let us not forget, nuclear rocket artillery from the United States.[313] Yet, in their introduction and diffusion, such work systems have been translated and transformed.[314] In due course, they have been adapted to production system templates upon which the domestic economy has converged.

Institutional work systems have changed over time. What has not changed are the differences between societies that are so crucial in a cross-sectional comparison to gauge convergence and divergence. Such differences may even have become more pronounced. Societies not only undertake the translation of supposedly international best practices or supranational regulation into their domestic contexts. They have come to specialize in specific branches of industry and services, market segments, and strategic niches. As they have done so, organization theory leads us to expect that the institutions furnishing organization, socialization, and industrial relations spaces have also come to diverge. This has indeed occurred. As a consequence, it has also become more difficult to compare this furniture across societies; if their contextual and strategic references have become different, then it is also more difficult to find pairs of matching enterprises, in terms of the contextual and environmental likeness necessary for matched-case comparisons.[315]

It is not as easy now as it used to be to find comparable plants in different countries that are well matched on the basis of near-identical products, production systems, or plant or company size. Large-scale, standardized automobile production has declined in Germany to some extent and moved to Spain, Britain, or the Czech Republic, in addition to countries such as Mexico. Standardized component production has also emigrated either south or east. When we compare populations of work systems and organizations, we find ourselves more and more comparing the incomparable. This is because the dialectical advance of internationalization is not only composed of the establishment of international templates but also a national differentiation of organizational populations. Societal effects not only turn up in the different social arrangements prevailing under identical products, size, and technology. They also manifest themselves as national and international actors evolve, select, and allocate to different societies work systems with different purposes, technical configurations, and institutional furniture. However, to scholars who have learnt to conceive of angles of comparison in terms of action systems, as explained in sections 5.3 and 5.4 above, the problem of this effect is not methodologically insurmountable.

It is easy to underestimate the effect when a new technology or organizational approach is internationally diffused as being state of the art. In the beginning, decontextualized international templates are depicted as being universal. This tends to affect technical configurations as well as institutional furniture, but the latter is usually addressed in vaguer form. To the extent that templates are diffused, they are invariably translated, adapted, and modified to suit locally specific purposes and accommodate existing institutions and culture. This tends to affect the engineering aspects, too.[316]

5.16 Summary

From a long-term perspective, German work systems have been exposed to the dynamics of a metatradition; this was prepared by the societal order of Germany in the Middle Ages and during its subsequent development. It is the contiguity and articulation of peer control and leadership within the close confines of provincial societal space that has provided a leitmotiv for the changing orchestration of work systems to date. From this basis, domestic and international effects have been so closely interwoven that it is difficult to describe one without referring to the other.

The regional fusion of hierarchical control with peer control and professional specialization, under societal horizons that are both provincial—by regulatory structures and retrenched societal horizon—and open to international horizons of action, has generated work systems with unique institutional furniture. They are comparatively simple, socially inclusive, based on or rooted in occupational identities. They link execution, management, and leadership by constructing careers in work, educational, and inclusive industrial relations, and they are geared to continuous improvement and piecemeal innovation. This artisanal background in provincial but internationalized layers of society has influenced the social construction of predominantly small and medium-sized firms. It has also extended to large enterprises, contrasts and conflicts between small firms and industrial juggernauts notwithstanding. This background does not vanish, even if the handicrafts were to vanish as an institutional corporation. A metatradition works by having its abstract properties become independent of the specific institutional shell that nurtured them; they then are cast into new institutions. As long as comparisons of work systems demonstrate that these systems emphasize continuity in careers, workflow organization, knowledge, and other subspaces between direct operation and conception, clients and producers, then the metatradition is alive, and institutions maintain their distinctiveness in an international comparison.

Next to primary and secondary work processes, enterprises have and are subject to a stratum of higher management or entrepreneurship and corporate governance. The construction of this stratum is not causally determined by the governance of work, nor does the latter causally determine the former. However, the strata of work processes, on the one hand, and corporate and management governance, on the other, are intimately related, for they have evolved from the same societal bedrock. The next chapter extends the analysis from work systems to corporate governance. As action systems, they are tightly coupled, but institutional domains and particularly institutional entities enjoy relative autonomy, which makes a separate treatment feasible.

6

Enterprise Management and Corporate Governance

6.1 Introduction

Just after being transferred to a regiment in Wittenberg in 1840, a young subaltern artillery officer in the Prussian army was asked by a colleague in the regiment to assist him in a duel, as a second. Under the social code of the time, it was a request the young officer could not refuse. Duelling was still endemic, not only among military officers but also civilians aspiring to bourgeois quasi-nobility. Although duelling was forbidden by law, the social code considered it an honourable and efficient way of settling disputes of a personal nature in areas where legal jurisdiction was difficult. It was an interesting case in which morality differed from modern law, which bestows a monopoly of physical force on the state. Morality required persons concerned by the estate-specific code not to refuse the offer of a duel.[317] It obliged them to enter into a private and tacit contract to settle a question of honour in this particular way, to be content with the outcome of the litigation thus set in motion, and not to betray it by subsequent recourse to official justice for whatever reason.

The economic efficiency of contracting to duel was much greater than busying courts with proceedings about slander or personal tort. The state saved resources, and so did individuals, who would otherwise have had to face the expense of courts, lawyers, and penalties, and possibly suffer a loss of freedom and above all dishonour by publicity. While the costs of duelling were lower, the private utility of duelling was greater, since it safeguarded the honour even of an obviously guilty culprit or loser better than a public trial or litigation could have done, without denying the initiating party its 'satisfaction'—a technical term then used to describe the moral result of the proceedings. Duellers did not contest the authority of the state in other respects at all, at least not at the time; the practice was part and parcel of ancient Germanic habits of feuding that had been a nuisance to generations of princes. Now, it was an optimal arrangement in a weak state and a liberal society of responsible and autonomous individuals.[318] University students were trained to duel in fraternities, where they learnt to fence with sharp weapons while protected by special equipment and clothing meant to prevent serious injury, so that such mock duels only left coveted and honourable facial scars.

Regrettably or otherwise, the duel in Wittenberg was reported to the authorities, and the officers concerned were court-martialled, Prussian fashion, oblivious to morality and the efficiency of governance. The artillery officer who had only acted as a second was sentenced to five years' confinement in a fortress (*Festungshaft*) in Magdeburg, although the duel had led only to minor injuries. 'Fortress confinement' was a penalty for infractions of the law deemed to have been committed with honourable intentions; it was different from custody in a 'normal' prison. In cases of duelling in the military, men acting as seconds were normally pardoned after half a year. Fortress confinement allowed greater personal freedom to move, socialize, and conduct activities which were socially useful or morally uplifting.

The young artillery officer made use of the time he had to serve at the Magdeburg citadel to conduct electrolytic experiments, which had commercially lucrative results and allowed him to finance further experiments. They were part of a line of research and development that he was pursuing. Later, after a war with Denmark over Schleswig and Holstein was over, a war in which he had proved useful as a technical 'boffin' for special operations, the officer resigned his commission and started a business that rapidly grew from a very small company to a multinational enterprise well known throughout the world. The opportunity that custody in the fortress offered would not have presented itself as readily had the officer done normal duty. Without his experimentation during his confinement, he would probably not have been assigned special technical tasks in the war, and without this experience and the intensive contact with the government and with the court that initiated it all, the young officer would have found it much more difficult to develop his enterprise, and we may never have heard the name Werner Siemens.[319]

This introduction has deliberately sought to unsettle conventional notions about contrasts and affinities, liberal and authoritarian order, free enterprise and constraints, and the relationship between any of these and German institutions and culture. This has been done because recent research and discussion on corporate governance and management certainly needs to be jarred from its fixation on simplistic contrasts of the type all topical discussions probably tend to make. This sets the scene for explaining the findings in the way we have established in this book, with reference to partitioning and recombination, internationalization and re-creation of domestic specificity. To begin with, a framework for the analysis of management, corporate governance, and (quasi)-public regulation is put forward. This framework contains elements that are often disregarded, and which are indispensable for understanding Germany. They relate to the recombination of liberal and non-liberal governance, and of internationalization and provincialization, in close proximity.

6.2 Managing and reducing uncertainty

6.2.1 *The public, private, and corporatist reduction of uncertainty*

Ideologically, many of us have come to consider a separation of public responsibility and private enterprise as natural, good, or at least a given. This is a liberal doctrine that has permeated functionalist theory, both economic and social, as presented by Parsons and his followers. It exemplifies one way of partitioning institutional space. But economic liberalism is not coterminous with partitioning of institutional space. Economic liberalism assumes a coarse-grained partitioning of institutional space, with a very systematic separation of public and private affairs. There are also economic orders that exhibit a more fine-grained partitioning of institutional space, that combine economic liberalism on some counts with corporatism and on others with mercantilism. This was demonstrated for Germany in Chapter 4. Such an order has peculiar implications for entrepreneurship and management. It is convenient to unravel such implications from what is supposed to be a central problem of management and entrepreneurship, particularly in an economically liberal society.

Entrepreneurs and managers have a highly ambivalent position vis-à-vis uncertainty: they suffer from it, they may profit from it, they try to reduce or manage it, and at the same time they willingly, unwillingly, or unwittingly reduce or increase it for others. In other words, the handling of uncertainty is dilemmatic, and economic actors—not only managers and entrepreneurs but others as well—are inevitably interdependent with respect to the reduction or management of uncertainty. This means that the measure of uncertainty accrued in a specific situation, and how it is experienced and managed, are truly social and societal constructions. The latter then incorporates soft and rigid institutional arrangements. As Streeck shows, the uncertainties of management relate to the management of uncertainties, and the latter includes the enactment and enforcement of public orders.[320] Management and entrepreneurship are therefore ill conceived as prevailing 'within' a public order. Instead, they also impinge on and even help to constitute or maintain a public order.

This action may be inherently problematic, such as when entrepreneurs 'conspire' against competition and public welfare at every opportunity, as Adam Smith famously pointed out. On the one hand, reduction or management of risk may amount to the reduction of innovation or welfare. On the other, it may increase welfare because the very diverse forms of social control and coordination lower transaction costs and alleviate agency problems. Should this happen, it is because public or private goods have been created that augment the working of entrepreneurship and management so as to generate and transact more utility. When public law enforcement increases the safety of transport from robbers and pirates, for instance, it stimulates trade and makes it happen more efficiently. In some parts of the world, piracy on the high seas still poses a great threat. This may be because no law is enforced since no government exists to do so. However, if the situation gets much worse, shipping companies might resort to organizing transport in convoys in some areas, accompanied by privately owned frigates to fire upon pirate ships. This might lead many pirates to change their line of work and enter the less risky business of convoy protection. In the Middle Ages, this was quite usual and necessary, as was the official licensing of pirates by governments to attack and plunder enemy or competing merchant navies.

Economic actors are not exposed to similarly stark threats and considerations in present-day western Europe, at least not most of the time, apart from petty theft, pilfering, and fraud. Entrepreneurship and management have become more civilized over the centuries, and this has happened by throwing killing, plundering, and war into a different and separate domain of society. Although Weber was criticized for being a representative of authoritarian state traditions in this respect, his depiction of the modern state as one with a monopoly over the use of force reveals a large amount of progress in civilization. Apart from that, the logic of action presenting itself to actors has remained identical. Entrepreneurs and managers have more or less vested interests, although different and shifting ones, in securing certain transactions in such a way that the costs and returns become more predictable and less uncertain. Government may also share this interest because it would like, for instance, to expand the tax base or to raise the level of satisfaction in the population. Securing transactions amounts to creating a public good when no transactor can be excluded from its benefits.

There does exist a large grey area between goods that are definitely public and those that are undeniably private. This grey area is partly filled with quasi-public goods produced by both collectively organized and privately contracted suppliers who, in turn, may be identical with or related to users. Suppose that an international maritime association organizes convoys accompanied by frigates, in return for a fee dependent on cargo value or tonnage, but open to any peaceful freight or passenger ship. This would still be a clear-cut case. Now imagine the situation of a maritime association running frigates and convoys but compelling all ships operating in certain areas to pay a fee, whether they join the convoys or not. Arguably, many ships may otherwise choose to operate close to convoys, free-riding on high-sea protection. Or alternatively, a secret deal between convoy protection businesses and pirates may make sure that those not paying the fee are hijacked or plundered.[321]

6.2.2   The dialectical complementarity of liberalism and corporatist governance

This little thought-experiment takes us right into what is central to corporate governance and entrepreneurship in the South Germanic bedrock. By virtue of the constitution of this society, the governance that became metatraditional implied a tight interweaving of legitimate rule and domination, as Weber was accustomed to call it, with guild or corporatist institutions. These have reasserted themselves as complements to more liberal practice, located in different corners of institutionally partitioned spaces. The rationale of this partitioning is that securing some transactions or provisions will help entrepreneurs face other risks or uncertainties more willingly. Such a dialectical theory of the management and reduction of uncertainty posits that actors are neither risk-takers nor risk-avoiders across the board. They countenance the acceptance and management of some uncertainty more willingly if they are insured or buffered against other kinds of uncertainty. Sometimes a separate state or insurance will cover some uncertainty. Sometimes enterprises will induce a state or other community to do this. Yet sometimes enterprises may collectively govern some of their operations on the basis of private or public contributions or inducements, in order to eliminate a specific type of uncertainty and thereby make other uncertainties more manageable.

Contrary to some liberal presuppositions, the meaning of corporatist practices has not overwhelmingly been to reduce the extent of competition, at least not in the dialectical perspective on the management of uncertainty. This is because—and this follows neatly from Streeck's analysis—entrepreneurs and managers are cognitively and morally unable to compete on all fronts at the same time. They will strive to obtain a number of certainties in order to manage better what remains uncertain. In this way, the management of uncertainty in one domain is dialectically linked to the creation of relative certainty in another one. Should uncertainty exist across the board, or the effort to tackle it take place in an integral fashion in a reasonably differentiated society, what is produced is an order which Weber classified as 'types of illegitimate domination'.[322] Now, why should Weber have called the government of a medieval (free) town illegitimate domination? Because the independence or autonomy of the town was often won by defeating a sovereign ruler? Was not such a rebellion then at least legitimate in the long run? It would be legitimate if those being ruled accepted it as such, which they patently did.

To distinguish legitimate from illegitimate domination, we need to recognize an additional aspect that Weber overlooked. As an occidental phenomenon, legitimate rule and domination require a certain amount of neutrality of that rule with regard to non-public interests. This neutrality need not be excessive, but it must be demonstrable and credible. Even dominant class interests are never entirely homogeneous. Their heterogeneity requires any collective representation of such interests to be different, in both substance and organization, from the more specific interests of some central actors. Yet at the same time, a close relationship with private interests also benefits the greater public interest, as the literature on corporatism, to which Streeck has referred and contributed, attests in many ways. In order for the whole corporatist apparatus not to become sterile or corrupt, it must be based on private enterprise dynamics—the management of new or different uncertainty—which is unleashed by the collective reduction of uncertainty that corporatist associations assume as quasi-public institutions; such dynamics must also be in the interest of the community.

As a mediator between private and public interests, corporatist governance would be stripped of legitimacy if the production of certainty were only to reduce the need for managing uncertainty. That would be a shift from uncertainty to certainty. Legitimacy is better established, at least in a 'modern' economy and society, if one kind of reduction of uncertainty enhances the management of another kind of uncertainty. This is a dialectical link between the two in the typical evolutionary mode of partitioning and recombination of opposites. But there are, to be sure, non-dialectical evolutions that are produced by a sheer reduction of uncertainty on all fronts. Weber has mentioned examples of these from German history, and those reading news reports on both post-Soviet societies and the public-private fraud and corruption in very liberal societies will quickly notice that they crop up again in the form of mafia-like protection insurance.[323] Protection insurance is mafia-like if the use of public authority, especially the use of its monopoly of force, is also mobilized by private business interests or vice versa.

In view of the dialectical relation between collective insurance against uncertainty and the management of uncertainty, corporatist constructions appear to walk a tightrope between the public and the private generation of generally available goods. They may strike a beneficial institutional balance between the private-public creation of public goods and the private generation and appropriation of goods. But what happens may also fade into the private appropriation of public goods, inefficiency in generating and distributing public goods, or even illegitimate governance. German history is full of examples of all these possible cases. Its metatradition has unfolded through a rich, diversified, and changing corporatist apparatus, for the purpose of organizing divergent interests in a coherent, institutional way that is closely intertwined with the functioning of the modern state. Enterprises thus contribute to the generation of public goods from which they also benefit, since uncertainty is reduced on a number of counts. In terminology which Marx used but would probably not have applied to corporatism within capitalism, this works if reducing uncertainty unleashes productive forces. It is only when productive forces are stifled that class antagonism becomes revolutionary. Whether the reduction of uncertainty does or does not unleash productive forces depends on more specific contingencies. But the metatraditional phenomenon as such is stable and has recurred in ever new forms. It has set the keynote for corporate governance and enterprise management and eluded the stylized contrasts between 'the market' and hierarchy, or between the public and the private domains.

The principal public goods that enterprises have thus helped to create are the following:

- Stable conditions for the valorization of invested capital, as far as supporting and coordinating entrepreneurial activities are concerned, and the assurance that labour will act as a production factor without any friction or at least that labour conflicts are carried out in an orderly fashion.
- A collectively defined pool of qualified and transferrable human resources, to an extent far above and beyond what an individual enterprise requires from a short-term perspective, including a pool of potential entrepreneurs.

As we have seen, a metatradition of institutional development means that countervailing tendencies are characteristically dominant in different eras. But their relative and time-specific dominance is reversible. It leads to the assertion of a contrary tendency, and development in the long run is characterized by a synthesis of such countervailing tendencies. Also, the reassertion of earlier tendencies that may have been temporarily overwhelmed by their opposite does not mean simplistic regression to earlier forms. This is because there emerge new sets of meanings, functions, and syncretic cultural and institutional practices. Older templates are generalized beyond their earlier restricted context, or they penetrate into new contexts, and they are mostly embedded in a context in which they function differently.

6.3   Entrepreneurship and top management, strategy, and organization

6.3.1   Family firms and impersonal juggernauts

Governance, entrepreneurship, and management have one main thing in common: the exercise of control. This opens a very wide field, differentiated by levels of aggregation, institutional domains, and control practices. Furthermore, control partly overlaps with the notion of coordination, which means that actors align their activities without being directly exhorted to do so by a directive authority or code. Kenneth Merchant has distinguished the dimensions of direct–indirect and personal–impersonal and combined them to generate a typology of control in a fourfold table. This is different from but partly coincides with a typology Mintzberg has supplied with regard to mechanisms of coordination.[324] In addition, there are political economy concepts of control and coordination, which mainly distinguish between control internal to an organization, external regulatory control, and market control.[325] Furthermore, we have the interpretation of control and coordination from the angle of interorganizational theory, which is concerned with networks and alliances.[326] If we further differentiate control by its origins, its legitimacy, and its execution, which takes us into the literature on industrial relations, we have a collection of salient notions that lead to an overly complex typology. Although it is possible with Herculean effort to integrate such concepts, it is nearly impossible to use the result to organize historically comparative work on entrepreneurship and corporate governance.

This situation is not improved by the fact that historians do not have much of a systematic comparative tradition in the strict sense defined in the previous chapter. It is very difficult to ascertain comparability and to distinguish the differences between reasonably comparable phenomena from the differences in the population of enterprises and institutions that we find in various societies. Let me propose a fast and, one hopes, not too dirty conflation of types into the following array. We find:

- small-firm entrepreneurship linking entrepreneurship and top management and featuring personal and direct control in independent firms;
- large-firm entrepreneurship featuring a greater or lesser differentiation between ownership and management and using impersonal and indirect controls internally, mostly as one descends in the hierarchy;
- district, putting-out, and stable outsourcing control and coordination between firms, using relational contracting and direct impersonal controls and coordination between firms;
- impersonal market controls;

- industrial or sectoral governance by public authorities;
- associational or quasi-public governance, involving chambers and associations for employers, industries, and employees, with individual or corporate membership and contributions.

These different forms can then be combined, more or less closely. At the end of a major survey article, Jürgen Kocka arrived at the following conclusion regarding Germany: 'One can say that in the brief decades between the end of the industrial revolution and the first World War there appeared central characteristics of management and entrepreneurship in organized capitalism which have continued to mark its development until today'.[327] This is a remarkable statement, given that Germany subsequently saw the further rise of cartel capitalism, a combination of very pronounced corporatist governance combined with central public planning (the latter during two world wars and also in preparation for the second one), a subsequent period of radical decartelization and goods-markets liberalization, an episode of economic deinternationalization in the Weimar Republic and the first years of Nazism, and then an episode of opening up to a European and a world economy. What then is it that makes a configuration of entrepreneurship and management appear stable over time?

Governance, entrepreneurship, and higher management have recently been interpreted as being subject to agency problems. This means that principals are confronted with the dilemma of how to institute controls which ensure that agents fulfil their roles and exercise their discretion in the interests of the principal. Principals may be governments or other authorities representing broader interests or merely individual shareholders. Now, the precise interests of a principal will depend on the principal's social construction. An economically 'neutral' government will be interested, for instance, in an optimal generation or distribution of welfare or both, and it will institute controls that elicit contributions from agents that are compatible with this interest. A shareholder of a company will potentially be interested in different things, depending on the relative size of the shareholdings, whether the shareholder takes an instrumental or intrinsic interest in the enterprise, and whether the shareholder is also involved in entrepreneurship or management. Since issues of entrepreneurship and governance are difficult to segment into smaller and specific arenas, any institutional arrangement that prevails will be the result of a political process in which the general and specific interests of different actors come into play.

The interesting thing about Germany is that it has evolved a particular industrial and firm-size structure. On the one hand, it has a fairly even spread of industries. But it has been a world leader in terms of the percentage of the labour force employed in industry since the formative period mentioned by Kocka. It has kept that position ever since, despite deindustrialization.[328] Germany appears to have evolved arrangements in entrepreneurship and corporate governance, as well as institutions governing work systems that give it some comparative advantages in a number of manufacturing industries and producer services. It appears to have developed such advantages not mainly in the fields where the organizational juggernauts operate, i.e. the large, diversified, and multinational firms, but primarily in 'flexibly specialized' small to medium-sized firms.[329] These typically are the enterprises which one finds in the engineering industries.

German definitions of medium-sized firms tend to extend rather deeply into what would be considered elsewhere as 'large'. An official EU definition of medium-sized firms puts the upper limit of the labour force at 250 employees. German definitions range from up to 500 to just under 1,000 employees. While different definitional conventions are to some extent arbitrary, they are also significant social constructions. The idea of the medium-sized firm is close to that of *Mittelstand*. This not only includes companies of a small or medium size, but also the close involvement of owners in management. Furthermore, such an enterprise is ideally imagined to constitute a community of fate binding together different classes. Just as it is expected that an owner should not frivolously abandon his or her enterprise for the simple reason that investment in a different enterprise or fund is more lucrative at some point, it is also expected that efforts should be made to stabilize employment, at least in whatever can be defined as the core labour force.

In other words, the interests of the principal are not only instrumental but intrinsic. Since the work of principals is work, it would be surprising if it was not subject to intrinsic motivation. Entrepreneurs derive direct utility from the professional fulfilment, status, and reputation that running the enterprise confers, whether or not some narrower economic theories consider this a complication. As Marx said, any historical configuration to unleash productive forces is based on exploitation. Self-exploitation occurs when entrepreneurs invest their own labour to a degree that exceeds the tangible instrumental benefits. Many entrepreneurs and managers are subjectively or objectively required to do that, certainly when they are in a pioneering phase or in a price-competitive and highly contested market. In addition, some amount of entrepreneurial profit or managerial benefits is considered to be an indicator of commitment and achievement due to intrinsic work motivation.

Although all this makes a cost–benefit assessment of entrepreneurial activity messy, it may make the activity more productive. Furthermore, salaries and distributed earnings are not only of instrumental value but are basic to the acquisition and maintenance of status, reputation, and satisfaction; they are both tangible and intangible benefits at the same time. In view of the perennially difficult problem of entrepreneurial succession, such enterprises may often decline and falter because entrepreneurship may have become asset-specific to such an extent that its replacement is intractable. However, a personalized legitimation of entrepreneurial authority remains important. It can also be acquired by non-owning managers on the basis of professional competence. If entrepreneurs do not translate their own asset specificity into a monopoly rent but engage in some measure of self-exploitation, they not only enhance dynamic productivity but the legitimacy of capitalism as such. In an order which remains capitalist, regardless of the variety, that is objectively seen as a public good.

The grooming of entrepreneurial succession requires attention in companies where entrepreneurship, management, and ownership are linked. In an economy such as Germany's has come to be, one in which employment, economic returns, and exports are greatly centred on medium-sized enterprises with overlapping management and ownership, we can expect to find a widespread practice of grooming successors. It is a part of culture and a soft institution, if not sanctioned through more rigid institutions.

The grooming may take different forms. Families who own businesses have a habit of providing hand-picked successors with good vocational training and higher education in technology, law, or business, and with experience in other companies or abroad in addition to varied experience in the target enterprise. Emphasis is placed on familiarity with details as well as general perspectives. This sort of grooming is very much contingent on the available potential, and it is also to be found in non-engineering industries. Consider the example of a company whose business involves forestry, holiday resort infrastructure, urban property, and assorted capital interests. It manages all this on behalf of an old aristocratic family that has withdrawn from management but has maintained an intrinsic interest in some invested property. Although medium-sized, this company is nevertheless located in various different national and international locations. The successor was personally selected by the predecessor on the basis of personal qualities, training, and a doctorate in law, which was considered vital in view of the complications arising through capital investment in various ventures and the ensuing transactions. The successor was then required to become familiar with the operational basics of the business property (infrastructure in Alpine resorts, forestry, and some urban real estate) by obtaining qualifications in three subjects: hunting, skiing, and company taxation. This man then worked as assistant to the manager for ten years before succeeding him. Likewise, the owner of a brewery would groom a son for succession by sending him to a technical university to study brewing technology and business administration and then by having him work in other breweries.[330]

Entrepreneurship in Germany has rightly been described as a highly personal syndrome. It has been construed as something that cannot be 'taught' in educational or training courses. University education for prospective managers has been comparatively widespread by any standard. However, this has been seen as providing basic or additional knowledge for specialization and authority, not for actually creating candidates to fill the positions of top management or entrepreneurship. For a long time, the latter have retained an aura of personal charisma for which there is no training or formal education.[331] At the same time, the ascription of entrepreneurship has not been limited to the selection of people to fill important posts. Grooming has been part of this development all along; it has combined early selection with long-term exposure to experience that is construed as bringing about entrepreneurial competence. It has been based less on a specific idea of generalism than on a more cautious idea of multi-specialization, to be built up step by step. Until recently, German entrepreneurship has rejected the idea that MBA courses constitute an 'inside lane' or 'fast track' to top positions. In this respect, medium-sized and owner-managed companies have been similar to large joint-stock companies.

The governance pattern found in and perpetuated by such medium-sized companies possesses a highly personalized element of control that is linked with ownership and consists of extensive socialization. In addition to safeguarding their independence as much as possible, such enterprises are also embedded in relational contracting and in associational and quasi-public governance. Rather than tying them only into relational and regulatory schemes, the latter types of governance have also sustained the commercial and technical manoeuvrability of these companies. Such a pattern is not absent in other societies. However, the corporatist governance that has evolved in the South Germanic bedrock, together with the social construction of entrepreneurship, has made this a pervasive and institutionally very tangible pattern. This pattern may be a source of strength if it dialectically unleashes entrepreneurial forces on fronts other than those for which greater certainty is made to prevail. Of course, it may also be a weakness if a complex apparatus of governance and administration or specific arrangements render entrepreneurs immobile.

Even large enterprises are under the influence of this pattern because it is, after all, geared to create a smooth link between entrepreneurship and top management, on the one hand, and work systems, on the other. As authors on the varieties of capitalism have shown, the pattern does make it somewhat difficult to introduce more radical technical or organizational change, but it also supports more incremental change. Moreover, it is linked to lower profitability in comparison with Anglo-American capitalism, which is explained by the structural need for self-exploitation. Although there should be no need for this in multinationals, their profitability is also lower when they are German, which attests to the importance of societal institutions compared to the international context.[332] However, this heightens the social legitimacy of this form of capitalism so that, as the press and other media in Germany have pervasively demonstrated during recent unfriendly takeover bids, socially illegitimate forms of capitalism are generally branded as foreign.

In the recent literature on shareholder value capitalism, which is different from the pattern sketched out for Germany and notably its backbone of medium-sized enterprises, there are not yet any findings on how entrepreneurship and top management generally have changed under its impact. There has been research on joint-stock companies and particularly on large and publicly traded ones, but there is nothing on how new forms of capitalism have affected the backbone of the German economy, meaning the enterprises that are not joint-stock and publicly traded. The few existing large enterprises attract extraordinary attention, but this should not prevent us from dealing extensively with change in this less important segment later.

6.3.2   Leadership, specialization, and management

Entrepreneurship and top management are linked with work systems through transmission belts. Transmission belts can metaphorically be seen to transmit both force and information from the top down and vice versa. Two main transmission belts are imaginable: leadership and management. The difference between them is simple but often disregarded. Leadership presumes that the leader is part of the collective which is being led. There is no subject–object division creating a fundamental distinction between them. Accordingly, they can identify with each other, to a great extent at least. This commonality may be built on similar experience and knowledge, but it also needs a normative orientation. Even a herd of cows being led to the meadow by a farm boy will accept his direction only by symbolic acknowledgement of such a commonality, and it is crucial that the cows perform it.[333] Leadership evokes symbolic unity, tacit knowledge, intuition, and emotion.

Management is different in that it posits a subject–object relationship between the manager and the managed. A manager creates cognitive distance between himself and those he manages in order to enable more sober and calculative consideration of action. Management evokes an objectified view, affective neutrality, and rational understanding. We can manage computer files, budget accounts, the flight of an aeroplane (e.g. selecting a course, speed, altitude, and climb and descent patterns to achieve fuel economy) as much as we can an organizational entity consisting of people. The implication is not that management and leadership are separate activities. They are typically linked, but leadership or management may be given different weight in different jobs or encounters. It involves behavioural diligence to keep them together and apart at the same time and to make choices on when to activate which pattern and how to change from one to the other without losing credibility and effectiveness. This set of issues is one of the most discussed and debated in both the practice and theory of management and organization.[334]

Different languages have different terms for the notions implied. Before the advent of American managerial practices, the German language did not have strictly equivalent terms for management. A similarly objectified and rational posture was, to be sure, inherent in the notion of *Verwaltung* or administration, but it was used more with regard to non-human objects and implied a static, mechanical, and reactive posture. It was more concerned with execution than with the open and proactive weighing of alternatives. A term for leadership—*Führung*—was, however, used extensively. This is not identical with the ideologized Nazi notion of the *Führerprinzip*, contrary to the more recent convictions of both foreigners and Germans. *Führen* was coined to refer to, and still refers to, a broad range of activities, including the driving of a car, the flying of an aeroplane, and the control of a machine, as well as the leading of a group or larger collective. The implication is not merely one of mechanical and rational submission; the connotative emphasis has been on the 'feel' activated when coming in contact with a steering-wheel, the 'touch' of the controls of the aeroplane, the physical sensation of handling a metal-cutting machine, and the either authoritarian or participative empathy with the human group or collective.

The irony is that, with respect to the commonplace and mundane activities of controlling tools and machines, Germans have kept the term *Führung*, as in

Führerschein (driving licence), *Maschinenführer* (machine operator), and *Flugzeug-führer* (aircraft pilot), whereas it has slipped out of use with regard to leadership in human groups and collectives: the *Betriebsführer* has become a *Betriebsleiter* or *Betriebsingenieur*, the *Gruppenführer* a *Gruppensprecher* or *Gruppenleiter*, only *Geschäfts-führer* (managing director of a limited liability company) has been kept as a technical term in law. With regard to human leadership, the term has been gradually forced off the stage. While this undoubtedly denotes a cultural shift to greater participa-tion, it does not mean that the cultural and institutional phenomenon of empathetic leadership based on commonality as such has been eroded. Where work systems characteristically breed commonalities through overlapping roles and careers, nothing else would fit in. It also has to be understood that empathetic leadership is not the opposite of the exercise of authority. It certainly is not in a German societal context, which is why the occupational logics within organizations and careers contrive to link authority with occupational solidarity.

Commonality can be vested in different symbolically meaningful characteristics. It may be a 'family firm', but the most prevalent transmission belt between top 'management' and work systems continues to be a specialized profession or occu-pation (*Beruf*). This notion is very modern, although it dates back linguistically to Lutheran doctrines and vocabulary. It emerged and became official towards the end of the nineteenth century. There are thus several transmission belts, distinguished by specialized occupations or larger occupational fields. Such occupational fields emphasize commonalities between higher and lower positions in the hierarchy. Their construction (see the previous chapter) thereby enables people to advance continually in their occupation by acquiring further education and training in the field. If a hierarchy rests on professional and occupational specialization and advancement, it is necessarily linked to an emphasis on leadership. Where occu-pational commonalities are strong up or down the hierarchy, management alone is seen as inadequate and unsatisfactory because of the distance it posits between those who manage and those being managed. In a German scheme of things, leadership, through the commonality it supposes, thus means sharing in something, which boils down to participation. In order for commonality to work, the subordination that inevitably exists in companies must be complemented by a sizeable element of leadership in those vertically constructed occupational fields and specialties. In other words, leadership is the legitimation for the subordination found in com-panies, but it works through participation.

Countless publications have reiterated that individuals can no longer expect to remain in the same occupation for their entire working life. Yet, outside the civil services, such occupations have been very infrequent anyway; the depiction of individuals engaging in the same occupation all their working lives has been little more than a caricature, at least to the extent that increasing longevity has enabled people to reach retirement age. Even in the older civil and public services, locomotive drivers were always required to have first completed a technical apprenticeship, and policemen who had no further education also had first to complete an apprenticeship of some kind. Similarly, there were clearly defined occupational paths for military staff to enter public and private services.[335] For a long time, Germany has had an impressive degree of occupational mobility, be it from rural to urban occupations, from public to private services or vice versa, from direct production to technical and other fields, from handicrafts to industry. Such occupational trajectories have been institutionalized in a broad array of occupational fields by requiring further education and training in addition to a more 'basic' occupation. Throughout this development, the occupational construction of transmission belts between the top echelons of management and work systems has been left intact; if certain specific occupations dwindle in importance, they are not replaced by an accidental patchwork of jobs but by trajectories in occupational fields.[336]

On this basis, it is understandable that top management, as the top end of different occupational transmission belts, has pervasively exhibited a functional subdivision of roles: technical directorship, commercial directorship, law and personnel directorship, for instance; or a more elaborate set-up with research and development, production (the technical functions), sales, accounting and finance (the commercial functions), etc. Occupations have followed this functional subdivision of tasks and knowledge. This has also been reflected in a comparative study of middle management in Germany and Britain. German middle management is simpler. It stabilizes organizational structures but focuses on the management of processes; it is less organizationally but more professionally conscious; and it has greater familiarity with and interest in operational matters. Career progression from non-managerial to managerial jobs happens within a field of occupational practice. Managers therefore have a more functional-occupational identity than a generalist one.[337] This was established in the 1990s and corresponds to comparisons made much earlier. There does not appear to have been any comparative change with respect to practice in another country during any period of time.

For quite a while, well past the onset of Americanization, any business management that lacked leadership was discredited under such a regime. In the 1950s, 'management' and 'manager' still had pejorative connotations. Managers were dubious characters because they could supposedly neither train nor lead subordinates. The terms were reserved for those who ran itinerant road shows or funfair establishments, for example.[338] Scepticism towards management has been focused particularly on general management. In practice, this function, which exists in all enterprises notwithstanding social ideology, was often performed collectively in medium-sized firms by a team of *Geschäftsführer*, some of whom were trained technicians and some of whom were commercial, financial, and accounting experts. The only individuals who acted as true general managers were the chairmen of boards of management in joint-stock companies (*Aktiengesellschaften*) and the rare divisional chairmen in conglomerates.[339]

Although this pejorative attitude toward management has been tempered over the years, the distinction between management and leadership is still clearly maintained in many domains. What in a British football enterprise (to avoid using the term 'club', since that term is no longer appropriate in the upper divisions of football) has come to be called the manager is called the *Trainer* in Germany; conversely the *Manager* of a German football team is a director in charge of the football division, as it were, and he might also be called the *Sportdirektor* or *Technischer Direktor* (sports or technical director). This shows how concepts become established as symbolic enactments, although what a British football manager does is presumably not very different from what a German *Trainer* does. This is what our functionalist mind tells us, not robust comparative research. In both countries, the responsibility for acquiring and selling players would be a reason for attributing managerial labels more plausibly, but characteristically in Germany this responsibility has been shared by *Trainers* for a long time. There may well be conflict with 'management', but prominent *Trainers* insist on being very closely involved in hiring and firing decisions. This in itself is already a significant difference.

The term *Manager* has come increasingly into use, however, in German enterprises that are internationally active and have international staff; so too has use of the English language as a *lingua franca*. This has happened as responsibility has increasingly focused on specific products or services, world regional markets, or other segments of a business combining commercial and technical responsibilities. This has meant a crossing of functional and occupational principles of organizational subdivision by integrating responsibility for product areas or world regions, and, in the same vein, by devolving general management functions. Over time, the general idea of management has acquired greater legitimacy, even penetrating the reaches of middle management. Although comparative information is still lacking, my impression is that this has not meant a decline of leadership as a legitimating idea and a form of practice.

Recent studies do show that the importance of basic vocational education through apprenticeship among the top management of small and medium-sized companies has been reduced over time, that the importance of university education has increased greatly, and that the more commercial and general managerial competencies have become more important compared to the technical ones. To that extent entrepreneurship and top management in small and medium-sized companies exhibit tendencies which are also present in other countries. On the other hand, the share of top managers and entrepreneurs combining apprenticeship with a university education is still at a comparatively substantial level. Both having 'learnt a trade' from the bottom up (*von der Pike auf*) and recruitment of entrepreneurs out of familial backgrounds that are already entrepreneurial have retained their importance. This has not prevented more paternalist views and practices from mutating towards co-management ideas, i.e. the idea that the works council should move from a representation of employee interests to greater entrepreneurial responsibility. But this is what many works councils have already done informally. While shareholder value thinking is evident in the greater importance attached to capital markets and to outsourcing and core competence policies, the social texture of enterprise communities and of leadership has not changed; its salience has if anything become more consciously realized as entrepreneurs and management confront imported shareholder value doctrines.[340]

We must not confuse a general tendency across different economies and societies with the extent of differences between them. We have always had intersocietal tendencies with societally specific origins that have become internationally pervasive and set the keynote in many countries; but this has not meant that differences are reduced. Societies and economies may be moving in a roughly similar direction, but precisely because they do, the differences between them are not diminished. A part of this argument is theoretical: evolutionary change is one of opposite principles being creatively combined. The posture of German management is, then, to combine 'true' management with leadership. One must not be fooled by the increasing frequency with which the word *Manager* is used in German as a job description. This is the emic aspect of a cultural and institutional phenomenon, which tends to be combined with a translation into a somewhat different etic code.

The resilience of leadership and occupational transmission belts, moreover, can be expected to remain particularly important vertebrae in the backbone of the German economy, namely in the wide spectrum of medium-sized companies featuring a substantial concentration of ownership and owner management. One of the advantages of such enterprises is that management can 'run a tight ship' and harness the socio-organizational cohesion of staff. This remains an effort requiring strong transmission belts, and these work as part of the machinery of occupational orders.

6.3.3 *Changing enterprise architecture*

Enterprise architectures invariably combine different principles, such as in the structuring of functional, matrix, and divisional organizations. In the microcosm of a company, we can find a qualitatively distinct combination of such types and subtypes. This is subject to a partitioning and recombination of institutional templates over time. What applies to the evolution of societies and economies also applies to the evolution of companies, though probably to a lesser extent. It is convenient at this point to discuss enterprise architecture as it is linked with work systems; in the previous chapter these were described as being governed by occupational subdivision, meaning a functional subdivision of the organization.

At least as far as rhetoric is concerned, the 1950s and 1960s in Germany were very much marked by genuine curiosity about everything that came from the United States. Just as this curiosity reached its climax, a report by the consultants Booz, Allen, and Hamilton was published and discussed. This report attested to the fact that enterprise architecture and business methods had become far less Americanized than could be presumed on the basis of the liberalization of product markets, the internationalization of economic activity, and notably the spread of multinationals. In practice, both curiosity and rhetoric had led to limited results. German firms came under attack for having either domesticated or simply discarded American templates. Functional organization abounded, whereas matrix and divisional organization were rare. A firm's product, institutional, and stakeholder traditions were respected; dense networks of various stakeholders held sway over top management; quantitative methods of operations research, control, and planning were rarely found or were unsophisticated; management development was a personal matter; and MBA degrees obtained during career progression were very infrequent.[341]

Interestingly, one of those in Germany disposed to look upon the introduction of American methods more favourably, Heinz Hartmann, criticized the report at the time (1973) as expressing a certain measure of 'cultural imperialism'. His argument was that the superiority of American concepts was hard to ascertain; so why should we be surprised not to see them spread as much as rhetoric made us believe they had done? From then on, the drift of discussion changed, not only in Germany but also abroad. German enterprise architecture was discovered as exhibiting not only delays or lags of adaptation to a presumed international best practice, but as also containing a logic that was no bad match for a new supranational context.[342] The collapse of the Bretton Woods Agreement with its fixed currency exchange rates, the oil crises, and the evolution of product markets that many western countries faced led to the decline of Fordist accumulation. All this resulted in a transition from stable or expanding mass production to more segmented and differentiated markets, a transition that could be seen to favour retention of the German organization and management template: primacy of technical functions, continuous adaptation of products to seek out more specific market niches, strategies to cope with greater volatility on the basis of a loyal and versatile workforce. Suddenly, the fact that a large German enterprise was more often than not an overgrown medium-sized firm became an asset rather than a liability.

This was not yet a time when the deconglomeration of conglomerates was expounded propagandistically, either in the United States or in Germany. American management templates still followed the idea of the conglomerate company. For example, in the Boston Consulting Group concept, companies were to possess and control a portfolio of different products and services, some of which were to be more of the 'cash cow' type, i.e. those generating revenue on the basis of a proven design and marketing pitch. The revenue from these was then to help finance the development of immature products. Cross-subsidization of product and services lines within a conglomerate was an accepted fact.

A number of large enterprises in Germany did follow this concept of a conglomerate and were highly integrated vertically or laterally. The German practice of occupational specialization and its preponderance, with substantial overlap of competence between adjacent jobs and occupations, retained its attractiveness as a way of keeping conglomerates flexible and allowing them to evolve in different directions without losing their identity and manageability. Let us consider a simple example. RWE (Rheinisch-Westfälische Elektrizitätswerke AG) was a dominant utility enterprise supplying electricity primarily to Germany's core industrial region at the time. It also controlled Rheinbraun, a local mining company extracting soft coal in open-cast mines in the region; the coal was used to produce electricity. Furthermore, RWE had its own telephone communication system, as all utility companies did, in order to assure communication lines of a higher standard of reliability than the public telephone system could guarantee in a sensitive network of power plants. When the market for telephone communication radically expanded and changed in the 1990s, RWE went over to offering telephone services to the public at large. Before it did, it could still interpret itself within a German conceptuality as a conglomerate with 'related' diversification, for everything appeared to hinge on the generation of energy and the stabilization of inputs, outputs, and related products and services, with regard to this technical core. The policy was to create a flexible conglomerate, rather than to deconglomerate enterprise architecture by product lines or in the supply chain.

Similarly, at Daimler–Benz in the 1980s, the preferred policy was to be an integrated supplier, not only of high-standard cars, lorries, and other utility vehicles, but also—by acquisition—aeroplanes and aerospace products, military equipment, and electronics. The idea was that 'synergy' between product areas in the course of innovation was to keep the management of the wide portfolio feasible. In a nutshell, this was still the old Boston Consulting Group idea of a balanced portfolio permitting enterprise growth by cross-subsidization and cross-fertilization of new business opportunities. At both Daimler–Benz and RWE, the idea, which was still 'American' to some extent, was to achieve growth by relying on 'related' rather than 'unrelated' diversification, thus avoiding the threat of unmanageability seemingly inherent in the latter, and by keeping the various product areas related on the basis of the synergy concept. Such concepts represented, in a way, an inseparable combination of both German and American approaches, and they shaped big business very much during the period that was later said to have given birth to the post-1945 'German model'.

Despite the propagandistic slant given to the ideas of relatedness and synergy, these were also tangible phenomena. The technical-occupational relatedness of activities in a German scheme, with many transient overlaps, made these ideas realistic up to a point. The policy was therefore one in which 'German' work systems might make an 'American' product portfolio feasible, and this had a notable affinity with practices used in some large German companies in the past. In the 1980s, we witness again an eclectic combination of domestic and foreign models. It has also been evident in financial services with the nascent concept of *Allfinanz*, i.e. a financial institution and strategy that includes not only all manner of banking services but also insurance. Curiously enough, this reached its climax very recently, in 2002, with the friendly takeover of Dresdner Bank by Allianz, the largest insurance company. Similarly Deutsche Bank has established a preferential alliance with an insurance company. This at least is contrary to the new rhetoric about core business and the segmentation of the supply chain or vertical disintegration.

Vertical and lateral integration were not the only concepts. Some large enterprises deliberately went about taking apart product portfolios and supply chains, and focusing their management on business cores, much earlier than the current discussion about German business history is prepared to remember. However, the idea that a business needed to have a strong core and that 'the product' played the greatest role in defining a company was widely accepted in Germany before the term 'core business' was coined in English. Those that survived took it to heart. In the 1950s, Siemens and AEG were not only part of the proud and important inheritance from the wave of industrialization using the 1900 version of the 'German model'; they were also more comparable, since both were large and fairly all-round suppliers of electrical and electronic products for households, public utilities, and commercial clients. It was AEG that produced PAL as the first and most frequently used standard of colour television in western Europe. But then, they parted company. Whereas AEG continued its strong diversification, Siemens did not. It more or less jettisoned domestic appliances such as washing machines, consumer electronics, and other household goods. It had identified and implemented a 'core business' of non-household goods as early as the 1970s and sought product niches where constant innovation would assure de-maturity and better strengthen barriers against competition. 'De-maturity' means to rejuvenate products through constant piecemeal innovation in order to prevent them from becoming mature and thus more liable to price competition by entrants new to the respective market. As has been explained to me by older Siemens managers, AEG dug in precisely where margins and profit opportunities were being increasingly squeezed, whereas Siemens abandoned such markets and products in favour of a set of core products that were kept de-mature by ongoing development in order to keep the margin of price over costs sufficiently large.

Siemens labels are still found on some household goods, but these have been transacted to a new joint venture with Bosch, following a different template and including growing production in foreign countries. The demise of AEG (via a merger with Telefunken, then sale to Daimler-Benz and its eventual disappearance for all practical purposes) was already well understood inside Siemens in the beginning of the 1980s. They saw their rival as having clung to household products, whereas Siemens had dropped these or started new alliance-based ventures for them, and focused on investment goods which fitted an enterprise template of continuous improvement and innovation that generated and sustained profit margins. A more recent example of this strategy is the hiving-off of microelectronic components development and production to Infineon. It is distinctive that Siemens did not opt to be a rapid-innovation firm in a supposedly high technology area itself. What it retained were fields of gradual innovation in goods where 'conventional' engineering and new techniques mixed, such as railways signals and control systems, a variety of industrial controls for processing industries, energy generation equipment, and medical diagnostic and treatment equipment. Such product specialization was then the occasion for the forming of divisions.

According to business theory, conglomerates can be managed to the extent that their different components are professionally 'related' to one another, reposing as they do on organizational methods and occupational identities that are strongly similar or overlapping[343]—for these feed into the top managerial processes that assure manageability. Arguably, German enterprise architecture can thus continue to keep conglomerates viable for a long time with the help of the work systems that it rests on, although a refocusing of the profile would be advisable at certain points, as the Siemens–AEG comparison shows. Now in relation to its substantial industrial economy, Germany has had fewer of these conglomerates. Yet one can argue that the ones it has had were viable for a long time because the construction of work systems and superimposed top management made it possible to take interrelatedness for granted or extend it. Daimler-Benz in the 1980s is a case in which strategies overextended the enterprise architecture and, as business theory predicts, made growth more likely to fail since it was being brought about by acquisition (MBB in aerospace and AEG-Telefunken) rather than by a 'natural growth' out of a previous, more limited portfolio.

Where conglomerates have emerged by endogenous growth rather than merger or acquisition, they are, with some plausibility, socially constructed to remain viable for a longer time. Paradoxically, this viability has been founded on the fact that German conglomerates have long retained characteristics of medium-sized firms. They are less like true conglomerates in the sense that they do not strongly resemble an acquired or self-mixed cocktail of more or less related activities and enterprise cultures, with the exception of consumer industries, notably foodstuffs. Instead, German conglomerates have been greatly extended medium-sized and large companies, or at least they have often been treated as if they were. Allied 'trust-busting' after the end of World War II was conducive to this, since it forced a number of large firms to give their business a narrower, sharper focus. Still, this was but another step in an evolution that had started nearly one and a half centuries ago, when German industrial companies emerged as rather monolithic and endogenously growing enterprises, often led by one technically trained and oriented entrepreneur who worked closely together with a financier or commercially experienced colleague.[344]

The example of RWE shows how the nexus of a conglomerate may be viable until the moment the dynamics of some markets, products, or techniques are such that they rapidly increase the factor of unrelatedness with regard to some established template. For instance, RWE has been forced to become an increasingly heterogeneous business because different competencies and organization are required to be a successful provider of mobile telephone services, compared to running a terrestrial system attuned to the high expectations placed on a company dealing in the generation of nuclear power as well. The moment RWE abandoned its ownership and operational control of the telephone company it had established, this signalled its deconglomeration. Such a process of deconglomeration could be observed over a longer period. Veba (a conglomerate *par excellence* with its collection of utilities, glass manufacturing, transport, and chemical industries) went through this process, as did some pharmaceutical companies such as Hoechst (with its core ending up as a new 'life sciences' multinational set up together with a French concern) and Schering (also focused on pharmaceuticals and selling off assorted chemical products, particularly agro-chemicals, to other industrial groups).

As conglomerates went out of fashion and the 'core business' or business process re-engineering became the new fashion, established German templates were not threatened across the board. As far as simpler and more streamlined enterprise architecture and product portfolio were concerned, the deconglomeration process took German enterprises back to their roots, to a more consolidated occupational and industrial base and a simpler architecture. Certainly with regard to simplicity of structure and the 'empowerment' of workers in the productive core, there was comparatively little for them to learn, when compared with enterprises in the countries that coined such newfangled slogans. But the return to the roots of their business may have been something of a shock to those whose memories had adjusted to the more recent value of stability in big enterprises and internal labour markets. The development could nevertheless be construed as precisely this, a return to the roots, although in the interest of increasing stock prices during a period when shareholder value capitalism was predominant—a point we will return to later—company public relations experts would have presented it as a ferocious exercise in Anglo-American downsizing and cut-and-thrust. However, focus on a core business is a traditional concept for medium-sized firms.

Some firms managed to do both, i.e. downsize enterprise architecture and ensure the continuation of co-determination and social peace. Schering greatly reduced its labour force and sold off various businesses to its competitors in the respective industries, with transition compensation and other assurances to employees, as part of its renewed focus on pharmaceuticals. This happened at the beginning of the 1990s without any confrontation, labour unrest, or public discussion or protest.[345] Here, too, one has to distinguish the rhetoric and hype from the practice. The practice existed in Germany before the rhetoric gave it a new name.

Another interesting change in enterprise architecture has been the spread of divisional organization in Germany, as compared to that in Britain and France. This has been studied extensively by Mayer and Whittington, who use time series on major companies quoted on stock markets.[346] At first, the story for German enterprises was very similar to what Booz, Allen, and Hamilton had determined at the beginning of the 1970s: notwithstanding size, German companies preferred functional organization and were averse to the divisional form. In my own work in Britain in the late 1970s, I observed formal divisions and matrix structures in situations where they would have been unthinkable in Germany at the time, and especially in German enterprises of similar size and product line.[347]

Even then, the managing director at one British site speculated about what officially came much later, i.e. a differentiation of wages and other conditions between divisions on the same site on the basis of different degrees of profitability. At the time, this idea was controversial among the board members, and the production director notably advised against it. However, in 1976, the practice of having two different, moderately sized divisions (a few hundred people each) share the same site was already accepted in Britain; so was the matrix organization in the British chemicals site. In Germany, just the idea of having different divisions on the same site would have appeared pretentious, and the chemicals site was organized according to a straightforward, functional principle (operations–maintenance–instrumentation), with de facto overlap of responsibilities occurring in the commonly shared field of chemical engineering, by linking chemistry and operations management with maintenance and mechanical engineering.

In the mean time, as Whittington and Mayer showed, large German companies moved to catch up with respect to divisional organization at the top levels of management. Divisional organization is applied at the top, but one would be unlikely to find the profusion of business units usually expected as a more disaggregate example of the divisional principle of organization or matrix structures. The increasing adoption of the divisional principle was shown to be particularly noteworthy for Germany, but this was only demonstrated for the top echelons of large companies. So, if we wish, we can say that Germany has indeed followed a sort of international best practice constituted by Anglo-American rivals. What we lack to date are comparisons of what divisional organization structures stand for in different countries, of their precise meaning in matching enterprises. Lacking this, it is difficult to draw conclusions with regard to societal convergence or divergence.

The phenomenon of a delayed and then eagerly promoted diffusion of models is not new for Germany, as we have seen. That country characteristically, almost recalcitrantly, asserts its preference for domestic models over foreign ones, and is also eager to adopt, translate, and domesticate the latter. What is more, German society generally alternates between and intertwines more traditional and domestic practices, on the one hand, and decontextualized international approaches, on the other. So, the question is whether we can expect much that is new in this respect with regard to evolving enterprise architecture. Matched-case studies would be helpful, but unfortunately we do not have any. Also, despite the increased pace with which German multinationals have recently been investing directly into other countries, it has become clear that the method of control they use over their rather far-flung empires still bears the imprint of their national society of origin. In this, they are no different from other multinationals from other countries; they only differ in the form such control takes.

The country-of-origin factor explains modes of coordination and control, even over the broad spectrum of international enterprise. Little else does. Strategies of internationalization (the steps proceeding from more cautious distribution and maintenance outlets to elaborate foreign subsidiaries, by direct investment or alliance) are best explained by industries.[348] German multinationals have historically treated their subsidiaries more like 'clones', which have had to follow their 'parent' technically and commercially, learning from it rather than operating independently. The subsidiaries have been more likely to emerge as internal start-ups, rather than as acquisitions or mergers. In the international arena of multinationals, what has been observed for the industrialization of Germany has again shaped the process of internationalization. We see that the behavioural template of the medium-sized and endogenously growing firm extends directly into the reaches of complex multinational enterprises. This has not been found elsewhere to the same extent.

6.4   Company finance, banks, and shareholders

6.4.1   The banking system

A basic question confronting any capitalist order is how to generate savings and channel them into productive investment. This question engages the financial action system of society and its economy, which is furnished with institutions governing the behaviour of banks and insurance companies as well as the financial side of company and consumer dispositions. The nature of such institutions is one of the central ingredients in varieties of capitalism.

This wider field of institutions in Germany follows from its distinctive process of societal and economic development. Again, we find the general characteristics already mentioned:

- There is an intricate web of institutional entities and provisions that mediate between or articulate private dispositions and entities, on the one hand, and those representing a public interest, on the other.
- Entities, particularly in the public or quasi-public sphere, have a strong regional demarcation, and regionally autonomous entities are tied up with state-or national-level entities in a layered financial institutional system.[349]
- A great deal of relational contracting occurs, mainly through stable and trust-based relations between banks and other enterprises. This is focused on the *Hausbank* principle, in which enterprises entertain privileged relations with one or more banks to obtain credit, and to monitor and support financial and non-financial dispositions.

The first characteristic, which can be summarized as financial corporatism, primarily involves a few publicly owned banks that promote particular missions, such as reconstruction, industrial or regional policies, and an elaborate system of savings banks, set up by towns or larger governmental districts. These have a commercial purpose as well as the goal of supporting the public policies and projects of towns and larger districts. Smaller savings banks (*Sparkassen*) are again associated with larger organizations supervised by states (*Landesbanken*), which pool funds from the smaller entities to engage in more voluminous and concentrated banking business. Furthermore, there are cooperative banks, which are also very regional institutions but which also have nodal entities that deal with specific types of business. These are typical suppliers of services to small business; since they are owned by their clients, they are also bound to relational contracting. Roughly one-third of the financial volume in bank balance statements rests with the purely commercial banks, one-third with the public savings bank system including the *Landesbanken*, and another third with the cooperative banks. Regionalization in the public and cooperative banking systems has already been mentioned. Relational contracting is typical throughout, as it is in purely commercial banks.

Historically, the roots of this financial system can be found in the nineteenth century, and the difference from Britain is again very informative. This has been nicely summed up in the following sentence: British banks are there to care for the money of those who have it already; German banks were set up to make money available to those who have less than they need.[350] The implication is that the debit side of banking (acquiring funds) was not a problem for British banks but the credit side required attention (deciding on where and under which conditions to invest money or give credit); for Germany, the implication is that attracting money from clients (the debit side) was considered problematic and required attention whereas granting credit may have been considered less problematic, possibly because the opportunities for placement were considered plentiful and secure or securable.

Such differences touch on socially constructed relations between banks, enterprises, and public regulation—the keynote of section 6.2 above—in this case with regard to the assurance of security of transactions and placements. Where banks compete for generating new funds, they will invest in the security of their credit business in order to put new depositors at ease, which they do by regulation of terms and by relational networking with and control of their debtors. Where banks take clients as given and concentrate on assuring them of acceptable returns, they minimize transaction costs by filtering secure opportunities rather than enhancing the security of opportunities. This is visible in the involvement of banks in financing manufacturing industry. British banks often found industrial enterprises to be incalculable risks, which is why their involvement in the financing of industrial investment was limited. They were more specialized as real estate, trading, and merchant banks. Funds for the development of industrial companies thus had to come from raising venture capital or from retained profits. That could happen through networks of friends, family, business partners, and other acquaintances, or it could happen in a less personal way, such as via the stock exchange.

In Germany, the banking system networked with and controlled the manufacturing system in such a way that it could secure the credit business. In the less munificent segments of financial markets, these relations were particularly dense, either implying a strong overlap of bank ownership, credit, and debit clients (in cooperative banks) or a strong link between public and private economic purposes (in local savings banks and specific public banks). This is how the picture evolved of German banking as featuring strong relational contracting and as being constructed in the sphere of 'merit goods', i.e. goods which become public ones to some extent because public and quasi-public relational contracting and regulation assures a more plentiful, secure, or efficient supply. In terms of the previously mentioned example of convoys to protect ships against piracy, these are the ships that cannot afford and are not willing to invest in guns on board, but are willing or forced to share in the costs of protective gunboats or a frigate.[351]

As a result of such differences in industrialization patterns, we arrive at the more recent categorization in the varieties-of-capitalism literature of equity and credit-based financing of manufacturing and service enterprises.[352] Given the extensive linkages with the larger corporatist apparatus connecting the exercise of public authority with the pursuit of economic gains, local or regional universal banks could find it easier to adopt an important role in industrialization within the closer confines of the provincial layers in German society. This helped them better assess and hedge against risk, monitor firms in the vicinity, and provide credit and capital participation on that basis. Given the greater specialization of banks in commerce and real estate in British society, this was less institutionally viable, and therefore the result was direct intermediation between the demand for and supply of industrial capital by personal contact or through the stock exchange. For Germany, the institutional furniture that resulted in the financial action system was modelled on the same patterns that emerged in industry and other services, with the added feature of an extensive and refined corporatist intermediation between public purposes and private interests. It led to a more plentiful supply of both financial and human resources, although the assumption from the start was a scarcity of funds for investment.

In his account of capital formation in German industrialization throughout the nineteenth century, Tilly has shown how such dialectics worked to convert scarcity into a more plentiful supply. Until 1850, financial procurement was largely directed at investment in real agricultural capital (buildings, tools, working capital) and public infrastructure, whereas investment in industrial capital trailed behind. The latter became much stronger and relatively more important after 1850. Yet, he suggests that 'it is interesting to speculate on the connection between industrial investment and the availability of social overhead capital—in particular, the railways. To what extent was the former a delayed response to the latter, not only with respect to the 1850s and 1840s, but for the century as a whole?'[353] This interpretation, which Tilly has formulated on the basis of extensive capital-formation analysis, attributes a particular role to financial systems in the promotion of industrial and other development in Germany. It corresponds with the pervasiveness of corporatist patterns in confined provincial layers and the link that these have provided between civil society and government. Society and subsocieties in Germany have tended throughout history to prepare the ground for stages of capitalist development by promoting capital productivity in the relatively more traditional sectors of the time—such as agriculture in the nineteenth century—and in public infrastructure. As close relations were constructed between public and private goods, public infrastructure could relate to the successive development of profitable private ends, although relations remained invariably tense and contested at any point in time. The implied or intended model of coordination is far from being based on rational planning and is constituted to a great extent by conflictual harmonization.[354]

Such institutional patterns appear to recur time and again; the redevelopment of East Germany after the accession of the former GDR states to the Federal Republic is the most recent case in point. A possibly much more abundant injection of capital into public infrastructure and formerly traditional socialist industries, even without any relation to foreseeable enterprise creation and regional income growth, has been occurring for a period which can safely be predicted to last much longer than two decades. If Tilly is right and this can be taken to be a long-term regularity in Germany, we can possibly expect a take-off in East Germany in a matter of five to ten years.

There is a tendency, in neo-liberal discourse, to suspect complex public–private intermediations of being a waste of public resources and a distortion of market forces. This may well be one of its drawbacks. However, there is no systematic comparison between open corporatist intermediation between the private and the public sphere, on the one hand, and the collusion between public authorities and private interests in what are termed more liberal economies, on the other. Such less visible intermediation often requires investigative journalism to bring it to public attention and may be a more pernicious disturbance of market forces than visible corporatism. A conservative position would be that such different orders have to some extent functionally equivalent but also functionally divergent methods and structures in generating and allocating waste, wealth, and poverty. At any rate, what the South Germanic pattern appears to achieve is more evenly distributed development, in which the contrast in munificence and performance is not so stark between regions or industries, and between wealthy and poor sectors.

What the financial system in Germany does not lack despite its high measure of corporatist formation, however, is competition. All sources point out that the profitability of banking in Germany is low, that the profit margins are very limited. Foreign banks are reluctant to enter the German market, except by acquisition or in the special area of no-frills direct banking. This is sometimes ascribed to the existence of the aforementioned tier of savings banks, which are guaranteed by public authorities and therefore do not have to hedge against risk and form reserves as much as do private banks. In whichever way it has to be assessed in terms of a liberal order, the mixed public–private financial system of Germany has at least had the effect of maintaining open and intense competition.[355] The relation between savings banks and public authorities is about to be altered in compliance with EU directives, which makes it difficult to make any definitive statements at this point. Undoubtedly the character of some institutions will change, as it always does. But it would be extremely surprising to see any changes that would diminish the importance of a differentiated banking population in monitoring and servicing local business.

6.4.2   *Investment financing and capital ownership*

There are three major ways to finance investment: bank credit, retained profits, and new issues of share capital or debentures. It has been pointed out that Germany's share of bank credit financing is strikingly higher than in other countries. This is a reflection of the fact that the same constellation of institutions has persisted since the beginning of industrialization. In Germany, the issuance of new shares or stock options has been seen more as an inevitable step needed to maintain a sound balance between debt and equity and less of a conversion to a proper financial-capitalist method. In this vein, there have been waves of popularizing share ownership in joint-stock companies throughout the entire existence of the Federal Republic. But such waves have not turned the balance in favour of shares and against credit financing in a sustained way.

Naturally, the financing of investment depends greatly on taxation, not only of companies but also of different saving opportunities. A discussion on the relation of taxation to corporate finance has been going on for centuries rather than decades. It has been a point of discussion and concern for a long time that the joint-stock company (*Aktiengesellschaft*) and its means of raising capital by issuing shares are discriminated against. Despite a number of reforms, the debate has never subsided. Some differences have also come about in the South Germanic bedrock: possibly as a result of more advantageous taxation, joint-stock company ownership has become much more dispersed in Switzerland. This is also a model acclaimed to achieve more advantageous taxation and popularization of shares. Corporation tax on distributed profits has been set at a level equivalent to the income tax of shareholders, but the corporate tax for retained profits is set at the maximal rate. This may be a prevalent reason for the propensity to finance investment by issuing shares or by bank credit; bank interest is a deductible expense whereas retained profits are liable to high corporation taxes. So, naturally, the South Germanic bedrock does not explain all the differences between Switzerland and Germany, nor do the types found in the varieties-of-capitalism literature, such as the socially coordinated market economy.

Höpner and Jackson have shown that German joint-stock companies traded on the stock exchange have established an earnings and stock-price 'equilibrium' that is lower than that of Anglo-American companies: the former have had a policy of accepting lower share prices and generating lower earnings on the basis of a smaller equity capital.[356] This has been fundamentally different from the Anglo-American equilibrium of aiming towards high earnings and prices on the basis of more substantial equity capital. Despite different 'equilibriums', the profitability of investing in company stock is still comparable. It is not disturbing for markets, even highly internationalized markets, to have institutionally differentiated segments at different price levels as long as their profitability of investment is comparable. To that extent I disagree with Höpner and Jackson, who find that 'a German "equilibrium" is not sustainable under an open market for corporate control'.[357] In economic theory and reality, market segments persist at different prices as long as the expected profitability of investment is the same.

However, the segmentation of markets with similar levels of investment profitability but different prices may be upset if enterprises deliberately, even if only temporarily, place greater importance on equity finance. They may do this, and have indeed done so in the past because, during a period of steeply rising share prices, the costs of procuring equity capital were lower for a firm in the Anglo-American stock market segment than the costs of procuring capital through credit. This has also happened in Germany, but it is far from clear to what extent the shift to equity finance is going to be sustained and durable. We will say more about this later. It was not the international integration of financial markets as such that caused sharp reactions in Germany, nor was it the profitability of investment in share capital, for it did not diverge much. What so enticed German companies and others to seek more equity capital was its low cost of procurement for firms in shareholder-value-governed systems, during the period when investors thought they could expect sustainable benefits from continuously rising share prices and new issues of shares.

Compared to most other countries in Europe or North America, Germany has had strikingly few joint-stock companies and few joint-stock companies whose stocks are publicly traded. Its stock exchange does not compare to the economic size of the country, and far fewer German than Dutch joint-stock companies are traded on the New York Stock Exchange. More than in many other of the '27 wealthy economies' compared, share ownership in joint-stock companies is characterized by a 'block vote' due to concentrated ownership.[358] In other words, even the few joint-stock companies that exist have less of the impersonal character of capitalism that prevails when ownership is widely distributed and owners treat their property in an instrumental way. This is obviously related to the fact that financial intermediaries tend to be large and concentrated and invest under longer-term auspices.

Moreover, the block vote and concentrated ownership have helped to maintain the equilibrium between low earnings and low share price mentioned above. The biggest perceived threat to a company tends to be the unfriendly takeover. This threat is easier when the amount of capital necessary to gain control of the company is lower and reasonably priced; it is more effectively deterred when a stable block vote exists and ownership is concentrated in relatively few hands. Germany does not yet have the plethora of pension funds that invest in share capital and thereby comprise one of the major sources of distributed holdings in Anglo-American contexts. But the result is still highly counterintuitive. Given that Germany has fewer quoted joint-stock companies, they could well have been subject to dispersed ownership and financial-capitalist influences to a rather large extent. Although they are comparatively large in terms of employment, they are undercapitalized. In most cases, controlling actors have tried to prevent both high exposure to stock markets and a dilution of future earnings through a high degree of capitalization.[359]

It requires a lot of effort to stabilize stock ownership, for undercapitalized enterprises can otherwise be taken over easily as the objects of future turnaround when their share price is low or when their earnings–price ratio is favourable or expected to improve. To achieve such stabilization, companies need to be linked in a cooperative scheme, to hold each others' shares out of a mutual, quasi-public interest. It is habitual to refer to this phenomenon as part of an 'organized capitalism', which it certainly is. Yet it is an organization in which the personal interests and preferences of the family owners, and the intrinsic and long-term commitment to ownership, be it for strategic, traditionalist, or intrinsic interests, are strong.

Despite and possibly because of the earlier pervasive liberalization of product markets, the degree of soft or rigid institutional organization has become as high in financial space as the institutionalization governing work systems has been. In human resources, organization, technology, and financial action systems alike, the provision of production factors have been cast in institutional moulds. Actors have always striven to stabilize ownership relations. Private and limited liability (*GmbH*) companies offer this opportunity anyway, through the exclusion of an impersonal market of corporate governance. Quoted joint-stock companies have also had several instruments to achieve this, such as different types of voting rights and shares. Some large companies in Germany set up systems of interlocking capital participation, again governed by relational contracting that prohibited the use of these shares in an instrumental way, allowing only coordinated methods.[360] This lasted until well into the 1990s, after which a wave of shareholder-capitalism rhetoric and practice reached Germany.

6.5   The translation of shareholder capitalism into the German societal context

6.5.1   *Stakeholders and shareholders in corporate governance*

Stakeholders literally hold a stake in a gamble or a game. Their fate and fortune is affected by the outcome of a game in which they are not necessarily influential actors. Whether they do have any influence on the outcome depends on the rules of the game, their own access to the game, and their compliance with norms. The metaphor suggests that stakes are committed to a game in a fortuitous way: if someone opens a shop in Detroit, he acquires a stake in or places a bet on the American automobile industry. In this sense, business and organization theory has tried to explain the external influences on organizations in terms of the interests of stakeholders who are taking a gamble on a focal organization, whether or not they have formally justified claims on that organization. However, it is not hard to see the empirical fact of stakeholdership being interpreted as interdependency and translated into consultation or participation rights.

Another perspective is a normative one. Some people conclude that it would be fair or would facilitate communication between stakeholders and a focal organization if formal procedures and entitlements for stakeholders were instituted through which they could influence the bet or game in a way they find positive. A normative stakeholder perspective would thus suggest that it is both in the community's and the organization's interest to take stakeholders' interests into consideration on the basis of their formal participation. A contrasting perspective would argue that public welfare is built on competitive markets and that markets are more likely to be competitive when issues are clear. So, public welfare would be augmented if General Motors could concentrate on competing in the business of producing and selling automobiles, instead of being lumbered with the fate of shopowners in Detroit. The latter should preferably be dealt with in separate markets or other spheres to be treated separately from competition between car manufacturers.

A shareholder perspective is thus not only an explanatory one but also a normative perspective that tells us which claims should be secured by formal entitlements. It proposes ways and means of gearing the action of agents to the well-understood interests of the principal, the latter being, of course, the shareholders. Shareholders are thought to be interested in the maximization of their returns and ideally not intrinsically interested in ownership. If I buy KLM shares because I am an aviation enthusiast who would appreciate going to annual meetings and being in symbolic touch with the oldest airline in the world still operating under its original name, then I would not behave in a way which makes shareholder capitalism work. KLM would appreciate it, but if many people had similar motives for investment, this would render the market less transparent.

Although the example sounds curious, it sheds light on an important ingredient in the promotion of shareholder value capitalism: it is in the interest of firms and of speculative sellers of shares to promote or tolerate any rhetoric that purports to prove that the behaviour of the firm conforms to shareholder value concepts, for this is a convenient way of ensuring that share prices keep rising. To respond to the whims and fashions of the stock markets makes share prices climb or prevents them from falling. It does not matter whether we are talking about a love of aviation tradition or a preference for specific management concepts; companies can adapt to any whim or fashion, and the stock exchange is the best place on Earth for converting such beliefs and sentiments into real resources, at least temporarily. Companies thus have an objective interest in investors who are loyal, gullible, and easier to appease. When a company has issued shares at prices advantageous to itself, this particular deal has an enduring effect on the investors because these people have parted company with their money. When the price of the asset falls, this puts the owners of the 'value' obtained through the previous share-price increases in a 'poorer' position, but not the company in which the money was invested. Shareholder value policies, if used intelligently by companies, may thus enrich company assets but, in the medium term, impoverish those shareholders who are not skilled speculators. Therefore, shareholder value doctrines may turn out in the long run to be ideologies from which the financial position of companies and top management profits more than the shareholders.

Although shareholder value concepts can be criticized for propounding a limited and distorted view of actors, this is not a very penetrating criticism. Most economic theories have that limitation, and so do other social science theories. Here, the points which are to be raised lie at the interface between German corporate governance and shareholder value capitalism, both as rhetoric and as a practice. In a common-sense way, shareholder value capitalism is inherent to any practice in any capitalist economy that has publicly and openly tradeable shares. Likewise, it is clear that the instrumental economic value accruing from share ownership and transactions can be derived in three main ways, depending on the institutions:

- by receiving distributed profits or dividends;
- by receiving options for shares or new shares under advantageous conditions, on the basis of shares already owned in an enterprise;
- by an appreciation of the market value of shares or other entitlements owned.

Finance theory greatly emphasizes the adequacy of a discounted cash-flow concept of evaluating future returns and integrating them with present-day information. A rational shareholder will try to estimate any predictable future disbursement or value change of a title held, within a time horizon that may vary. He will then discount such benefits to the present day and obtain the value of a particular share. In addition, shareholder value theorists have alerted us to the role that rising stock prices play as part of the benefits that shareholders can expect. Moreover, there have been more specific 'theories' relating stock performance to managerial measures such as downsizing, accounting standards, pay rewards for managers who contribute to generating dividends and increasing stock value, mergers establishing superior market position, reorganization of the value chain according to core competencies, the introduction of market control rather than hierarchical control, cost reduction including wage reduction, and many more.

Much of this is reminiscent of what a stylized Anglo-American variety of capitalism stands for. For this reason, it is quite understandable why Streeck asked in the early 1990s whether the German type of capitalism could withstand the onslaught of shareholder value capitalism. The internationalization of economic activities during this period was marked above all by a rapid increase in the international mobility of financial capital. Financial markets, it could be argued, were certainly potentially more homogeneous and thus more contestable than those for goods, and they could be interpreted as becoming more and more unified or contestable. This was said to advantage 'disembedded' participation in transactions, a participation more bereft of intrinsic motives than entrepreneurship or other types of work. Such market types were thought to be spreading, and it was here that Anglo-American capitalism had cumulative advantages, sharper concepts, and institutional influence worldwide.[361]

In connection with shareholder value capitalism, there also emerged the more general idea that capitalist accumulation had entered a new era. The Internet made possible considerable improvements in productivity. Communication via the Internet was to enable rationalization and flexibility of intrafirm processes, intercompany communication and control (of stocks, supplies, standards, work processes, delivery times, technical specifications, etc.) and contact between consumers and enterprises. There was a rash of start-ups and diversification in the fields of Internet software, portals, communication tools and other designs, and manufacturing and maintenance of information technology. Concomitant productivity increases and the emergence of new markets were considered by many to be sustainable in the long term, so that continuous appreciation of share value was imagined to be a realistic scenario.

It was also argued that 'globalization' was so pervasive not only in financial markets but also in product markets that internationalization of economic activities would lead to the emergence of transnational firms and alliances that were focused on specific products, services, and techniques. It was also predicted that internationalization would bring about market expansion, new markets, and productivity increases. This would relegate the diversified and more nationally active firm to an inferior position. Also, there were drives to denationalize, deregulate, and privatize economic activities, to expose them to the discipline of markets. As a result, a whole syndrome of interrelated ideas and practices evolved that tied together shareholder value capitalism, Internet applications and related industries, 'globalization' and 'lean management' concepts, core competencies, and the re-organization of value chains.

Shareholder value concepts, particularly in so far as they reiterated the import-ance of aiming at sustainable increases in stock prices, were thereby provided a concept of how such sustainable appreciation was to be viable, bearing in mind that a 'real economy' had, after all, to provide the foundations of financial capitalism. This was crucial because the wise investor or analyst of institutions had to remem-ber that share price increases might be speculative and temporary. However, long-term perspectives have never been attributed to Anglo-American economic institutions or considerations in which economic actors engage. Such perspectives were, however, more important outside this context, where fundamental con-cepts were examined against long-term viability. Germany is a society with strong leanings towards long-term orientations, which is why an argument about stock price appreciation being sustained by a real economy is important in order to diffuse the idea and the practice abroad. Conceivably, this argument furthered the legitimacy and acceptance of shareholder capitalism in countries not only like Germany, but also elsewhere.

Even when Germany's coalition government of Social Democrats and Greens took office in 1998, it welcomed the syndrome with open arms, making the establishment of joint-stock companies easier, auctioning telecommunication rights in a perfectly capitalist manner, supporting immigration of telecommunica-tions and software specialists, and encouraging share ownership transactions by company taxation changes. This was not a big surprise, though, because Social Democrats and trade unionists may have thought that the 'wonder years' of the 1950s and 1960s were coming back: if there are substantial productivity increases, then redistribution is much easier. From their standpoint, shareholder value capit-alism may have looked like a new set of institutions enhancing growth and productivity, just as Fordism appeared to be in the 1950s. In such a scheme, whatever institutionally enmeshed an individual company in arrangements beyond its individual control was forgotten or discounted, be it corporatism, relational contracting, the intrinsic interests of shareholders in entrepreneurship and invest-ments, or anything else.

To this extent, one had to presume that the clash between such rhetoric and practice and German types of capitalist legitimacy and functioning was going to be fierce. Most of the things advocated, with some nuanced exceptions regarding the concepts of lean management, empowerment of the workforce, and tight internal control, could be viewed as being alien to what the stylized 'German model' of this period had come to represent. It was not by accident that this stylized model came under Anglo-American attack just at that moment; it was criticized for standing in the way of all that the progress of capitalist development promised at the time.

6.5.2 *Crooked paths in German shareholder capitalism*

At the instigation of Streeck, a number of studies have been conducted that are highly pertinent to questions concerning the effect of shareholder value capitalism and its further associations in Germany.[362] These show that the changes wrought were probably some of the most substantial since the establishment of the social market economy, yet I would not go so far as to say that they were the most important ones since then. The finishing touches of what would be called the 1978 version of the 'German model' were only just being applied; one example was the passage in 1976 of what eventually became the Codetermination Act for large joint-stock companies. Since 1945, there has hardly been a decade in which the alarm bells have not been sounded by concerned analysts who worriedly point out the fundamental importance of recent changes in policy.[363]

First, the authors of the above-mentioned studies show that there is a relatively consistent and interdependent syndrome of promoting the practice of some shareholder value concepts in very large enterprises. This syndrome is characterized by the following:[364]

- adopting US accounting standards, including greater transparency with regard to specific business lines or divisions;
- conducting elaborate investor relations;
- giving primacy to profitability management by more specific business units;
- adjusting the compensation of employees to achieve compatibility with profitability and shareholder value goals.

Although the syndrome itself is consistent, its relationship to internationalization is not close. In the first place, internationalization has two dimensions: 'real economy' and financial internationalization. While these are correlated, there are wide divergencies. However, there are relatively few enterprises that are internationalized less through exports or direct investment than in financial respects. The enterprises that exhibit a high level of internationalization in the real economy dimension also have a greater scatter or higher variance with regard to financial internationalization.[365] This might indicate that, as real economy internationalization progresses, financial internationalization increasingly hinges on a policy choice, rather than on some general constraint. But we do not yet have inter-temporal comparisons to corroborate this. There are also industrial-sectoral patterns; for example, the chemical and pharmaceutical enterprises score the highest on both dimensions of internationalization.

The decision to adopt shareholder value orientations is thus related to the measure of financial internationalization, as would be expected, although the motive is far from clear. There are two major reasons why enterprises may adopt shareholder value policies. One is to finance investment more easily from an advantageous source. The other is the intention to follow a best practice, based on other experience or legitimized concepts, which supposedly leads to greater competitiveness and profitability. The first motivating reason is related to the costs of investment capital procurement; the second to results and how to achieve them.

Höpner has somewhat deemphasized the capital cost motive. His argument is that, if anything, the importance of owners' capital decreased in relation to debt during the 1990s.[366] This is a very significant finding. It shows that shareholder value orientation has not led to a modification of the long-standing German practice of relying on debt financing more than on equity, in comparison with Anglo-American and other societies. This is very counterintuitive and shows the resilience of this trait of the German variety of capitalism. Höpner has thus rightly reiterated that a combination of financial and real economy motives for adopting new practices was linked to the quest for managerial benefits, power, and control.

Still, it must also be acknowledged that enterprises anticipated lower costs of procuring capital for investment via the issue of shares. Capital markets do not have to be tight in order for firms to look more actively for capital in the form of equity. The motive may be more closely related to relative prices than to scarcity across the board. If investors calculate that share prices will rise, this will have two major advantages for a firm issuing shares. Investors will pay high prices for shares because they expect that shareholder value will accrue through future share price increases. *Ceteris paribus*, this also means that dividends to be paid in future are relatively less important as part of the total value to be generated. If there is a persistent expectation that the price of a company's shares will rise, then it means that such a firm is receiving a great deal, indeed a disproportional amount, of financial backing for each nominal share it sells. This expectation must have played an important role in firms' calculations. This was particularly noticeable in the United States, where a 'bubble' gradually formed with regard to the relation between stock prices and the replacement cost of capital (measured by Tobin's q). In equilibrium, this relation would be measured at 1; but as the bubble grew, it rose to more than 2. This implies abnormally low costs of procuring investment capital via stock markets, and naturally, enterprises in other countries competed for attracting similarly advantageous funds.[367]

As long as the bubble was growing or at least holding steady, there was a functional motive for firms to acquire funds through stock markets rather than by bank loans, and the internationalization of financial markets extended the effect into all the countries affected by their spread. Yet it also has to be expected that prudent companies will avoid overcapitalization in order not to become targets of incalculable takeover bids when a bubble bursts. This explains the trend that Höpner found among large German companies not to change the equity-to-debt ratio over the long run. Overcapitalization runs the risk of 'dilution' of capital, and this may lead to a sharper drop in stock prices. Other motives mentioned by Höpner also operate: investors consider shareholder value orientation more effective per se and reward it. Under such conditions, this is a method of preventing hostile takeover, which is a threat when equity at stock market prices exhibits what markets consider undercapitalization. In such a case, it pays to take over a firm, at least when future returns are considered satisfactory, with or without a turnaround having taken place.

We thus have contrasting findings: shareholder capitalism has made substantial inroads in Germany but only in the large, publicly quoted, joint-stock enterprises, which are less important. However, the equity-to-debt ratio has not risen in Germany. It appears that enterprises made use of the shareholder value wave and advantageous costs of capital procurement to increase equity, but they did so in order subsequently to raise debt capital. As a result, the ratio of equity to debt did not change appreciably during the 1990s. This pattern is again familiar. Earlier waves of popularizing shares[368] had also been instrumentalized to justify incurring greater debt after this was secured by a higher level of equity and its market capitalization.

Another striking finding is that the cross-ownership of shares between companies has declined significantly. Companies had used cross-ownership to prevent hostile takeovers and to stabilize corporate control and the interests to which they were subject. Now, however, large banks in particular have stopped investing substantially in industrial and service companies, as Beyer has shown.[369] This is a significant break with the practice of relational contracting among large firms for the purpose of collectively enacting a stable set of ownership and control relations. What thereby becomes evident is the greater degree of individualism among enterprises and a change in the role that banks play in monitoring and stabilizing other companies. It appears reasonable to conclude that monitoring has to some extent been relegated to financial markets.

Shareholder capitalism has also affected the composition of management boards in joint-stock companies. Previously, top management in large German enterprises ascended to that rank primarily by promotion from inside the company and, with regard to the occupational backgrounds of management, technical occupations were on a par with commercial ones. However, during the 1990s a notable change occurred in this pattern. The most striking increase was the number of board seats filled by top managers recruited from outside the enterprise. It is a phenomenon one would expect when very serious policy changes occur or a complete change of policy or a turnaround is undertaken. The share of financial specialists in top positions also visibly increased, but only until 1996. After that, it decreased again and then remained stable in 1998 and 1999.[370] Although the authors of the studies cited here tend to conclude that the importance of financial management has increased, the trend is far from monotonic. It might also be that after the achievement of substantive 'financialization' of large enterprises, the question now is how to generate surpluses by means other than financial operations, particularly since the glamour of that method has vanished in the wake of collapsing stock prices. It is highly likely that the real economy is coming into its own again. This should inspire ideas for 'the future', rather than encouraging reliance on analyses of the pre-collapse past.

6.5.3   Implications for industrial relations and employee benefits

On the supervisory boards of many German firms, shareholder value policies had initially and programmatically conflicted with co-determination, one of the pillars of German industrial relations. Those promoting Anglo-American concepts were the vanguard in this conflict. In the large enterprises investigated, however, it turned out that the correlation between the intensity of co-determination and that of the shareholder value orientation was very small and insignificant.[371] This is again counterintuitive, at least for the intuition that had accepted the two as being diametrically opposed concepts. There were, of course, convincing examples of enterprises reducing vertical integration in the value chain, reducing firm size, and changing industries in order to evade co-determination as it existed in the coal and steel industry (full parity of employee representatives on supervisory boards) or in large companies (near-parity). Nevertheless, again we have a finding that shows the overall compatibility of economically liberal and corporatist patterns. Works councillors and the employee members of supervisory boards have been critical of many new policies, to be sure, but their involvement has not been destructive to shareholder value policies in the specific form in which they materialized.

Accordingly, there does not appear to have been any broad attempt by owners and top management to reduce the influence that works councillors and employee members of supervisory boards have achieved, in so far as it is possible to draw this conclusion from a cross-sectional analysis. This fits in with much earlier findings: before or upon its introduction, co-determination had regularly been perceived as conflicting with profitability, competitiveness, and the smoothness of strategic decision-making. Yet as it evolved and as experience in working with it accumulated, management found that usually co-determination generally supported and improved managerial action. Employee representatives made sure that decisions were better conceived, on the basis of a greater dissemination of information, and that the implementation of those decisions was less problematic. Therefore, in the concepts of institutions over a decade ago, we again see that opposing practices were recombined, programmatically and conceptually.

A frequent topic in debates in Anglo-American contexts is the effect that shareholder value policies have on the distributive position of wage labour relative to capital. As expected, there is an inverse correlation between the deterioration of this distributive position in very large companies in Germany and the extent to which shareholder value policies were pursued. However, upon closer inspection, it turns out that the average wage level per capita of employees has not deteriorated. Shareholder value policy-makers have noticeably implemented vertical disintegration by selling subsidiaries or other components and outsourcing activities, thereby reducing the size of the workforce. This policy is mainly responsible for the decline of total wages and their importance as part of total expenses. It can also be safely assumed that, to some extent, the activities and employees relocated under new ownership will often have had to accept less lucrative conditions of employment, although this aspect was not covered by the studies carried out. Remaining employees did not experience any extensive deterioration of conditions.[372] Furthermore, in the payment systems adopted, there was overall a shift in the direction of performance-related compensation. This did not mean the introduction of piece rates, but of more sizeable wage components in the form of bonuses in various forms for groups, plants, or enterprises.[373] It could also be seen that the popularity of schemes promoting employee shareholdings in the company grew with the backing of both management and works councillors.

Two major shifts have occurred that imply a change in practice. One has been a shift from employment creation or maintenance in the company to profitability; the other has been from the maintenance of general norms and standards to company individualism within industrial relations policies. This definitely is a change in the direction of Anglo-American patterns. However, decentralization of wage bargaining is also part of a long-term trend that has prevailed in Germany and elsewhere and that, in Germany, has been quite pronounced in the chemicals and pharmaceuticals industries and weaker in the metal and engineering industries. To this extent, it is not radically new. It offers the options of combining central and regional bargaining with company agreements. Furthermore, it is difficult to establish whether wage bargaining in Germany has been decentralized at a more rapid pace than in Britain or the United States.

Generally in Germany, there has been a gradual erosion of the uniformity of collective bargaining; more and more exceptions have worked their way into agreements or even outside of them and have been approved and co-implemented by local works councils in company-specific pacts. As anyone who has observed Germany for some time might have expected, works councils were on the whole supportive in this exercise, despite some criticism.

So, in a way, the roles of unions and collective agreements, on the one hand, and works councils and their input, on the other, have been inverted. Whereas previously, unions bargained for industrial and regional agreements that were supplemented by local agreements reached by works councils, with or without 'opening clauses' in the collective agreement, now collective agreement standards have become identical with the higher standards that large companies can accept in view of their greater capital intensity and relatively small labour-cost percentage, and works councillors negotiate and implement local reductions of such standards. This is a change that affects employee interests. However, the industrial relations system as such has not changed much in its characteristic dualism of local and regional industrial bargaining: collective agreements and statutory co-determination are still intertwined in the various individual companies, despite the inversion observed.[374]

It is important to consider the qualitative reconstruction of industrial relations, rather than a shift along one dimension such as company individualism. Despite enterprise individualism in levels and methods of compensation and despite the fact that very large enterprises can 'in principle' afford enterprise individualism better than can small and medium-sized firms, notably in industrial relations, it turns out that large enterprises with higher or lower degrees of internationalization and shareholder value orientation have now emerged as the standard bearers of collective bargaining at regional-industrial levels. Whereas the small and medium-sized companies in labour-intensive industries, depressed regions, and especially eastern Germany have become notorious for undercutting collective agreements and leaving employer federations altogether, the large enterprises have still clung to regional collective bargaining. One particular example was the dilemma into which IG Metall (the metal and engineering industries union) manoeuvred itself in 2003 and which triggered a profound crisis among the union's board members due to an unsuccessful attempt to organize a strike in the east. When the strike collapsed and a controversy over succession within the board followed, it was significant that employers quickly and publicly exhorted IG Metall to put its house in order and do its job because, after all, the union was badly needed. No one would ever have seen this genuine corporatist care bestowed upon a union during the Thatcher or Reagan eras in the United Kingdom or the United States.

It has always been a matter of contention whether small and medium-sized companies carry a greater weight in employer federation decision-making than do large enterprises. At the moment, it almost seems as if regional collective bargaining is being maintained by large enterprises, although one would assume that small and medium-sized companies could profit from it most, at least theoretically. If wages are taken out of competition, the firms that gain from this are the more labour-intensive ones that, by themselves, have less significance in labour markets. As previously mentioned, the tendency in collective bargaining appears to be to accede to union wage claims because they can be shouldered by large and capital-intensive enterprises, and it is considered crucial to preserve industrial peace. That, in turn, is only a pertinent consideration if the bargaining and strike power of unions is still relatively threatening, despite massive unemployment. We can explain the dynamics thus far. Yet once again, it is a profoundly German institutional phenomenon that large enterprises are thus convinced they should heed employers' associations and to stick to regional collective agreements in order to avert strikes, when faced with a trade union that only guarantees peace and cooperation in return for regional bargaining. In this respect, the effects of shareholder value practices are quite different from what we observe elsewhere.

6.5.4   The durability of recent changes

The authors of the studies cited here have stressed two things. One is that more familiar German patterns have been creatively combined and intertwined with shareholder value practices. The other is that changes which have taken place will in all likelihood be sustainable. The latter interpretation is worth some scrutiny. From a long-term perspective, one is inevitably struck by the phenomena of inversion and of the reincarnation of older institutional patterns in new forms. With respect to industry–enterprise dualism, continuity and inversion are even intimately linked. Likewise, during the period studied by Höpner, the importance of having board members with backgrounds in technical occupations and financial occupations first increased and then declined again, as described above. This demonstrates that the importance of financial board members has not increased monotonically but started to decline again even before the 'bubble' burst. Could it be that top management was wise enough not to take shareholder value strategies as seriously as its rhetoric did? The tendency towards achievement-related bonuses, however, had already begun before shareholder value was widely discussed as an option. This may well be a long-lasting trend. With regard to both monotonic and temporary tendencies, the question therefore still remains open whether they are reversible and directly ascribable to shareholder value policies.

At the time of writing, share-option schemes for top management are being questioned as a consequence of recent experience. As newspapers report, not only is Siemens re-evaluating its policy, so too is Microsoft in the United States. It appears that such schemes encourage short-term profit maximization on the part of management—even to the point of manipulating financial statements—more than shareholders appreciate. Following the recent scandals about the manipulation of company statements and the collaboration of accountants in such manipulation, it also appears that the propaganda about transparency and veracity of accounting in facilitating shareholder value may have been overdone. This would fit in well with a quasi-theorem of highly regulated accounting: complex requirements increase the potential for manipulation, because such requirements are inherently conflict-ual and dilemmatic, and are thereby likely to create opportunities for discretion and manipulation. From this point of view, too, it is highly questionable how sustain-able some practices will be. Any observer schooled in the partitioning of institu-tions, their inventive recombination and translation into different contexts over a longer time, would expect to see shareholder value practices creatively adapted to local culture and institutions. Precise and truthful accounting requires social safe-guards rather than greater bureaucratic complexity. Social safeguards are, however, domestic German products rather than Anglo-American imports. They emerge from a world of relational contracting and the collective creation of quasi-public goods.

We will have to wait another decade to see what is sustainable and what is not. At the moment we can only guess. It would be a surprise, though, if the manifest worldwide collapse of stock prices, new economy enterprises, and possibly some other related concepts did not have any consequences. Well-known German companies such as Telekom and Bertelsmann have shed top managers who were financial and public relations geniuses and have once again hired proven oper-ational managers of a very familiar type. This was to be expected at a time when the 'bubble' has burst and losses (both operational and those due to the depreciation of assets) are more the order of the day than profits. Even serious liberal periodicals such as *The Economist* have acknowledged the existence of a 'bubble' for years and have predicted that it will burst sometime.[375] The only question is when and to what extent.

The question now is what effect the bursting of the bubble will have. Financially at least, the basis on which both the rhetoric and policies of shareholder value capitalism once flourished has shrunk, meaning that the period in which raising funds by issuing shares was more advantageous than credit finance has passed. The analysis of changes due to shareholder value capitalism has not yet been able to include the more serious test of a crisis. That shareholder value policies in their recent form rest on speculation and hype more than sustainable enterprise competitiveness in the real economy is already quite clear, according to informed industrial economists such as Van Witteloostuijn.[376] However, it is hard to find other observers who have taken a bubble into account and considered the possibility that such changes will be reversed or combined with subsequent changes not emanating from a standard, liberal shareholder value concept. A sustained effect of this concept has at least been relativized to the extent that it has been linked to an extravagant bubble originating in the United States,[377] to which German companies appear to have 'adapted'. In their enquiries, Höpner, Hassel, Rehder, Streeck, and others had pointed to the fact that new and established patterns were being combined. This was already evident from data for the period before the bubble burst. What remains to be done is to distinguish which effects are due to more sustainable shareholder value policies, which are temporary, and which are sustainable but possibly only tenuously connected with shareholder value.

What the long-run consequences will be for corporate governance in institutional and company policy is impossible to predict for Germany or for any other society. It will again depend upon the culturally and institutionally conditioned and embedded responses of a number of actors. This is where 'the games real actors play' come in, i.e. the open-ended side of actor-centric institutionalism;[378] it is impossible to extrapolate societal characteristics from societal analysis in a straightforward way. Considering historical experience, we think it is a safe bet to suggest that whatever happens in Germany will probably amount to a creative combination of liberal and non-liberal approaches and a domestication of imported approaches and concepts in the usual way. Imports have always implied more questions than answers, and the translation of foreign concepts into domestic practice has had to provide such answers.

6.6   The unending story of institutional partitioning and recombination

At this moment, one can approach shareholder value, the 'new economy', and 'globalization' in two main ways. One is to suggest that 'Anglo–American capitalism has done it again' and left an indelible mark on many or most economies and societies by generating institutions and practices that are superior as long as markets prevail and are therefore more universal. This would mean that new forms of liberal economic institutions are crowding out corporatist, socialist, or governmental-interventionist practices and institutions.

The other perspective is different and not yet well established. It is that new forms of liberal governance and their underlying assumptions have contributed to the creation of a bubble that has now burst, in the same way that other bubbles have burst before, whether capitalist bubbles or not. It is tempting to formulate something like a theorem in connection with this: as soon as a clear-cut and stylized template of economic and social development has not only taken root but been put forward in a programmatic statement, its demise as a stylized form is certain, and its eclectic combination with countervailing forms is under way, thanks to the catalyst of major or minor crises and other requirements for adaptation. History has a nasty and ineradicable habit of refuting tidy models, whatever they are. It is easy to show something in retrospect, which is why the recognition of change in 'models' is banal. It is a much more onerous task to say something pertinent about the future. It is dubious to predict the future as nothing other than a continuation of the most topical and recent trends when the basis for such trends, which themselves changed an earlier 'model', has undergone a crisis, such as the recent bursting of stock exchange bubbles.

Just as Japan was being lauded as a record-breaking, trend-setting, and sustainable 'model', the country was caught in a bubble created by financial investment in real estate and notorious 'economizing with the truth' of company financial statements. Just after the 'German model' started to be peddled in a historically short-sighted and simplistic form, it exhibited severe flaws that became particularly pernicious in coping with the aftermath of unification. This would lead us to suggest that any 'model' (set of institutions that appear to be interdependent for a period) will contain a flaw somewhere in its institutional texture. This flaw will prove destructive to the 'model' just as its implementation and application is becoming entrenched, or the flaw may accumulate destructive potential over time. In the short or medium term, this potential need not lead to changes because actors will underrate its importance. This is due to the self-assurance typically exhibited by actors when they perceive a high amount of interdependency among institutions and therefore come to believe they are dependent on the chosen path. It leads them to accept slack, waste, and malfunctioning as costs supposedly linked to benefits, even when these benefits shrink or are demonstrated to be only tenuously related to the costs in question.

Within such tendencies, organized actors and government tend to make policy choices, not by the discriminate weighing of discrete alternatives that can be decoupled, but in the more summary spirit of evaluating one supposed 'model' against another. This may delay or hamper the more finely tuned creation of institutions and practices, which history has shown tends to occur in any case to the extent that crises are overcome and new 'productive coalitions'—to use a term coined by Streeck for Germany—are forged.

When interpreting what has happened in Germany during the last decade or so, it is tempting to turn back to Karl Marx; this is particularly enticing at a moment when conventional, partisan, and self-confident interpretations of Marx have very fortunately gone out of fashion. One of the central dilemmas of capitalist production, according to Marx, is the dialectical decoupling and re-coupling of use value and exchange value. In free markets, the exchange value of a good and of money may considerably outpace or lag behind its use value. *Pace* Marx, not only capitalism but also other types of economies generate bubbles that consist of a temporary and rapid build-up of the exchange value of goods or money. In the short term, such exchange values can also be converted to use value by selling share capital, the value of which has greatly appreciated at a propitious moment. In this way, use value can be generated because the money earned can be used for substantial consumptive or investment purposes.

Marx was a Prussian born in 1818 just at the historical moment when, after the Napoleonic Wars, the development of institutions was marked by a surge of economic liberalism. This environment must have been a decisive influence in Marx's own life and outlook. It corresponded with what his friend Engels observed in contemporary England, and after Marx emigrated to London, he saw this experience strongly confirmed by his intensive study of records and literature in the British Museum.[379] Although Marx was very vague about what he envisaged as a likely or politically advisable order of socialism and it would be wrong to try to fill the gaps by poring over the exegesis of his works by his former imitators, he did consider it inevitable that free associations of producers would arise, that they would intertwine with political domination, and that political recognition would be given to the working classes, for they were essential contributors to welfare. At the time, it was hard for him to conceive that moves in these directions would ensue as consequences of further 'revolutions from above', starting in 1866. In particular, he did not live to see the full corporatist consequences of the collapse of Germany's post-1872 unification boom.[380] What entrepreneurs, unions, and diverse governments have done since then amounts to a programme of preventing the drifting apart of use and exchange value by way of collective organization and links to the government.

The possibility that such a divergence of use and exchange values could occur and that financial markets could become more important than the real economy are nightmares that have plagued social forces in Germany. These fears were used to collectively enact exchange value as use value and to create greater esteem for producers than for speculators. They thereby bore the imprint of the provincial layers within a society with a long record of economic self-regulation but one beleagured by different and frequently debilitated currencies. Such fears were rekindled by devastating hyperinflation after World War I and by inflation and currency reform after World War II, in addition to the other catastrophes mentioned. Temporary reconciliation of use value with exchange value was mostly achieved through a fortuitous combination of revolution from above (including that instigated by US military government) and renovation of intermediate associations. This was far from textbook socialism, but it built on the foundation of the South Germanic bedrock and featured many overtones deriving from the sharper Prussian dialectics shown in Chapter 4. Despite the Prussian tradition of bestowing revolutions on society from above, remarkable affinities exist between this and some Marxist analyses, much as its various proponents may have hated the idea.

In the mean time, we have witnessed another confrontation between the real economy and financial capitalism and have watched use value drift away from exchange value. Marx is hardly on the agenda any more, and most German actors are consciously more concerned with breaking away from handed-down domestic wisdom and traditions than with making use of them. For precisely these reasons, it is safe to expect their reinvention and re-enactment in novel forms.[381] As asset prices and revenue fluctuate, actors will rediscover and mobilize various dispositions to hedge against some of the uncertainties facing them in order to manage better other uncertainties or more specific ones. In the South Germanic bedrock, the occurrence of anything else would be highly surprising.

In this spirit and on the basis of what has been discussed in the earlier chapters, it is also advisable to keep in check the enthusiasm over the ongoing reconstruction of institutions and culture in Germany and probably in many other societies. Wave after wave of economic development and innovation has broken upon the domestic shores of Germany, be it the wave of internationalization, business models, financial relations and institutions, or many another. We can still argue about the pervasiveness of such developments in German society, for the segment directly affected has been relatively circumscribed, and we do not have any comparative evidence about changes in small and medium-sized enterprises and in companies other than joint-stock concerns. A more general comparison, conducted by Guillén, of corporate governance changes over time in Asian, Anglo-American, and Continental countries came to the conclusion that no evidence exists to support the idea of convergence in the sense of 'net' convergence.[382]

This appears to correspond to what has happened in Germany more specifically, and it conforms to what we have encountered on many historical occasions: a temporary 'model' is introduced and then replaced to some extent with a novel amalgamation of it and existing institutions. However, this recombination is viewed more soberly once we have learnt to accept the process of partitioning and recombining as a common evolutionary mechanism, as historical normalcy. Although the discussion on convergence of governance in internationalization has intensified, the pace of research has not. We still do not have a sufficient number of comparative studies that adhere to accepted standards of comparison and are suitably specific about changing institutions and culture. It is extraordinary, was probably predictable, and remains definitely deplorable that rigorous international comparison has gone into decline just as 'globalization' has become conceptually more and more prominent. Where are the comparisons of corporate governance in firms defined to be substantively comparable? How could it be that the rhetoric of globalization and unbridled theoretical universalism has cast a shroud over monographic investigations of specific types of enterprises in particular societies?

The first evidence regarding specific enterprises and thereby some characteristics of the general landscape in Germany indicates that general evolutionary mechanisms and some metatraditions of German society have again emerged. It is correct to say, as Christel Lane has been saying, that the version of the 'German model' established after 1945 and acknowledged to be such only after 1977 has more or less vanished.[383] Such 'models' tend to be outdated as soon as they are proposed.[384] The history of social science in the Federal Republic has been littered with books whose titles begin with phrases such as 'the end of' or 'the crisis of' and often end with a question mark, and which analyse the crisis and downfall of one important institutional pillar or another in Germany, such as *Meister*-type foremen, engineers with an earlier vocational apprenticeship and diploma, or pay-by-results. It is also entirely correct to state that the Deutschland AG 'model' is finished, as researchers of the Max Planck Institute for the Study of Societies point out in less academic publications. However, one could also contest whether it ever existed in the first place in a form remotely comparable to Japan Incorporated, the 'model' that originally coined the phrase.[385]

Just because coordination between the government and private enterprises is institutionally less visible in a liberal order such as that of the United States, we should not be fooled into believing, in the absence of systematic comparative proof, that coordination is weaker for internationally exposed sectors. In the few fields where the United States is highly competitive in international markets on the basis of a positive balance of trade, there are not many companies that do not benefit from a strong impetus and subsidies provided by the defence establishment, at least in the early and formative phases of the development of technology or more generic products. Probably even Siemens had less of that, despite his military background, apart from the time and space he had in his Magdeburg 'prison' and the interesting challenges in a brief war.

6.7 Summary

A great deal of change has taken place, triggered by international exposure and emerging national weaknesses at the same time. New specific phenomena surprise those who have come to take a well-established 'model' for granted or as stable over time, in very concrete sets of characteristics. But temporary and concrete 'models' always imply change and alterations of recent changes. It would be highly surprising if more of that did not occur in the future, just as the economic liberalism of Prussia was thoroughly revised on subsequent occasions. Furthermore, as in earlier periods, new phenomena are being intricately combined with more established and mutated characteristics in other respects. Some features of the earlier 'German model' are being harnessed in order to cope with more recent challenges, a point that a number of authors have made about industrial relations in a period of internationalization and shareholder value development.[386] The more long-lasting metatradition explains ongoing partitioning of spaces and the recombination of institutional facets, and the characteristic toing-and-froing between openness and closure, international incursions, and domestic resilience. This yields new concoctions and reactions of different substances. The combination of what is temporarily international or national, liberal or non-liberal, German or foreign, will undoubtedly give rise to another invention of a 'German model'—maybe a 2020 version to sum up the highlights of an amalgamation that will have drifted into decline at least five years before that date.

Recent imports are syncretically bound with institutional or cultural features that have already been declared 'German' because their foreign origins have been forgotten. This will undoubtedly happen with regard to those changes that are at present still considered as foreign imports, and when this does, it will signal the end of an era. One survey on the way shareholder value affects certain business systems also reaches this conclusion and argues in favour of establishing 'hybridization' as a pertinent concept.[387] According to the experience of reconstructing business systems, the present analysis adds that hybridization includes a reaction producing new domestic institutional originality, rather than a position in between. Any domestic concoction now diagnosed, in retrospect, as embodying the domestic originality of a 'German system' also resulted from a reaction between imported and domestic substances during the process of hybridization, in which a novel substance was derived from the combination.

Let us return briefly to what was said in the introduction to this chapter: in some respects the situation of Siemens in the middle of the nineteenth century was governed by liberal principles to a much greater degree than the situation of a new entrepreneur today. Understanding the metatradition, we can analyse evolution better, for it thrives on opposites which escalate each other, such as liberalism and non-liberalism. The true challenge is not to advance towards greater liberalization per se, but to ensure that the articulation of a new kind of liberalization includes its opposite in an adjacent domain.

Another lesson illustrated by the anecdote at the beginning of this chapter relates to what might be called a German dialectic of entrepreneurship and constraints. At a certain stage of complex uncertainty it is not only conceivable but inevitable that entrepreneurship should develop well under a system of regulatory constraints. The creative combination of innovation and constraints has been illustrated, somewhat provocatively, by the necessity of Werner Siemens being in something like a prison in order to conduct innovative experiments.[388] This leads us to the dialectics of the reduction and management of uncertainty and to the more visible institutional form this has taken in Germany.

From this, it is not difficult to elucidate how international changes have been translated into concoctions that have acquired the character of esteemed national treasures by reacting with domestic substances. This metatradition is fairly robust for entrepreneurship, management, and industrial relations. Likewise, the world of finance and banking also shows features of institutional partitioning of spaces and the recombination of distinct characteristics. It would be completely out of the ordinary to expect Germany to produce something over time other than corporatist or relationally contracted, quasi-public goods in order to counter some of the uncertainties of management, so that the management of others can be improved.

7
Making Sense of Internationalization

7.1 Introduction

The foreign correspondents of newspapers are a type of expatriate in multinational enterprises. They are symptomatic of societies that are coming together by developing a closer interest in each other, yet which still remain different. In 1989, Pascale Hugues, a young French journalist working for *Libération*, a French daily newspaper, was posted to Bonn. According to public opinion polls, France and Germany are each other's most favoured foreign nation, and they are linked with each other to an extent that even goes beyond EU treaties. Hugues herself had a family background that was partly Alsatian; so to her, Germany was not exactly an alien country. But by her own account, she was unsure how to come to grips with her job, given that Frenchmen approached Germany ambiguously, with an almost sanctimonious, overt friendship ('la grand-messe franco-allemande') cloaking an undercurrent of uncertainty and apprehension. One evening when she 'had the blues', a Danish colleague gave her a piece of advice which gave her the key: 'Try to look at Germany as an exotic country, and all will be well.' At first, she thought that he was mocking her. But then, 'the advice was to become precious to me. Germany has not bored me for a single moment.'[389] This meant that she kept detecting, unravelling, and explaining differences.

Considering the country one works in as exotic may indeed be a brilliant approach for foreign journalists. It may keep you from 'going native', taking things as self-evident and thus ending up with not much to wonder and write about any more. A country is exotic, not as such, but in the eye of the beholder. Exoticism characterizes the adopted perspective of the beholder rather than the properties of the country. What grounds are there for maintaining this perspective, even when familiarity increases and even though you may not be a foreign correspondent? This chapter summarizes some of the conceptual lessons presented in this book and identifies what may be peculiar to Germany in the more general conceptual picture.

7.2 Types of theory, history, and the future

The discussion on internationalization involves the past, the present, and the future. Contributions mainly do one of the following things:

- they analyse past processes and states of internationalization;
- they diagnose and explain recent and present-day internationalization;
- they predict or anticipate future tendencies of internationalization.

Such aspects may be addressed individually or combined with each other. The present contribution, although relying on cross-national comparative studies, greatly emphasizes the fruitfulness of a strongly diachronic analysis. However, this study is not strictly historical. In order to anticipate future processes or states, any treatment that is not limited to pure historiography needs theory. The social sciences have many types of theory to differentiate and compare phenomena along a number of different dimensions. This book is avowedly eclectic in the sense that it considers it highly fruitful and necessary to combine theories of different types in order to discuss and explain a specific class of phenomena, including more general or wider evolutionary tendencies.

The theories combined here have been of the following main types:

1. 'Grand theory' or *social theory* is a highly general type of theory, geared to account for relations and tendencies of high generality across substantial ranges of space or time and applicable in different disciplines. This was used in the specific form of conceptually and empirically identifying metatraditions as reasonably stable but dialectical and paradoxical tendencies. Such tendencies emerge through the institutional partitioning of societal spaces and the recombination of distinct institutional elements.

2. This was combined with a number of more specific theories, or *theories of the middle range*, dealing with the development of more specific arrangements or practices. They come from the disciplines of sociology, notably the sociology of work, organization studies, industrial relations, economics, and political science. This is in keeping with the drive in societal analysis to relate phenomena in different institutional domains to one another in an interdisciplinary endeavour.

3. While both social theory and theories of the middle range strive to be applicable across frames specific to time and place and adopt a universal posture, *historiography* underlines the specificity of such frames. It does not believe in accounting for historical events as specific manifestations of universal regularities. It points to the inevitable limitations, caused by the specifics of time and place, of any regularity we may come up with.

In addition, there are the acknowledged differences among theoretical currents or approaches, among positivistic, interactionist, and interpretive theories, and among those that regard collectivities as consisting of conflicting and negotiating parties or as functionally integrated wholes.[390] While the foundation of societal analysis is strongly interactionist, none of the different theoretical postures dominates the analysis. Sometimes, historiography has the upper hand, as when the origins and results of wars or broader political conflict are being taken into account. These exemplify the fact that some 'interdependencies' are not functionally necessary but incidental and specific to periods and the constellations of social forces within these. At other times, social theory prevails, as when the recurrent mechanism of institutional partitioning and the non-identical reproduction of metatraditions in the South Germanic bedrock are emphasized. Last but not least, theories of the middle range are essential for facilitating the piecing together of the manifold aspects. The concrete indeterminacy of historical tendencies and the paradoxical character of social theory are the reasons why combinations of middle range theories 'tip the balance' in favour of the application of different and competing types of social theory, explaining in more specific terms the way in which institutional partitioning and recombination occur. Grand theories are not distinguished very much by being either fundamentally right or wrong. However, they may be more or less useful, and their usefulness is a function of the degree to which they help us integrate theories of the middle range.

The application of such distinct theory types should not be seen as subject to a reductionist order. Reductionism means that one type of theory follows from a more fundamental theory. Their relations are instead governed by recursiveness: any kind of theoretically specific posture makes it necessary to revert to a different posture. This means that a particular theoretical argument is predicated on other types in an iterative process. As such, there is no type of theory that is more fundamental. The foundation is paradoxical in the sense that it is composed of generality (social theory), specificity (historiography), and the area in between (middle-range theories). The quest for a robust foundation is necessary but, because of its paradoxical nature, it is unending and leads to iteration between the different foundations mentioned; this process can only be stopped arbitrarily should a temporarily satisfactory solution appear and need to be publicized.

The treatment implemented here builds on the complementarities among the different strands of theory. The experience gained through this type of analysis leads us to the supposition that we do indeed have a great many adequate theories. The problem is to be familiar with them and to combine them adequately in order to investigate phenomena with a broad scope such as internationalization. Societal analysis, in the way it has been posited and further developed here, responds to such experience. It does not constitute an approach that plays up its distinctiveness from others in order to compete with them. It does insist on acknowledging the importance of the societal aspect of whatever phenomenon is being studied, including that which is trans- or supra-societal. It brings together many approaches and theories in order to explain this aspect. This programme amounts to a different kind of consistency of approach. Nearly every social science approach would emphasize its generality, theoretical consistency, and elaboration, in addition to the empirical corroboration or pertinence of the approach. Status and reputation tend to depend on the ability to put forward a concept that is distinct, logically consistent, and widely pertinent. This applies to social theory and middle-range theories alike.

The methodological argument underlying the present societal-analysis approach is different. It is eclectic in a clinical sense. It argues that a great many of the explanatory or practical problems with which social science deals are inadequately addressed if a single approach is used that pretends to integrate pertinent knowledge into one general, logically consistent, and distinct body of theory. It argues that we need a deliberate multiplicity of more self-contained bodies of theory; that the theoretical multiplicity of social science is a virtue rather than a deficiency; and it probably tallies with the subject matter it deals with. The problem is that too many scholars seek to identify some chosen topic or problem with an existing or new body of theory.

Therefore, it would be advisable to dedicate more effort to the pooling and conceptual integration of different bodies of theory, a skill in which neither students nor scholars are adequately trained. I call this 'clinical' because in medicine, notwithstanding medical specialization, an adequate diagnosis and solution also tends to require access to and pooling of theoretical knowledge of different sorts. Such a clinical orientation is transversal to, but does not necessarily conflict with, non-clinical or not directly clinical bodies of knowledge such as physiology, anatomy, biochemistry, and genetics. Some types of professional ethos in social science emphasize a clinical orientation more than others. Max Weber's work was surely not devoid of it, nor is the work of many proponents of socio-economics. A clinical orientation is not restricted to what is often called 'applied sciences'. It also includes basic research and is apparent in some high-level research institutes.[391] On a more modest level, it is inherent to the ethos of *bedrijfskunde*, a multidisciplinary business administration approach in the Netherlands within which I have worked since about 1990.

Note that this does not mean that social science will be manoeuvred into a backwater of theoretical stagnation by combining theories rather than developing them further.[392] In line with the postulated recursiveness, the approach consists of going from one theory type to another in the argument, rather than confining oneself to one specific theory. The clinical combination of theories, of which there are already a great many, requires judicious selection, the adequacy of which varies for different problems. The act of combination itself thus poses research problems and points towards a specific kind of theorizing. Conceivably, this could be called middle-range theorizing based on all the other types; it would be a manner of theorizing and conducting research which, although middle-range, is distinguished from others of the same type by appreciating historiography on its own terms and by handling distinct social theory approaches with ease.

In a classic and highly influential treatment of social mores, practices, attitudes, and beliefs in the late Middle Ages, based mainly on sources from Burgundy, which in that era included the Low Countries and territories in both France and the Holy Roman Empire of the time, Huizinga diagnoses how it closely combines religious fervour and rational reflection, piety and self-indulgence, temperament and discipline, morality and immorality, cruelty and politeness, as well as other stark contrasts.[393] This could be construed as an analysis of a period of transition from the Middle Ages to modernity. The title of the book, *The Autumn of the Middle Ages*, encourages this interpretation. Yet another message may emerge: periods are always transitory, and in social formations we always find a striking combination of contrasts coexisting in close proximity. Earlier beliefs and practices are not simply reduced but recombined with newly emerging ones. In this respect, Huizinga may have suggested the Kamchatka effect, which was indeed of central importance here. The announcement of new eras should not fool us into assuming that new orders crowd out established behaviour or are less internally riven and contradictory. The novelty of new institutions and culture resides in the novel syntheses of old and new elements. This message is strengthened here.

In all these respects, this book has programmatic conclusions to offer. It seeks to convince the reader that a treatment may be more convincing when we deliberately and diligently seek out a combination of existing approaches and bodies of knowledge and integrate them into a combination that sheds light on the phenomenon from different angles. While this makes the treatment theoretically more complex, it may help to keep the theoretical complexity and fragmentation of the social sciences in check. It guides us towards an interpretation of socio-economic change in which continuity coincides with change, such that societies re-enact themselves in novel ways, despite and because of the onslaught of internationalization.

7.3 The international constitution of societal specificity

My analysis has shown that, particularly in the case of Germany and its societal predecessors, it is hard to find culture and institutions in the worlds of work, organization, and the economy that have been devoid of decisive international influence. However, this is not just because Germany has had very blurred boundaries throughout its history, which makes it difficult to differentiate between internal and external phenomena.

In addition, we see that the specificity of institutions in the South Germanic bedrock is a consequence of the institutional partitioning of government and governance within a characteristic pattern that alternates between the overextension and provincialization of societal space. The characteristic fusion of hierarchical control and lateral coordination in this society was made possible by provincialized rule being intertwined with corporatist representation and governance. This form and transformation of feudalism depended on settlements after wars and other conflicts, which were by definition international, affected the balance of forces inside Germany, and increased the salience of intermediate layers of societal aggregation.

Interdependent with its own kind of societal and political layering, Germany has all along been open to foreign incursions of different kinds. There are probably very few institutions that have not experienced a more or less substantial influence imported from other societies or have not entailed trading and communication across the thin span of a broader European, Eurasian, and later Atlantic horizon. In other words, what is original about German institutions is not the ingredients as such, but the reaction of substances with one another. Such reactions have implied specific kinds of institutional partitioning and recombination. The most creative periods of institution-building have been when foreign incursions have been particularly noteworthy, such as during and after the Thirty Years' War and the Napoleonic Wars, after World War II, and in the course of building the European Union. Throughout German history, it has been the international transcendence of society that has provoked the formation of domestic culture and institutions.

This serves to make the point that the development of societal specificities was triggered by the extension of horizons of action and of society. In turn, the importing of foreign solutions was enacted on the basis of domestic conditions. Internationalization has helped to make society more distinctive. This fundamental mechanism has been present throughout the ages; it has not occurred in a uniform way but has implied qualitative shifts, such as a differential emphasis on non-liberal or liberal economic institutions. To this extent, development has been far from unidirectional. However, it has implied ever new variations around a leitmotiv constituted by a metatradition.

A metatradition only constitutes path dependency in an ambiguous and para-doxical way. It tends to approximate innovation and change to a path that is historically established. Due to the nature of qualitative shifts, incidental shocks, and creative development of recombinations, it is not a straight path and not necessarily a clear path, either. It may twist and turn during its course through history. It is better compared to a path such as the so-called Ho Chi Minh Trail, which was a territory consisting of many trails and having many routing options.[394]

This interpretation fundamentally questions the weight and pertinence of any discussion that highlights the tensions between internationalization and domestic specificity. These undoubtedly exist. Yet, they are being continuously transformed into new institutional concoctions, which are interpreted after a while as being coherent and consisting of functional interdependencies. Still, they are always historically temporary or episodic. Path dependency allows us to identify temporary equilibria in an analysis that economists term 'comparative statics', but it does not take us into a dynamic analysis.

Steps of internationalization are necessarily restricted to specific domains. Their consequences include domestic responses that imply greater domestic specificity. Increases in international interdependency are, in turn, interdependent on provin-cialization and the domestic specificity of institutions; domestic specificity is thus developed on fronts other than those affected by internationalization. It has also been possible to see that extensive diffusion of foreign models is conditional upon their 'socialization' or translation, i.e. mutual adaptation between them and pre-vailing meanings and practices.

7.4 Layering of societal space

A fundamental dilemma is that social actors, in principle, like their societal horizons to be nearby, while at the same time they extend horizons of action and bring far-flung interdependencies to bear on societal entities. This dilemma has led to layered societal constructions, such that non-layered societies are a historical rarity.

Germany and its predecessors have constituted one of the most significant and long-lasting, albeit qualitatively changing but altogether stable, lineages of societal layering, according to a mainly territorial principle of subdivision.

As we have seen, this layering has been linked to severe conflict over the relative importance of layers and boundaries between entities. Yet it is the arbitrariness of boundaries that has been conducive to societal integration. It is important to distinguish the intensity of layering from the stability of boundaries demarcating societal entities. In Germany, it appears that fuzzy, contested, and perennially changing intermediate entities of societal community have helped to entrench layering in a way that has not fundamentally counteracted but supported national and international integration.

In the South Germanic bedrock, layering clearly follows from traditions of feudalism and their transformation. From feudalism it is not far to federalism, both linguistically and in the evolution of political forms. In a way, federalism is the political aspect of societal layering, at least in the South Germanic bedrock, where sovereignty of political rule and domination has historically been feeble at the level above the individual states or older estates of the realm. Even American federalism has similar roots, in that it built on a somewhat overextended system of colonial rule which strove for a balance between sovereign royalty (or the Union) and the more provincial government in colonies (or states). Some observers would link Germanness to severity and the running of a tight institutional ship. The intention has indeed been there throughout history, but it has to be seen against the dialectical backdrop of perennially contested rule in both feudalism and federalism, the constant redrawing of boundaries, and fundamental upheaval. This backdrop and the institutional template of tightly linked hierarchical and lateral control have together brought forth a popular penchant for order and leadership.

We have seen that the strength of intermediate or lower layers of societal inclusion and government under the German variant of feudalism was decisive for the constitution of structures of economic, social, and political governance. It led to a provincial articulation of sovereign rule with peer control in the economic and social spheres. This laid the foundation for the close intertwining of hierarchical and more lateral social control in a provincialized society with strong subcentres. It is a phenomenon still seen today, and it is a metatraditional theme affecting cultural dispositions and formal institutions, as well as the distribution of economic, political, and social power. It is particular to a society in which national elites tend to be the more functional elites and the provincial elites the more diffuse.

This does not mean that the institutional apparatus of governance within Germany is irrevocably interdependent on strong internal federalism. The characteristic decoupling of historically established linkages may inevitably affect the relationship between institutions of governance and federalism in Germany. Yet the possible and likely decoupling does not mean that the two tendencies are thereby weakened. For Germany, federalism may well become more European, while the institutions in the governance of work, the economy, and related domains become more national in nature. This could again be a creative development on the basis of a metatradition, one implying that the governance of work, organization, business practices, industrial relations, etc. have 'always' been more local than has the top tier of legitimate rule and domination. With respect to Germany, that top tier has come to be a European one. This is not to be interpreted as a prediction of the future. However, a more dynamic perspective can be derived from the present analysis in order to envisage possible new variations on a metatraditional theme.

7.5 Convergence and divergence in close proximity

The idea that domestic societal specificity is always internationally constituted and that the construction of internationalization depends on domestic conditions runs counter to the antinomy between convergence and divergence. It is possible to see that striking convergence through the importation of foreign models has led to divergent forms of implementation and to recombination with other practices. This has consequences for the interpretation of ongoing or future trends in internationalization.

There are always convergent tendencies in the transfer of experience and models within or across societies, and they affect concrete practices in societies. This observation is virtually banal. In the present historical period, the main tendencies toward convergence can be summed up as follows:

- the spread of multinational enterprise;
- the decontextualization and international transfer of technical, business, managerial, and industrial relations models;
- the imposition of law and regulation by supranational government.

Basically, such tendencies and their effect upon concrete domestic culture and institutions have produced convergence in this sense ever since the Roman Empire imposed a new infrastructure and supra-tribal law and recruited local tribes into imperial service in lands which are now German, French, Belgian, Dutch, or English. We have also seen how the pre-German societal formations in such lands have been subjected to convergence imposed by new feudal elites and the spread of best imperial or international practice throughout the ages, whether that practice was Roman, Frankish, Arab, or northern Italian. A good rule of thumb is that any concrete practice appreciated as domestic, familiar, 'traditional'—one of the most inept terms in social science, which has been qualified and differentiated in this volume—and indigenous is the result of convergent tendencies. This occurred throughout the Middle Ages, and modern cases in point are those of the Napoleonic occupation, the phase of economic international liberalization before World War I, Americanization after World War II, European integration, and financial internationalization in the 1990s. All these convergent tendencies have evoked divergent responses.

The dialectics of convergence and divergence are nicely epitomized by Prussia at the beginning of the nineteenth century: convergence with France was more pronounced during and after the Napoleonic Wars although it was highly partial;

while in the subsequent time of peace, the trend shifted to divergence, at least where economic institutions were concerned. Severe crises may encourage or lead to convergence with the (former) enemy, whereas peaceful relations may reduce the pressure to emulate competing institutional sets. The same thing occurred after World War II. Piecemeal convergence may rest on peaceful relations and international order, but the historical evidence is also that convergence is more radical during the onslaught and aftermath of war or severe conflict. 'Cultural imperialism' can then be seen as a short-term convergence-enhancing, and by that token long-term divergence-producing, 'continuation of war by other means', to paraphrase Clausewitz.

More enlightening than positing divergence against divergence is to ask how convergent tendencies are conditioned by and contributive to divergent settings. One of the best established and yet most neglected facts is that such dialectical effects occur. Furthermore, it is necessary to acknowledge that such effects occur in close proximity. This means that we find results of convergence and divergence so closely interwoven that it may be extremely difficult to distinguish them within specific empirical manifestations. This is what we called the Kamchatka effect. The Technical University of Karlsruhe, for instance, originated as a *Polytechnikum* modelled on French technical elite education. It then mutated into a *Technische Hochschule* following a neo-German model after 1880, with a different type of student recruitment, training concept, and status.

The importance of convergent and divergent tendencies may change over time. As we investigate specific practices or entities, we are concerned with what may be called 'gross' convergence or divergence. Now, it is always easy to demonstrate gross convergence when a decontextualized model or practice is just beginning to spread internationally. Again, this observation is banal. The question then is how to assess 'net' convergence or divergence, including the further-flung effects that occur over time as a new model is being mutually adapted with respect to other institutional and cultural patterns. Net convergence or divergence is a more serious question, for it points to societal change.

This question is not only more serious but virtually intractable because the number of specific changes that occur tends to become so great and their conjoined effect so diffuse that it is almost impossible to ascertain net convergence or divergence. Thus, any such findings tend to be a research artefact conditioned by the period of study and by the range of adaptive processes covered. As a consequence, it is advisable within a deeper investigation to drop the issue of convergence versus divergence and replace it by asking which kinds of convergent tendencies are interdependent on which kinds of divergent ones. This is based on a more stable evolutionary mechanism. We have known about interdependency for a long time, and yet, curiously, any time that something new happens, researchers tend to suggest that it means the end of history—for this is what the end of the interdependency of convergence and divergence would amount to.

The entire argument—from the international constitution of societal specificity to the interdependency of convergence and divergence—is summed up concisely and precisely in Pascale Hugues' dictum mentioned at the beginning of the chapter: the methodological rule of thumb is that anything which at first looks familiar ought to be considered exotic. This is particularly apt in matters to do with internationalization or in any cross-societal comparison. By neglecting this dictum, researchers continue to discuss issues in terms of convergence versus divergence. For local 'traditions' turn out to reveal exotic origins, and it is only a few steps from the import of an exotic, decontextualized, and convergence-enhancing phenomenon to an adaptation that blends into a local scenery with surprising ease and even increases its specificity. This is because the reaction of external imports with domestic substances, through translation and reciprocal transformation, leads to new and original substances. According to the Kamchatka effect, we will find within these new combinations contrasting elements in close proximity.

7.6 A metatradition for the South Germanic bedrock

The importance of metatraditions has not gone unnoticed in social science. The most prominent example might be Michel Crozier's interpretation of French socio-political institutions alternating between strict, central, and standardizing control, on the one hand, and spontaneity, idiosyncrasy, and revolt, on the other.[395] This is another result of a particular type of society-building. It has its own persistent structural antagonisms and, in a general, ambiguous, but powerful way, set the scene for the ongoing development of institutions. D'Iribarne has emphasized the importance of long-lasting tradition by focusing on expectations and behaviour that recur regularly over the ages;[396] this is continuity, whereas Crozier highlights continuity and then fluctuation. In a paradoxical treatment of metatradition, continuity and fluctuation are combined. Note that this treatment excludes direct and unequivocal relations between any heritage or tradition and concrete manifestations of behaviour at a specific point, because such relations are always mediated by the dialectics inherent to the ongoing partitioning and recombination of culture and institutions. Notions such as 'national character' or culture are one-sided since they neglect paradox and its consequences.

Even long-running metatraditions are time- and place-specific phenomena particular to societies. Historiography is indispensable for the identification of metatraditions, and it must be accepted on its own terms. Historiography insists on specifying the time and place of certain forces and constellations, thus making it an eminently clinical discipline—one that should be reflected through the mirrors of the more general theory found in economics, sociology, or political science. This does not mean that we use general theory to explain historical evolutions. We cannot do this, for we do not seem to have theory that is sufficiently elaborate and general. No discipline or type of theory is more fundamental than another. The will to improve one theory inevitably points to another one. This is what recursiveness implies.

The metatradition for Germany, Austria, and Switzerland has been shown in this volume to exemplify societal aggregation in a process that alternates between overextension and retrenchment, so that intermediate societal layers become particularly salient. With the development of feudalism and absolutism, this process transformed older and more Germanic institutions of lateral coordination and weak rule into a striking coalescence of lateral and hierarchical elements and into a division of labour between princes and estates, between rule and socio-economic governance. This is the heritage that has affected the oscillation between and recombination of liberalization and corporatism, the latter having had national-liberal, fascist, communist, and social-democratic variants.

This metatradition has therefore also affected the evolution of the governance of work, management, and enterprises. It brought about a coalescence of hierarchy, professional authority, and lateral professional coordination, combined within a stakeholder approach and more communitarian business traditions that culminated in co-determination and collective regulation. This fusion would not have been as tight had it not been catalysed by vicious conflicts about the identity and borders of society and, more recently, by severe societal stress and strain caused by war and reconstruction, before and after defeat.

This is what we can ascertain for Germany. If we were to look at another society, a different metatradition would emerge. The treatment so far has been representative, but it has theoretical boundaries in terms of time and space that limit its application to analysing a specific metatradition. Still, the general conclusion deserves to be emphasized: metatraditions are powerful; they do not exclude but integrate power relationships and economic forces. We ignore them at our peril; for to ignore them means to fall prey to the ahistorical myopia from which some areas of social science have suffered. The classics, however, intended and practised something different. This means that we should not consider specific evolutions to be universal and unidirectional. They can be that only in a very abstract sense, one that embraces paradox. Instead, such evolutions should be visualized as contingent and dialectical, but they are nonetheless meaningful along the crooked path that a metatradition implies.

7.7 European and German biases

Out of respect for historiography, we may inevitably make a theoretical scheme less general than is desirable. The theory of societal aggregation through layering is, on the one hand, fairly general because we do observe layering around the world. However, the criteria of layering may differ according to region and populace, and according to ethnicity, culture, and kinship. Through the particularities of feudalism, layering in Europe in general and in the South Germanic bedrock in particular has become dominated by territorial entities that have constituted and generalized loyalties, identities, practices, and norms, and also their enforcement.

In other parts of the world, layering has evolved differently. Ethnic, cultural, and kinship commonalities have become or remained more important. In this respect, this study has clear limitations. The interplay of overextension and retrenchment in societal community has led to different societal structures elsewhere. We can only acknowledge that and be cautious about applying elsewhere the theories used here. The overriding importance of territoriality in the layering of European societies is a case in point. Where layering is based on ethnicity or other criteria distinct from territoriality, different concepts are appropriate. To a large extent, the present treatment is one of internationalization in Europe, the building up of a European layer of societal community, and of the place Germany holds in its midst.

In eastern Europe, there were particular types of societal aggregation and disaggregation, notably the refined territorial subdivision of settlement based on ethnicity or culture. Societal homogenization across diverse settlements in eastern Europe has featured cruel episodes of ethnic cleansing and annihilation. These have worked against layering in the trivial but horrific sense that if an ethnic or cultural entity is wiped out or expelled, layering becomes less important and the foundation for more severe societal rifts is laid. The final result is societal division rather than layering. This is a different variant of the dialectics of extending horizons of action, on the one hand, and societal retrenchment, on the other.

Presumably, the interdependency of internationalization and layering is therefore stable, even more stable than counter-examples suggest. Wherever nation-building has been a declared aim, be it in former African colonies or currently in Iraq, ethnic, cultural, kinship, and religious entities always appear to have come back with a vengeance, or the prospects of successful nation-building have remained very tenuous. Internationalization may thus contribute less than we have thought to the development of national specificity; in fact, it may well be connected with the promotion of more segmental specificities.

Without wanting to dabble in a field of knowledge that cannot be further developed here, I merely suggest that the general mechanism may indeed apply outside Europe, but in a form that is specific in time and place. It may contribute to the maintenance or revival of segmental societal entities below the level of the nation state or of entities purporting to be nation states. In short, internationalization may create more havoc outside Europe than the present analysis for Europe suggests. Even here, the problems of integration facing Europe in the wake of EU extension and the controversial debate about an EU 'constitution' show that renationalization is a potent force and that limits to central European government and harmonization of policies are becoming increasingly apparent, specifically in the internal governance of member nations. Still, to continue de Tocqueville's reasoning with regard to the United States, limits to central government and to harmonization in a number of domestic policy fields may be required in order to achieve unified European responsibility on other fronts, such as foreign policy and defence. Note also that the periods of internationalization witnessed by Europe and in particular by Germany in the past were not free from havoc. Some of the chapters in this volume have made it sufficiently clear that horrific havoc has been part and parcel of internationalization, and there is nothing that Europe in general or Germany in particular has not already had to learn about death and destruction as corollaries of societal aggregation.

7.8 An evaluative balance of topical German feats, predicaments, and prospects

The common association of fear, contempt, admiration, and sympathy with respect to things German is not restricted to consumers of tabloid newspapers or war films, but is also found among social scientists and other specialists. Research and theories on Germany have explicitly or implicitly reflected such concerns. The present analysis is not directly concerned with whether German culture and institutions are successful or deficient, admirable or atrocious. It is typical of a culture and its institutions that their heritage lasts longer than do success, failure, or fashion. Specific adaptations of culture and institutions, or their absence, may change a success story into an episode of failure, or vice versa.

Yet, readers are accustomed to linking a neutral evaluation of a society with more short-term impressions and facts relating to the performance of that society in the international league. Topical success is related to a presumption of stability, and lack of success to the idea that fundamental change is desirable or can be expected. Nothing of the kind conforms to more general experience in a rigorous way. Yet it is probably inevitable that we should comment briefly on how the present analysis can be linked to a topical perception of feats and predicaments.

First, we can see that the development of institutions features a recombination of distinct elements following from different principles and coexisting in close proximity. This goes against the grain of theories and popular conceptions that presume further-flung and more stable interdependencies between institutions in different domains. The creative ability of societies to decouple and recombine institutional and cultural facets highlighted here combines tight coupling within and across action spaces with ongoing and surprising institutional modification. This process continuously breaks with temporarily established institutional interdependencies, and it temporarily erects new ones. This vitiates any conceptualization of societal change as happening uniformly across the board on the basis of stable interdependencies between concrete and specific institutions. Evolutionary interdependencies exist between actors and in a more ambivalent way within a metatradition, but not between concrete institutions. In a dynamic perspective, evolution is paradoxical; since we know this, there is no reason to be surprised by changes in 'models'.

Second, aspects of institutions in the governance of work, companies, and the economy have proven astoundingly stable and productive despite the critical developments that accumulated in public regulation during the 1970s and 1980s and that were exacerbated by the way German unification was publicly handled. Nevertheless, Germany never stopped being a leading exporting country: it reduced its backlog in the presence of multinational companies with direct investment in other parts of the world, and firms in western Germany remained surprisingly healthy. It had little difficulty surviving the oil and currency crises of the 1970s that finished *les trente glorieuses*, and became a regional beacon of diversified quality production. This was the time when the image of Germany was exaggerated as a model social market economy with good economic growth, high levels of employment, good technical and industrial performance, and well-functioning practices in training, education, and industrial relations.

Just prior to 1990 and reunification, when the country was being governed by a Christian Democratic–Liberal coalition, Germany was certainly not at the bottom of the league as far as national economic performance in an age of increasing liberal reform was concerned. It had modest liberalization policies. Still, these were comparable in intensity at the time to those of the Netherlands, the country that for a while was a new regional exemplar of growth, liberalization, and deregulation. It was the vitality of its businesses, in addition to a burst of public deficit spending after unification in the early 1990s, that covered up dangerous deficiencies in German public regulation. Germany nevertheless paid its share of expenses for the Gulf War and set out to achieve rapid harmonization of wages and welfare in East Germany. The government thought, more or less, that it could manage all this by temporary increases in deficit spending and by establishing a temporary supplement to the income tax (the *Solidaritätszuschlag*). But this plan did not work; instead it drove the country into deficit spending and caused an extraordinary increase of non-wage labour costs. As the OECD acknowledged, Germany has had below-average growth since the collapse of the post-unification boom, and the low growth 'reflects a desynchronization of economic activity between Germany and the other EU countries in the early 1990s on account of the economic shock associated with reunification'.[397]

The way Germany handled reunification and avoided dealing with a number of regulatory deficiencies would probably have broken the back of any other comparable country much sooner. It could do what it did by relying excessively on institutions to function as they should in the governance of work, business, and the economy, as described in Chapters 4–6. That reliance was excessive but it took another decade in order for it to become clear to everyone that a more radical overhaul of regulatory institutions and policies was necessary. This much can be said for the functionality of institutions in the governance of work, organization, management, and industrial relations. They were overburdened but did their job, as resilient institutions often do. Likewise, the way the population submitted to the burden of reunification—at first jubilant and then gritty or sullen—probably constituted an unsurpassed example of patriotic compliance in peacetime. After reunification, year by year, about 150 billion Euro on average went from the West to the East, as subsidies and as transfer payments to new states and public authorities devoid of sufficient tax income of their own. This sum is roughly equivalent to the extra budget implemented by the much larger United States to cover the costs of the Iraq war in 2003. It suddenly put Germany at the top of the European table of gross national product devoted to the public sector. No other state would probably have gone so far for so long to welcome home and integrate one-fifth of its new total population of 83 million citizens, emerging as they did from the rubble of state socialism, without suffering major political controversy.

The stark fact is that, in addition to a period of internationalization, the 1990s for Germany were a period of tenacious and largely silent patriotism, a subdued patriotism in Europe rather than against it, although popular acclaim for European integration waned. This was articulated in phenomena of subliminal emotional refuge from the stresses and strains of unification, such as the greatly increased frequency and apparent popularity of television shows airing what is called *Volks-musik*.[398] Without overstretching the application of the dialectic of internationalization and domestic specificity, we can see how significantly the two went together. But this was not widely discussed as such. There was no agenda of national reform to combine internationalization, national integration, and adaptation of public regulation within one consistent package. Above all, Germany seems to have a problem with consistency and reform of national welfare policy. This is the current impediment, not internationalization issues as such.

What, then, were the public regulatory deficiencies?[399] Already in the 1970s, an increasing share of the fiscal burden of social welfare was being placed on contributions imposed on wage labour, paid by wage earners and employers. Notably, non-wage labour costs were rapidly increasing. The relative disadvantaging of the use of labour as a factor of production and the increasing fixity of labour costs led to inelastic and deficient creation of employment opportunities. This did not mainly affect the competitiveness of the internationally exposed sectors of the economy, but it did affect employment for two main reasons: the heavy fiscal and social security burden on labour discouraged the development of labour-intensive services, and it encouraged the use of 'black market' labour, unrecorded employment for which taxes, social security, and health insurance contributions are not paid. Numerous firms in internationally exposed settings relocated activities or made new investments abroad to some extent. This was because the comparative advantage of foreign labour increased by leaps and bounds, to the same extent as did domestic non-wage labour costs. Nevertheless, employment in internationally exposed businesses held up well, which attests to the ongoing competitiveness of German firms; this was definitely not the central problem of the 'German model' of the time.[400]

After reunification, governments again continued or even increased the tendency to shift the burden of welfare and active labour market policies onto the shoulders of labour, including employer contributions for the benefit of labour. The increasing longevity of the population and rising health costs, sluggish economic growth and development of employment, and massive and persistent subsidization of eastern Germany then caused a relative increase in the public fiscal burden, including taxes, social security, and health insurance contributions, to an extent that at the time was unparalleled in Europe and the OECD. The absolute financial weight of the burden can be compared to a purely hypothetical US decision to fight an Iraq-type war for at least twenty years. This led to a vicious spiral of an increasing fiscal burden, especially in labour costs, in spite of wage restraints, low growth, welfare-financing problems, and employment reduction.

While this conundrum was well known and studied, it was swept under the carpet. This is all the more surprising when we consider that students of the conundrum and theorists of reform were closely linked to the major parties (Miegel and Biedenkopf to the CDU, Scharpf and Streeck to the SPD). However, the problem also has ramifications for the vicissitudes of party competition in the federal system and in the welfare-financing and management corporatism of Germany, one of its many corporatist institutions. The effect of these vicissitudes was that both large parties found it preferable to evade the conundrum rather than address it in political debate and campaigns, for fear of being outdone by the other populist party and losing the support of specific corporative interests.

All the while, the conundrum has had specific and well-understood roots; it is not linked to homogeneous and generally applicable characteristics. In German federalism, public fiscal responsibilities are mostly shared by the federal government (controlled by the second parliamentary chamber) and state governments (controlling the first parliamentary chamber at federal level, which also has to approve at best approximately two-thirds of federal legislation). When there are different majorities in the two chambers, as there often have been due to swings of public opinion after federal elections in successive state elections, policy-making becomes a tortuous, protracted, and substantively messy and evasive affair. An opaque patchwork of responsibilities, which has evolved to conduct decision-making while safeguarding the particular interests of a multitude of actors, has been criticized as undemocratic, wasteful of resources, and perennially bordering on subtle or crude forms of corruption.[401]

Although the changes required are pervasive, they are nonetheless specific and focused on dealing with sufficiently identifiable problems ranging from muddled federalism to the excessive burden of social security and welfare contributions on labour as a production factor. There is no need to obscure this precise analysis by calling into question a broader range of institutional arrangements per se. Federalism is certainly part of the current problem, with its muddled cross-level sharing of responsibilities, but not all or even most of the socio-economic institutions affecting work, management, and industrial relations are problematic.[402] In recent years, Germany has been criticized by institutions advocating more pervasive liberalization policies, notably the OECD. Such criticism has addressed the regulation of utility markets (gas, electricity, water), financial markets, and corporate governance, among others. The OECD did, however, acknowledge that 'Germany emerged among the pioneers in product market reform and market opening in Europe'.[403] Although one may contest the neo-liberal inspiration of OECD documents, its report on Germany reflects the characteristic partitioning of institutions in the economy of the country, namely the cooperative, corporatist, and governmental regulation of the generation of factors pertaining to both capital and labour, combined with liberal regulation and contestable markets for consumption and investment goods. This combination, hugely promoted in the post-war years and quite influential since then, has supported a high degree of economic competitiveness. To this extent, and more than the OECD admits, social coordination has been useful in counterpoising the liberalization which serves competitive markets. However, in the long run, the failure adequately to address specific problems may put all kinds of institutions under pressure, though this is functionally dubious. In a true revolution, everything may be turned upside down, without any regard for targeted solutions to specific problems.

In short, Germany is not a normative model in most respects, not even in the analytical sense, except for periods of no more than a few decades. Neither are other societies. Germany has recently performed unique feats and been subjected to unique predicaments. Both the feats and the predicaments are indirect and highly mediated derivatives of the South Germanic bedrock, which have had positive effects in specific situations and at specific times and negative effects in other situations and at other times. A syndrome of high productivity and competitiveness has recently become even more acute, as shareholder-value dynamism has declined and real economic productivity re-emerged.[404] In Germany, the high productivity syndrome has helped maintain dysfunctionality and slack in employment-enhancing public regulation and in aspects of federalism. This is another phenomenon of partitioning: the virtues of some things stabilize the pathologies of others.

The acknowledgement of feats and predicaments does not stand in the way of a sober assessment of the country intended to discern and explain patterns of internationalization that are distinctive for societies. It is hoped that the present analysis supplies enough useful tools and insights of a more general nature to be applied elsewhere. It appears certain that the general mechanisms and metatraditions presented here will also be useful in the future in a general way. What precisely will happen is, as Streeck points out, very much a question of whether and in what way elites face their responsibilities and work together to meet the challenges. Streeck, however, is somewhat pessimistic about the capacity of actors to make choices as radical as in the periods before and after the world wars.[405] Conceivably, the threat of a collapse of the welfare state and public finance, which is currently more evident for Germany in view of its particular predicament than for Scandinavia, might unleash more creative forces. At the beginning of the 1990s, the case of Sweden was also being discussed on the premise that the Swedish 'model' of the welfare state and egalitarian centralized wage bargaining had collapsed.[406] Sweden now exemplifies a new combination of the welfare state with market forces and less conglomerate industry. The current discussion in the German public media, in its search for likely solutions to social security and welfare, general education, employment services, taxation, and other public revenue-generation problems, is little influenced by models from Anglo-American countries. Instead, there is a fascination with Denmark, the Netherlands, Finland, Switzerland, and Austria, the closest neighbours in or very near the South Germanic bedrock.

7.9 A conclusion on internationalization

Major evolutionary tendencies typically encapsulate opportunities and constraints. These are not necessarily distinct. In a dialectical approach to evolution, its parameters are paradoxical in virtue of shading from opportunities into constraints. The 'shading into something else' phraseology expresses the fact that such dialectics are actor-centric. This means that opportunities shade into constraints and vice versa by the nature of their perception, construction, and enactment, rather than on the basis of a supposedly objective nature independent of actors' perception and volition. Certain actors see constraints where others see opportunities. A closer retrospective analysis of courses of action shows that constraints are indeed inter-actively adopted along with the choice of specific opportunities. One implies the other, and specific institutions and culture evolve during the course of making successive choices that entail specific constraints and of submitting to specific constraints that confront actors with choices to be made.[407]

To come back again to Hugues' dictum noted at the beginning of the chapter: the answers to whether internationalization acts as a constraint or as an opportunity, and how dialectical combinations of opportunities and constraints are adopted in a process, are not given per se, but are inherent in the construction of actors, institutions, and culture. The construction of all of these develops within the heritage of a metatradition. Societies always enact some kind of continuity of the metatradition. This can be used in retrospect to explain an evolution, but it can also be used in order to do two other things.

One is to provide a correct and balanced diagnosis of acute phenomena of internationalization that embraces both constraints and opportunities, not as dis-tinct and contradictory phenomena, but as interlinked. Such a diagnosis can be the basis for realistic suggestions of courses of action, for public actors, enterprises, associations, trade unions, and others. It is important to note that such a realistic diagnosis and such suggestions cannot be made individually; they require concerted effort. Another is an attempt to predict, to the extent that a measure of specificity is feasible, along which 'path'—with a breadth at least metaphorically similar to that of the Ho Chi Minh Trail—novel partitioning and the recombination of opposites is likely. This involves conditional statements and thus overlaps with the develop-ment of contingent courses of action.

It would appear that the discussion in Germany and elsewhere, in scholarship and in practice, has much to gain from such an approach. It translates a fundamental lesson taken from the dialectical process of internationalization and turns it into an explanation of things that have happened and a topical and prospective conceptu-alization of things to come. This lesson needs to be demonstrated to students and decision-makers alike. The latter especially tend, overtly and intuitively, to over-estimate internationalization as a constraint rather than an opportunity. They remain silent about the policy errors that they themselves have cumulatively built up in the past, except when one step in the build up can be blamed on a different party.[408] They may deduce from it either the need to introduce abundant and encompassing measures on behalf of liberalization or the need to take what turns out to be frustrated and helpless action in niches that constraints have supposedly not affected. Internationalization is eminently reversible; however, its reversibility is partial in the long term. It goes together with the institutional partitioning of societal spaces, and it involves the partitioned recombination of opposites existing in close proximity. It requires and breeds societal specificity, although learning from foreign practice is essential. In the past, this has meant learning from France or the United States, and now it possibly means learning from Denmark and Finland. This is the way history has worked so far, and it is unlikely to stop working this way. Whatever actors specifically do or can do has to be explained and conceived within the framework of such general dynamics.

Notes

1 Yourcenar (1968: 310–11). Translation:

'The deceased prior . . . could have had no way of knowing to what extent you had elected to live your life in a state of revolt,' said the canon almost acrimoniously. 'You must surely have lied to him many, many times.'

'You are wrong,' said the prisoner, with an almost hostile glance at this man who had wanted to save him. 'Our contradictions never kept us apart.'

2 For an overview of co-evolution theory and literature from an organization theory point of view, see Lewin and Volberda (1999).

3 See Rorty (1989: pp. xiv–xv). The style of the present book is deliberately ironic in places, conforming to Rorty. Irony however does not mean agnosticism or nihilism. In my reading of Rorty, it suggests that sacred fundamentals are not for us to define, that profane fundamentals should be open to critical discourse, and that profanation cannot decisively harm what is sacred, as long as it is subject to a critical discourse which in turn is an enactment of something sacred. The expression of fundamental wisdom is thus inevitably ironic. This irony has been central for both God-fearing rabbis and an agnostic such as Nietzsche.

4 Stark (1996) has suggested a fundamental mechanism of 'recombination' in the evolution of socio-economic orders, implying the combination of opposite institutional character-istics. I concur with Stark but develop the idea of recombination within an action theory framework in the following chapters.

5 Smelser (1994) brings together central theories and findings on polity and society, economy and society, and institutional and cultural processes. While 'globalization' does not figure in the title, the tension between internationalizing forces and the retention or increase of domestic distinctiveness, and between universal and societally specific tendencies, emerge as key themes.

6 See the introduction to Davies (1997).

7 Ruigrok and van Tulder (1995).

8 See Smelser (1994: 287–8).

9 The debate and its inconclusive outcome or countervailing tendencies are well summar-ized by Streeck (1998: ch. 1).

10 See Bartlett and Ghoshal (1989) for a ground-breaking conceptualization, as well as subsequent publications by the authors. While their work has been influential in striking the key note, the sample they covered was not large.

11 This is another lesson from Ruigrok and van Tulder (1995).

12 Rugman (2000).

13 Dowling, Welch, and Schuler (1999: 18) show that there is no US multinational in the international top ten of foreign investment related to total investment.

14 Richard Whitley, a student of national business systems, has therefore come to refer to it, in seminar presentations, as 'globaloney'.

15 The notion of dialectics is explained below. Dialectical unity implies that when the conflict between productive forces and productive relations becomes too great, a 'revo-lution' re-establishes a new mode of production, consisting of new productive relations

better able to tap into productive forces. While Marx should not be taken on board in a dogmatic fashion, this is by and large still a viable heuristic for analysing socio-economic change. See e.g. Cohen (1978).

16 See Inglehart (1990) and other publications cited therein.

17 A recent book from the group is Halman and Hevitte (eds, 1996). This also cites previous publications.

18 Hofstede (2001).

19 See Smelser (1994: chs 15, 17), especially the analysis of the dialectics and syncretism of secularization and religious identification (pp. 308–9).

20 This is a literal translation of *Entzauberung*, i.e the removal of magic from interpretations of the real world, a notion used by Weber.

21 For example, the French word for 'head', *tête*, is derived from the Latin *testa*, meaning a piece of broken pottery. It is the same as saying the word 'nut' is, in the Queen's English, the proper word for 'head'.

22 Boyer (1998).

23 Soskice (1999).

24 See Weber (1964: vol. 1, 16–17).

25 Knowledge can be divided into explicit (codified or scientifically corroborated) and implicit or tacit knowledge. Jorna (2000) has provided a convincing systematization.

26 See van Heigenoort (1972: 45). This reasoning is logical. But since logical terms are necessary in order to give a coherent picture of the 'real world', it also has an epistemological extension. This philosophical argument was used by Poole and van de Ven (1989: 563) in organization and management theory.

27 This is 'permanent dialectics'as defined and reiterated by Vieira da Cunha, Clegg, and Pina e Cunha in Clegg (ed., 2002: ch. 2).

28 See Poole and van de Ven (1989). This article also argues that in order to be explained sufficiently, any real-world phenomenon has to be addressed using conflicting theories. Explanatory completeness thus takes us through paradox, not as a last resort, but always to paradox in a circle of logical and empirical examination.

29 I have adopted the actor/agent distinction from Hollis (1994: 19).

30 See Clark (2002). This is an eclectic discourse that addresses more specifically cross-national comparisons and institutionalist analysis, which are also crucial in my analysis.

31 I have made this point with a colleague (Sorge and van Witteloostuijn 2004) with regard to organizational change rhetoric. It can be generalized to other fields with ease.

32 See Lanciano *et al.* (1998), Maurice (2002), Maurice *et al.* (1977, 1982), Maurice and Sorge (2000), Maurice *et al.* (1980), Sorge and Warner (1986).

33 Plessner (1959) showed that belated nation-building had led to uncertainty in a number of civic and political orientations, lack of self-assurance, a sort of collective inferiority complex, and aggressive self-assertion. While he rightly pointed to the role of feudalism in preventing nation-building, he neglected the force of traumas of foreign incursions, ravages, and domination, which increased both feudal authority and particularism, on the one hand, and lack of self-assurance and aggressive self-assertiveness, on the other. See Chapter 4 of this volume.

34 There is a substantial amount of literature which does this, and an early, almost classic sociological treatment of it can be found in Dahrendorf (1965). He argued that national, cultural, and institutional heritage had worked against liberalism and acceptance of conflict. As subsequent chapters of my book show, this is only part of the story, rather

than the whole of it. While Dahrendorf's argument was well presented, it underrated the dilemmatic origin of non-liberal heritage and the fact that its force came from being closely enmeshed with opposed orientations. This will also be developed in the middle chapters of my book.

35 See Albert (1991).

36 This goes for the Hohenzollern, who became electors and kings of Brandenburg-Prussia, the Habsburgs, who were German emperors for centuries and also rulers in Austria and Hungary, the Wittelsbach, who at first ruled over the Rhenish Palatinate and then also Bavaria, the Luxemburgs, who became kings of Bohemia, and the Burgundians, who became vassals of both the French kings and the emperor of the Holy Roman Empire of the Middle Ages.

37 Streeck (1997: 54). Unfortunately, this statement is buried in a footnote. All the same, it is fundamental.

38 Leaving aside caricature, the first methodologically sound demonstration of German familial authoritarianism by international comparison was Devereux *et al.* (1962). In more popular treatments, it is the goose-step that has become a symbol of aggressiveness and authoritarianism, stylized such as in Davies (1997: 612). Anyone who has seen British soldiers 'square-bashing', i.e. performing turns or halting with demonstrative and noisy tramping on the ground—thighs lifted so high that they form an acute angle with the torso, and the legs then being snapped back into the vertical position so that the boots strike the ground with a resounding thump, is not struck by any quantitative difference in the amount of artificial, puppet-like movement between this manoeuvre and the goose-step.

39 As will be shown in Chapter 5, and much to the surprise of both foreigners and Germans themselves, German enterprises were revealed to be tightly but consensually run, with a simple, flat hierarchy and a large amount of spontaneous mutual adaptation, and on the basis of organized workforce participation. This could not have been due solely to ideologically instilled belief in harmony and authority, not even in the first instance.

40 Lammers (2003: 1400).

41 Davies (1997: 470).

42 See Hillmann (2000: 372) and other sources quoted therein.

43 Davies (2000: 1135).

44 Lévi-Strauss (1963: 229).

45 Esser (1993: 324–6) gives a classic definition of society in the analytical sense.

46 The original draft by Jefferson read: 'We hold these truths to be sacred and undeniable...' (Davies 1997: 678). The appeal to the sacred was thus replaced by an appeal to self-evidence as an Enlightenment concept. But both versions appeal to myth; more on that later.

47 It is probably inept or cowardly to state this in a footnote, but other references in these notes will make it clear: the theoretical foundation I use owes a great deal—more than I feel competent to explain in the beginning—to the philosophy of American pragmatism, beginning with John Dewey and branching out into the Chicago School of sociology and social psychology.

48 This is a response to what lies behind the concept of 'sociology without society' put forward by Touraine (1981). In an interactionist perspective, there is a notion of society that is meaningful although the idea of 'societal variables' at a separate and elevated level is abandoned.

49 See Smith (1759/1976). König (1967: 106) considers this to be one of the first major advances towards sociology, in which the natural law concept of society was rejected in favour of the postulate that society was based on moral sentiments, in the sense of moral integration into a societal community.

50 Karl Weick (1979) emphasizes that actors pragmatically make sense of the arrangements which they confront, interacting with the sense or meaning that they enact through their own behaviours. In this way, coherence between arrangements and individual action is not given in an objective way but constituted or 'enacted', meaning that it comes out in the act itself and need not be premeditated. Thus sense or meaning is not simply given to human actors but imputed within integrated behavioural and sense-making action.

51 Mead (1997) is a basic text which explains the relation between personal knowledge and society, the micro- and the macro-level as it were.

52 See Giddens (1986), which is fundamentally concerned with the duality of structure. The present analysis is concerned with the duality of institutions. Giddens (1986: 28–9) deals with institutions in a similar way, directly and indirectly going back to the present theoretical foundations.

53 This work (Berger and Luckmann 1971) is one of the classic, ground-breaking texts in positing knowledge constituted within a societal horizon as necessary and central to any treatment of institutions, order, and structure.

54 See Burrell (2002: 32–3), in reference to his work and that of Morgan, where the distinction is made between objectivistic and subjectivistic approaches in organization studies as well as in social sciences more generally.

55 See Merton (1968). This is also one of the earlier programmes of theory-building that expounded the value of nomothetic theories of the middle range.

56 Hübner (2001) has provided what I take to be the state-of-the-art treatment of myth in relation to classes of knowledge that aim for rational discourse and empirical corroboration.

57 Compare Descartes' idea that 'I think therefore I am', or Kant's definition of the Enlightenment as 'man's exit from self-induced irresponsibility *[Unmündigkeit]*'. Both are myths.

58 Berger and Luckmann (1971: 72).

59 See Oliver (1996, 1997). The dialectically inspired management literature has thus revived interactionist theory more effectively to some extent than sociology, which remains more exclusively positivist. Again, there is no harm in positivism but Oliver shows that interactionism can offer useful inspiration.

60 DiMaggio and Powell (1983) unilaterally associated the notion of institutions with the Weberian iron cage. But Weber saw this iron cage manifested in modern bureaucracy, rather than in institutions per se.

61 This point is well made by Giddens (1986: 14–16). Both symbolic and resource power become socially pertinent by being enacted by knowledgeable actors. Conceptually, domination and power enter in as institutional forms which are always related to patterns of legitimation and signification on more 'structural' and interactional levels (1986: 28–9).

62 Lewin (1948) had analysed this process for decision-making criteria, processes, and outcomes in groups. But it can be generalized beyond the level of groups, as has in fact been done by the notion of the succession of habitualization, objectivization, and sedimentation in institutionalization put forward by Tolbert and Zucker (1996). I down play this terminology in order to help readers avoid the pitfalls of prevalent unidirectional

evolutionism and the obscuring of the dialectical nature and reversibility of the process, aspects that are too often neglected by institutionalists. Lewin, however, was at least emphatic about reversibility. For a fruitful institutionalist analysis of issues in 'globalization', see the introduction, chapter 1, and conclusion in Djelic and Quack (eds, 2003).

63 The term 'partitioning of institutional space' is derived from the 'partitioning of resource space', as a concept in population ecology: here, organizations divide up resource space and different types specialize in qualitatively different segments of this space. See Carroll (1985).

64 This is not to argue against every manifestation of culturalist comparison, such as the more famous ones detailed by Geert Hofstede (2001). These are useful points of departure. But they need to be immediately differentiated and qualified as norms which are very specific and different from situation to situation. Only then can valid bridges be built between general values and individual manifestations of behaviour. One of the most tedious tasks is therefore to reiterate the point that types of behaviour observed in different societies happen to coincide with general value differences.

65 The original German version is *Dienst ist Dienst, und Schnaps ist Schnaps*, which translated more literally means 'duty is duty and booze is booze'.

66 This is explained by the 'structurationist' approach put forward by Giddens (1986), which is in fact rather similar to that of Berger and Luckmann.

67 This also includes the contribution of d'Iribarne (1989), which focuses on what I will later explain as a metatradition understood as soft institutions and culture.

68 Parsons (1964).

69 König (1967: 106–7, 126). The bias against the endogenous origin of rule and domination and in favour of exogenous origin, through superposition of invading tribes and rulers, is influenced in central Europe and other regions by the historic fact that aristocratic rulers extended and consolidated their reign against dwindling regional confederations. The clearest exceptions to this were Switzerland and the Netherlands until the Napoleonic conquest. See also König (1980: 132–3) for the argument, derived from the research of Marc Bloch, that society emerged when *communitas* came into being.

70 See Hofstede (1997). This title expresses a principal message of the book much better than that of the English original, *Cultures and Organizations*, which attests to the value of translation.

71 March and Simon (1958) have proven the salience of limits to rationality, which simply means that we can enact rational choice only to the extent that this extends over a small range of action parameters and is firmly embedded in something else: intuition, custom, ideology, unreflective practices. Many scholars pay lip service to this principle but do not heed its implications. Action theorists and interpretivists would express those implications as follows: rational choice is always the enactment of tradition, values, or unreflective institutions that prevail beyond the horizon of rationality and are evoked by its very practice. How this works was brilliantly demonstrated by the author of a classic work in organization sociology (Gouldner 1976), a study that has been given less attention than it deserves, as it may be Gouldner's most profound work.

72 See Czarniawska and Joerges (1996).

73 See Saka (2003). Mueller (1994) and others have posited that organizational effects work in close proximity to and against societal effects. I contend that cross-national organization effects trigger societal effects.

74 The basic exposition of this is found in Luhmann (1972).

75 The phenomenology of Luhmann's ideas has been well analysed and to some extent rectified by Eley (1972).

76 Lockwood (1964). This author conceived social integration around fundamental values, in line with the structural-functionalist theory of the time. I propose not to restrict the focus to values but to include basic understandings on a more general basis, i.e. to include evaluatively more neutral 'practical knowledge' as Giddens calls it.

77 See Münch (1980). I have refrained from quoting a lot of social theorists because for me the paper by Münch is authoritative. It lays out neatly much of the preceding discussion and allows me to keep a certain distance from the overspecialized niceties of general theory, which would prevent me from moving on to empirical reality.

78 Although analytically very clear about his distinction between social integration and systems integration, Lockwood (1964: 247–8) also criticizes the 'artificiality' of the distinction when authors focus on only one type of integration. He showed us that we cannot consider how or why one type happens without referring to the other. I try to follow his advice here.

79 See de Leeuw (2000: 104–5).

80 See Sorge (1985). I have also taken up the idea of interpenetration from Münch and, indirectly, from Parsons, and have contrasted it with crystallization, a high amount of conflation of the division of labour and the division of meaning.

81 Cf. Carrère d'Encausse (2000). This is now also accepted by many postsocialist scholars.

82 See Scharpf (1997).

83 The notions of tight and loose coupling were introduced by Karl Weick (1979). Loose coupling means that a change in any subsystem does not immediately or strongly affect other subsystems. Tight coupling means that any change in any subsystem leads to immediate and marked changes in other subsystems.

84 See Boje (2002: 359). It was primarily organizational symbolists who conceived of rhizomatic linkages between paradigms, such as positivism and interpretivism. Symbolic meanings were seen as subterranean links between diverse and overtly autonomous institutions.

85 Maurice et al. (1982) introduced the notion of spaces into the analysis of societal effects. In French sociological theory on work, space (espace) denotes a decidedly non-institutional or cross-institutional space defined by a clear reference to constitutive meaning. It is an abstract space, whereas concrete behaviours always have to be seen as set within multiple spatial references and thus part of a potentially unlimited array of spaces.

86 A partitioning of institutional space is analogous to the 'partitioning of resource space', familiar from population ecology, meaning that species specialize in more finely grained resource niches. See Carroll (1985).

87 This is an assessment on which a variety of thinkers concur, such as Berger and Luckmann (1971), one of whom has more evident Christian inclinations, and the philosopher-theologian Hübner (2001). Hübner has sought to demonstrate that myth is an inevitable grounding that is implied, tacitly or expressly, by any doctrine. As such, it does not constitute a value judgement. Again, the use of the term is therefore not meant to throw a smokescreen of myth over substantiated insight and disparage either the foundations of social solidarity or religion.

88 König (1967: 126–7). This had been pointed out, on the basis of historical experience, by scholars as diverse as Alexander Rüstow and Ibn Khaldun.

89 This happened in AD 212 and had been prepared by the emperor Marcus Aurelius, who had died earlier. See Davies (1997: 165).

90 Davies (1997: 185) sums this up: 'As Rome waned, the provinces waxed'.

91 Streeck (1998: 21) called this the 'coextensive economic community, community of values, and coercion of the nation state' (*die ko-extensive Wirtschafts-, Werte- und Zwangsgemeinschaft des Nationalstaats*). This stylizes an established idea quite well. It is an idea that seems to have left a mark on much of social science, be it as an ideal, a state to be reached, or a definitive equilibrium.

92 I am not aware of any study which has convincingly proved, by comparison, that disturbances through deficient societal coordination occur less often in more perfect nation states than they have done in more layered societies. This is probably what gave the nation state its mythical quality.

93 Crozier (1971) argued that it is the oscillation between national and orderly structuring, on the one hand, and spontaneous and temperamental counter-reaction, on the other, that comprises a long-running constant in French society. This says something about the particular coordination problems resulting in a model nation state.

94 Tourists can learn more about him by visiting the statue commemorating him in a battle in a less tropical jungle, in which a few Roman legions were annihilated but which in all likelihood took place somewhere else. The statue's location is revealed by a song composed by a former British soldier in Germany in the 1960s, with the remarkable refrain: 'Hermann the German stands on a hill, just a mile out of Detmold'.

95 As Lord Palmerston is reputed to have said, no one quite understood the intricacies of the problem save 'the Prince Consort, who was dead, a German professor, who had gone mad, and himself, but he had forgotten all about it' (Davies 1997: 931). The local population certainly had no intention at the outset of ending up under Prussian rule, as they eventually did. But later they did not show any inclination to throw off that rule, except those living in the northern Schleswig strip that was 'returned' to Denmark in 1920. This is more than could be said for Danish rule over the two territories.

96 This idea had already been put forward by Alexis de Tocqueville (1951: pt IV, chrs. 2–5) in his reflections on democracy in America: the nation is singularly strong, in the (admittedly limited) authority it commands and the allegiance it mobilizes, on the basis of the local and state autonomy that it grants and assures. This gives it even greater legitimacy in the institutional domains which it claims and pursues.

97 I myself have had the experience of speaking French to waiters in Montreal and being answered in English. This confused me thoroughly, since my French is not much worse than my English.

98 On convergence and divergence, see Pugh and Hickson (1996).

99 These ethnically different origins are recognizable, for example, in Brandenburg in the names of places such as 'Deutsch [German] Wusterhausen' or 'Wendisch [Slav] Rietz'.

100 Thomas and Znaniecki (1918).

101 See König (1967: 126).

102 In this regard, it is probably not a historical novelty that Germany currently shares the lead with Switzerland in immigration and the mixing of societal origins in Europe (Hillmann 2000). Note, though, that excessive nationalism need not result from a lack of migration and ethnic mixture but from a great deal of it, if for specific reasons it becomes problematical.

103 Whilst Julius Caesar was a masterful writer in addition to being a shrewd politician and resourceful military leader, Charlemagne, another millenary political figure just over eight hundred years later, probably had the writing skills of a present-day primary school pupil with no prospect of receiving a secondary education.

104 The Franks were not really a tribe but a societal segment which split off from a number of tribes to conquer new territory. This pattern, in which cohorts of conquerors split off to conquer territories and societies without losing touch with their society of origin, appears to be a very Germanic institution. The Normans excelled in it, as did other tribes invading the older Roman Empire. See the following note.

105 See Vollrath (2002: 2–3). The naming of the Empire 'of the Franks and Lombards' at the coronation of Charlemagne as emperor in AD 800 was thus tribal rather than generically Germanic. There was no indication of any degree of Germanness in any way whatsoever. Rome provided the model, and the Franks and Lombards supplied the chief rulers. Note that the Italian province of Lombardy derived its name from the Germanic tribe called Langobardi ('the long beards'), which had conquered the territory and put it under subjection.

106 See Aner *et al.* (1997: 54).

107 My friend and colleague Wolfgang Streeck has come to profess privately an allegiance to the western Roman Empire. This overlaps to some extent with the Frankish Empire, and it was equally formative in laying the foundation for the institutions and culture that are presently considered valid for a European Union. While my friend's remark is purely anecdotal, it undoubtedly reflects an acute perception of a European Union as distinct from the eastern Caesaro-papist tradition (in the eastern Roman Empire).

108 Rokkan (1970). Much of the research on nation-building in political science has followed this tradition, and it has strong links with comparative historical analysis. Anderson (1974) has published an influential treatment that tends to take more of a political economy angle.

109 See van der Loo and van Reijen (1990).

110 Robertson and Khondker (1998: 28).

111 Mintzberg (1995) has described the dilemma in vivid and precise terms, suggesting that Canada is composed of different cultural communities, rather than culturally different provinces. This is more specific than what I have proposed for the sake of simplicity. Canadians will understand, I hope. But his argument also boils down to an admittance of the legitimacy of layering in society and a refutation of a monoculture within a nation state.

112 This is subtly expressed by the motto on the number plates of cars in Quebec: *Je me souviens* (I remember).

113 It is both breathtaking and amusing to see how the humiliating carnage of several battles of Highland Scots against 'the English' is laboriously and fondly commemorated at Stirling (Scotland) and its surroundings, in memorial constructions, festivities, and other highly symbolic events.

114 Davies (1997: 695).

115 This was the Garde-Schützenbataillon, recruited in the canton of Neuenburg or Neuchâtel, which had opted to choose the Prussian king as a more symbolic ruler at a distance. Berliners used to call the soldiers of the battalion 'Neffchateller' even after 1866, when the link was severed and recruitment in Switzerland halted.

116 Bohemia had a mixed population in which nearly one-third were Germans and the rest Czechs. The Germans lived mainly in Prague and in the mountains of the border region. The first university to be founded north of the Alps in the older *Reich* was in Prague. It was multilingual, just like Bohemia until 1945.

117 See Aner (1997: 24).

118 See Aner *et al.* (1997: 24).

119 Macfarlane (1978) has established quite plausibly a cultural anthropological link between Tacitus' *Germani* along the Rhine and the 'origins of English individualism'.

120 See E. A. Thompson (1965).

121 The Germanic term *Herzog* is more specific than the Roman term *dux*, the source of terms such as *duc, duce* and *duke* in Latinate languages. A *Herzog* is someone who leads an army (*Heer*) on the move and in battle.

122 Even such a sober and calculating politician as Bismarck used such romantic ideas. See his 'Reichstagsrede über Unitarismus und Partikularismus vom 16. April 1868', in Schätzel (ed., n.d.: 348); when advocating public voting in elections, he argued that it would be worthy of free Germans, much like the ancient gatherings of the *Thing*.

123 Eckstein (1966: 26).

124 Before the Nazis brought back the swastika, a symbol long used by the Finnish air force, and other Nordic mythology, Kaiser Wilhelm II loved to tour Norway and was apparently remembered as a jovial and decent man in the Westland of Norway. I owe this information to Eli Moen, a Norwegian social historian, who is not from the Westland and is therefore at the necessary scholarly distance.

125 See e.g. Aner *et al.* (1997: 48). The non-Celticized Germanic peoples came into western Europe from habitats in the east, at least east of the River Oder, which in conjunction with its tributary, the Neisse, currently constitutes the border between Germany and Poland.

126 Rather than designating a more traditional tribal order, the name given the Franks, as suggested earlier in the text, denoted certain qualities: it means 'the wild ones', 'the bold ones', 'the impetuous ones'. See Vollrath (2002: 2) and also Davies (1997: 298–9.).

127 Vollrath (2002: 1) thus pinpoints this as the beginning of 'German history in the Middle Ages'.

128 Even eminent historians well aware of the differences have conflated Germans and Germanic peoples; see e.g. E. A. Thompson (1965).

129 Note that 'peer' is derived from the French word *pair*, which the Normans brought to England; it dates back to the Latin *par* (= equal), i.e. someone of equal rank or status. Whereas in a British political context 'peer' has become more associated with members of the House of Lords, *Genosse* was used for all social strata and, with the advent of modernity, increasingly among the lower social strata.

130 The pervasiveness of guild formation as a principle at all levels is described by Vollrath (2002: 25).

131 In Aner *et al.* (2002: 197); my translation.

132 See Aner (2002: 106–7) for the state of fragmentation in 1661, and Aner (2002: 122–3) for the same at the end of the eighteenth century. If there is change, it is an increase of fragmentation.

133 The term 'partitioning of institutional space' is derived from the 'partitioning of resource space', as a concept in population ecology. Here, organizations divide up resource space

and different types of organizations specialize in qualitatively different segments of this space. See Carroll (1985).

134 The same is true for the development of Dutch as a codified and coherent language, which was given an impetus by the official translation of the Bible sponsored by estates in Holland (the Statenbijbel).

135 To this extent, the contribution of Crozier (1971) is important; Crozier tells us that we should not look for homogeneous characteristics in a country's heritage but for typical pairs of opposites that recur and alternate to the extent that they are interdependent and predictable. As it were, one firm order conditions the next uprising and vice versa.

136 March and Olsen (1976) introduced the notion of the 'garbage can' into organization theory in a non-pejorative way. It means the heterogeneous repertoire of knowledge and experience that actors seek in a rather unsystematic way to retrieve recombined problem typifications and solutions.

137 See Weber (1964: vol. 1, pp. 16–17).

138 See the German original:. Das streng traditionale Verhalten steht—ganz ebenso wie die rein reaktive Nachahmung . . .—ganz und gar an der Grenze und oft jenseits dessen, was man ein 'sinnhaft' orientiertes Handeln überhaupt nennen kann. Denn es ist sehr oft nur ein dumpfes, in die Richtung der einmal eingelebten Einstellung ablaufendes Reagieren auf gewohnte Reize. Die Masse alles eingelebten Alltagshandelns nähert sich diesem Typus, der nicht nur als Grenzfall in die Systematik gehört, sondern auch deshalb, weil . . . die Bindung an das Gewohnte in verschiedenem Grade und Sinne bewusst aufrecht erhalten werden kann: in diesem Sinne nähert sich dieser Typus dem von Nr. 2 [Affekt] (Weber 1964: vol. 1, p. 17).

139 d'Iribarne (1989). Rather than being something that societal analysis had neglected, as d'Iribarne used to think, it is something that fits into it.

140 The outstanding exception is Mecklenburg, which was ruled by the Obodriten, the one and only dynasty that was able to retain control over one and the same territory from before the High Middle Ages until 1918. It was a dynasty of Slavic princes already in place when Germanic immigrants arrived on the scene.

141 See Schmidt in Aner *et al.* (2002: 218 19).

142 Sandboxes were used by writers of letters or documents to pour sand over the ink to make it dry.

143 In his drama *Der Prinz von Homburg*, Heinrich von Kleist nicely alluded to this memory in his treatment of the battle of Fehrbellin in 1675, a Brandenburger victory over Sweden. Sweden is pictured as the side that had razed the country to the ground in the Thirty Years' War, a war that had ended just twenty-seven years before that battle.

144 The Hohenzollern electors and kings were Calvinists, whereas the overwhelming majority of their subjects were Lutheran (with the exception of French Huguenot immigrants and reformed Protestants in some western territories). Until the first half of the nineteenth century, when Lutherans and reformed Protestants established a united church in Prussia, the religion of the rulers and most of the ruled was therefore different. This fact is not often appreciated. It was the origin of religious tolerance in Prussia.

145 See Gorsky (1993). This article also makes it clear that Prussian disciplinary revolution had overwhelmingly foreign roots: the Great Elector was educated in Holland and imported not only a Dutch wife but also Dutch civil servants and practices. At the symbolic level, there is no place in the world that commemorates the Dutch dynasty and rulers as much as Brandenburg (note place-names such as Oranienburg and

Oranienstrasse, Oranienplatz and Moritzplatz in Berlin). The last major instance of institutional transfer was in the 1820s, when the organization of the united Lutheran and Reformed church in Prussia was modelled on the Presbyterian order of the Dutch Reformed church.

146 Djelic and Quack (2002).

147 The word 'Gothic' originated as a disparaging epithet coined by Italians. At the time, no one in France or Germany had any relation to the Goths. But Italians had known the Goths as another Germanic tribe originating from eastern Europe that had left a swath of destruction across the Roman Empire. The Goths were good at knocking down buildings, not erecting or refining them. When French architects invented the style, which was a departure from Romanesque architecture, it was given this name by jealous Italians, presumably in the hope of damaging the reputation of the French in architecture as much as the Goths had wrought havoc in the Roman Empire.

148 In his long series of both epic and cabaret-like poems, *Deutschland—ein Wintermärchen*, Heinrich Heine (both a romantic and republican poet living as an expatriate in Paris) poured scorn on the project to finish the cathedral, arguing that it symbolized a distasteful coalition of all the reactionary forces that Germany could muster, including Rhenish Catholicism, Swabian romanticism, and Prussian feudalism.

149 Friedrich Engels was born and grew up in Barmen and Elberfeld in a family of merchants and manufacturers. But his experience of working in Manchester proved far more formative for his analysis of capitalism.

150 The mountains of Berg are usually the first ones on the Continent to be reached by weather fronts coming in from the sea, so that rain is frequent and abundant, which was ideal for bleaching and also provided a rich supply of water tumbling down numerous mountain streams at considerable speed.

151 In a German historical context, much as in the English one, the term 'non-conformist' can be applied to Protestant denominations that deviated from an established Protestant church. In Berg, Reformed or Calvinist churches enjoyed less toleration or privilege than Lutheran ones, except when territories were historically under Dutch or Brandenburg-Prussian rule or influence.

152 This is recounted in local yearbooks with unabashed frankness and great pride. Having grown up in the area, I have been exposed to these attitudes.

153 Prussia was always keen on Berg, not only for its industry, but also because its religious character, more Reformed than Lutheran, strengthened Calvinism, as the variant of the Christian religion which the dynasty did not share with many of its subjects, apart from the Huguenot refugees from France, who were a bulwark of loyalty to the monarchy.

154 See Behnen, in Vogt (ed., 2002: 398).

155 Folklore in Düsseldorf has it that Napoleon expressed his appreciation of the recent urban development there, which used French examples, by saying that this was 'a small Paris'. Inhabitants of the town still proudly relate this story.

156 Behnen, in Vogt (ed., 2002: 398).

157 All kinds of intermediate organizations had been firmly abolished in France by a conjunction of Jacobin doctrine and Napoleonic absolutism, which had led to the loi le Chapelier. This was also tried in German territories in the Confederation of the Rhine, but apparently without much success.

158 Behnen, in Vogt (ed., 2002: 399).

159 Behnen, in Vogt (ed., 2002: 403).

160 See von Eck (1879: 5–6).

161 See Aner *et al.* (1997: 152).

162 Until World War I, loss of life in military forces was as likely to be due to illness as to dying in battle.

163 All this is described with great accuracy and detail in von Eck (1879). This book is the result of a *Winterarbeit*, a desk-bound job that officers in the Prussian army of the Second Reich (1872–1918) had to do during the winter. In its length, rigour, detail, and interpretative skill, this work was at least as good as any doctoral thesis of the time.

164 This episode was reported by the nationalist historian Treitschke (n.d.: 192).

165 Co-evolution means that phenomena are coupled together in the course of evolution. In organization theory, it means that internal organization, strategy, and contextual and environmental characteristics evolve together on the basis of interaction or reciprocal conditioning. For an overview, see Lewin and Volberda (1999).

166 This was well expressed by the government motto: *Suum cuique*, 'to each his own (entitlements and duties)'. It is easy to disparage this from a later, modern point of view. At the time, it also contributed to the rule of law and the protection of civilians against the horrors of war and despotism.

167 Liberal and socialist-minded literature has come to use this term in a pejorative way. But in the Netherlands, a country with a greater liberal and bourgeois tradition, aristocrats still use the designation of *jonkheer*.

168 See Kürschner (1902: 138).

169 The main instigator of Prussian militarism, Friedrich Wilhelm I, the 'soldier king', never actually went to war except when asked by the emperor. To him, the army was a deterrent that was only to be used as a last resort. As a young prince, he had fought in the Battle of Malplaquet at the beginning of the eighteenth century, on behalf of a coalition built by the emperor. Horrified by the carnage on both sides in a battle that was unprecedented at the time for loss of life, he walked away with a firm reluctance to wage war and with a distrust in the emperor's word.

170 The Hohenzollern received their first major feudal title when they became *Burggrafen* (counts) at Nuremberg, i.e. rulers over the countryside around Nuremberg.

171 See Behnke, in Vogt (ed., 2002: 400–1).

172 See Behnke, in Vogt (ed., 2002: 403–4).

173 This quiet social revolution has been described with great sensitivity by Theodor Fontane, a journalist and novelist of Huguenot extraction and therefore infused with a Prussian patriotism that in no way dampened his liberal inclinations. The title of the novel is *Vor dem Sturm* (Before the Storm).

174 The Berlin district of Kreuzberg is replete with street names commemorating places of battle and leading generals of this war, overlooked by a memorial on the top of Kreuzberg Hill that gave the district its new name, after the Iron Cross (*Kreuz*) which was introduced to honour the bravery of volunteers and the ranks in battle.

175 Gneisenau had even undergone his formative military experience in North America in a German contingent hired out to the British army. This had alerted him to less conventional forms of warfare and the importance of manoeuvring and of sustaining morale among voluntary combatants.

176 See the contributions to Streeck and Yamamura (2001).

177 See the chapter by Geoffrey Jackson in Streeck and Yamamura (2001: 123).

178 Hardenberg was an ardent admirer of Adam Smith, and although promotion of industry and trade was an unmistakeable ingredient of policy, it was unequivocally liberal in the constitution of contractual freedom. See the chapter by Lehmbruch in Streeck and Yamamura (2001: 48–9).

179 Kocka (1978: 512) also refers to this.

180 Treitschke, who was a nationalist but also a keen economic and social historian, pointed out this curiosity. He was a Saxon born and bred and a great admirer of Prussia at the same time. See Treitschke (n.d.: 454–5).

181 Pollard (1978: 150–1.) clearly shows the ebb-and-flow pattern of the tightening and relaxation of regulation. His main point is that employers had contractual freedom above all because there was an oversupply of labour and this also affected regulation. For the more skilled types of work that were emerging, job demarcation, the restriction of occupational access, the de facto control of job territories by craftsmen and their unions, and other related phenomena are too widely known to allow easy generalizations about greater freedom of economic contracting, at least when comparing Continental Europe and Britain. See also the chapters in Wood (ed., 1982), notably that by Littler (ch. 7).

182 Rokkan (1970: 87).

183 Streeck, 'Introduction', in Streeck and Yamamura (eds., 2001: 1–38).

184 More programmatically, some commentators in Germany after 1872 suggested that Germany should follow its own path, between Western and Eastern concepts. While the propagation of 'third ways' has acquired an incomprehensible cachet (from co-operative economy doctrines, through mixed economy doctrines, down to more recent Blairist hype), the German 'third way' of the time also involved tampering with democratic principles and alignment with Western democracy, which is why it became politically incorrect to identify with it. While Streeck and others play with the word, they do not have this context in mind. But it is of course true that some of those who advocated corporatism in Germany may also have been considering some measure of departure from parliamentary responsibility or other Western democratic principles. This discussion requires a great deal of honesty. Care must also be taken not to decontextualize ideas more than is legitimate, which could imply that a *Sonderweg* led more or less inevitably to Nazism.

185 Anderson (1974).

186 'It was first used to describe a group of radical patriots, cooped up at Cadiz as refugees from the French invasion of 1808' (Carr 1980: 1).

187 This is well documented by Chang (2002). Even today, the political apostles of free international trade refrain from practising it in those industries in which other countries could out-compete the firms in the political economy of which they have to heed domestic interests.

188 It is conceivable that Sweden is a much-underrated case, demonstrating a similar bureaucratic service class ethos, dedication to the rule of law, and a strong king—although its service class lacks an aristocratic origin. I would gladly concede that Prussia is much less distinctive than is generally presumed, but it remains one of the illustrative cases within a Baltic pattern of rule.

189 In his own account of the Napoleonic Wars, Treitschke, as a nationalist historian who was undoubtedly mirroring widespread sentiment in Prussian circles, castigates as especially treacherous, retrograde, and ineffectual everything that the Habsburgs, Metternich, and their generals did, rather than vilifying Napoleon or especially France.

190 Bismarck is frequently and correctly ascribed the authorship of many policies between 1850 and about 1888. Bismarck, through many confrontations and quarrels, was still able to impose his view on King Wilhelm I, who trusted Bismarck most of the way and was also aware of his own limits.

191 This intelligentsia invented the German tricolour of black, red, and gold, an eclectic combination of colours that were important in medieval times. These were the colours used by the *Burschenschaften*, the nationalist student societies.

192 Musgrave (1967: 48).

193 Lehmbruch, in Streeck and Yamamura (eds, 2001: 49).

194 Bismarck frequently evoked, in court and government circles, the necessity of being able to legitimate war aims to common soldiers. This relates back to the trauma Friedrich Wilhelm I suffered from the Battle of Malplaquet at the beginning of the eighteenth century, and unconsciously at least, this was also the lesson drawn from the warmongering of Friedrich 'the Great' (Friedrich II), who escaped defeat by the skin of this teeth, specifically by the fact that Russia halted its campaign in the Seven Years' War (1756–63) because the new tsar was a fervent admirer of everything Prussian. After that, Prussia 'only' had Austria and France to contend with.

195 In summarizing the path to unity under Bismarck, I have used the depiction found in Engelberg (1987: chs 6–9).

196 A. J. P. Taylor described the history of modern Europe as having been shaped by three 'Titans': Napoleon, Bismarck, and Lenin. Of these, he said, 'Bismarck probably did the least harm'. See Davies (1997: 842).

197 See the beginning of Chapter 2.

198 Non-German historians have a habit of calling this war 'Franco–Prussian'. It was, of course, Franco–German, and there was no reluctance on the part of any German state or its populace to enter into it.

199 See Behnen, in Vogt (2002: 494–5).

200 This earlier wound was inflicted on the core of the country by a coalition of the English and the Burgundians in the Hundred Years' War. It was resolved with the appearance of Joan of Arc.

201 See Behnen, in Vogt (2002: 512–13).

202 See Behnen, in Vogt (2002: 461–2).

203 Kocka (1978: 563).

204 Kocka (1978: 563). See also Wengenroth, in Vogt (ed., 2002: 356–7).

205 Clark (1940). This contribution was fundamental and was developed later in Germany by the notion of *funktionsfähiger Wettbewerb*, following Kanzenbach (1960), who also was a long-serving chairman of a monopolies commission.

206 As do the contributors to Streeck and Yamamura (eds, 2001).

207 Wengenroth, in Vogt (ed., 1992: 358).

208 See Lane (1998).

209 Even former allies or parts of Germany saw fit, after World War II, to nationalize all German property. The best example of this is the expropriation of the Hermann-Göring-Werke (HGW) in Austria after World War II Austria had been part of Germany from 1938 to 1945 (thanks to one of the most welcome military occupations in history), and the government had supported the industrialization of Austria through the HGW. After expropriation, the new public enterprise (VOEST) became the mainstay of Austrian heavy industry.

210 Streeck (1992: ch. 1). See also Sorge and Streeck (1988).

211 Lee (1978: 455–6).

212 Stein (1975: 51). This is based on calculations presented by Reichstag member Eugen Richter.

213 Lee (1978: 456). See also Stein (1975: 75).

214 Winkler (1970: 54).

215 It is usually contended that the Chancellor and ministers were formally only appointed by and responsible to the emperor. But the Reichstag did have control over the budget and the laws. It can then be said that the position of political power in Imperial Germany was close to that in the USA, and the US President conceivably had greater power than the German Emperor, who was not an elected figure. But authoritarianism in Germany is likely to be due, above all, to the unlimited trust placed by citizens in the competence of professional bureaucracies.

216 Lee (1978: 456).

217 Charles Maier (1975: 83) writes: 'The Germans brought a model of civil service leadership into the factory: the state hierarchy legitimized the rankings of private enterprises. While French relationships did not allow for mingling between employers and workers or any other groups that stood on the different divides of the command structure, the German patterns allowed subordination and dependence to be noninvidious, visible and even honorific. Employers could mingle directly with their workers and take pride in their common sharing of productive efforts and imposed hardships.'

218 This is the classic neo-corporatist pattern, described by authors such as Lehmbruch, Schmitter, and Streeck. See Streeck (1992), as well as his other publications cited therein.

219 See Crouch (1993) and Streeck (1992). I also distinctly remember a talk with Rudolf Meidner, one of the architects of the 'Swedish model', who simply and calmly stated that a small group discussed the major structures at national union headquarters and then had it implemented by the party.

220 Aner *et al.* (1997: 161).

221 Aner *et al.* (1997: 160).

222 Without wishing to take part in debates about a European constitution and how this Union should be classified, I simply take a federation to be what it has always meant: a temporally indefinite combination of separate political entities, in which the representatives of federating entities 'swear' (i.e. sign highly official and compelling documents), for themselves and their successors, to keep together in common solidarity and operate common policies in domains to be defined.

223 Probably the best-known and earliest analysis of organized capitalism was provided by Hilferding (1927), more readily available to the international reader as Hilferding (1981). This author not only diagnosed financial capitalism as conflicting with real economic development but also suggested that collective organization and control on the supply side of commodity markets had supplanted competition between enterprises. The point to be made here is that in partitioned institutional space, organized capitalism co-exists with market competition.

224 Djelic (2001).

225 A vivid symbol of American 'trust-busting' in Germany is the former headquarters of IG Farben at Frankfurt on Main. As the enterprise was broken up, this expansive building became a centre of US military command and administration in Germany.

226 Djelic (2001: 170).

227 See Lawrence (1980).

228 Fordism has two strands that may not always come together. One is a mass production system using transfer lines in a flow-line arrangement for assembly or other operations. This can be very productive. The other strand is a macroeconomic coordination which makes productivity increase coincide with buying power, so that an economy is in a high-growth equilibrium. On the second, the macro-regulation strand of Fordism, see Boyer (1990).

229 See e.g. Barjot (2002). Sometimes the development of productivity policies had highly political overtones, as is shown in Barjot (2002) in the chapter on Norway by Moen. For the Netherlands, Karsten and van Veen (2003) show that productivity policies, replacing earlier efficiency promotion, were considered indispensable for extricating the country from post-war stagnation, and were an important part of a new, centralized, and tight-economic-planning corporatism.

230 Djelic (2001: 146).

231 Djelic (2001: 180).

232 See Streeck (1997), as well as other publications by this author referred to therein.

233 See Windolf (1994) for an empirical analysis of such cross-holdings and their functions, before they were abandoned or reduced in a wave of shareholder-value practices, core business policies, and promotion of international alliances and mergers.

234 Whitley (1992, 2002).

235 Starting in the early 1980s, the GDR had increasingly come to rely on West German loans and transfer payments in order to keep itself financially viable. Some West German politicians may have entertained the hope that one day the GDR would have to default on its loans and thereby make a 'takeover bid' possible. If they did, they were absolutely right, and the massive crowds demonstrating against the GDR government in the streets in 1989, among other things, averted the less pleasant situation of such a bid, which would have been interpreted as an aggressive act.

236 After Austria had lost its empire in 1918, it could easily have joined Germany. Whereas this occurred in 1938 and lasted till 1945, both the Allied settlements imposed in 1918 and 1945 prevented it.

237 Prussia was blamed for a militarism that had made aggression possible, or better, sustainable. In a realistic view, the tools of aggression and annihilation would not have been as powerful without the Prussian organizational and military heritage. But Prussia was not the mastermind behind political crime and genocide. The abolition of Prussia was mainly instrumental in reducing de facto centralization of political functions due to the size of Prussia relative to the other states.

238 See Hesse (1967: 87–8). While the ability of unitary federalism to facilitate effective political decision-making is increasingly contestable, the main structures and processes diagnosed at an early stage by Hesse are still in place.

239 Piore and Sabel (1984).

240 This is based on the analysis in Chapter 2.

241 Miller and Rice (1976) looked at work systems as being decomposable into technical and sentient subsystems. This does not imply the same distinction as that between action and institutional systems. However, their principle of 'joint optimization', as 'a contrived coincidence of task and sentient boundaries' (p. 255), implies tight coupling

through systemic and social integration within the same boundaries. This was an action-systemic concept used as a basis for the demarcation of institutional subentities.

242 See Thompson (1967: 10): 'For the purpose of this volume, then, we will conceive of complex organizations as open systems, hence indeterminate and faced with uncertainty, but at the same time as subject to criteria of rationality and hence needing determinateness and certainty.' Thompson was, of course, not an action theorist. But the idea of simultaneous closure and openness is attributable to him. The subsequent differentiation of action and institutional systems makes that idea easier to grasp.

243 See de Leeuw (2000).

244 This figure was translated and developed from the one in Lanciano *et al.* (1989: 21).

245 This is the way Lanciano *et al.* (1989: 21) explain the Figure.

246 The original concept is from Maurice *et al.* (1982). This has been successively extended, and here I use a version I included in Sorge (1998).

247 See Dunlop (1958).

248 See Woodward (1965: 36).

249 See the chapter by Marc Maurice, 'The Paradoxes of Societal Analysis: A Review of the Past and Prospects for the Future', in Maurice and Sorge (eds, 2000: ch. 2), as well as Maurice (2002).

250 Maurice (2002: 1215–17). The original research question was how it came about that France and Germany had significantly different wage inequalities, even in comparable industries and enterprises.

251 This sort of conversion happened very frequently, painfully but successfully, and is nowadays too often forgotten. For example, both Heinkel and Messerschmitt, formerly dominant aircraft makers, produced small cars in the 1950s and 1960s that to an imaginative observer looked like fighter cockpits on three wheels and were the first motor cars which less wealthy people could afford.

252 See e.g. Maurice *et al.* (1980, 1982) or Sorge and Warner (1986).

253 See Soskice (1999) and his chapter in Maurice and Sorge (eds, 2000: ch. 10), and also Whitley (2002) and Whitley and Kristensen (1997).

254 A brief but excellent discussion which I have found inspiring is provided by van Raaij (2001: 45–8). See also Roethlisberger (1977) and Weick (1995) for more classic authors, as well as Gunnesson (1991).

255 Blalock, a classic nomothetic methodologist who strives for nomothetic causal statements, has summarized his insistence on the pertinence and feasibility of these, despite some doubts: 'it seems useful to attempt to state the ideal and to clarify issues and objectives even when present practices fall short of the mark' (1972: 196). To repeat, I am not arguing against idealistic ambitions, but maintaining that the search for nomothetic causal statements leads us away from generalization and toward statements specific to time and place; generalization is more viable if we leave questions of causality to individual constellations.

256 See Harbison *et al.* (1955).

257 Harbison *et al.* (1955: 36).

258 Harbison *et al* (1955: 34–5).

259 Harbison *et al.* (1955: 33).

260 Cf. the last sections of Chapter 4.

261 As pointed out by Görlitz (1977), the Prussian and German army probably adhered the least to the principle of keeping staff work separate from line authority. In the US army,

commanding officers have executive officers or deputy commanders who are different from chiefs of staff, as the latter do not have command authority. In the Prussian and German armies, chiefs of staff have been also second in command.

262 See Görlitz (1977).

263 This is well analysed in organizational terms and on the basis of historical material by Brouwer (2003). Their relative effectiveness in combat was established by the comparisons Dupuy (1977) made for both world wars. Facile clichés have however been spread by authors such as Morgan (1997: 15–16). First, mechanistic army drill and organization was not first reintroduced in modern times in Prussia but by Prince Maurice (Maurits) in the Netherlands, one and a half centuries before Friedrich II. Second, it was not Friedrich II who introduced it into the Prussian army but his father, the soldier king who never started a war. Pathologies of excessive enforcement of discipline and demotivated soldiers pressed into service have wrongly been compared to other armies in the special circumstances of the Seven Years' War (1756–63). This was when Prussia was struggling without effective allies against almost every power in the vicinity (Austria-Hungary, Saxony, Russia, and France), which almost broke the back of the country. The support given by its only ally, the UK, was restricted to a bit of financial assistance and did not include troops, although the Treaty of Westminster between the UK and Prussia had caused the war, the main beneficiary of which was the UK: it could take Canada from France because French military effort was absorbed by Prussia. Then, while the period between 1763 and 1806 was an interlude of organizational and leadership rigidity, after learning from the defeat by Napoleon, the Prussian army introduced, more rapidly and systematically than any other regular army in Europe, the decentralization of responsibility and flexibility of strategy and tactics down to the level of, eventually, infantry platoons and squads.

264 See Markovits and Hellerman (1995/6). See also Clark (1987), who traces suggestive parallels between the evolution of football from a civilized kind of brawl between males from different villages in medieval England into a variety of sports, on the one hand, and management innovation in different societies, on the other. Both accounts home in on the distinction between the perfectionism of set-pieces versus the artful variation of spontaneous tactics and mutual adjustment, as far as the contrast between the US and Europe is concerned.

265 Among those who participated in NATO manoeuvres with more substantial forces during the heyday of the Cold War, the story circulated that a German commander on the 'wrong' (attacking) side, the red side which always has to lose, found himself tempted to ruin the manoeuvre by launching a surprise attack on an American unit. That would have won the battle for the red side. Of course, in 'good' manoeuvres and wars, the winner is always the one that is in the strategically defensive position. Certainly in army tactics and strategy, German forces in NATO never really emulated American doctrine. The only army that was consistently admired for indefatigable effort and enormous sacrifice and bravery was the Red Army. This is another case of institutional learning happening between opponents rather than allies.

266 The army has traditionally distinguished three levels of learning: a basic level of 'school-type' learning, with careful explanation and exercise; a 'drill' level for rapid exercise and habitualization; and a 'combat level' where habitualized routines are adapted to exacting and changing contingencies such as foul weather, noise, extreme temperatures, pressure, social isolation, lack of food or sleep, etc. According to this doctrine, learning moves

from standardization through habitualization to situationally specific and discretionary adjustment. It starts with formal schemes and set-pieces but moves towards discretion.

267 It will be objected that the military social order of Germany in 1966 was the same as the one that prevailed until 1945. Certainly, a great deal of arbitrariness and rigidity in discipline will have vanished. However, when relating my own experience to my father (in 1965–6), I was struck by how many times he said, with a smile: 'This is what we had, too.'

268 The most influential study affirming such tendencies was Kern and Schumann (1970).

269 The first major international study to make this point was Harbison and Myers (1959), with regard to the material base of society and above all the industrial relations system.

270 I was therefore representing Britain in the larger team, not Germany. But I must say that this has almost taught me more about Germany than having lived there for nearly thirty years.

271 See Maurice *et al.* (1980).

272 For more detailed results, see Maurice *et al.* (1977, 1982) and Sorge and Warner (1986).

273 See Lane (1989).

274 This has also involved a criticism of societal analysis, as in Lallement (1999), Lane (1998, 2003) and Lane's chapter in Maurice and Sorge (eds, 2000: ch. 11).

275 Affinities between nationally distinct organizational and management patterns and work-related values have been suggested by Hofstede (2001: 377).

276 D'Iribarne (1991) mistakenly thought they were not part of societal analysis, which touched off an unnecessary controversy. D'Iribarne has been interested in the cultural and stable residue of long-running metatraditions and their recurrent themes; undoubtedly these exist. They are one aspect of societal analysis within its dialectical framework set out here.

277 See Gordon (1996), also cited and discussed in van Witteloostuijn (1999: 202).

278 See Sivesind (1997), which provides a culturalist explanation of differences. I hope that what I say here will continue our dialogue by convincing him of the use of extending this into institutional settings and the construction of society.

279 One of these regiments, his favourite, was the 2. Westfälisches Husarenregiment no. 11, which was mentioned in Chapter 4.

280 Sorge (1979) and Dirrheimer *et al.* (1980). The latter states that this research orientation emerged from an analysis of the first results or claims concerning microelectronics, which were at extreme variance with each other. It was then claimed that microelectronics meant the end of the socio-economic world as we knew it, either for better or for worse.

281 Sorge and Warner (1986: 162).

282 Maurice *et al.* (1986).

283 Maurice and Sorge (1990). A more complete report was presented in Maurice and Sorge (1989).

284 See Maurice *et al.* (1988).

285 Campbell *et al.* (1989).

286 Sorge (1989).

287 See Marry (1993).

288 Daubigney *et al.* (1972).

289 See the chapter by Hiroatsu Nohara in Maurice and Sorge (eds, 2000: ch. 12).

290 Jacqueline O'Reilly has presented an argument that amounts to conceiving of gendered space as an independent space in the societal division of meaning, one which interacts with others. This is a pertinent development of societal analysis. See her chapter in Maurice and Sorge (eds, 2000: ch. 20).

291 In the final chapter of his magnificently detailed and coherent comparison, Dore (1973) emphasizes, strangely enough, the late development effect and gives it much greater prominence than it deserves. The US was also a late industrial developer, roughly at the same time as Germany after its unification in 1872. Yet it shared economic and social institutions with England to a much greater degree than did Germany or Japan.

292 See Herrigel (1996).

293 See Streeck and Rehder (2003).

294 See Hartmann *et al.* (1970/1).

295 Sellier (1972). At a time when many Germans were debating the relative merits of works councils and collective agreements and shifts from one to the other, Sellier perceptively emphasized their interdependencies.

296 One of the earliest observers was Lawrence (1980), whose findings have not been disconfirmed.

297 See Hancké (1999); Soskice (1999).

298 See Panic (1976).

299 See Cox and Kriegbaum (1980).

300 See Loveridge (1983). This article showed how British engineering firms developed through a gradual transformation and subordination of occupationally autonomous gangs, which in a way operated as quasi-independent firms in an industrial district, into loosely integrated ensembles that kept a high amount of segmentation of functions, work groups, sites, or plants.

301 See the various contributions in Brussig *et al.* (eds, 1997).

302 See Lane (1998), as well as the chapter by the same author in Maurice and Sorge (eds, 2000: ch. 11).

303 The most up-to-date comparison for Europe is Crouch *et al.* (2001). According to this work, the differences between districts can be explained by the emphasis on how relational contracting addresses the supply chain and by the emphasis on supportive institutions.

304 Piore and Sabel (1984). We (Sorge and Streeck 1988) had distinguished differentiated quality production, also possible in larger and non-networked firms, from the context of specialized production in small firms that are tied into districts. These have different logics of operation.

305 For the period of the Federal Republic, this was discussed and analysed by Lehmbruch (2002). The interplay between regional competition founded on autonomy and distinctiveness, and solidarity implying institutional homogeneity, collective solidarity, and responsibility, has been characteristic in German history. This is the dialectical unity of the 'unitary federation' already mentioned in the previous chapter.

306 See Sorge *et al.* (1983: ch. 6), one of the earlier studies attesting to the importance of a small firm and craft context in the adoption of applications of microelectronics. Previous electronic programming systems in metal-cutting had been much more involved with larger firms.

307 For the account that follows, see Maier (1987). The references to Tuttlingen in that text are somewhat sketchy, but I have also relied on an oral account by the author, who had studied archival material and historic texts.

308 For a historical account of the district, see Eichhorn *et al.* (2003: 72–3).

309 See Eichhorn *et al.* (2003).

310 See Geppert, Matten, and Williams's chapter in Geppert *et al.* (eds, 2002: ch. 2), and the chapter by Becker-Rittersbach, Lange, and Lohr in the same volume (ch. 3).

311 See Geppert, Williams, and Matten (2003), and also Williams, Geppert, and Matten (2003). The latter paper makes the point that, while German production organization and industrial relations have faced an uphill struggle, some actors are also aware of its relative advantages and make strategic use of them in multinationals.

312 Streeck (1997: 53) suggested the following: 'There are indications that the German vocational training system is about to be dramatically transformed by internationalization, among other things by European Community "harmonization" of skill profiles in the unified European labour market.'

313 The latter was, of course, a German invention, transplanted to the United States shortly after its creation in Peenemünde, along with its leading pioneers, Wernher von Braun and others.

314 See the chapter by Edward Lorenz in Maurice and Sorge (eds, 2000: ch. 14).

315 See sections 5.3 and 5.4 above.

316 See section 2.3.4 above, and also Czarniawska and Joeges (1996) and Saka (2003).

317 This morality and practice goes back to ancient Germanic social order. To some extent, Anglo-American societies have preserved it better, being more liberal than those in the South Germanic bedrock, by the relative leniency practised in cases of bodily harm. Germanic duels are nowadays most fondly recollected in two standard highlights of most American media productions, the fist fight and the shoot-out. A duel must not be confused with a vendetta; duels were conclusive whereas vendettas might go on endlessly.

318 A less sanguine opinion was advanced by Theodor Fontane in his novel *Effi Briest* (1895), the best-known dramatization in German of the antecedents and consequences of a duel next to Austrian *fin-de-siècle* authors. This novel was based on a real case of a duel initiated by one Armand Léon von Ardenne, an officer who had also served in the 2. Westfälisches Husarenregiment no.11, mentioned in Chapter 4.

319 In his autobiography, Siemens gratefully remembered the opportunity and acknowledged its importance (1966: 31–3). When he was pardoned after serving six months, he asked the commanding officer of the citadel to be allowed to occupy his cell for another few days so that he could finish the experiments. He was promptly evicted the same night and dumped in the streets of Magdeburg by an exasperated superior who thought Siemens was ungratefully mocking not only regulations but also clemency.

320 See Streeck (1987), from which much of what follows in the text is derived.

321 This situation is very real and can be observed in the streets of central Nairobi at night. When a car is parked, a friendly man casually loitering on the pavement in the vicinity solicits a small sum of money to protect the car from burglary and serious damage. It is a highly efficient and reassuring, tacit and trust-based way of reducing uncertainty, which is also utterly charming in view of the pleasant banter with the unofficial 'attendant', who is usually far from officious or threatening. There is always service with a smile.

322 See Weber (1964: vol. 2, pp. 923–4). An interesting point that Weber left unexplained is that town and urban corporations are discussed under this heading.

323 In German history, these were exemplified by robber barons (*Raubritter*) in phases of development where the distinction between the rule of legitimate authority and gainful activity was obliterated. Robber barons could be hired to conduct feuds or run protection rackets.

324 See Merchant (1985) and Mintzberg (1983).

325 See Grandori (2002). She has already linked organizational concepts with those of political economy. But the combination remains daunting.

326 Sydow (2002) provides an overview.

327 Kocka (1978: 589).

328 Actually, Liechtenstein's percentage has been higher, but I disregard it here.

329 Porter (1990) comparatively demonstrated this on the basis of supply and demand factors as well as lateral relations with cooperating firms and supportive institutions.

330 I have personally seen this happen in both cases.

331 Hartmann and Wienold (1967) have made this point abundantly clear, as has Hartmann (1959).

332 See Soskice (1999), and also the chapter by the same author in Maurice and Sorge (eds, 2000: ch. 10). Lower levels of profitability for German multinationals are reported in Harzing (1999: 325–6).

333 I am quite aware that some variants of the psychology of work and organization have been branded as 'cow psychology' in a way which I perceive as grossly unfair to cows. By using cows here, I imply that even superficially submissive cows require legitimacy of leadership. The only conceivable setting for managing people without giving them leadership is in a purely punitive prison.

334 It has been suggested that work groups instantaneously differentiate between instrumental and expressive leadership, but combinations are required and work differently under different circumstances. For a summary, see e.g. Yukl (1994).

335 In the case of my grandfather (see previous chapter), this meant that most of the clerks working in the Provinzial group of insurance companies were former non-commissioned officers from one of the regiments stationed in Düsseldorf or Krefeld. Many publications on social and occupational mobility over time, notably from the Max-Planck Institute for Educational Research in Berlin and written by Hans-Peter Blossfeld, Karl Ulrich Mayer, and others, have shown that social mobility was more pronounced from the end of the nineteenth century until the middle of the twentieth, before its pervasiveness was held up as a 'new' tendency. From the 1960s on, the mobility of native Germans has declined rather than accelerated.

336 In his well-known socio-historical studies of Siemens, Kocka (1969) stressed the background of leadership in military organization and discipline. This is undeniable. But it is also striking that the social order of the military emulated feudal society including urban guilds; as the 'backbone of the German army', the non-commissioned officer was thus parallel with the master craftsman, carried great authority, was a residue of flexibility, and could not be demoted arbitrarily by superiors. The implication is thus not unilaterally one of discipline and submission but also of flexible autonomy. This side of German institutions has been neglected by left-liberal writers, whereas neo-conservative writers may have overrated them. My own approach is to stress the intimate relation between the two, a unique combination that brought forth both

unheard-of compliance with evil potentates and enthusiasm for participation. It just depended on where the pendulum was at a given moment.

337 This was shown in a comparison by Kieser *et al.* (1996).

338 See Hartmann (1959), the first in-depth, post-war empirical analysis of West German management, for a vivid description and analysis of such views and practices.

339 For a contrast of Germany with Great Britain, see Sorge (1978).

340 The most recent details and views on such matters have been contributed by Gergs and Schmidt (2002).

341 See Booz, Allen and Hamilton (1973), who also included critical comments appended by Heinz Hartmann.

342 Lawrence (1980) had made this point vividly on the basis of his earlier studies of engineers and engineering in the Federal Republic.

343 The classic and well-accepted demonstration of this is Rumelt (1974).

344 Landes (1960) made it clear just how distinctive this was for Germany when compared to Britain. Kocka (1978) argued that general managers or financiers had also been important for starting up German industrial concerns. But what he shows is that most frequently there exists a coalition of a more technical person and a more commercial or financial figure. This indeed is the classic combination and division of competences, which has remained important in many companies. Depending on the company's needs at the time, one or the other partner in such a management duo has the upper hand.

345 This case appears to be largely unresearched, although it would merit an article in the *Harvard Business Review*, as an example of combining shareholder value and core business concepts with co-determination, social responsibility, and social peace. The personnel manager in charge of the HRM and industrial relations side, Dr Knuth Dohse, was formerly a researcher at the Wissenschaftszentrum Berlin, a former colleague of mine. The transformation in question was more or less concluded at the beginning of the 1990s. Luckily, it was thereby spared the less sensible propaganda and stock market crazes, which only built up steam in the course of the 1990s.

346 Mayer and Whittington (1999).

347 See Sorge and Warner (1986), especially chs 5 and 6 on organizational structures.

348 See Harzing and Sorge (2003).

349 This is exactly parallel to the balance between national and regional levels of aggregation in the organization of interests of artisanal firms. See Streeck (1992: ch. 4).

350 This sentence is attributed to Adolf Weber by Herbert Oberbeck and Nestor d'Alessio in Knights and Morgan (eds, 1997: 102). I am grateful to Glenn Morgan for alerting me to this splendid dictum.

351 See Musgrave (1959: 43–4). Merit goods are public goods in which the exclusion principle does not apply completely, which is the reason for free-riding. In turn, this may lead to their elevation to public goods because they 'merit' this form, in order to improve their supply and conform with norms of justice.

352 See Zysman (1983), as well as the chapter by Soskice in Maurice and Sorge (eds, 2000: ch. 10), and also Whitley (2002).

353 Tilly (1978: 429).

354 The reader who finds it odd to modify the noun 'harmonization' with the adjective 'conflictual' should be aware that such word combinations are going currency in German society. Witness words such as *Konfliktpartnerschaft* (partnership in and by

conflict) and *Streitkultur* (a culture both of and in controversy). See the interesting observations in this respect by Pascale Hugues (1998).

355 On a note of personal experience, I have found the services provided by German banks to me as a customer to be, on the whole, better than those in the other three European countries in which I have had experience, namely Britain, France, and the Netherlands.

356 See Höpner and Jackson (2001), especially §2, pp. 10–14.

357 Höpner and Jackson (2001: 14).

358 See La Porta *et al.* (1998), especially tables 3 A–D. Germany even exceeds in this respect some much smaller neighbouring countries such as the Netherlands and Switzerland.

359 Spectacular and recent exceptions are described and explained by Höpner and Jackson (2001).

360 See Windolf (1994).

361 See Streeck (1997), in particular the questioning of German corporate governance and industrial relations towards the end of the article.

362 These were conducted at the Max-Planck Institute for the Study of Societies. During my stay at the Institute while writing this book, I was fortunate to have the opportunity to meet the researchers involved and discuss these questions with them.

363 This is a profoundly German phenomenon. Conceivably, it can be related, again, to past traumas of war, devastation, expropriation, foreign occupation, expulsion, galloping inflation, and other such events. It appears to be an unending succession of interpretations set off by the Thirty Years' War and what were perceived as somewhat repetitive events, although their cruelty and viciousness have declined. But traumas become functionally autonomous with regard to 'real' phenomena. See also Chapters 2 and 3 above. Germans are compelled to diagnose crisis and collapse in order to show that they are not ignorant of the past. This does not mean that they competently address truly fundamental problems in a concerted way. Analysts and public opinion may have become suffused with the diagnosis of fundamental shifts or crisis so much that they are less able to tell the difference between subtle shifts and major problems, such as the unemployment problems discussed in the next chapter.

364 Höpner (2003: 36–67).

365 Beyer (2001).

366 Höpner (2003: §3.4).

367 See *The Economist*, 24 June 2000, p. 112, and the underlying study by Smithers and Wright (2000).

368 In the 1960s, the federal government issued *Volksaktien* (the 'people's shares', a stock market equivalent of the VW beetle) of partially denationalized enterprises (VW and Veba) to people below a certain income threshold in order to popularize stock ownership. Later the stock exchange sales tax that had hindered transactions was abolished, and corporation tax reform changed a general and high tax rate to the taxation of distributed profits according to the income level of individual share owners. Still, all these reforms have not achieved a major breakthrough in popular stock ownership.

369 See Beyer (2002).

370 Höpner (2003: 126).

371 Höpner (2003: 162–4).

372 See Beyer and Hassel (2001).

373 Kurdelbusch (2001).

374 See Rehder and Hassel (2001) and Streeck and Rehder (2003), and compare these with Hartmann (1970/1). See also the preceding discussion in the text about the unending debate on the decentralization of industrial relations.

375 See e.g. 'Profits of Doom', *The Economist*, 2 Jan. 1990, p. 68. This article made the point that the stock market had overheated, especially in the USA. See the same periodical, 15 Apr. 2000, p. 13, and other articles, which argued against the idea that any 'new economy' paradigm supported the stock-value appreciation observed.

376 Van Witteloostuijn (1999) provided an entertaining and factually detailed analysis of the phenomenon, showing that its spread owed more to hype and mystique—transformed into objective and real factors by the stock exchange—than to economic performance.

377 See *The Economist*, 15 Jan. 2001, pp. 15–16, and 15 Apr. 2000, pp. 13–14.

378 This renders the application of Scharpf's (1997) ideas useful.

379 The expulsion of Marx from Prussia is another case of trenchant Prussian dialectics. Marx had been intellectually at home in left-liberal Hegelianism, which was one of the academic ideologies of Prussian reform. He was also married to the sister of a Prussian Minister of the Interior, not a *Junker* but a higher aristocrat by the name of von Westphalen, whose family ostracized him and his wife. Despite the tribulations inflicted on him by the government and academic colleagues in Germany, he never felt at home in England but never got an academic position there, either. His experience was completely the opposite of that of his friend, colleague, and supporter Engels, who was a well-liked and successful businessman in Manchester and enjoyed the lifestyle of an English country gentleman, including fox-hunting, for which he is fondly and ironically remembered by Mancunians.

380 He died in London in 1883.

381 I hope readers will forgive the lack of detail, for I am not trying to outdo Marx in trying to accomplish an impossible mission, as his followers have done.

382 See Guillén (2000). This is probably the richest and most pertinent study available with regard to the countries, time period, and governance parameters covered.

383 Lane (2003). This paper is one of the better examples of a veritable flood of work proclaiming convergence and pervasive change, most of which not only offers no comparisons to prove this, but also fails to recognize the categorical difference between the two. Lane's treatment is based on more extensive comparative experience.

384 In their introduction to Yamamura and Streeck (eds, 2003: 1–50), the editors write: 'what may look ex post like a logical and even the only possible development in the liberalization, internationalization and hybridization of nationally embedded capitalism, may appear impossible and may even be outright unimaginable ex ante' (50). Precisely. Or, in other words, by the time scholars have understood the world, it tends to appear in a different form. Scholars tend to take that as evidence of pervasive change.

385 Japan Incorporated included a whole range of coordination and pooling activities, between *keiretsu*—but not only within them—and between them and complex chains of suppliers and the state. This included research and development and even decisions about which industries should engage in export campaigns. Japanese exports had strategically been focused on a very restricted range of subindustries and products. Concertation of research and development is much less visible between major industrial groups in Germany, and export activity is a hallmark of most industries rather than being concentrated in a selective number of industries and products.

386 See the contributions in Müller-Jentsch and Weitbrecht (eds, 2003).

387 See Aguilera and Jackson (2003).

388 That innovation should thrive in a German prison would be appreciated as a neat joke in British comedy, in keeping with much of its post-1939 imagery about Germany. I trust British readers to take the joke as an opportunity, in the best paradoxical traditions of British comedy, to understand that contrary to expectations, some German prisons were so liberal that their inmates hated to leave them. The most outstanding application of paradox in comedy can, of course, be found in *Monty Python's Flying Circus*. The relevance of *Monty Python* for paradoxical organization theory was shown by Sorge (2000*b*).

389 Hugues (1998: 11); translations mine.

390 This variety has been well systematized and discussed by Burrell (2002), primarily for organizational paradigms. But this can be extended more generally with regard to social science paradigms.

391 For example, note the way in which Scharpf (1997) has embedded game theory in a range of alternative and complementary theories.

392 Some of the critics of *bedrijfskunde* would argue this point, not without empirical justification in some cases.

393 Huizinga (1947).

394 The Ho Chi Minh Trail was a band of territory with thick forests used by the North Vietnamese to transport forces and supplies to South Vietnam in order to replenish and equip the 'Viet Cong' and North Vietnamese government forces fighting in the South.

395 Crozier (1971).

396 D'Iribarne (1989).

397 OECD (2003: 23).

398 Once again, the phenomenon is not new. Plagued in the 1950s by the aftermath of World War II, Germans sought distracting refuge from the acute stress and despair by watching *Heimatfilme*, i.e. films set in scenic Alpine areas which happily resolved traditional conflicts over things like inheritance of farmland or hunting rights and the choice of marriage partners within rustic milieux. The classic and pioneering piece in this genre, from another romantic period coinciding with the aftermath of the Napoleonic Wars and occupation, is the opera *Der Freischütz* by Carl Maria von Weber.

399 Here, I rely on the research of members of the Max Planck Institute for the Study of Societies in Cologne, mainly Scharpf, Streeck, Manow, Ebbinghaus, and Trampusch. A large number of publications have appeared, mostly after 1995, which have established the scenario that follows in the text. It is advisable to visit the website of the Institute (<www.mpi-fg-koeln.mpg.de>) for sources because it is impractical to quote all of them here. For an earlier work which shows how old the basic analysis and some of the predicaments basically are, see also Scharpf (1983), and see also Scharpf (2002), a more recent comparative analysis.

400 See Scharpf (2002), particularly figure 5 and his discussion of it.

401 The most articulate and detailed criticism along these lines has been provided by Arnim (2000).

402 A good analysis and evaluation of strengths and deficiencies is provided by the various contributions to Harding and Patterson (eds, 2000), and the summary of the editors in ch. 8, in particular this remark, is to the point: 'The German "model" has assimilated a massive and underdeveloped economy and made macro-economic errors of judgment in the unification of the two currencies. Yet it is still the largest exporter in the world, it

has had consistently low inflation since 1995, its balance of payments is in massive surplus' (128). However, 'The real root of these weaknesses emanates from the macro-level coordination between policy-makers, industry and worker representatives' (ibid.).

403 OECD (2003: 21).

404 Czipin & Proudfoot consultants reported: 'Germany overtook the USA as the most productive country last year . . . Almost two-thirds of working time was productively used. In this respect Germany is at the top world-wide. . . . With respect to work morale, only Australia scores better . . . Work morale is most problematic in American organizations.' Note that German management did not come out on top whereas work systems did. See 'Manager: Schlechte Noten', *Die Zeit*, no. 51 (11 Dec. 2003), p. 32.

405 See the final passage of his introduction to Streeck and Yamamura (eds, 2001: 38).

406 At the time, this was candidly conceded even by one of the inventors of Swedish macroeconomic coordination and the welfare state, Rudolf Meidner.

407 Although this is the essence of dialectical action theory, as expressed by the Chicago School and revived in organization studies by Karl Weick (1979), its genealogy takes us back to Martin Luther. In his tract *Von der Freiheit eines Christenmenschen*, he clearly suggests that the freedom of Christians points to submission (to the constraints posited by God), and the central constraint God imposes is to make use of the freedom he generously offers. Dialectical action theory is, in fact, a secularized version of this concept. For Luther, it has a liberating effect. Decision-makers can expect the same liberating effect, but they often appear to vacillate between scholasticism and arbitrariness.

408 Note this statement by the prime minister of North Rhine-Westphalia, the largest state in Germany: 'Trapped between irreversible globalization, the increasing longevity of our society, increasing public debt with corresponding interest payments and weak growth, the welfare state no longer works the way we have become accustomed to'. (*In dem Schraubstock einer irreversiblen Globalisierung, zunehmender Überalterung unserer Gesellschaft, steigender Staatsschulden mit entsprechenden Zinslasten und einer schwachen Wachstumsdynamik funktioniert der Sozialstaat nicht mehr so, wie wir das gewöhnt sind.*) See Peer Steinbrück, 'Etwas mehr Dynamik, bitte', *Die Zeit*, no. 47 (13 Nov. 2003), p. 18. The prime minister did not mention the problems accruing from heavy subsidization, such as that of coal mining one thousand metres underground north of the River Emscher, on the outskirts of the old Ruhr region, nor any of the other aforementioned problems, all of which are domestic in origin.

References

Aguilera, Ruth, V., and Jackson, Gregory (2003), 'The Cross-national Diversity of Cor-porate Governance: Dimensions and Determinants', *Academy of Management Review* 28, 447–65.

Albert, Michel (1991), *Capitalisme contre capitalisme* (Paris: Éditions du Seuil).

Anderson, Perry (1974), *Lineages of the Absolutist State* (London: New Left Books).

Aner, Ekkehard, *et al.* (1997), *Großer Atlas zur Weltgeschichte* (Braunschweig: Wester-mann).

Arnim, Hans-Herbert von (2000), *Vom schönen Schein der Demokratie. Politik ohne Verantwor-tung—am Volk vorbei* (Munich: Droemer).

Barjot, D. (ed.) (2002), *Catching Up With America: Productivity Missions and the Diffusion of American Economic and Technological Influence after the Second World War* (Paris: Presses de l'Université de Paris-Sorbonne).

Bartlett, Christopher, A., and Ghoshal, Sumantra (1989), *Managing Across Borders: The Transnational Solution* (Boston, Mass.: Harvard Business School Press).

Bendix, Reinhard (1970), *Embattled Reason: Essays in Social Knowledge* (New York: Oxford University Press).

Berger, Peter, L., and Luckmann, Thomas (1971), *The Social Construction of Reality: A Treatise in the Sociology of Knowledge* (Harmondsworth: Penguin).

Beyer, Jürgen (2001), 'One Best Way oder Varietät? Strategien und Strukturen von Großunternehmen im Prozess der Internationalisierung', *Soziale Welt* 52, 7–28.

—— (2002), *Deutschland AG a.D.: Deutsche Bank, Allianz und das Verflechtungszentrum großer deutscher Unternehmen*, MPIfG discussion paper 02/4, available at <www.mpi-fg-koeln.mpg.de/workpap/wp02-4.html>.

—— and Hassel, Anke (2001), *The Effects of Convergence: Internationalization and the Changing Distribution of Net Value Added in Large German Firms*, MPIfG discussion paper 01/7, available at <www.mpifg.de/pu/mpifg_dp/dp01-7.pdf>.

Blalock, Hubert, M. (1972), 'Theory Building and Causal Inferences', in *Methodology in Social Research*, H. M. Blalock and A. B. Blalock (eds), (London/Llubljana: McGraw-Hill and Mladinska Knjiga), 155–98.

Booz, Allen and Hamilton, (1973), 'German Management: Challenge and Response. A Pragmatic Review with an Appraisal by Heinz Hartmann', *International Studies of Management and Organization* 3: 1–2, 1–150.

Boyer, Robert (1990), *The Regulation School: A Critical Appraisal* (New York: Columbia University Press).

—— (1998), 'Hybridization and Models of Production: Geography, History, and Theory', in *Between Imitation and Innovation: The Transfer and Hybridization of Productive Models in the International Automobile Industry*, R. Boyer, E. Charron, U. Jürgens, and S. Tolliday (eds) (Oxford: Oxford University Press), 23–56.

Brouwer, J. J. (2003), *Schaduwen over de woestijn. Strategie, management en organisatie van het Duitse en Britse leger van Versailles tot El Alamein: theorie en praktijk* (The Hague: CinC Management Consultants).

Brussig, Martin, Lohr, Karin, Semlinger, Klaus, Sorge, Arndt, and Strohwald, Udo (1997), 'Bestandsbedingungen und Entwicklungspotentiale' in Brussig *et al.* (eds) (1997), 17–290.

—— *et al.* (eds) (1997), *Kleinbetriebe in den neuen Bundesländern* (Opladen: Leske + Budrich).

Burrell, Gibson (2002), 'Organization Paradigms', in *Organization*, A. Sorge (ed.) (London: Thomson Learning), 25–42.

Calori, Roland, Lubatkin, Michel, and Véry, Paul (1994), 'Control Mechanisms in Cross-border Acquisitions: An International Comparison', *Organization Studies* 15, 361–80.

Campbell, Adrian, Sorge, Arndt, and Warner, Malcolm (1989), *Microelectronic Product Applications in Great Britain and West Germany: Strategies, Competence and Training* (Aldershot: Gower Press).

Carr, Raymond (1980), *Modern Spain: 1875–1980* (Oxford: Oxford University Press).

Carrère d'Encausse, Hélène (2000), *La Russie inachevée* (Paris: Fayard).

Carroll, Glenn R. (1985), 'Concentration and Specialization: Dynamics of Niche Width in Populations of Organizations', *American Journal of Sociology* 90, 1262–83.

Chang, Ha-Joon (2002), *Kicking Away the Ladder: Development Strategy in Historical Perspective* (London: Anthem Press).

Child, John (1996), 'Strategic Choice', in *International Encyclopedia of Business and Management*, v (London: Routledge-International Thomson Publishing), 4556–71.

Clark, John M. (1940), 'Toward a Concept of Workable Competition', *American Economic Review* 30, 241–56.

Clark, Peter A. (1987), *Anglo-American Innovation* (Berlin: Walter de Gruyter).

—— (2000), *Organizations in Action: Competition Between Contexts* (London/New York: Routledge).

Clegg, Stewart R. (2002), *Management and Organization Paradoxes* (Amsterdam/Philadelphia: John Benjamins).

Cohen, G. A. (1978), *Karl Marx's Theory of History: A Defence* (Princeton: Princeton University Press).

Cox, Joan G., and Kriegbaum, Herbert (1980), *Growth, Innovation and Employment: An Anglo-German Comparison* (London: Anglo-German Foundation for the Study of Industrial Society).

Crouch, Colin (1993), *Industrial Relations and European State Traditions* (Oxford: Clarendon Press).

—— LeGalès, Patrick, Trigilia, Carlo, and Voelzkow, Helmut (2001), *Local Production Systems in Europe: Rise or Demise?* (Oxford: Oxford University Press).

Crozier, Michel (1963), *Le Phénomène bureaucratique* (Paris: Seuil).

—— (1971), *La Société bloquée* (Paris: Seuil).

Czarniawska, Barbara, and Joerges, Bernward (1996), 'Travel of Ideas', in *Translating Organizational Change*, B. Czarniawska and G. Sevón (eds) (Berlin: Walter de Gruyter), 13–48.

Dahrendorf, Ralf (1965), *Gesellschaft und Demokratie in Deutschland* (Munich: Europäische Verlagsanstalt).

Daubigney, Jean D., Fizaine, Françoise, and Silvestre, Jean-Jacques, (1972), *Comparaison de la hiérarchie des salaires entre l'Allemagne et la France* (Aix-en-Provence: Laboratoire d'Économie et de Sociologie du Travail).

Davies, Norman (1997), *Europe: A History* (London: Pimlico Random House).

Devereux, Edward C., Bronfenbrenner, Urie, and Suci, George J. (1962), 'On Parental Behaviour in the United States and the Federal Republic', *International Social Science Journal* 14, 488–506.

DiMaggio, Paul J., and Powell, Walter, W. (1983), 'The Iron Cage Revisited: Institutional Isomorphism and Collective Rationality in Organizational Fields', *American Sociological Review* 48, 147–60.

D'Iribarne, Philippe (1989), *La Logique de l'honneur* (Paris: Seuil).

—— (1991), 'Culture et effet sociétal', *Revue française de sociologie* 32, 599–614.

Dirrheimer, Angela, Hartmann, Gert, and Sorge, Arndt (1980), *Qualitative Veränderung der Arbeit durch neue Informationstechnik*, IIM/LMP discussion paper 80–3 (Berlin: IIM/LMP).

Djelic, Marie-Laure (2001), *Exporting the American Model: The Post-war Transformation of European Business* (Oxford: Oxford University Press).

—— and Quack, Sigrid (2002), *The Missing Link: Bringing Institutions Back into the Debate on Economic Globalisation*, Wissenschaftszentrum Berlin für Sozialforschung discussion paper FS I 02-107 (Berlin: Wissenschaftszentrum Berlin Für Sozialforschung).

—— —— (2003), *Globalization and Institutions: Redefining the Rules of the Economic Game* (Cheltenham/Northampton, Mass.: Edward Elgar).

Dore, Ronald (1973), *British Factory—Japanese Factory: The Origins of National Diversity in Industrial Relations* (London: Allen & Unwin).

Dowling, Peter J., Welch, Denice E., and Schuler, Randall (1999), *International Human Resource Management: Managing People in a Multinational Context*, 3rd edn (Cincinnati, Ohio: Southwestern College Publishing).

Dunlop, John T. (1958), *Industrial Relations Systems* (New York: Holt, Rinehart and Winston).

Dupuy, T. N. (1977), *A Genius for War: The German Army and the General Staff* (London: Macdonald and Jane's).

Eck, N. N. von (1893), *Geschichte des 2. Westfälischen Husarenregiments Nr. 11* (Mainz: Militärverlagsanstalt).

Eckstein, Harry (1966), *Division and Cohesion in Democracy: A Study of Norway* (Princeton. Princeton University Press).

Eichhorn, Friedhelm, Hessinger, Philipp, Finke, Michael, and Feldhoff, Jürgen, (2003), *Regionale Knoten in globalen Warenketten. Industriedistrikte im Spannungsfeld von Global Players und lokalen Akteuren: Medizintechnik in Tuttlingen und maritime Industrie in Rostock* (Munichen: Rainer Hampp).

Eley, Lothar (1972), *Transzendentale Phänomenologie und Systemtheorie der Gesellschaft: Zur philosophischen Propädeutik der Sozialwissenschaft* (Freiburg im Breisgau: Rombach).

Elias, Norbert (1977), *Über den Prozess der Zivilisation*, 2 vols (Frankfurt am Main: Suhrkamp).

Engelberg, Ernst (1987), *Bismarck: Urpreuße und Reichsgründer* (Berlin: Akademie-Verlag).

Esser, Hartmut. (1993), *Soziologie: Allgemeine Grundlagen* (Frankfurt am Main: Campus).

Ferner, Anthony (1997), 'Country of Origin Effects and Human Resource Management in Multinational Companies', *Human Resource Management Journal* 7, 19–37.

Geppert, Mike, Williams, Karen, and Matten, Dirk (2003), 'The Social Construction of Contextual Rationalities in MNCs: An Anglo-German Comparison of Subsidiary Choice', *Journal of Management Studies* 40, 617–41.

—— Matten, Dirk, and Williams, Karen (eds) (2002), *Challenges for European Management in a Global Context: Experiences from Britain and Germany* (Basingstoke: Palgrave Macmillan).

Gergs, Hans-Joachim, and Schmidt, Rudi (2002), 'Generationswechsel im Management ost- und westdeutscher Unternehmen: Kommt es zu einer Amerikanisierung des deutschen Managementmodells?', *Kölner Zeitschrift für Soziologie und Sozialpsychologie* 54, 553–78.

Giddens, Anthony (1986), *The Constitution of Society* (Berkeley/Los Angeles: University of California Press).

Glassmann, Ulrich, and Voelzkow, Helmut (2001), 'The Governance of Local Economies in Germany', in Crouch *et al.* (2001), 79–116.

Gordon, David (1996), *Fat and Mean: The Corporate Squeeze of Working Americans and the Myth of Managerial 'Downsizing'* (New York: Free Press).

Görlitz, Walter (1977), *Kleine Geschichte des deutschen Generalstabes* (Berlin: Haude und Spener).

Gorski, Philip S. (1993), 'The Protestant Ethic Revisited: Disciplinary Revolution and State Formation in Holland and Prussia', *American Journal of Sociology* 99, 265–316.

Gouldner, Alvin W. (1976), *The Dialectic of Technology and Ideology: The Origins, Grammar and Future of Ideology* (London/Basingstoke: Macmillan).

Grandori, Anna (2002), 'Agency, Markets and Hierarchies', in *Organization*, A. Sorge (ed.) (London: Thomson Learning), 160–78.

Greenwood, Royston, and Hinings, C. Robert (1996), 'Understanding Radical Organizational Change: Bringing Together the Old and the New Institutionalism', *Academy of Management Review* 21, 1022–54.

Guillén, Mauro F. (2000), 'Corporate Governance and Globalization: Is there Convergence across Countries?', in *Advances in International Comparative Management* 13, J. L. C. Cheng and R. B. Peterson (eds) (Stamford, Conn.: JAI Press), 175–204.

Gummesson, Evert (1991), *Qualitative Methods in Management Research* (Newbury Park, Calif.: Sage).

Haar, J. (1989), 'A Comparative Analysis of the Profitability Performance of the Largest U.S., European and Japanese Multinational Enterprises', *Management International Review* 29, 5–19.

Halman, Loek, and Nevitte, Neil (eds) (1996), *Political Value Change in Western Democracies* (Tilburg: Tilburg University Press).

Hancké, Bob (1999), 'Varieties of Capitalism Revisited: Globalization and Comparative Institutional Advantage', *Lettre de la regulation* 30, 1–3.

Harbison, Frederick H., and Myers, Charles A. (1959), *Management in the Industrial World* (New York: McGraw-Hill).

—— Köchling, Ernst, Cassell, Frank H., and Ruebmann, Heinrich C. (1955), 'Steel Management in Two Continents', *Management Science* 2, 31–9.

Harding, Rebecca, and Paterson, William E. (eds) (2000), *The Future of the German Economy: An End to the Miracle?*, (Manchester/New York: Manchester University Press).

Hartmann, Heinz (1959), *Authority and Organization in German Management* (Princeton: Princeton University Press).

—— and Wienold, Hanns (1967), *Universität und Unternehmer* (Gütersloh: Bertelsmann).

—— Hetzler, H. W., Pöhler, Willi, and Neuloh, Otto (1970/1), 'Industrial Relations im kommenden Jahrzehnt', *Soziale Welt* 20/1, 425–36.

Harzing, Anne-Wil (1995), 'The Persistent Myth of High Expatriate Failure Rates', *International Journal of Human Resource Management* 6, 457–75.

—— (1999), *Managing the Multinationals: An International Study of Control Mechanism* (Cheltenham/Northampton, Mass.: Edward Elgar).

—— and Sorge, Arndt (2003), 'The Relative Impact of Country-of-Origin and Universal Contingencies on Internationalization Strategies and Corporate Control in Multinational Enterprises: World-Wide and European Perspectives', *Organization Studies* 24, 187–214.

Heigenoort, John van (1972), 'Logical Paradoxes' in *Encyclopedia of Philosophy*, P. Edwards (ed.) (New York: Macmillan), 45–51.

Herrigel, Gary (1996), *Industrial Constructions: The Sources of German Industrial Power* (Cambridge: Cambridge University Press).

Hesse, Konrad (1967), *Grundzüge des Verfassungsrechts der Bundesrepublik Deutschland* (Karlsruhe: C. F. Müller).

Hickson, David (1993), 'Many More Ways than One', in *Management in Western Europe: Society, Culture and Organization in Twelve Nations*, D. Hickson (ed.) (Berlin: Walter de Gruyter), 249–62.

Hilferding, Rudolf (1927), *Das Finanzkapital* (Vienna: Verlag der Wiener Volksbuchhandlung).

—— (1981), *Finance Capital: A Study of the Latest Phase of Capitalist Development* (London: Routledge and Kegan Paul).

Hillmann, Felicitas (2000), 'Vom internationalen Wanderungsraum zu transnationalen Migrationsnetzwerken? Der neue europäische Wanderungsraum', *Kölner Zeitschrift für Soziologie und Sozialpsychologie*, special issue 40, (363–85).

Hodgson, Geoffrey M. (1997), 'Evolutionary Theories of the Firm', in *IEBM Handbook of Organizational Behaviour*, A. Sorge and M. Warner (eds) (London: International Thomson Business Press), 88–94.

Hofstede, Geert (1997), *Lokales Denken, globales Handeln: Kultur, Zusammenarbeit und Management* (Munich: Beck/dtv).

—— (2001), *Culture's Consequences: Comparing Values, Behaviours, Institutions and Organizations across Nations*, 2nd edn (Thousand Oaks, Calif./London: Sage).

Hollingsworth, J. Rogers (1997), 'The Institutional Embeddedness of American Capitalism', in *Political Economy of Modern Capitalism: Mapping Convergence and Divergence*, C. Crouch and W. Streeck (eds) (London: Sage), 133–47.

Hollis, Martin (1994), *The Philosophy of Social Science: An Introduction* (Cambridge: Cambridge University Press).

Höpner, Martin (2003), *Wer beherrscht die Unternehmen? Shareholder Value, Managerherrschaft und Mitbestimmung in Deutschland*, Schriften des Max-Planck-Instituts für Gesellschaftsforschung 46 (Frankfurt am Main: Max-Planck-Instituts für Gesellschaftsforschung).

—— and Jackson, Gregory (2001), *An Emerging Market for Corporate Control? The Mannesmann Takeover and German Corporate Governance*, MPIfG discussion paper 01/4 (Cologne: Max-Planck-Institut für Gesellschaftsforschung).

Hrebiniak, Lawrence G., and Joyce, William, F. (1985), 'Organizational Adaptation, Strategic Choice and Environmental Determinism', *Administrative Science Quarterly* 30, 336–49.

Hübner, Kurt (2001), *Glauben und Denken: Dimensionen der Wirklichkeit* (Tübingen: Mohr Siebeck).

Hugues, Pascale (1998), *Le Bonheur allemand* (Paris: Seuil).

Huizinga, J. (1947), *Herfsttij der middeleeuwen: Studie over levens-en gedachtenvormen der veertiende en vijftiende eeuw in Frankrijk en de Nederlanden*, 6th edn (Haarlem: Tjeenk Willink & Zoon).

Inglehart, Robert (1990), *Culture Shift in Advanced Industrial Society* (Princeton: Princeton University Press).

Jorna, René J. (2000), 'De "zwarte" doos in de bedrijfskunde: cognitie in actie', unpubl. inaugural lecture, University of Groningen Faculty of Management and Organisation.

Kantzenbach, Erhard (1967), *Die Funktionsfähigkeit des Wettbewerbs*, 2nd edn (Göttingen: Vandenhoeck & Rupprecht).

Karsten, Luchien, and van Veen, Kees (2003), 'Management Consultancies in the Netherlands in the 1950s and 1960s: Between Systemic Context and External Influences', in *Management Consulting: Emergence and Dynamics of a Knowledge Industry*, M. Kippling and L. Engwall (eds) (Oxford: Oxford University Press), 52–69.

Kern, Horst, and Schumann, Michael (1970), *Industriearbeit und Arbeiterbewusstsein*, 2 vols (Frankfurt am Main: Europäische Verlagsanstalt).

Kieser, Alfred, *et al.* (1996), 'A Comparison of British and German Managerial Roles, Perceptions and Behaviour', in *Managing Across Cultures: Issues and Perspectives*, P. Joynt and M. Warner (eds) (London: International Thomson Business Press), 202–11.

Knights, David, and Morgan, Glenn (eds) (1997), *Regulation and Deregulation in European Financial Services* (London: Macmillan).

Kocka, Jürgen (1969), *Unternehmensverwaltung und Angestelltenschaft am Beispiel Siemens, 1844–1914* (Stuttgart: Enke).

—— (1978), 'Entrepreneurs and Managers in German Industrialization', in Mathias and Postan (1978), 492–589.

König, René (ed.) (1967), *Fischer-Lexikon Soziologie* (Frankfurt am Main: Fischer).

Kürschner, Peter (1902), *Armee und Marine: Ein Ratgeber für alle Wehrpflichtigen* (Braunschweig: Ludwig & Lohmann).

Kurdelbusch, Antje (2001), 'Variable Vergütung bedeutet Wettbewerb und Risiko', *Die Mitbestimmung* 47, 22–5.

Lallement, Michel (1999), *Les Gouvernances de l'emploi* (Paris: Desclée de Brouwer).

Lammers, Cornelis J. (2003), 'Occupation Regimes Alike and Unlike: British, Dutch and French Patterns of Inter-organizational Control of Foreign Territories', *Organization Studies* 24, 1379–1404.

Lanciano, Caroline, Maurice, Marc, Silvestre, Jean-Jaques, and Nohara, Hiroatsu (1998), 'Introduction: L'analyse sociétale de l'innovation', in *Les Acteurs de l'innovation dans l'entreprise: France–Europe–Japon*, C. Lanciano, M. Maurice, J.-J. Silvestre, and H. Nohara (eds) (Paris: L'Harmattan), 125–44.

Landes, David S. (1960), *The Structure of Enterprise in the Nineteenth Century: The Cases of Britain and Germany*, IIR reprint no. 152 (Berkeley: Institute of Industrial Relations).

Lane, Christel (1989), *Management and Labour in Europe: The Industrial Enterprise in Germany, Britain and France* (Aldershot: Edward Elgar).

—— (1998), 'European Companies between Globalization and Localization: A Comparison of Internationalization Strategies of British and German MNCs', *Economy and Society* 27, 462–85.

—— (2003), 'Institutional Transformations and System Change: A Study of the Changing Form of Corporate Governance in Germany and its Consequences for the German Business System', paper presented at the Workshop on National Business Systems in the New Global Context, Oslo.

La Porta, Rafael, Lopez-de-Silanes, Florencio, and Shleifer, Andrei (1998), 'Corporate ownership around the word', Harvard Institute of Economic Research Paper no. 1840, available at <http://papers.ssm.com/sol3/delivery.cfm/98062502.pdf?abstractid =103130>.

Lawrence, J. W., and Lorsch, Paul R.. (1967), *Organizations and Environments* (Cambridge Mass.: Harvard University Press).

Lawrence, Peter (1980), *Managers and Management in West Germany* (London: Croom Helm).

—— (2002), *The Change Game: How Today's Global Trends are Shaping Tomorrow's Companies* (London/Sterling, Va.: Kogan Page).

Lee, J. J. (1978), 'Labour in German Industrialization', in Mathias and Postan (1978), 442–91.

Leeuw, A. C. J. de (2000), *Bedrijfskundig management: Primair proces, strategie en organisatie* (Assen: Van Gorcum).

Lehmbruch, Gerhard (2002), *Der unitarische Bundesstaat in Deutschland: Pfadabhängigkeit und Wandel*, MPIfG discussion paper 02/2 (Cologne: Max-Planck-Institut für Gesellschaftsforschung).

Lévi-Strauss, Claude (1963), *Structural Anthropology* (New York: Basic Books).

Lewin, Arie Y., and Volberda, Henk (1999), 'Prolegomena on Co-evolution: A Framework for Research on Strategy and New Organizational Forms', *Organization Science* 10, 519–34.

Lewin, Kurt (1954), *Resolving Social Conflicts: Selected Papers in Group Dynamics* (New York: Harper Brothers).

Lockwood, David (1964), 'Social Integration and Systems Integration', in *Explorations in social change*, G. K. Zollschan and W. Hirsch (eds) (London: Routledge & Kegan Paul), 244–57.

Loo, Hans van der, and Reijen, Willem van (1990), *Paradoxen van modernisering: Een sociaalwetenschappelijke benadering* (Muiderberg: Coutinho).

Loveridge, Ray (1983), 'Sources of Diversity in Internal Labour Markets', *Sociology* 17, 44–62.

Luhmann, Niklas (1972), *Soziologische Aufklärung: Aufsätze zur Theorie sozialer Systeme*, i, 3rd edn (Opladen: Westdeutscher Verlag).

Macfarlane, Alan (1978), *The Origins of English Individualism* (Oxford: Blackwell).

Maier, Charles S. (1975), *Recasting Bourgeois Europe: Stabilization in France, Germany, and Italy in the Decade after World War I* (Princeton: Princeton University Press).

Maier, Hans E. (1987), *Das Modell Baden-Württemberg: Über institutionelle Voraussetzungen differenzierter Qualitätsproduktion*, Wissenschaftszentrum Berlin discussion paper IIM/LMP 87–10 (Berlin: Wissenschaftszentrum Berlin).

March, James G., and Olsen, Johan P. (1975), *Ambiguity and Choice in Organizations* (Oslo: Universitetsforlaget).

—— and Simon, Herbert A. (1958), *Organizations* (New York: John Wiley).

Markovits, Andrei S., and Hellerman, Steven L. (1995/6), 'Soccer in America: A Story of Marginalization', *Entertainment and Sports Law Review* 13, 225–55.

Marris, R. L. (1997), 'Managerial Theories of the Firm', in *IEBM Handbook of Organizational Behaviour*, A. Sorge and M. Warner (eds) (London: International Thomson Business Press), 79–97.

Marry, Catherine (1993), 'Peut-on parler autrement du "modèle" allemand et du "modèle" français de formation?', *Formation et Emploi* 44, 23–8.

Mathias, Peter, and Postan, M. M. (eds) (1978), *The Cambridge Economic History of Europe. Volume VII. The Industrial Economies: Capital, Labour and Enterprise. Part 1* (Cambridge: Cambridge University Press).

Maurice, Marc (2002), 'L'Analyse sociétale est-elle encore d'actualité? L'historicité d'une approche et son évolution', *Economies et sociétés*, series *Economie du travail* 22, 1213–39.

—— Sellier, François, and Silvestre, Jean-Jacques (1977), *La Production de la hiérarchie dans l'entreprise: Recherche d'un effet sociétal* (Aix-en-Provence: Laboratoire d'Économie et de Sociologie du Travail).

—— —— —— (1982), *Politique d'éducation et organisation industrielle en France et en Allemagne: Essai d'analyse sociétale* (Paris: Presses Universitaires de France).

—— and Sorge, Arndt (1989), *Dynamique industrielle et capacité d'innovation de l'industrie de la machine-outil en France et en RFA: Analyse sociétale des rapports entre "espace de qualification" et "espace industriel"* (Aix-en-Provence: Laboratoire d'Économie et de Sociologie du Travail).

—— —— (1990), 'The Societal Effect in Strategies and Competitiveness of Machine-tool Manufacturers in France and West Germany', *International Journal of Human Resource Management* 1, 141–72; revd version repr. in B. Kogut (ed.), *Country Competitiveness: Technology and the Organizing of Work* (New York/Oxford: Oxford University Press, 1993), 75–95.

—— —— (eds) (2000), *Embedding Organizations: Societal Analysis of Actors, Organizations and Socio-economic Context* (Amsterdam: John Benjamins).

—— —— and Warner, Malcolm (1980), 'Societal Differences in Organizing Manufacturing Units: A Comparison of France, West Germany and Great Britain', *Organization Studies* 1, 59–86.

—— Eyraud, François, d'Iribarne, Alain, and Rychener, Frédérique (1986), *Des enterprises en mutation dans la crise: Apprentissages des technologies flexibles et émergence de nouveaux acteurs* (Aix-en-Provence: Laboratoire d'Économie et de Sociologie du Travail).

—— Mannari, Hirsohi, Takeo, Y., and Inoki, T. (1988), *Des enterprises françaises et japonaises face à la mécatronique: Acteurs et organisation de la dynamique industrielle* (Aix-en-Provence: Laboratoire d'Économie et de Sociologie du Travail).

Mayer, Arno J. (1981), *The Persistence of the Old Regime: Europe to the Great War* (New York: Croon Helm/Pantheon Books).

Mayer, Michel, and Whittington, Richard (1999), 'Strategy, Structure and Systemness: National Institutions and Corporate Change in France, Germany and the UK, 1950–1993', *Organization Studies* 20, 933–60.

May-Strobl, Eva, and Paulini, Monika (1997), 'Das Gründungsgeschehen in den neuen Bundesländern—Wachstumstypen und Beschäftigungsbeitrag', in Brussig *et al.* (eds) 1997), 323–56.

Mead, George Herbert (1997), 'The Self as Social structure', in *The Classical Tradition in Sociology: The American Tradition*, J. Alexander, R. Boudon, and M. Cherkaoui (eds), (London: Sage), i, 214–19.

Merchant, Kenneth A. (1985), *Control in Business Organizations* (Cambridge, Mass.: Ballinger).

Merton, Robert K. (1968), *Social Theory and Social Structure* (Glencoe, Ill.: Free Press).

Miles, Raymond E., and Snow, Charles C. (1978), *Organizational Strategy, Structure, and Process* (New York: McGraw-Hill).

Miller, Eric J., and Rice, A. K. (1967), *Systems of Organization: The Control of Task and Sentient Boundaries* (London: Tavistock).

Mintzberg, Henry (1983), *Structures in Fives: Designing Effective Organizations* (Englewood Cliffs, NY: Prentice Hall).

—— (1995), *Les propos d'un 'pur coton': Essai sur la problématique canadienne* (Montreal: Québec/Amérique).

Morgan, Gareth (1997), *Images of Organization*, 2nd edn (Thousand Oaks, Calif./London: Sage).

Mueller, Frank (1994), 'Societal Effect, Organizational Effect and Globalization', *Organization Studies* 15, 407–28.

Müller-Jentsch, Walter, and Weitbrecht, Hansjörg (eds) (2003), *Changing Contours of German Industrial Relations* (Munich/Mering: Rainer Hampp Verlag).

Münch, Richard (1980), 'Talcott Parsons und die Theorie sozialen Handelns II: Die Kontinuität der Entwicklung', *Soziale Welt* 31, 3–47.

Musgrave, P. W. (1967), *Technical Change, the Labour Force and Education: A Study of British and German Iron and Steel Industries, 1860–1964* (Oxford: Pergamon Press).

Musgrave, Richard A. (1959), *The Theory of Public Finance: A Study in Public Economy* (New York: McGraw-Hill International).

Musselin, Christine (2001), *La Longue marche des universités françaises* (Paris: Presses Universitaires de France).

Nelson, Richard R., and Winter, Sidney (1982), *An Evolutionary Theory of Economic Change* (Cambridge, Mass.: Belknap Press).

OECD (Organization for Economic Cooperation and Development) (2003), *OECD Economic Surveys: Germany. Volume 2002, Supplement no. 4* (Paris: OECD).

Oliver, Christine (1992), 'The Antecedents of Deinstitutionalization', *Organization Studies* 13, 563–88.

—— (1996), 'The Institutional Embeddedness of Economic Activity', in *Advances in Strategic Management* 13, J. A. C. Baum and J. E. Duttton (eds) (New York: JAI Press), 163–86.

—— (1997), 'Sustainable Competitive Advantage: Combining Institutional and Resource-based Views', *Strategic Management Journal* 18, 697–713.

Panic, M. (ed.) (1976), *The UK and West German Manufacturing Industry 1954–72* (London: National Economic Development Office).

Parsons, Talcott (1964), *The Social System* (New York/London: Free Press/Collier-Macmillan).

Pettigrew, Andrew M. (1985), *The Awakening Giant: Continuity and Change in ICI* (Oxford: Blackwell).

Piore, Michael J., and Sabel, Charles F. (1984), *The Second Industrial Divide: Possibilities for Prosperity* (New York: Basic Books).

Plessner, Helmuth (1959), *Die verspätete Nation* (Stuttgart: Enke).

Pollard, Sidney (1978), 'Labour in Great Britain', in Mathias and Postan (1978), 97–179.

Poole, Marshall Scott, and Ven, Andrew H. van de (1989), 'Using Paradox to Build Management and Organization Theories', *Academy of Management Review* 14, 562–78.

Porter, Michael E. (1980), *Competitive Strategy* (New York: Free Press).

—— (1990), *The Competitive Advantage of Nations* (London/Basingstoke: Macmillan).

Pot, Ferrie (1998), *Continuity and Change of Human Resource Management: A Comparative Analysis of the Impact of Global Change and Cultural Continuity on the Management of Labour between the Netherlands and the United States* Tinbergen Institute Research Series paper no. 188 (Rotterdam: Tinbergen Institute).

Pugh, Derek S., and Hickson, David (1996), 'Organizational Convergence', in *International Encyclopedia of Business and Management*, iv, M. Warner (ed.) (London and New York: Routledge), 3899–903.

Raij, Erik M. van (2001), *The Implementation of a Market Orientation: Designing Frameworks for Managerial Action* (Enschede, Netherlands: Twente University Press).

Randlesome, Collin, Brierly, William, Bruton, Kevin, Gordon, Colin, and King, Peter (1990), *Business Cultures in Europe* (Oxford: Heinemann Professional Publishing).

Rehder, Britta, and Hassel, Anke (2001), *Institutional Change in the German Wage Bargaining System: The Role of Big Companies*, MPIfG working paper 01/9, available at <www.mpifg. de/pu/workpap/wp01-9/wp01-9.html>.

Robertson, R. and Khondker, H. H. (1998), 'Discourses of Globalization: Preliminary Considerations', *International Sociology* 13, 25–40.

Roethlisberger, Frederick K. (1977), *The Elusive Phenomena* (Cambridge, Mass.: Harvard University Press).

Rokkan, Stein, with Campbell, A., Torsvik, P., and Valen, H. (1970), *Citizens, Elections, Parties: Approaches to the Comparative Study of the Process of Development* (Oslo: Universitetsforlaget).

Rorty, Richard (1989), *Contingency, Irony and Solidarity* (Cambridge: Cambridge University Press).

Rugman, Alan (2000), *The End of Globalization* (London: Random House).

Ruigrok, Winfried, and Tulder, Rob van (1995), *The Logic of International Restructuring* (London/New York: Routledge).

Rumelt, Richard R. (1974), *Strategy, Structure and Economic Performance* (Cambridge, Mass.: Harvard Business School Press).

Saka, Ayse (2003), *Cross-national Appropriation of Work Systems: Japanese Firms in the UK* (Cheltenham and Northampton, Mass.: Edward Elgar).

Scharpf, Fritz W. (1983), 'Institutionelle Bedingungen der Arbeitsmarkt-und Beschäftigungspolitik', in *Institutionelle Bedingungen der Arbeitsmarkt-und Beschäftigungspolitik*, F. W. Scharpf and M. Brockmann (eds) (Frankfurt am Main: Campus), 213–33.

—— (1997), *Games Real Actors Play: Actor-centred Institutionalism in Policy Research* (Boulder, Colo./Oxford: Westview Press).

—— (2002), *Obstacles to Low-skill Employment in Continental Welfare States*, unpubl. MPIfG discussion paper.

Schätzel, Walter (ed.) (n.d.), *Der Staat: Was Staatsmänner, Politiker und Philosophen über den Staat und seine Probleme gesagt haben* (Wiesbaden: Dieterich'sche Verlagsbuchhandlung).

Schmoller, Gustav (1962), 'Das Wirtschaften und die Volkswirtschaft', in G. Schmölders, *Geschichte der Volkswirtschaftslehre* (Reinbek: Rowohlt), 217–25.

Sellier, François (1972), 'La Fonction de négociation dans la codécision "simple" en Allemagne Fédérale', *Droit Social*, 11: 487–99.

Seo, Myeong-Gu, and Creed, W. E. Douglas, (2002), 'Institutional Contradictions, Praxis and Institutional Change: A Dialectical Perspective', *Academy of Management Review* 27, 222–47.

Siemens, Werner von (1966), *Lebenserinnerungen*, 17th edn (Munich: Prestel).

Sivesind, Karl-Henrik, (1997), 'The Indispensable Role of Culture: Explaining Different Organizations and Understandings by Comparison of German and Norwegian factories', unpubl. doctoral thesis, Department of Sociology and Human Geography, University of Olso.

Smelser, Neil J. (1994), *Sociology* (Cambridge, Mass./Oxford: Blackwell).

Smith, Adam (1976), *The Theory of Moral Sentiments*, D. D. Raphael and A. L. MacFie (eds) (Oxford: Oxford University Press).

Smithers, Andrew, and Wright, Stephen (2000), *Valuing Wall Street: Protecting Wealth in Turbulent Markets* (New York: McGraw-Hill).

Sorge, Arndt (1978), 'The Management Tradition: A Continental View', in *Manufacturing and Management*, M. Fores and I. Glover (eds) (London: HMSO), 87–104.

—— (1979), *Technical Change, Manufacturing Organization and Labour Markets: Effects and Options of Microelectronics*, IIM/LMP discussion paper 79–15 (Berlin: Wissenschaftszen-trum).

—— (1985), *Informationstechnik und Arbeit im sozialen Prozess: Arbeitsorganisation, Qualifikation und Produktivkraftentwicklung* (Frankfurt am Main: Campus).

—— (1991), 'Strategic Fit and the Societal Effect: Interpreting Cross-national Comparisons of Technology, Organization and Human Resources', *Organization Studies* 12, 161–90.

—— (1998), 'La Construction sociale de l'innovation et des innovateurs en Allemagne et en Grande-Bretagne', in *Les Acteurs de l'innovation dans l'entreprise: France–Europe–Japon*, C. Lanciano, M. Maurice, J. J. Silvestre, and H. Nohara (eds) (Paris: L'Harmattan), 125–44.

—— (1999*a*), 'Mitbestimmung, Arbeitsorganisation und Technikanwendung', in *Mitbestimmung in Deutschland: Tradition und Effizienz*, W. Streeck and N. Kluge (eds) (Frankfurt am Main: Campus), 17–134.

—— (1999*b*), *Organizing Societal Space in Globalization: Bringing Society Back In*, MPIFGT working paper, available at <www.mpi-fg-koeln.mpg.de/publikation/working_papers/wp99-10/index.html>.

—— (2000*a*), 'The Diabolical Dialectics of Societal Analysis', in Maurice and Sorge (2000), 37–56.

—— (2000*b*), 'Editorial: OS, its First Twenty Years and Into the Next Millennium: Something Not So Completely Different', *Organization Studies* 20, pp. v–vii.

—— Hartmann, Gert, Warner, Malcolm, and Nicholas, Ian (1983), *Microelectronics and Work in Industry: Applications of CNC Machine Tools in Great Britain and the Federal Republic of Germany* (Aldershot: Gower).

—— and Streeck, Wolfgang (1988), 'Industrial Relations and Technical Change: The Case for an Extended Perspective' in *New Technology and Industrial Relations*, R. Hyman and W. Streeck (eds) (Oxford: Blackwell), 19–47.

—— and Warner, Malcolm (1986), *Comparative Factory Organisation: An Anglo-German Comparison of Management and Manpower in Manufacturing* (Aldershot: Gower).

—— and Witteloostuijn, Arjen van (2004), 'The (Non)sense of Organizational Change: An *essai* about Universal Management Hypes, Sick Consultancy Metaphors and Healthy Organization Theories', *Organization Studies* 25, 1243–60.

Soskice, David (1999), 'Divergent Production Regimes: Coordinated and Uncoordinated Market Economies in the 1980s and 1990s', in *Continuity and Change in Contemporary Capitalism*, H. Kitschelt, P. Lange, G. Marks, and J. Stephens (eds) (Cambridge: Cambridge University Press), 101–34.

Spender, J. C. (1989), *Industry Recipes* (Oxford: Blackwell).

Stark, David (1996), 'Recombinant Property in East European Capitalism', *American Journal of Sociology* 101, 993–1027.

Stein, Claus-Dieter (1975), 'Die Rolle von Staat und Unternehmern bei der Berufsbildung von Industriearbeitern in der Weimarer Republik', unpubl. Master's thesis, Department of History, Free University of Berlin.

Streeck, Wolfgang (1987), 'The Uncertainties of Management in the Management of Uncertainty: Employers, Labour Relations and Industrial Adjustment in the 1980s', *Work, Employment and Society* 3, 90–104.

—— (1997), 'German Capitalism: Does It Exist? Can It Survive?', in *Political Economy of Modern Capitalism: Mapping Convergence and Diversity*, C. Crouch and W. Streeck (eds) (London: Sage), 33–54.

—— (ed.) (1998), *Internationale Wirtschaft, nationale Demokratie: Herausforderungen für die Demokratietheorie* (Frankfurt: Campus).

—— (1992), *Social Institutions and Economic Performance: Studies of Industrial Relations in Advanced Capitalist Economies* (London: Sage).

—— and Rehder, Britta (2003), 'Der Flächentarifvertrag: Krise, Stabilität und Wandel', *Industrielle Beziehungen* 10, 341–62.

—— and Yamamura, Kozo (eds) (2001), *The Origins of Non-liberal Capitalism: Germany and Japan in Comparison* (Ithaca, NY/London: Cornell University Press).

Sydow, Jörg (2002), 'Inter-organizational Relations', in *Organization*, A. Sorge (ed.) (London: Thompson Learning), 127–45.

Thomas, William I., and Znaniecki, Florian (1918), *The Polish Peasant in Europe and America*, ii (New York: Knopf).

Thompson, Edward A. (1965), *The Early Germans* (Oxford: Clarendon Press).

Thompson, Edward P. (1978), *The Poverty of Theory and Other Essays* (London: Merlin Press).

Thompson, James D. (1967), *Organizations in Action: Social Science Bases of Administrative Theory* (New York: McGraw-Hill).

Tilly, Richard H. (1978), 'Capital Formation in Germany in the 19th Century', in Mathias and Postan (1978), 382–441.

Tocqueville, Alexis de (1951), *De la démocratie en Amérique* (Paris: Gallimard).

Tolbert, Pamela, and Zucker, Lynne (1996), 'The Institutionalization of Institutional Theory' in *Handbook of Organization Studies*, S. Clegg, C. Hardy, and W. North (eds) (London: Sage), 175–90.

Touraine, Alain (1981), 'Une sociologie sans société', *Revue française de sociologie* 22, 3–13.

Treitschke, Heinrich von (n.d.), *Deutsche Geschichte: im neunzehnten Jahrhundert* (Berlin: Safari-Verlag).

Vogt, Martin (ed.) (2002), *Deutsche Geschichte: Von den Anfängen bis zur Gegenwart* (Frankfurt am Main: Fischer Taschenbuchverlag).

Vollroth, Hanna (2002), 'Deutsche Geschichte im Mittelalter', in *Deutsche Geschichte: Von den Anfängen bis zur Gegenwart*, M. Vogt (ed.) (Frankfurt am Main: Fischer Taschenbuchverlay), 1–143.

Weber, Max (1964), *Wirtschaft und Gesellschaft*, 2 vols (Cologne: Kiepenheuer & Witsch).

Weick, Karl E. (1979), *The Social Psychology of Organizing* (Reading, Mass.: Addison-Wesley).

—— (1995), 'What Theory Is Not, Theorizing Is', *Administrative Science Quarterly* 40, 385–90.

Whitley, Richard (ed.) (1992), *European Business Systems* (London: Sage).

—— (2002), 'Business Systems', in *Organization*, A. Sorge (ed.) (London: Thomson Learning), 179–96.

—— and Kristensen, Peer Hull (eds) (1996), *The Changing European Firm: Limits to Convergence* (London: Routledge).

Williams, Karen, Geppert, Mike, and Matten, Dirk (2003), *Challenges for the German Model of Employee Relations in the Era of Globalization*, Nottingham University Business School International Centre for Social Responsibility research paper no. 05–2003 (Nottingham: Nottingham University Business School).

Windolf, Paul (1994), 'Die neuen Eigentümer: Eine Analyse des Marktes für Unternehmenskontrolle', *Zeitschrift für Soziologie* 23, 79–93.

Winkler, Heinrich August (1970), 'Mittelstand zwischen Liberalismus und Nationalsozialismus', unpubl. Habilitation thesis, Department of History, Free University, Berlin.

Witteloostuijn, Arjen van (1999), *De anorexiastrategie: Over de gevolgen van saneren* (Amsterdam/Antwerp: Uitgeverij De Arbeiderspers).

Wood, Stephen (ed.) (1982), *The Degradation of Work? Skilling, Deskilling and the Labour Process* (London: Hutchinson).

Woodward, Joan (1965), *Industrial Organization: Theory and Practice* (Oxford: Oxford University Press).

Yamamura, Kozo, and Streeck, Wolfgang (eds) (2003), *The End of Diversity? Prospects for German and Japanese Capitalism.* (Ithaca, NY/London: Cornell University Press).

Yourcenar, Marguerite (1968), *L'Œuvre au noir* (Paris: Gallimard).

Yukl, Gary (1994), *Leadership in Organizations* (Englewood Cliffs, NJ: Prentice-Hall).

Zysman, John (1983), *Governments, Markets and Growth: Financial Systems and the Politics of Industrial Change* (Ithaca, NY: Cornell University Press).

Index